THE FRIGHTFEST GUIDE TO MAD DOCTOR MOVIES

First published by FAB Press, August 2023

FAB Press Ltd.
2 Farleigh, Ramsden Road, Godalming
Surrey, GU7 1QE, England, U.K.

www.fabpress.com

Edited by Gavin Baddeley
Picture research and layout by Kevin Coward
FrightFest Guide original book design, layout, cover and pre-press origination by Harvey Fenton
Film cast and crew credits, additional research and index by Francis Brewster
Thanks also to Alan Jones and the FrightFest image archive

Author's Dedication:
To my wife Kate, my eternal partner in FrightFest, film, and life everlasting. If you didn't already exist I would have had to create you.
With all my love from your very own mad doctor.

Acknowledgement for visual material is due to the following organisations and individuals:
2929 Productions, 430 Productions, 775 Media Corp., A.J. Films-Paris, A24, AB-PT Pictures, Aetas Film Productions, AFB, Agincourt Productions, Alcide Bava, Alliance Distribution, Alliance Films, Allied Artists, Alpha Films, American International Pictures, American Mary Productions, Amicus, Aquarius Releasing, Inc., Associated Producers, Inc., Astor Pictures, Aurum, Automatik Entertainment, AVCO Embassy, Avis Film, Bad Badger, Beast of Blood Company, Beo Starling, BH Tilt Goalpost Pictures, Blind Wink, Border Film Productions, Brent Walker Film Distributors, British Lion, Bron Studios, Brooks Films, Cambist Films, Canal+ Espana, Caralan, Castle Rock Entertainment, Champs-Elysees Productions, Chromewood, CIC, Cine Artists Pictures, Cinemagia, Cinemagroup F.D., Cinemarque Entertainment (USA), Cinepix, Claussen + Wubke Filmproduktion, Columbia Pictures, Columbia-EMI-Warner, Comptoir Francais du Film Production Paris, Condor International Productions, Cornerstone Production Company, Cross Creek Pictures, Dark Castle Entertainment, Dark Rabbit Productions, Dead Films, Inc., Demarest Films, Deutsche Columbia Pictures Filmproduktion, Dimension Pictures, e-m-s, Eagle Film Distributors, Eclectic Pictures, Elgin International Productions, Embassy Pictures, Emerson Film Enterprises, EMI Film Productions, Empire Pictures, Ente Nazionale Industrie Cinematografiche, Eurocine, Evolution Pictures, Ezekiel Film Production, Favorite Films, Fenix Film Madrid, Film Futures, Film House Germany, FilmFour, Filmplan International, Films Manacoa P.C., Filmways Pictures, Inc., First Independent, First National, Focus World, Fontana, Fox Atomic, Frakas Productions, Frsco Productions, Furthur Films, Galatea Productions, Geffen, Gilbert Films, GO Video, Goldstar Productions, Group 1, Hallmark Releasing, Halyard Productions, Hammer Films, Hemdale, High5Films, House of 1,000 Corpses, LLC, Howco, I.G.A.P. Roma, IFC Films, IFC Midnight, Independent-International Pictures, Infinite Lives Entertainment, Instinctive Film, Jack Broder Productions, JCLW Virtual Movie Marathon, Jeff Rice Films, JVC Entertainment, Inc., Lady Film, Lakeside Pictures, Largo Entertainment, Laurel Productions, Lider, Lion's Films, Lions Gate Films, Lippert Films, Lira Films, Live Home Video, Logolite Entertainment, Lux Film, Magnet Releasing, Majestic Pictures, Marvel, Mayflower Dell, Media Releasing Distributors, Medusa Distribuzione-Rome, MKB Films, Momentum Pictures, Monogram, Motion Picture Capital, Movie World Promotions, Naked Lunch Productions, National Screen Service, Nebel Productions, Nervous Tick, Network, New Line Cinema, New Normal Films, New Realm Distributors, New World Pictures, Omnia, Orion Pictures, OTL Releasing, Pacific Western, Parade Pictures, Paramount Pictures, Parallel Zide / Lion Share Productions, Pathe Pictures, Petit Film Rouge International, Ponycanyon, PRC Pictures, Premier Releasing, Prisma, Producers Releasing Corporation, Rank Film Distributors, RCA, Re-Animator II Productions, Re-Animator Productions, Inc., Recorded Picture Company (Productions) Limited, Redwire, Regency Enterprises, Rep 12, Republic Pictures, Rhombus Media, RKO Radio Pictures, Rochelle Films, Safran Company, Sandy Howard Productions, Sceptre Industries, Screencraft Enterprises, Seven Arts Pictures, Sigma, Simian Films, Sirena Studios, Six Entertainment, Skouras Pictures, Societe Nouvelle de Cinematographie, Sony Pictures Classics, Summerstorm Entertainment, Target International Pictures, Tartan Films, TF1 International, Tigon Pictures, Trans World Films, Trans-Lux, Trimark, Twentieth Century-Fox, Twins Twins Productions, Twisted Pictures, United Artists, United Film Distribution Company, Universal, Valiant Films, Vamanos Films, Vecteezy.com, Vitaphone, Voltage Pictures, Voodoo Pictures, Warner Bros., Wild Street Pictures, Wild Bunch, World Northal, XYZ Films, Zanuck/Brown, Zeitgeist Video, Zevs Film.

Front cover illustration:
Italian theatrical release poster art for L'orribile segreto del Dr. Hichcock aka The Horrible Dr. Hichcock (1962)
Frontispiece illustration:
American one-sheet theatrical release poster art for Re-Animator (1985)

Printed in India

A CIP catalogue record for this book is available from the British Library

hardcover: ISBN 978 1 913051 31 0
paperback: ISBN 978 1 913051 32 7

-THE DARK HEART OF CINEMA-

FRIGHTFEST® GUIDE

MAD DOCTOR MOVIES

Dr. John Llewellyn Probert

-THE DARK HEART OF CINEMA-

FRIGHTFEST®

Throughout its 24 years of programming the cream of the horror, science-fiction, thriller and fantasy genres from around the world at its three hugely anticipated yearly mega-events (as part of the Glasgow Film Festival in Scotland every March, in Central London every late August Bank Holiday and its Halloween Shocktoberfest) and online too, FrightFest, the United Kingdom's biggest, best and most prestigious Party Central for fear fans has premiered thousands of movies.

Now, after covering in detail the Exploitation, Monster, Ghost, Werewolf, Grindhouse and Vampire genres, The FrightFest Guide books add Mad Doctor Movies to their highly acclaimed and beloved roster. And it's one with a very unique twist indeed because it comes from noted medic, surgeon, biochemist and horror expert Doctor John Llewellyn Probert. Who better than an actual practitioner of the Hippocratic oath to assess everything hypocritical in the vast clinical celluloid cosmos? To uphold every director, producer, scriptwriter and star in assorted horror hospitals to the ultimate in ethical standards? To swear by the healing gods that hard-won scientific gains won't be totally desecrated by the horror deities in search of ever more expanding terror therapies? To respect the dodgy fever charts in surgeries pointed at by quacks, diagnose the alien ailments from other worlds and cure the weird sicknesses in society for the economic stability of the mad doctor film industry? I know whom I'd trust to be my critical doctor of such medical mayhem!

Over the years FrightFest has been a veritable shock corridor for the Mad Doctor genre. A few examples: Brian Yuzna's **Beyond Re-Animator** (2003), Leigh Whannell's **Upgrade** (2018), Vincenzo Natali's **Splice** (2009), and Bernard Rose's **Frankenstein** (2015). From intensive care units, emergency wards and sanatoriums to gynaecologists, psychiatrists and the morgue, FrightFesters have visited them all in some demented virtual form or another. For crazy clinicians, psycho patients, strange symptoms, terrifying transplants and neurotic nurses have been staple subjects for the vast array of titles you will read about in Doctor Probert's unusually probing analysis. All the infamous Doctors are here, including Caligari, Jekyll, X, Hichcock, Mabuse, Renault, No, Phibes, Blood, M, Frankenstein and Orloff. But there will be many movies you probably won't be expecting like **Fedora** (1978), **The Doctor in the Nude** (1973) and **Sssssss** (1973) too.

The beauty of Doctor Probert's handpicked list is it's the perfect antidote to whatever might ail you. Just look through this catalogue of chronic conditions and tick a box! Cabin fever, schizophrenia, hydrophobia, photosensitivity, shivers? You've got chills? Are they multiplying? They should be, especially after Doctor Probert will keep you overnight, not for observation, but reading his cure-all for medical movie mania. It's just what the Mad Doctor ordered.

And who better to write the foreword to such a groundbreaking forensic analysis than the most controversial director on the planet. Tom Six entered pop culture history with **The Human Centipede**

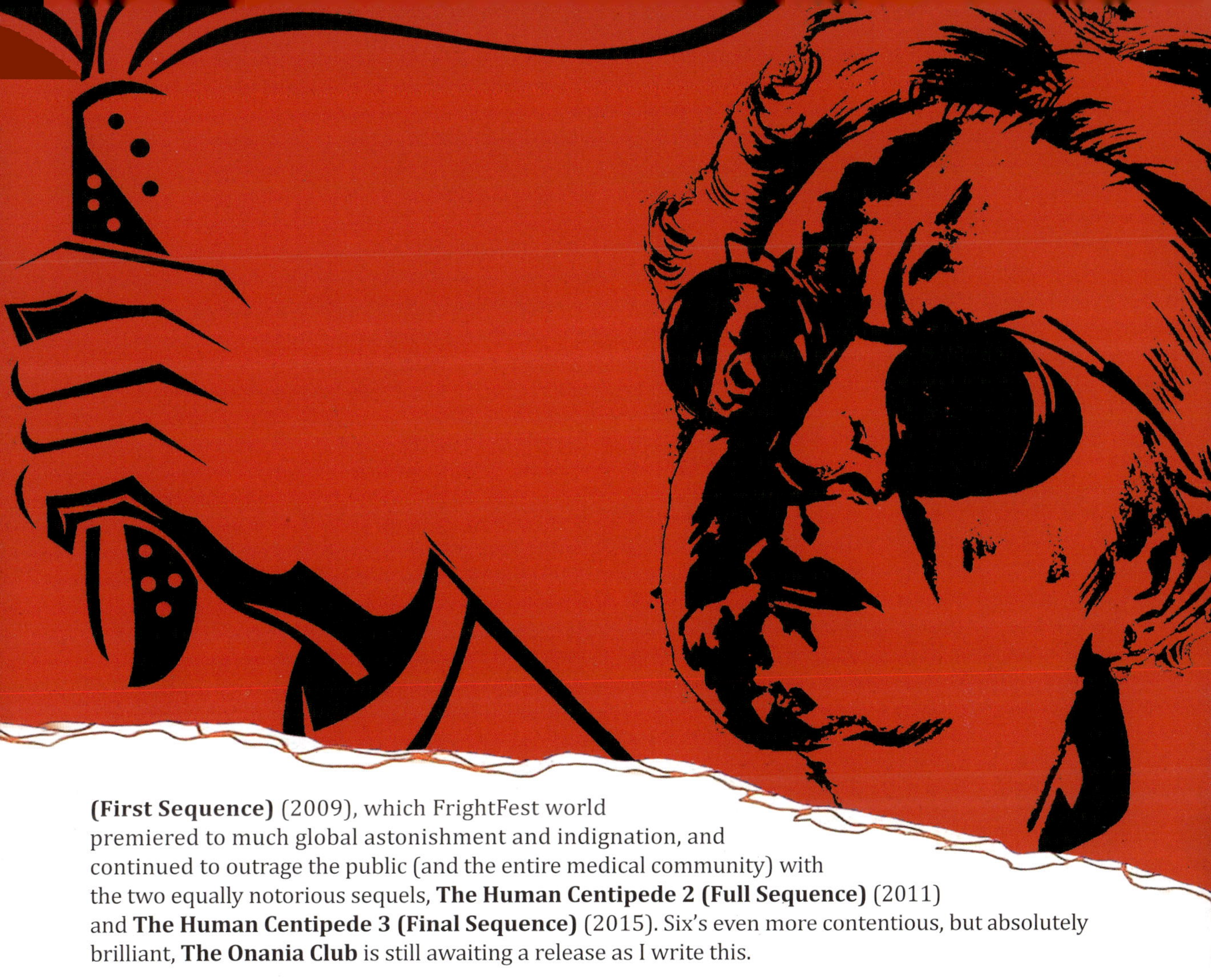

(First Sequence) (2009), which FrightFest world premiered to much global astonishment and indignation, and continued to outrage the public (and the entire medical community) with the two equally notorious sequels, **The Human Centipede 2 (Full Sequence)** (2011) and **The Human Centipede 3 (Final Sequence)** (2015). Six's even more contentious, but absolutely brilliant, **The Onania Club** is still awaiting a release as I write this.

So, come up to the lab
And see what's on the slab
I see you shiver with antici......pation...

'The FrightFest Guide to Mad Doctor Movies' is the seventh volume in a collectible series intended to build the knowledge of the curious spectator and the cult connoisseur alike – the exact same maxim with which we meticulously produce our annual events that are globally famous, currently listed as one of the Top 25 greatest, and used by the international film industry as a litmus test for the future of the horror genre and the best way to position their titles.

Enjoy this latest respected roundup of all things fractured, intravenous, glandular, malignant and acute, written with the same passionate enthusiasm that sets FrightFesters apart from the mundane fest rest. But you should know by now that FrightFest is not just a film festival or the friendliest community you could ever wish to join. It's also an ever-increasing super brand that includes FrightFest Presents, our multi-platform/VOD entertainment label that has released such diverse and popular titles as **Some Kind of Hate** (2015), **My Father Die** (2016), **Boar** (2017), **The Siren** (2019), **Videoman** (2018), **The Wind** (2018), **12 Hour Shift** (2020), **Bitch-Ass** (2022), **Initiation** (2021), the cultural phenomenon **The Love Witch** (2016) and the critically acclaimed **Relic** (2020), **You Are Not My Mother** (2021) and **The Harbinger** (2022).

~ Alan Jones, FrightFest co-director

Dr. John Llewellyn Probert

When John Llewellyn Probert was ten years old he saw Kurt Neumann's **The Fly** (1958) and it made him want to be a mad scientist when he grew up. Two years later, the brain transplant scene from Terence Fisher's **Frankenstein and the Monster from Hell** (1974) made him want to be a surgeon. Obviously nothing could top this, so when John was eighteen he went to the University of Nottingham, where he obtained basic bachelors degrees in medicine, surgery, and biochemistry (because he thought biochemistry might also be useful). A few years later, after doing all the right things and passing all the right exams, he was made a Fellow of the Royal College of Surgeons of Edinburgh. That still didn't feel like enough letters after his name, so John headed to the University of Pittsburgh, Pennsylvania, where he obtained his postgraduate doctorate in molecular biology before returning to the UK. He is currently a Consultant Urological Surgeon in the South West of England and because one job just isn't enough for him, he is also an Honorary Senior Lecturer at the University of Bristol, where both undergraduate and postgraduate surgery students get to enjoy his lectures once a week.

All through this John has maintained his lifelong love of horror movies. He remembers staying up until three in the morning during his undergraduate finals because Channel 4 was showing a rare screening of Amicus's **Tales from the Crypt** (1971). He just had time between Royal College examinations to dash out to a nearby multiplex to catch John Carpenter's **In the Mouth of Madness** (1995). John chose the University of Pittsburgh for his science doctorate because he could spend his spare time scouting the locations of George Romero's movies, pictures from which made it into his inaugural university lecture on his return to the UK, breaking up all the stuff about PCR techniques and the regulation of cytochrome activity.

Once his thesis doctorate was submitted, John found himself at a bit of a loose end, so he decided to fulfil a lifelong ambition to become a writer – for some reason having peer-reviewed papers published in scientific journals didn't seem to count. He had his first short story published nearly twenty years ago, and has since published over a hundred more, along with three novels – *The House That Death Built* (2013), *Dead Shift* (2016) and *How Grim Was My Valley* (2022) – as well as six short story collections and six novellas. His first short story collection, *The Faculty of Terror*, won the 2006 Children of the Night award for best work of Gothic Fiction, and in 2013 he won the British Fantasy Award for his novella *The Nine Deaths of Dr. Valentine*.

His non-fiction writing has included monographs on Herbert J. Leder's 1967 shocker **It!** and Douglas Hickox's **Theatre of Blood** (1973). The latter is his favourite film of all time, though surprisingly features no surgery at all (well, perhaps a little bit). John also has an online review site, *House of Mortal Cinema* – now into its second decade – where he gets to talk about the latest film releases and festival screenings.

He is married to Kate, aka the author Thana Niveau. Soon after they met they formed *Teatro Proberto* to reimagine hard-to-see British classics like **Corruption** (1968) for live audiences, condensing the films down to fifteen minutes and playing all the parts between the two of them. This, and their pantomime version of **Blood on Satan's Claw** (1970), have been performed on stage both in Brighton and London. They currently live in a Gothic mansion in deepest Somerset, with one room for the Blu-ray library, another for the books, and still another for the dressing-up box.

Dr. John Llewellyn Probert's never-ending manic work ethic can perhaps be best explained by Conan Doyle's Sherlock Holmes, who once said "My mind is like a racing engine, tearing itself to pieces because it is not connected up with the work for which it was built." You now hold in your hands the latest piece of work that has helped to keep its author sane.

FOREWORD BY TOM SIX

Why was I asked to write a foreword for this bible about mad doctor movies?

Is it because I wear panama hats and linen and silk suits daily? Or because I smoke tons of handmade Dominican cigars? Maybe because I live in Amsterdam? Probably not! I am the film dictator and madman who created the infamous pop culture **Human Centipede** film trilogy and I know a thing or two, or three, about the subject. And I am proud to be a part of this. Ladies, gentlemen and every other lifeform, this glorious guide is the medicine you so desperately need. Will it fully cure you from your obsessive love of macabre cinema? Highly unlikely! But it's preferential to a lobotomy.

Now to prove I'm worthy; since I was a kid I have been obsessed with movies. I literally live for and off of them. Usually what scares you is the thing that fascinates you the most. I will admit I'm terrified of hospitals and doctors, so a lot of my favourite films feature doctors. From comedy doctors like Dr. Frederick Frankenstein (**Young Frankenstein**) and Dr. Michael Huffuhrer, sorry Hfuhruhurr (**The Man with Two Brains**), to the more sinister Dr. Moreau (**The Island of Dr. Moreau**) and Dr. Christian Szell "Is it safe?" (**Marathon Man**), along with doctors straight from hell, like Dr. Hannibal Lecter (**The Silence of the Lambs**) and my very own creation, Dr. Josef Heiter "Feeeed her!" (**The Human Centipede (First Sequence)**).

For the few people on this planet who do not know what a Human Centipede (a human insect?) has to do with a mad doctor, let me explain. I got the basic idea for the film while watching a sadistic and very active pedophile on television getting away with a very light sentence. I thought that a much more suitable sentence would be for him to have his mouth sewn to the anus of a fat truckdriver. Being fed fresh poop while begging on his hands and knees for mercy. Lightning struck and demons sang! A brilliant and original film concept was born. I photoshopped three pictures of my ex-girlfriend posing on her hands and knees into a chain, sharing one digestive system. It looked like a centipede. A human centipede! I immediately knew a mad doctor had to be involved.

My late grandfather was an absolute Dutch hero who managed to escape from a forced labour Nazi camp in Berlin during World War II, and walked all the way back to Amsterdam, where he lived, which is close to 400 miles. As you can imagine he told me a lot of unbelievable war stories, so naturally my villain doctor had to be German. I read a lot of books about the Nazi doctors, mainly focused on Dr. Josef Mengele a.k.a. *the angel of death.* He was a flamboyant, very sadistic bastard who totally lacked empathy and performed nightmarish experiments on prisoners in the infamous Auschwitz II-Birkenau concentration camp.

He focused primarily on (identical) twins with absolutely no regard for the health or safety of his victims. A female witness once described how Dr. Mengele sewed two Romani twins together, back-to-back, in a crude attempt to create conjoined twins. Both children died of gangrene after several days of suffering.

If you have seen the first **Human Centipede** film, you are probably starting to notice a few similarities. I wanted my masterpiece to be 100% medically accurate because it would make for an iconic tagline, and it would mean the film was way more scary. This is why I consulted one of the top Dutch vascular surgeons, who happened to be my ex-girlfriend's father. He almost choked on his coffee when I told him about my mouth-to-ass film concept. After a few nights of little sleep, he told me he would help me on one condition: that he would stay anonymous. I knew a lot of doctors are somewhat sadistic. Deal! He wrote a very extensive surgery report and told me he could actually perform this operation in his hospital. They would need compatible blood types and immunosuppressive drugs to avoid rejection. The biggest risk however would be sepsis, meaning blood poisoning. I couldn't be more excited and I really wanted to get this completely right so I had written down a ton of extra questions for him. He consulted a gastroenterologist colleague and friend about them. This doctor researched human stool transplants for curing patients with bowel and other diseases. If the donors are healthy and the faeces is not attacked by outside bacteria it wouldn't kill the victims inside a human centipede, but they would need IVs with fluids and vitamins. This final seal of approval granted me the official tagline "100% medically accurate". You have got to see **The Human Centipede (First Sequence)** to believe it; it's all in there. I saw a lame Australian GP in the press claiming the film was not a 100% medically accurate but he is dead wrong. The film is fiction but I have the backing of medical specialists who are right to back it up.

This is also a perfect moment to give a special shout out to the late German actor Dieter Laser, who played Doctor Josef Heiter. This legend was a force of nature, an incredible actor and my partner in creative crime! Did you know all my movies feature doctors? It is an unhealthy obsession. **The Human Centipede 2 (Full Sequence)** features a pedophile psychiatrist and **The Human Centipede 3 (Final Sequence)** features a dodgy prison doctor who works without his license. My latest movie, **The Onania Club**, features a vile oncologist who is based on a real Dutch neurologist who deliberately gave patients wrong diagnoses. People died from receiving the wrong treatment, while others committed suicide because they were given such bleak prognoses. He was part of the biggest medical trial in the Netherlands to this day. If you think I am crazy for coming up with all these insane film ideas, real life is much more insane.

If these anecdotes fascinated you, excited you, maybe even turned you on, you will eat this book raw! I said it in my intro and I am going to say it again – this guide is the definitive bible of mad doctor movies. Even this film dictator discovered some movie titles and a lot of background information I knew nothing about so as a final medical warning this guide may cause severe adverse effects like wanting to see every movie mentioned. Enjoy and try to relax, so it won't hurt!

I'll pass the scalpel to you, Dr. Probert.

~ Tom Six
"an unhealthy mind in an unhealthy body"
The Netherlands, 2023

Writer/producer/director Tom Six started his career in television, being one of the pioneer directors for the original and highly successful reality TV show 'Big Brother' in the Netherlands. As directing consultant, he was responsible for the start of 'Big Brother' shows in the U.S., Germany, Denmark, Norway and South Africa. Tom Six successfully pursued his true passion of filmmaking. He created three Dutch films before moving on to his first English spoken film: **The Human Centipede**. *A concept so crazy, it has become part of pop culture all over the world. His latest movie,* **The Onania Club** *– another film that will have the world talking – has yet to be granted a release at the time of this book's publication.*

FRIGHTFEST GUIDE

MAD DOCTOR MOVIES

INTRODUCTION

I. ON A PERSONAL NOTE

When I was five years old I had to have a blood sample taken. The GP was elderly and her sight wasn't too good, and she used a blood pressure cuff as a tourniquet, inflating it to produce the necessary pressure. I think she failed with the needle at least three times before I, blood running down my arm, began to cry, and my mother told the doctor that was enough. A few years later I was admitted to hospital with appendicitis and needed an IV line putting in. The junior doctor assigned the task had several attempts on my left wrist before someone else managed to get one in on the right side. My memory of the sensation was, to quote the once-famous English horror writer R. Chetwynd-Hayes, 'like a knife being forced through teak'. At least by that age I was able to understand the benefits – I needed my appendix out or I would die from peritonitis. Something akin to a blunt pencil being shoved under the skin of my wrist was a small price to pay in order to live. So was the incision in my right side I still have to this day. That hurt for quite a bit as well, incidentally.

Those are my early memories of doctors, and I expect everyone reading this will have a few of their own. Not the ones where all you recall is a smile and some reassurance, but the ones that were painful, or required the consumption of some bitter-tasting medicine or undergoing a procedure that, if not excruciating was at the very least uncomfortable, and quite likely undignified as well. There's hardly anyone alive who hasn't had a needle stuck into them, either for the sake of a blood test or the administration of a vaccine. In some cases it's not so much the needle itself that was scary, as the fact that someone was quite

above: This book had a major impact on the young Dr. Probert, particularly the story 'Manderville'.

prepared to pierce your skin with one. Because, not only do such people understand that it's going to be uncomfortable (a 'sharp scratch' as my anaesthetist colleagues are fond of saying beforehand) but also that they know exactly where they need to stick it. Doctors know more about your body than you do, and if they know where your blood vessels are, then surely it follows that they know where the nerves go too. That if they wanted to, they could cause even more pain than they already are. Not that a doctor would ever dream of doing such a thing, of course.

Unless, perhaps, if they were mad.

Of course, it's not just needles that doctors stick into us. Fingers are placed where no one would ever imagine placing them, except perhaps in consenting situations for the purposes of sexual pleasure. But as the Canadian director David Cronenberg (and there will be much more on him later in this book) observed – the only person who knows the anatomy of the woman in your life as well as you do is a gynaecologist. Better, in fact, because they know what to look out for in terms of disease processes, and their ability to detect such things is based at least partly on the experience of having done the same kind of examination many times before.

I'm a urologist, another specialty that involves intimate examinations. I've been in this specialty for long enough now that I can confidently claim to have examined thousands upon thousands of men's prostate glands. That means that thousands of times I have placed the increasingly-experienced index finger of my right hand inside a man's rectum in order to detect pathology.

It goes without saying that the world needs people like me, as well as my gynaecologist colleagues, and all my other compatriots who are willing to put their fingers in places most would find shocking, in order to detect disease, monitor for cancer recurrence, and make decisions about a patient's welfare. Oh yes, thank heavens there are people who aren't fazed by this sort of thing and are willing to do it, all for the benefit of the individual we are examining.

But what if we specialists were mad?

II. APPOINTMENTS WITH FEAR

Piercing needles and probing fingers are used by doctors pretty much across the board, but many specialties come with their own unique aspects of the intimate, the distasteful, and on occasions the painful. As you will read over the pages which follow, horror cinema has done its utmost to exploit any fears inherent in what the more insane members of those different specialties might get up to. I became a urologist partly because of an occasion where, as a junior doctor in training, I was privileged to witness a procedure in which a patient's urinary bladder had to be removed as a curative treatment for cancer. What, then, was to be done with the ureters (the tubes that drain your kidneys) that could now be described, as we surgeons tend to say, as 'flapping in the breeze'? The answer was to separate a segment of the patient's own small intestine, refashion it into what is known as a pouch, anastomose the ureters into the back of that pouch, and connect the front to the patient's remaining urethra. I was blown away by this complex, inventive, clever, and intricate procedure that gave a patient a functioning organ created from another part of them. As someone who had grown up loving David Cronenberg's films (there's that name again) perhaps it was inevitable that I would find such a procedure fascinating. Indeed, it appealed so much, both to my intellect and as a challenge to my practical skills, that I soon felt compelled to enter the specialty myself.

Such construction and reconstruction is not confined to urology. Patients with narrowed coronary arteries undergo bypass grafting, where the long saphenous vein is removed from the leg,

top right: Vaccines have long inspired anxiety, as illustrated by this 1802 James Gillray cartoon satirising the fears of an early 'anti-vaccine society'.

and segments are stitched onto the arteries to allow blood to bypass blocked areas. Orthopaedic surgeons fix fractures and replace worn-out joints, plastic surgeons work wonders with burns patients, and vascular surgeons can now connect the main artery in your armpit to the main one in your leg (the femoral artery, memorably described in Stephen King's short story 'Survivor Type' as 'like a fucking turnpike') if there's a blockage somewhere in between that stops the blood getting through.

Surely, if these highly-qualified, highly-skilled individuals happened to be mad, it would be just a short step from there, to doing something that could restructure parts of our bodies into something strange and horrifying? (And possibly 'beautiful' if your name was David Cronenberg.)

Because I perform surgery myself, I spend a lot of time with anaesthetists, who bring with them their own world of exploitable horror potential. An anaesthetist can put you to sleep and, more importantly, is in total control of how long you sleep and when (or if) you wake up. While you are under an anaesthetic you are powerless and utterly unaware of what is being done to you. Or at least you should be, but part of the process of anaesthesia is paralysis, so it's quite conceivable that you could be completely aware of everything, but totally unable to respond to or do anything about it.

From the body to the mind. Psychiatrists are there to help manage our mental health, but to do that they need to get inside our heads, metaphorically if not physically. What might they find lurking there? What about the secrets that really we'd rather they didn't know about, even though it might be essential for them to be aware of them in order to give us the right treatment? What other thoughts might they leave in there once they claim they've finished? Especially if they themselves are the mad one? How are we to know? And then there are the (sometimes heavily sedating) medications they use, drugs that in sufficient doses can render you almost as incapable as an anaesthetic, with no memory of who you are, where you are and, perhaps worst of all, with no desire or energy to be able to do anything about it. If those don't achieve the desired effect, there's always ECT (electroconvulsive therapy) to fall back on. You're supposed to have that under anaesthetic, but obviously if you happen to be in the clutches of a madman they might conveniently forget.

A mad cardiologist can stop your heart, then start it again, make it beat in all kinds of strange rhythms, and install a pacemaker that can be used to regulate both the rate and rhythm. A mad dermatologist might be giving you topical cream to make that irritating rash worse, just to see how bad it can get. Some drugs that are used to treat cancer are so powerful that they are capable of causing cancer themselves, if given in dangerous doses. Cancers that are drug resistant or unsuitable for surgery can sometimes be treated with radiotherapy, where a tumour is given X-rays. But if it's the wrong dose or the wrong type of X-rays, there's always the danger of 'atomic mutation'.

And, apart from the doctors themselves, what about the institutions in which they practice? Psychiatric institutions with security so efficient that once you get in it can be difficult to get out. Those huge old Victorian hospitals with their

top: Adaptations of Stephen King's 'Survivor Type' include a 2012 short and this animated segment of the 2020 *Creepshow* series.

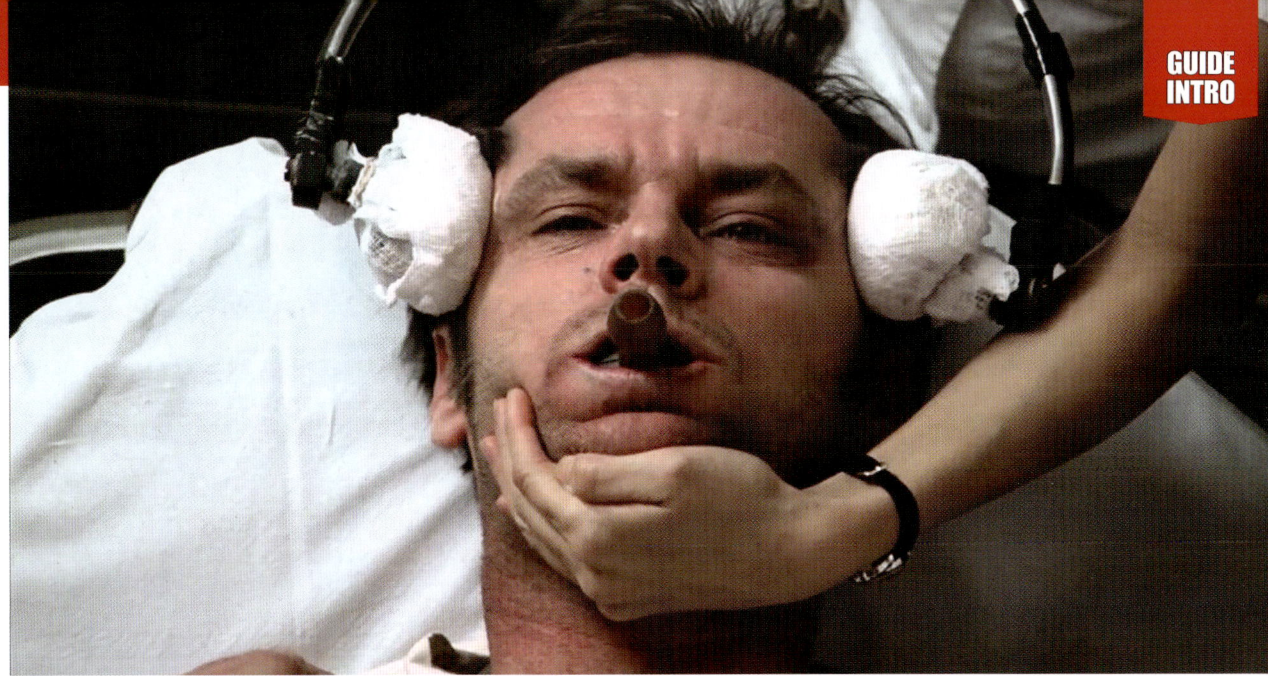

winding, poorly-lit corridors that may not lead where you're expecting. Now imagine being chased down them by someone, not at all sane, and carrying a very large needle.

Yes, it's not surprising that many of us harbour a fear of doctors. The thought of what a mad medic might do to you invokes the kind of very visceral, primal fear, that beats at the heart of the horror genre. Which probably explains why there are so many horror films about doctors, and not so many about mad bank managers or accountants. There are a few about lawyers, but I'm sure that will be dealt with in another book. Doctors are clever, doctors are skilled in doing things that can hurt us, and yet we must trust them when we are at our most vulnerable. To misquote Douglas Adams, you might think you're vulnerable in the shower, but that's just peanuts compared to when you have something seriously medically wrong with you.

The idea of placing trust in someone whom you believe has greater knowledge than you has long been a fine source of potential terror and fearful situations, predating our age of science and reason. There are numerous suitably unpleasant examples depicted in the arena of horror cinema: one need look no further than Michael Reeves' **Witchfinder General** (1968), Michael Armstrong's **Mark of the Devil** (1970), or Ken Russell's **The Devils** (1971), all of which illustrate the horror of misdiagnosis by the era's 'experts', leading to accusations of witchcraft. However, even the most meticulous and rational of scientific researchers can get it wrong sometimes, especially when the world of the supernatural is concerned: witness the physicists of John Hough's film of Richard Matheson's **The Legend of Hell House** (1973) or Nigel Kneale's **The Stone Tape** (1972). We trust teachers to look after our children in the daytime, handing them over to babysitters if we want to go out in the evening. We trust those who prepare our food not to poison it, or to make it out of the most unappetising of ingredients (one of the many factors that makes Tobe Hooper's **The Texas Chain Saw Massacre**, 1974, such an effective film). We trust our loved ones, our friends, ourselves. So many instances of trust, and all ripe for exploitation by skilled horror filmmakers.

But it's not mad religious zealots or chefs that we're here to talk about, it's mad doctors. Before we get to the fleshy, blood-infused, meat of this introduction – in which you're going to be led gently by the hand though a history of mad doctor cinema – please allow your author to embark on a short diatribe on the plethora of medical mistakes that he has encountered during a lifetime of moviegoing. Medical howlers which have, on occasion, threatened to drive him into a very special, cinema-viewing-induced state of madness.

Some may find it rather odd that a man who spends his days seeing the insides of people might enjoy the prospect of watching faked versions of the same for pleasure in his spare time. Yet the distance between reality and fantasy is in fact so vast that this beloved genre of ours has long

top: ECT has featured in numerous stories, including **One Flew Over the Cuckoo's Nest**, with Jack Nicholson in the lead.

provided me with a welcome respite from the more mundane everyday horrors I sometimes encounter. However, from time to time I do find that, no matter how hard I try to suspend disbelief, my surgical knowledge has intruded on my enjoyment of a movie.

I'm not talking about what one might term 'dramatic license' here – those little lapses in logic or realism that allow the filmmakers to keep the action moving. Such as in Breck Eisner's 2010 remake of **The Crazies**, where star Timothy Olyphant receives an extremely unpleasant penetrating stab wound to the palm of his hand and is then seen using that same hand without any discomfort at all a few scenes later, as if he had received no more than a pinprick to his thumb. I'm willing to forgive those. It's the more subtle details, the ones that are only wrong because no one has bothered to check that they're correct, that get me twitching a little when they pop up on screen.

"To know life, Otto, you must first fuck death – in the gall bladder!" as dear old, endlessly quotable Udo Kier famously states in Andy Warhol's 3D all-colour all-guts-out **Flesh for Frankenstein** (1973). Quite how Udo actually manages to do that has always been something of a mystery to me, as the incision in actress Dalila Di Lazzaro's abdomen is on the wrong side to allow him to... er... gain access to that particular part of her. Either that or the size of Udo's organ would suggest that the creations in his laboratory have not been the only subjects of his surgical attentions.

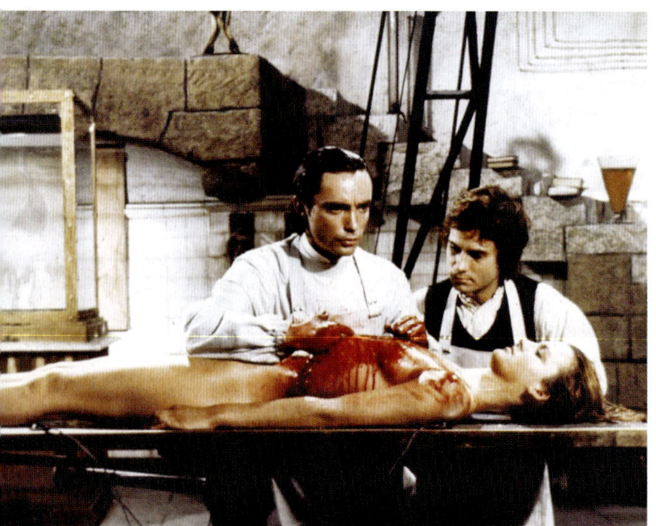

And it's not just low-budget Italian movies shot by Warhol acolytes that are marred by such mistakes – they occur in more recent Hollywood movies too. In John Stockwell's 2006 **Turistas** (UK title – **Paradise Lost**), a crazed Brazilian surgeon removes organs from helpless teenaged backpackers to sell on the black market. The incisions he uses would be extraordinarily ineffective for achieving the job, and are in fact rather less dramatic than the ones surgeons actually use, which has the specialist in me wondering if anyone with any knowledge of such procedures was ever asked for their advice by the filmmakers concerned.

Contemporary movies are littered with common medical mistakes. The one that causes me the most ire is probably where the blood is either the wrong colour or the wrong consistency, and when it's hung up in a bag for transfusion it should never be see-through. Who on earth thinks you can see through a bag of blood? People for whom verisimilitude is merely a word they don't know how to pronounce let alone spell, that's who. Chest X-rays being held up or put on a light box the wrong way round, so that the heart points to the wrong side, comes a close second. Pete Walker's 1974 movie **Frightmare** manages to go one better than that, by having Dr. Lytell (Leo Genn) looking at an abdominal X-ray that is both the wrong way

above: Udo Kier (left) examines some **Flesh for Frankenstein** in 1973.
top: Aztec priests removing a sacrificial victim's heart.

round and upside down. If you freeze frame the next time you watch it, note that the metalwork in the patient's hip is at the top of the screen when it should be at the bottom.

I don't doubt that some mistakes are deliberate and included to heighten dramatic impact. At least I hope they are, otherwise Mel Gibson really does think that hearts still beat once they have been wrenched from the chest cavity (**Apocalypto**, 2006), and George Romero did believe it was still possible for Joe Pilato to find the breath to shout "Choke on them!" once the zombies had divested him of his lungs in **Day of the Dead** (1985). And while we're on the subject, vocal cords can't be cut, and lungs can't inflate and deflate of their own accord (the diaphragm is responsible for that by contracting inside the chest cavity, aided by the movement of the ribs). Plus the severed hands that are the progeny of Robert Florey's 1946 **The Beast with Five Fingers** and its ilk cannot crawl around because the fingers are flexed by the flexor digitorum longus muscle, which is in your forearm.

Happily, not all of my movie medical observations have led to frustration. On the commentary track to his 2007 **Planet Terror**, director Robert Rodriguez suggests that star Rose McGowan's character probably operates her machine-gun leg by using pelvic floor exercises, something which I think might just be possible. Anyone interested in exactly how she might be able to achieve that is welcome to write to me care of the publisher for a more detailed explanation.

But enough of the things in films that make this particular doctor mad. It's now time to turn our attention to the antics of those onscreen doctors who are either already mad or end up that way during the course of a movie's running time. Let's start with a definition. For the purposes of this volume, I thought it best to largely limit things to the horror and science fiction-related antics of individuals either in possession of a medical degree, or those who have gained a doctorate in another subject but whose work has led to horrific consequences for other human beings. This may be as a result of overambitious research, accidents during or the side effects of said research they could not have foreseen (even if we the viewers most likely saw it coming), or simply because someone annoyed them and they were moved to put their experience and training into practice in an inappropriate – and therefore for us horror fans often entertaining – way. A few supremely unqualified but enthusiastic amateurs have also been included in the mix. Believe me they have earned their place. As we proceed there will also be comments as to the accuracy and feasibility of the medical dialogue, procedures, and deaths that have been depicted in genre cinema over the years. So, if you want to know if it's actually possible to rip a still-beating heart from a victim's chest and hold it up before their horrified gaze, or you're just interested in whether tetrodotoxin or curare is the best drug to create zombie slaves, you've come to the right place.

III. A BRIEF HISTORY OF MEDICAL MOVIE MAYHEM

The first movies to explore the horrors that medical experts might get up to were, unsurprisingly, short subjects. One of the earliest examples is **The Doctor's Experiment**, a French film from 1908 in which individuals are given monkey gland injections and regress to ape-like beings. It ran a grand total of eight minutes. Fourteen years later the great Lon Chaney Sr. would star as Dr. Arthur Lamb, attempting to do something similar to the hapless Raymond McKee in the now thought lost **A Blind Bargain** (1922). In 1910 Georges Méliès made **Hydrothérapie fantastique,** a 13-minute movie in which an overweight man visits a doctor for help and ends up being subjected to a very primitive form of liposuction, after which he is blown up and then put back together again. In the early years of cinema, literature was often used as the inspiration

top: Tetrodotoxin – a neurotoxin found in pufferfish – is allegedly a key ingredient in creating zombies.

Number 431. COMPLETE. One Penny.

DICKS' STANDARD PLAYS.

FRANKENSTEIN.

BY R. B. PEAKE.

ORIGINAL COMPLETE EDITION.—PRICE ONE PENNY.

*** THIS PLAY CAN BE PERFORMED WITHOUT RISK OF INFRINGING ANY RIGHTS.

LONDON: JOHN DICKS, 313, STRAND.

for mad doctor movies, most notably Mary Shelley's 1818 novel *Frankenstein: or, The Modern Prometheus*. First off the mark was the 1910 silent American short **Frankenstein**, 'a liberal adaptation of Mrs. Shelley's story for Edison production' as the opening intertitle puts it. Directed by J. Searle Dawley, it ran for 16 minutes, and starred Charles Ogle as the Monster, who comes to life from a barrel of gloop in an animation scene where it looks as if a dummy has been set on fire and the footage run backward. This is actually more in keeping with how the creature is created in Mary Shelley's novel than the lightning that would soon become almost *de rigueur* in movie versions. (The monster itself bears a passing resemblance to the one Peter Cushing would create – played by David Prowse – in Hammer's 1974 **Frankenstein and the Monster from Hell**.) The second adaptation of Shelley's novel, also from America, was **Life Without Soul** (1915). A feature length film directed by Joseph W. Smiley, and starring Percy Darrell Standing as 'the brute man', it's now considered lost, although some stills survive. Also thought to be lost is the next adaptation, this time from Italy and released five years later. Eugenio Testa's **The Monster of Frankenstein** was also feature length, though cut to a running time of 39 minutes because of censorship issues.

We then come to James Whale's 1931 version of **Frankenstein**, the milestone of cinema that embedded an image of the Monster in the popular imagination that endures to this day, made an instant international star of Boris Karloff who played the Monster, and led a generation of cinemagoers to believe its creator's first name was Henry. It debuted hot on the heels of Tod Browning's unabashedly supernatural spinechiller **Dracula**, a movie that had also shocked mainstream audiences of the day. Previously, no matter how outlandish and outré the horrors suggested by the titles or tag lines of early Hollywood shockers, in true *Scooby-Doo* style, the denouement almost invariably showed any uncanny elements to have a rational, down-to-earth explanation. When Whale presented audiences with a man who really had 'made a monster!', a man who in a – frequently cut – line mused blasphemously on how he now knew how it felt like to be God, it's hardly surprising that pious 1930s filmgoers fainted in the aisles. Would audiences have found it less shocking if the Monster had been stitched together from live body parts – transplants if you will – rather than cadavers robbed from graves and organs rescued from jars? Bearing in mind religious sensibilities of the day, perhaps a poster line promising 'The man who created Man!' might have stirred up even more controversy. Accusations of impiety aside, the success of Tod Browning's **Dracula** had saved Universal Pictures from bankruptcy, and following the popularity of **Frankenstein**, the studio became synonymous with horror, though this didn't stop rivals from making their own contributions to the burgeoning genre.

The following year saw Paramount mounting its own classic mad doctor adaptation, Erle Kenton's **Island of Lost Souls** (from the 1896 H.G. Wells novel *The Island of Dr. Moreau*), which again faced censorship issues, particularly in the UK. That same year, Warner Bros. gave us an original mad doctor in the shape of **Doctor X**, directed by Michael Curtiz and starring Lionel Atwill and Fay Wray, whilst MGM adapted Sax Rohmer by casting Boris Karloff in **The Mask of Fu Manchu**. Meanwhile, Universal returned with Edgar Allan Poe's **Murders in the Rue Morgue**. It starred Bela Lugosi and was directed by Robert Florey (who were both originally in the frame for the studio's

top left: *Frankenstein* was a flop when first published as a novel, then became a hit on the stage, before becoming iconic on the big screen.

Frankenstein). In 1933, Lionel Atwill as Dr. Otto von Niemann, created life and tied Fay Wray to a chair in poverty row studio Majestic's **The Vampire Bat**. Universal's mad doctor offering for 1933 was another H.G. Wells adaptation, in which Claude Rains plays Jack Griffin, a research chemist driven mad as an unfortunate side effect of the procedure that turns him into **The Invisible Man**.

Fritz Lang's German film **The Testament of Dr. Mabuse** was released the same year, a sequel to Lang's two-part 1922 thriller **Dr. Mabuse the Gambler** (1922). (Lang would not revive the character again until 1960 with **The Thousand Eyes of Dr. Mabuse**, his final film.) Dr. Mabuse was originally conceived by the Luxembourgian writer Norbert Jacques, and intended to be a villainous mastermind in the style of other evil doctors like Fu Manchu and Guy Boothby's literary creation Dr. Nikola. To distinguish his villain, Jacques envisaged Mabuse as being not just one person, but several, with the suggestion that Mabuse is a nebulous, spectral entity that inhabits a series of hosts. When one is arrested or killed, another version of Mabuse appears.

There was little let up in the production of mad doctor movies in 1934. Sane psychiatrist Bela Lugosi was driven crazy by Boris Karloff in Edgar G. Ulmer's **The Black Cat**. Louis Friedlander's **The Raven** was released the following year, and also pitted Universal's biggest horror stars against each other. This time Lugosi plays a neurosurgeon, already mad at the start of the film, while Karloff was cast as his unwilling accomplice. While both films were billed as Poe adaptations, neither is particularly faithful to his work, with Ulmer's film in particular paying little more than lip service to its titular inspiration. Any audiences looking for something truer to Poe's prose – if decidedly lurid and tatty – could have watched Dwain Esper's **Maniac**, which as well as featuring a mad doctor trying to bring the dead back to life, included a meowing cat alerting the police to a bricked-up body.

In 1935, MGM gave us Peter Lorre performing hand and head transplants (or was he?) in Karl Freund's terrific expressionist **Mad Love**. That same year, in addition to **The Raven**, Universal gave the world the sequel it had been waiting for. **Bride of Frankenstein** managed to outdo its legendary

predecessor in every department, creating one of the most widely admired and adored films of all time, and ensuring director James Whale's eventual immortality, as documented in Bill Condon's 1998 biopic **Gods and Monsters**, adapted from Christopher Bram's novel *Father of Frankenstein* (1995).

Universal's 'first run' of horror films is generally regarded to have reached its end in 1936. Their mad doctor film for that year paired Karloff and Lugosi once more, in Lambert Hillyer's **The Invisible Ray**, a mixture of Gothic melodrama and science fiction. Michael Curtiz at MGM gave us Boris Karloff as a pianist executed for a murder he didn't commit, then brought back to life by Edmund Gwenn in **The Walking Dead**. In the same year the same studio gave us **Dracula** director Tod Browning's penultimate movie **The Devil-Doll** featuring Lionel Barrymore as an unjustly imprisoned businessman, who learns how to miniaturise human beings from his mad scientist cellmate, knowledge he uses to exact his revenge when he escapes. Meanwhile, Karloff went to the UK to make **The Man Who Changed His Mind** (1936) for director Robert Stevenson, re-titled – rather splendidly – as **The Brain Snatcher** when re-released in 1951. Presumably to belatedly cash in on the popularity of Robert Wise's 1945 film **The Body Snatcher**, which also starred Karloff. The story that inspired it was written by another Robert (Louis) Stevenson, and with the first cycle of

top right: The grave robbers Burke and Hare inspired numerous stories, including Robert Louis Stevenson's 'The Body Snatcher' (1884).

black and white talkie mad doctor pictures coming to an end, it's time to address another literary character who has enjoyed more than his fair share of screen adaptations.

Robert Louis Stevenson's *The Strange Case of Dr. Jekyll and Mr. Hyde* was first published in 1886, with the first film version coming out 22 years later. It's now believed lost, as are three more successive cinema adaptations, until 1912 when the earliest version known to still exist in its entirety went before the cameras. Director Lucius Henderson's 12-minute version of **Dr. Jekyll and Mr. Hyde** starred future film director James Cruze playing both title roles. (Though it has been claimed that Mr. Hyde is played by someone else in certain scenes, and watching the film today, it certainly isn't easy to tell when we are watching Mr. Cruze and when we aren't.) The transformation scene is done well, with Cruze's coiffed platinum-haired doctor degenerating into his loping, sallow-eyed alter ego. Another eight versions saw the light of a projector before the first phase of Universal's horror cycle came to an end. The most well-known include John Robertson's 1920 version starring John Barrymore, whose Dr. Jekyll provided a memorable transformation into a spider-like Mr. Hyde. In the same year, German director F.W. Murnau (who would famously go on to make an 'unofficial' – hence illegal – version of Bram Stoker's novel *Dracula* under the title **Nosferatu** in 1922) filmed **Der Januskopf**. The title's literal translation is 'The Janus Head', Janus being the Roman god with two faces. To avoid litigation the leads' names were changed from Jekyll and Hyde to Dr. Warren and Mr. O'Connor, both roles being played by Conrad Veidt. Veidt had made a memorable impression as the sleepwalking assassin Cesare under the control of another mad doctor – this time a hypnotist – in Robert Wiene's **The Cabinet of Dr. Caligari** just months earlier. On that basis alone, a Veidt interpretation of Jekyll and Hyde would be fascinating to see, but sadly this is yet another lost version of the story. Back in Hollywood, another silent version worth mentioning (and definitely worth seeing) is **Dr. Pyckle and Mr. Pryde** from 1925. A young Stan Laurel stars in this short comedy interpretation of the story, where the good doctor gets turned into a mischievous prankster. While Universal was busy with **Dracula** and **Frankenstein**, another studio, Paramount, was busy shooting the first sound version of Stevenson's classic novella. Rouben Mamoulian directed Fredric March in this 1931 film, which remains one of the most famous adaptations, featuring a revolutionary transformation scene between Jekyll and Hyde. March's performance in the title role is outstanding, winning him the Best Actor Oscar for that year, with the film's writing and cinematography also nominated.

The Motion Picture Industry Code – popularly known as the Hays Code after Will Hays, president of the Motion Picture Producers and Distributors of America – was just one element in a perfect storm facing horror cinema in the mid-1930s. The genre also faced diminishing box office returns, and an effective ban in the UK following controversies over the likes of **The Raven** and **Mad Love**. But, by the end of the decade, a lucrative re-release of 1931's **Dracula** and **Frankenstein** helped revive horror's fortunes, and mad doctors were soon back in business. Rowland V. Lee directed Basil Rathbone as the **Son of Frankenstein** (1939), the final Universal movie to feature Boris Karloff as the Monster. It was successful enough for Erle Kenton's **The Ghost of Frankenstein** to appear

left: Henry Jekyll, one of fiction's most eminent mad doctors.

in 1942, this time featuring Sir Cedric Hardwicke as Frankenstein's other son and Lon Chaney Jr. as the Monster. Bela Lugosi, who provided such a memorable performance as broken-necked Ygor in **Son of Frankenstein** was back, getting his brain transplanted into the Monster's body at the end. It therefore followed a kind of Universal monster logic that in the follow-up, **Frankenstein Meets the Wolf Man** (1943), the Monster should be played by Lugosi. The Monster was meant to speak with Lugosi's distinctive voice as well, but apparently when test audiences found Lugosi's dialogue hilarious, it was all cut. Roy William Neill, perhaps best known for making many of the Basil Rathbone Sherlock Holmes films (including one of the best, **The Scarlet Claw** in 1944) directed this battle of the titans. But Erle Kenton was back in the director's chair for the following year's **House of Frankenstein**. As was Boris Karloff, though this time as Dr. Gustav Niemann, escaping from the prison where he had been incarcerated for his brain transplant experiments, and intent on revenge on those who put him there. For that purpose he revives Dracula (John Carradine) from George Zucco's travelling circus, then thaws out both the Wolf Man (Lon Chaney Jr.) and the Frankenstein Monster (Western star Glenn Strange this time). It all ends in the local swamp where Niemann and the Monster get pursued by an angry mob.

Most of the monsters were back in 1945's **House of Dracula**, including Dracula, the Wolf Man and the Frankenstein Monster, all played by the same actors as in the previous film, and with Kenton directing again. This time they converge on the seaside mansion of Dr. Franz Edlemann (Onslow Stevens) who wants to help both them and his hunchbacked nurse Nina (Jane Adams). However, while trying to cure Dracula, he's inadvertently infected with the vampire's blood and becomes a madman, cackling with glee as he reanimates the Frankenstein Monster. The Wolf Man is cured, Dr. Edlemann gets shot, and the burning castle collapses on the Monster. The End. Not only of **House of Dracula** but of an entire movie cycle. After this the classic monsters would appear again, but only as comedy foils for Abbott and Costello.

Meanwhile, other studios were quick to cash in on the public's renewed appetite for mad doctors. Warner Bros. cast Humphrey Bogart in his only horror role in 1939's **The Return of Doctor X** (not a sequel despite the title). In the same year, the British company Argyle made **The Dark Eyes of London** (US title **The Human Monster**) which saw Bela Lugosi playing the struck off Dr. Orloff, up to no good beside the Thames. Boris Karloff, finally free of his Universal Frankenstein Monster make-up, embarked on a series of entertaining mad doctor movies for Columbia Pictures, including **The Man They Could Not Hang** (1939), **The Man with Nine Lives** (1940), **Before I Hang** (1940), (all three directed by Nick Grindé), **The Devil Commands** (1941) directed by Edward Dmytryk, and **The Boogie Man Will Get You** (1942) directed by **The Raven**'s Lew Landers. During this busy period

top left: The Hays Code, satirised in Whitey Schafer's 1940 photo.
top right: Mad doctor Bela Lugosi in **The Dark Eyes of London** (1939).

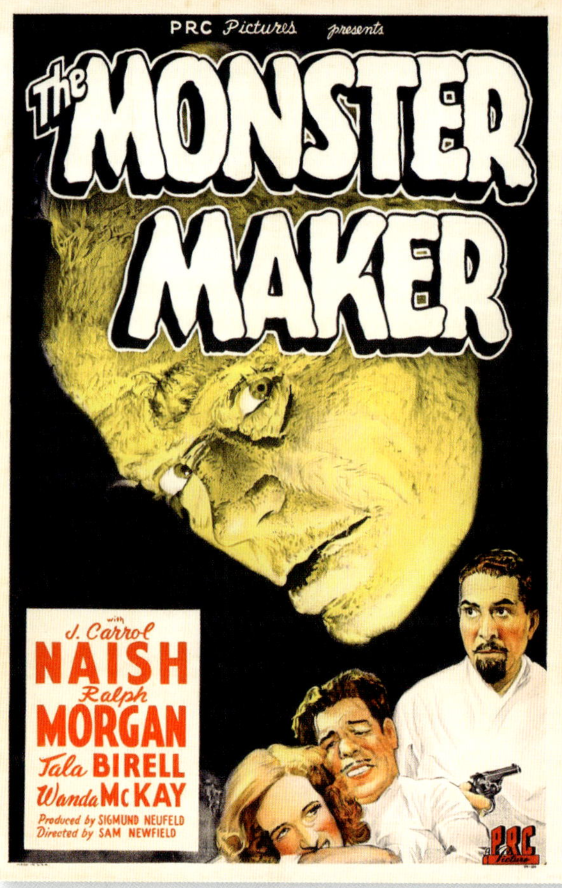

Karloff was also occupied transplanting the brain of a gangster into a college professor in Universal's **Black Friday** (1940), and experimenting with spinal fluid in **The Ape** (1940) for Monogram.

As well as their Frankenstein pictures, during the early-1940s Universal had plenty of other mad doctors up to no good for the public's entertainment. Lionel Atwill was Dr. Paul Rigas, filling up Lon Chaney Jr. with electricity in George Waggner's **Man Made Monster** (1941). Then Atwill was **The Mad Doctor of Market Street** (1942), relocating to a Caribbean island to continue his experiments in suspended animation. He popped up as another medical baddie in Universal's **The Ghost of Frankenstein** in the same year, and was red herring Dr. Fish in **The Strange Case of Doctor Rx** (also 1942). Meanwhile, George Zucco brought David Bruce back to life as **The Mad Ghoul**. In 1943 Universal released their **Captive Wild Woman**, in which John Carradine's Dr. Sigmund Walters turned a gorilla into a woman, proving successful enough in doing so that she appeared in two increasingly poor sequels.

Offerings from other major studios included Paramount's **Dr. Cyclops** (1940) which boasted tiny people in full colour. MGM remade **Dr. Jekyll and Mr. Hyde** (1941), with Spencer Tracy in the dual role and Ingrid Bergman and Lana Turner as the women in his life. Twentieth Century-Fox came up with **Dr. Renault's Secret** (1942) which was George Zucco attempting Moreau-like transformations of apes into men. Finally for the 1940s, Paramount produced a lavish version of Barré Lyndon's **The Man in Half Moon Street**, boasting a fabulous Miklós Rózsa score to accompany Nils Asther's attempts to keep himself eternally young.

The more modestly-budgeted end of Hollywood movie production also entered the 1940s mad doctor boom with gusto. Low rent outfit PRC (Producers Releasing Corporation) cast Bela Lugosi as Dr. Paul Carruthers, creator of giant bats who would kill anyone who wore his deadly aftershave in **The Devil Bat** (1940). Lugosi was back, trying to maintain his wife's youth with the glandular fluid of young women in **The Corpse Vanishes** (1942) for Monogram and producer Sam Katzman. More Lugosi Monogram madness was to be had in **The Ape Man** (1943), **Return of the Ape Man** (1944 and not a sequel), and perhaps best and most enjoyable of all, William Beaudine's **Voodoo Man** (also 1944). PRC released **The Mad Monster** (1942) in which George Zucco turned Glenn Strange into a werewolf, and 1944's **The Monster Maker**, in which J. Carrol Naish injected concert pianist Ralph Morgan with growth hormones to create an absurdly severe case of acromegaly. B-movie standbys director William Beaudine and star John Carradine were responsible for the last mad doctor of the 1940s, Monogram's 1946 **The Face of Marble**, a tale of voodoo and reanimation of the dead that doesn't make a lot of sense and is all the more worthwhile to watch because of it.

top left: Martha Vickers and John Carradine in **Captive Wild Woman** (1943).

The mad doctor movies of the 1950s suffered an inauspicious beginning as William Beaudine directed its title star in **Bela Lugosi Meets a Brooklyn Gorilla**. Lugosi played tropical island resident Dr. Zabor with an evil plan in store for Dean Martin and Jerry Lewis wannabes Duke Mitchell and Sammy Petrillo. Much better was 1953's **Donovan's Brain**, adapted from **Wolf Man** screenwriter Curt Siodmak's novel of the same name, in which scientists remove the brain of an evil tycoon, which then continues to influence those around it after death. Not at all good was the incomprehensible **Mesa of Lost Women** (1953). Still spoken of breathlessly by bad film enthusiasts, it's only watchable if you can stand the terrible music score. 1955 saw Bela Lugosi as Dr. Eric Vornoff creating a race of atomic supermen in a 'forsaken jungle hell' in Ed Wood's **Bride of the Monster**. Meanwhile over at Universal, mad professor Leo G. Carroll's solution for world hunger was to mess about with growth hormones, giving his assistant acromegaly (a condition that turns up more often in horror movies than most endocrine disorders) and creating a massive spider in Jack Arnold's **Tarantula** (1955), one of the best of the giant monster movies of the decade. The following year Universal completed its trilogy of movies featuring the Gill-man that had begun with 1954's **The Creature from the Black Lagoon**. John Sherwood's **The Creature Walks Among Us** had a group of bickering mad scientists capturing and vivisecting the Gill-man in this surprisingly gloomy and downbeat entry. There was a return to Gothic horror from low-budget outfit Bel-Air productions that same year. Reginald Le Borg directed a remarkable cast including Basil Rathbone, John Carradine, Akim Tamiroff, Lon Chaney Jr., Tor Johnson, and Bela Lugosi, in **The Black Sleep**. Rathbone's Dr. Cadman was trying to cure his wife's brain tumour (with some fun scenes of Victorian neurosurgery) while creating a dungeon full of 'mistakes' as he did so. In Jack Pollexfen's low-budget programmer, Robert Shayne's Professor Bradshaw turned death row's Charles 'The Butcher' Benton (Lon Chaney Jr.) into the **Indestructible Man** (also 1956). In 1957, producer Herman Cohen cast Whit Bissell as a mad scientist twice, first as hypnotherapist Dr. Brandon, causing Michael Landon to proclaim **I Was a Teenage Werewolf**, and then as a member of the American branch of the Frankenstein family, creating monster Gary Conway in **I Was a Teenage Frankenstein**. The film was made primarily in black and white, only transferring into colour at the end, providing audiences with a lurid final shot of the monster's face before the fade out.

Teenage Frankenstein's use of colour, plus a shot of a packing case labelled with the address 'Wardour Street' were nods to the fact that, as the 1950s progressed, something very special had started to happen on the other side of the Atlantic. Britain's Hammer Films, best known in the UK for making movie adaptations of popular radio and television programmes, had scored a big hit with their film version of the scary BBC science fiction serial **The Quatermass Experiment** (1955). But it was their next foray into fantasy cinema that broke office records all over the world, established them as a household name synonymous with the genre, and changed the face of cinema forever.

The Curse of Frankenstein (1957) was an interpretation of Mary Shelley's novel that went out of its way to avoid any suspicion that it had been inspired by James Whale's 1931 film (especially from Universal's legal department). A true team effort, Hammer's version had the critics recoiling in disgust (while still retaining the ability to write lengthy dismissive notices) and the audiences clamouring for more. Which they got the following year when most of the team (minus Lee's Creature, dissolved in acid

lower right: **The Quatermass Xperiment**, the 1955 sci fi shocker that helped launch Hammer Films into the horror game.

at the finale) returned for **The Revenge of Frankenstein**. This time the Baron's experiments in brain transplantation yielded a healthy individual (Michael Gwynn) who subsequently degenerates into cannibalism.

Back in the US, Edgar G. Ulmer's insipid **Daughter of Dr. Jekyll**, complete with giggling werewolf character, was a prime example of how desperately the genre needed a company like Hammer to revitalise it. Kindly local doctor Paul Beecher (John Beal) was turned into the much madder **The Vampire** (1957) when he took some vampire bat blood pills for a headache by mistake. In Boris Petroff's **The Unearthly** (also 1957), crazy Dr. Charles Conway (John Carradine) turned people into zombies while ostensibly trying to cure his patients' depression. Finally for that year, **The Man Who Turned to Stone** was one of a group of Eighteenth Century mad doctors who had kept themselves young by draining others' life force, but miss a treatment, leading to the effect rather spoilered in the title.

While Hammer were cashing in on their newfound success with **The Revenge of Frankenstein** (and going on to even greater success thanks to the casting of Christopher Lee in **Dracula**), 1958 saw numerous American filmmakers jumping on the Frankenstein bandwagon. Richard E. Cunha made the entertaining **Frankenstein's Daughter** in less than two weeks, featuring a monster that was supposed to be made from the body of a gorgeous woman played by a man who wasn't. Working with a bigger budget, director Howard Koch made **Frankenstein 1970** (apparently 'Frankenstein 1960' didn't sound futuristic enough) for producer Aubrey Schenck. This monster looked like the victim of a bad car accident (though not as bad as **Frankenstein's Daughter**), but the film was shot in CinemaScope and best of all had Boris Karloff as its creator. It was back to the UK for the rest of 1958's mad doctor movies. Capitalising on Hammer's success, producers Robert S. Baker and Monty Berman hired Jimmy Sangster to write their own Gothic horror. The result was **Blood of the Vampire**, in which Sir Donald Wolfit's Dr. Callistratus experimented on prison inmates and got to tie up Barbara Shelley. Producer Richard Gordon cast Karloff as Dr. Bolton, who researched anaesthetic agents in Robert Day's **Corridors of Blood**. Finally, the deliciously daft **Womaneater** had George Coulouris' Dr. Moran feeding women to the exotic plant he kept hidden in his Surrey basement to aid his experiments in reanimation.

The end of the decade brought another mad doctor remake from Hammer. **The Man Who Could Cheat Death** (1959) was a sexier, more melodramatic version of 1945's **The Man in Half Moon Street**, with Anton Diffring as the scientist trying to keep himself youthful. In the US, Vincent Price starred in William Castle's **The Tingler**, which saw the materialisation of a wobbling centipede-thing that could crush your spine if you didn't scream. Meanwhile George Macready was creating **The Alligator People** in the depths of Louisiana swampland in Roy Del Ruth's breezy monster picture. From Germany came **The Head** (**Die Nackte und der Satan** or **The Naked and Satan**) in which Horst Frank's Dr. Brandt dies but his assistant keeps his head alive using the

top left: **The Man Who Turned to Stone** (1957).
lower right: Vampires and Mad Doctors in **Blood of the Vampire** (1958).

doctor's techniques. Mexican director Fernando Méndez's **Black Pit of Dr. M** had two doctors researching the afterlife, and included a role for Abel Salazar, most famous to horror fans for his starring role in 1962's delirious **The Brainiac**. From the Philippines came the first in (eventually) a whole series of Filipino mad doctor movies with Gerardo de Leon's atmospheric reinterpretation of H.G. Wells' *The Island of Dr. Moreau* as **Terror Is a Man**. Finally, Jean Renoir wrote and directed **The Doctor's Horrible Experiment** aka **Experiment in Evil** aka **Le testament du Docteur Cordelier**, a modern-day retelling of the Jekyll and Hyde tale for French television.

As one decade ended with a Jekyll so did the new one begin. Hammer kicked off the 1960s with a fresh version of the story, scripted by acclaimed writer Wolf Mankowitz as perhaps the studio's bid for greater respectability. **The Two Faces of Dr. Jekyll** had Paul Massie going from hairy beardy decent doctor to smooth-faced pleasure seeker. It did not do well, either critically or financially.

The most influential mad doctor film of 1960 came from France in the form of Georges Franju's **Les yeux sans visage** (aka **Eyes Without a Face** and in the US as the splendidly Gothic **The Horror Chamber of Dr. Faustus**). The tale of Pierre Brasseur's mad surgeon trying to restore the face of his daughter, that he was himself responsible for ruining, turned a pulp horror plotline into the stuff of art, and influenced an entire subgenre of movies, including Robert Hartford-Davis' **Corruption** (1968) starring Peter Cushing, Jess Franco's **Faceless** (1988), and Pedro Almodóvar's **The Skin I Live In** (2011). Also from France, co-produced with Italy and filmed in part in Holland, came Giorgio Ferroni's **Mill of the Stone Women**, another tale of a mad doctor trying to cure his ill daughter, with an interesting line in 'artistic by-products'. The same year's **Seddok** (aka **Atom Age Vampire** and also from Italy) gave a variation to the Franju tale by having the girl be a stripper and the doctor have the ability to turn into a monster to help him abduct new victims. Mexico provided its own contribution to the wealth of movies based on Mary Shelley's most famous creation, with Rafael Baledón's **Orlak, the Hell of Frankenstein**, featuring a remote-controlled monster being used by a criminal for revenge.

1961 saw two more cinematic mad scientists from the UK. **Doctor Blood's Coffin** featured Hazel Court being threatened by a zombie in Cornwall at the climax, though the best thing about Sidney J. Furie's film was the title. It was better, however, than the same director's **The Snake Woman**, which featured cobras alive and biting in the Victorian North of England. The following year gave us, at one end of the budgetary spectrum, Terence Young's **Dr. No**, the first James Bond film, with Joseph Green's **The Brain That Wouldn't Die** at the other. From Italy came Riccardo Freda's necrophile Gothic fantasy **The Horrible Dr. Hichcock**, while in Spain Jess Franco began his exceptionally prolific career as a director with **The Awful Dr. Orlof**.

In 1963, Ray Milland had been encouraged to 'pluck it out' as Dr. Xavier in Roger Corman's **The Man with the X-Ray Eyes**. The following year **The Evil of Frankenstein** was Hammer's third in their cycle. It was conceived as what we would now call a reboot for the series, after a five-year absence from cinema screens, and therefore sadly didn't follow up on the intriguing promise of the previous entry. That same year Jess Franco unleashed **Dr. Orloff's Monster**, a sequel to the first film, and Martin Kosleck was a mad Nazi doctor dealing with little monsters (and one enormous one) in Jack Curtis' US production **The Flesh Eaters**. Victorian serial killer brain transplantation was the subject of Gino Mangini's Italian horror **The Hyena of London**, while India's **Mr. X in Bombay** had mad science turning someone invisible. Audiences saw the last in the Robert Lippert-produced trilogy of movies he began in 1958, based on George Langelaan's short story 'The Fly', with 1965's **Curse of the Fly**. That same year a new incarnation of Sax Rohmer's 'devil doctor'

top right: 007's foe Dr. Julius No in the first Bond film (1962).

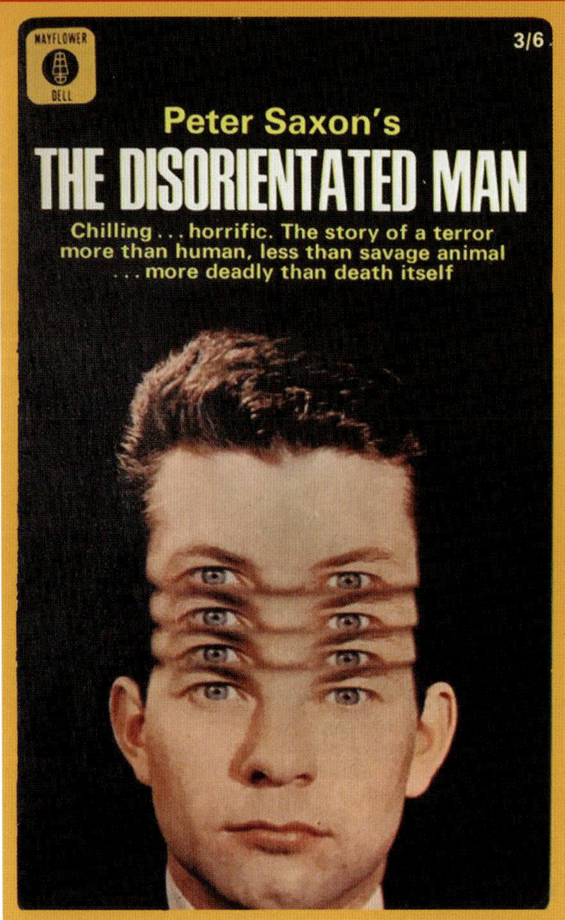

came to the screen in **The Face of Fu Manchu**, the first of five Anglo-German films to be produced by Harry Alan Towers and star Christopher Lee as the title character. Both this and **The Brides of Fu Manchu** the following year were directed by Don Sharp and were entertaining pulp adventures. Thereafter the series went downhill, with Jeremy Summers' **The Vengeance of Fu Manchu** (1967), with the final nails in the coffin of Fu being provided by two Jess Franco-directed pictures, **The Blood of Fu Manchu** (1968) and **The Castle of Fu Manchu** (1969).

In 1966 the Gothic giallo **The Murder Clinic** hailed from Italy, with more Franco (this time from France) in the shape of **The Diabolical Dr. Z**, while Herbert J. Leder made the rather silly but still somehow unnerving **The Frozen Dead** in the UK. Stateside, we got the final film from William 'One Shot' Beaudine, the memorably titled **Jesse James Meets Frankenstein's Daughter**. The following year saw more Peter Cushing, this time transplanting souls in Hammer's **Frankenstein Created Woman**, and investigating ludicrous giant moth murders in Tigon's **The Blood Beast Terror**, both from the UK. American expat Mel Welles directed the Spanish-German **Maneater of Hydra** aka **Island of the Doomed**, in which Cameron Mitchell created bloodsucking trees.

It took nearly ten years for Gerardo de Leon's **Terror Is a Man** to become a hit in the US (after being retitled **Blood Creature**). The demand for more Philippines-set horrors had resulted in **Brides of Blood** and then **Mad Doctor of Blood Island** (both 1968). **Mad Doctor** was yet another variation on the Moreau theme, but this time with chlorophyll creatures instead of ape men. It was successful enough to warrant a follow up entitled **Beast of Blood** shortly after. Meanwhile, from Mexico came **Snake People**, starring Boris Karloff in one of his final roles, as a mad doctor-cum evil voodoo priest. That sort of spoils the ending but I've just saved you 90 minutes of your life. From director Adrian Hoven (producer and star of the following year's **Mark of the Devil**) came the German-made **Castle of the Creeping Flesh**, in which mad aristocrat scientist Howard Vernon was trying to bring his raped and murdered daughter back to life. By 1969 the times they were a-changing and so was the face of horror, reflected by the eclectic bunch of movies made that year. Hammer and Peter Cushing gave us the best, grimmest, most nihilistic movie in the Frankenstein series so far with Terence Fisher's **Frankenstein Must Be Destroyed**. Meanwhile, rival studio Amicus, in collaboration with AIP, produced the fascinating **Scream and Scream Again**, an adaptation of the novel *The Disorientated Man* by Peter Saxon, admired by no less a creative force than **Dr. Mabuse** and **Metropolis** director Fritz Lang. From Argentina came Emilio Vieyra and Jerald Intrator's singular **The Curious Dr. Humpp**, in which a mad doctor needs the vital fluids he drains from people having sex to stop him from turning into a monster. Possibly inspired by cardiac surgeon Christian Barnard's ground-breaking research into cardiac transplantation (and then again, maybe not) René Cardona's **Night of the Bloody Apes** had a man's heart replaced by a gorilla's as a possible cure for leukaemia. Instead it turned him into, well, the title gives it away. Refusing to be outdone by any of this lunacy, the Japanese stepped up to the mark with Teruo Ishii's **Horrors of Malformed Men**, a loose adaptation of various story elements from

opposite top left: Edogawa Rampo – Japan's king of thriller fiction. (Say his pen name quickly to identify his main inspiration.)

the work of horror and thriller writer Edogawa Rampo. Did Rampo's work feature huge exploding flying penises? If so I don't believe the story that features them has been translated yet.

The 1970s opened with Hammer going back to where it all began with the minor misfire that was **The Horror of Frankenstein**, while Amicus cast Peter Cushing and Christopher Lee in Stephen Weeks' **I, Monster**, one of the most faithful adaptations of the Jekyll and Hyde tale despite changing the names of the lead character(s) to Charles Marlowe and Edward Blake. Also filming in the UK, AIP gave us Vincent Price in the delicious art deco revenge thriller that was Robert Fuest's **The Abominable Dr. Phibes**. From Canada came the curious contemporary-set **Dr. Frankenstein on Campus**, while France gave us one of the best mad doctor films of 1970, Claude Mulot's **La rose ecorchée** (another variation on **Les yeux sans visage**), as well as one of the worst in Pierre Chevalier's **Orloff and the Invisible Man**, a film so tatty and silly it's easy to mistake it for the work of a bored and disinterested Jess Franco. From the US, **The Incredible 2-Headed Transplant** had Bruce Dern as a mad scientist conducting research into head transplantation (this is not a field of actual research in case anyone is wondering) and popping the head of a psycho-killer onto the body of his caretaker's brain-damaged son. Who thinks these things up?

Hammer gave us a pair of Gothic mad doctor classics in 1971 with Brian Clemens' creatively kinky twist on a well-worn theme in the shape of **Dr. Jekyll and Sister Hyde**. Peter Sasdy made arguably the best film of his career (and certainly one of the best Hammers) with **Hands of the Ripper**, featuring Eric Porter as an increasingly mad psychiatrist, determined to get to the bottom of why Angharad Rees feels the need to regularly impale people with a variety of sharp objects. Robert Fuest and Vincent Price struck once more, this time taking their creative villain to Egypt with **Dr. Phibes Rises Again** for AIP. Meanwhile, the US was churning out plenty of old tat, such as Al Adamson's **Dracula vs. Frankenstein** and **Brain of Blood**, the latter intended to look like the latest 'Blood' picture from the Philippines despite being shot in Los Angeles. Del Tenney's 1964-shot, previously unreleasable, **I Eat Your Skin** was finally given life on a double-bill with David Durston's far superior **I Drink Your Blood** thanks to enterprising distributor Jerry Gross. Lowest budgeted of the lot was Don Barton's **Zaat** aka **Blood Waters of Dr. Z**, which featured the deranged Dr. Leopold creating swamp monsters in a bid for worst mad doctor film ever made. Italy kept audiences of a certain sophistication entertained with Mel Welles' sex and horror filled **Lady Frankenstein** and Fernando Di Leo's sex and horror and Klaus Kinski-filled **Slaughter Hotel**. The two films also starred Rosalba Neri, and very watchable she was in both.

The UK came up with a cracking pair of mad doctor pictures for 1972. Robert Powell tried to identify which of the four patients he spoke to was the recently-insane head of the **Asylum** from Amicus. While Tigon and World Film Services teamed Christopher Lee and Peter Cushing as competing

top right: Many thought Jack the Ripper had to be a medical man, such as improbable suspect Doctor Thomas Neill Cream.

brothers in Freddie Francis' **The Creeping Flesh**, one of the last great British Gothic horrors of the period. Spain's Paul Naschy came up with his own spin on the Robert Louis Stevenson story with (unsurprisingly for anyone familiar with his oeuvre) **Doctor Jekyll and the Werewolf**, while fellow Spaniard Jess Franco threw together **Dracula, Prisoner of Frankenstein**, which also featured a zero-budget werewolf as well as many of the director's by-now well recognised obsessions. Brian De Palma, on the way to developing a reputation as one of America's most stylish filmmakers, gave us the tale of Margot Kidder as conjoined twins under the control of William Finley in **Sisters**, while J.G. Patterson's **Doctor Gore** was a much lower budget American mad doctor picture. Meanwhile, in the Philippines, director Eddie Romero, still milking H.G. Wells' Dr. Moreau concept, turned Pam Grier into the panther woman in **The Twilight People**, while the Shenck brothers (George and Aubrey) filmed their own version in the same country in the same year, adding a dollop of 1932's **The Most Dangerous Game** and calling it **Superbeast**.

Mad doctor movies continued to proliferate around the world in 1973. From Spain, Paul Naschy starred in **The Hunchback of the Morgue**, Jess Franco directed **The Sinister Eyes of Dr. Orloff** and **The Erotic Rites of Frankenstein**, and Eloy de la Iglesia made the **Clockwork Orange**-like **Murder in a Blue World**. Richard Gordon produced **Horror Hospital**, which saw Michael Gough doing horrible things to people's brains in a British country house, while Graham Crowden was turning people into giant guinea pigs in a similar location in Lindsay Anderson's **O Lucky Man!**. Hammer produced their final Gothic horror, bringing back Peter Cushing to star in **Frankenstein and the Monster from Hell**. In the US, Strother Martin turned Dirk Benedict into a reptile in Bernard Kowalski's **Sssssss** aka **Ssssnake**, S.F. Brownrigg delivered a sweaty Deep South Gothic with **Don't Look in the Basement**, Eddie Saeta's **Doctor Death Seeker of Souls** brought the low-budget mayhem back to Los Angeles, while William A. Levey's **Blackenstein** was not a patch on AIP's **Blacula**. The most lavishly-budgeted US mad doctor movie for that year could be seen on the small screen, as Jack Smight directed Leonard Whiting as creator and Michael Sarrazin as the created in **Frankenstein: The True Story** (it wasn't). France's Alain Jessua cast Alain Delon and Annie Girardot in the social satire **Traitement de choc** (aka **The Doctor in the Nude**), while Andy Warhol lent his name (and members of his 'Factory') to the Paul Morrissey directed **Flesh for Frankenstein**, which was filmed in Italy. Finally, Mexican director Juan López Moctezuma (best known for the delirious **Alucarda**) directed **The Mansion of Madness** aka **Dr. Tarr's Torture Dungeon**, loosely based on a story by Poe.

In 1974, Donald Pleasence tried to cross humans with plants, creating **The Mutations** in Jack Cardiff's sleazy film. Mel Brooks directed one of the all-time classic horror comedies (and got to use some of the original Kenneth Strickfaden laboratory equipment) with the black and white **Young Frankenstein**, after shooting the hit **Blazing Saddles**. In Italy, Klaus Kinski was the mad scientist in Sergio Garrone's Gothic **The Hand That Feeds the Dead**, with the same cast and director reuniting for **Lover of the Monster**, released only a month later. Both films also shared some footage but are not alternate titles for each other. Meanwhile, Rossano Brazzi was Count Frankenstein discovering a Neanderthal man amongst other absurdities in Dick Randall's **Frankenstein's Castle of Freaks**.

top right: It's alive! Gene Wilder in **Young Frankenstein** (1974).
bottom left: **The Twilight People** (1972).

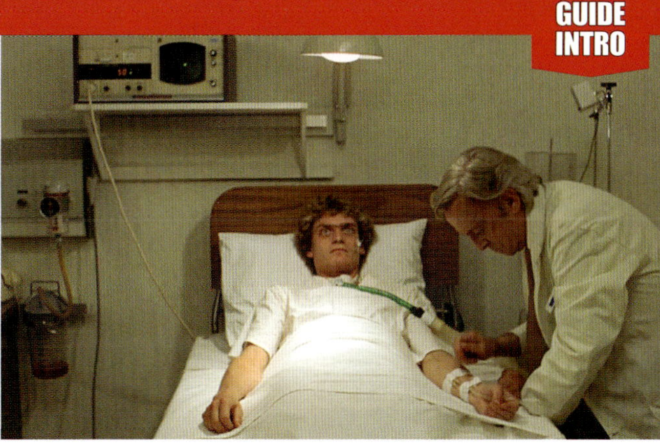

1975 had people singing along to Frank N. Furter's attempts to make a man with blond hair and a tan in Jim Sharman and Richard O'Brien's British piece of cult eccentricity **The Rocky Horror Picture Show**. Of all countries, it was Canada that had audiences either speechless or running for the cinema exits with a double dose of extreme horror from either end of the artistic spectrum in the form of **Shivers** – David Cronenberg's first foray into body horror – and Don Edmonds' nasty Nazi exploitationer **Ilsa, She Wolf of the SS**.

There was more blaxploitation from the US in 1976, as Bernie Casey turned himself into an Albino bloodsucker in William Crain's **Dr. Black, Mr. Hyde**. Rock Hudson grew Barbara Carrera in a lab in Ralph Nelson's **Embryo**, and Michael Pataki directed Richard Basehart in a variation on Franju's **Les yeux sans visage** as a doctor concentrating specifically on 'Les yeux' as he attempted to restore his daughter's sight, lost in an accident that was (of course) of his own doing in **Mansion of the Doomed**. Jess Franco contributed his version of the Whitechapel murders, starring Klaus Kinski as the title character in the Swiss-shot **Jack the Ripper**.

The year 1977 also proved a fruitful one for mad doctors from around the world. Director and star José Mojica Marins, most famous for his Coffin Joe pictures, made the sex and lurid mutilation-filled **Inferno carnal**. Thinking he could do better than all those Filipino versions (he could), Samuel Z. Arkoff produced a new adaptation of Wells' **The Island of Dr. Moreau**, directed by Don Taylor and starring Burt Lancaster and Michael York. Not quite the equal of the 1932 version, it was, nevertheless, an entirely creditable remake. Canada gave us more body horror with David Cronenberg's **Rabid**, but this time they left the nasty Nazisploitation to the Italians, who acquitted themselves admirably in that capacity (if such a thing can ever be considered admirable) with Luigi Batzella (directing as 'Ivan Katansky'), managing to make **The Beast in Heat** somehow filled with acts of bad taste while at the same time being really rather dull.

Junior doctor Geneviève Bujold uncovered an organ transplant conspiracy in Michael Crichton's movie adaptation of Robin Cook's novel **Coma** in 1978. Meanwhile in Australia, ballet megastar Robert Helpmann (from Powell and Pressburger's 1948 **The Red Shoes**, and 1968's **Chitty Chitty Bang Bang**'s Child Catcher, amongst many others) played Doctor Roget, studying the psychic powers of comatose patient **Patrick** in Richard Franklin's hospital thriller. The same year Billy Wilder contributed to the genre with **Fedora**, a film made in France and featuring José Ferrer as the disgraced Dr. Vando, whose 'youth enhancing' treatments may have contributed to the film star title character's unstable mental state.

Canadian director David Cronenberg was back in 1979, getting Samantha Eggar to somatise her rage in the form of **The Brood**, at the behest of Oliver

top right: Medical malpractice down under in **Patrick** (1978).

Reed's experimental psychiatrist Dr. Raglan. The same year, David Warner appeared as Dr. John Stevenson – aka Jack the Ripper – pursued across time by Malcolm McDowell's H.G. Wells in Nicholas Meyer's Hollywood science fiction thriller **Time After Time**. Also from the US, but on a much lower budget, came Gregory Goodell's **Human Experiments**, in which Linda Haynes found herself wrongly convicted, then subject to the attentions of mad prison doctor Geoffrey Lewis. Finally for 1979, Sergio Martino's **Island of the Fishmen** aka **Screamers** was another loose *Island of Dr. Moreau* adaptation from Italy. Despite the claims of the American trailers, viewers did not get to see a man turned inside out.

The following year brought more low-budget lunacy from Italy. First in the form of **Patrick vive ancora** (**Patrick Still Lives**), a sequel to Richard Franklin's 1978 picture that was as sleazy as it was unofficial. Director Mario Landi's film was matched for daftness by Marino Girolami's **Zombie Holocaust** aka **Doctor Butcher M.D.**, which managed to combine current trends for both cannibal and zombie movies. In France, the frequently vampire-girls-in-diaphanous-clothing-obsessed Jean Rollin made the gloomy, thoughtful, hospital-based horror **The Night of the Hunted**. It was left to the US to come up with some bigger-budgeted, far more lavish, mad doctor movies from name directors. Brian De Palma went Hitchcock crazy (and cheated a fair bit) with **Dressed to Kill**, while Ken Russell, never a director to hold back, sent William Hurt on an odyssey of the weird in **Altered States**.

The US contributions to the mad doctor genre proved considerably less ambitious and lower profile in 1981. Barbi Benton was stalked by a mad slasher doctor (quite possibly a first) in Boaz Davidson's **X-Ray** aka **Hospital Massacre**, while boredom-monger Jerry Warren made the eminently fast-forwardable (for those few who dared to watch it) **Frankenstein Island**. However, there were great directors making great mad doctor movies elsewhere. Cult Italian favourite Lucio Fulci gave us the immortal, if a bit loose at the seams, Doctor Freudstein, living in the basement of **The House by the Cemetery**. While in Canada, David Cronenberg worked with his biggest budget and scored his biggest hit to date with his exploding head movie **Scanners**. The Polish arthouse director Walerian Borowczyk came up with his socio-cultural perverse take on the Stevenson novella with **The Strange Case of Dr. Jekyll and Miss Osbourne**. In Australia, director Michael Laughlin had mad Arthur Dignam assisted by sexy Fiona Lewis in creating teenaged murderers in **Strange Behavior**. While finally, from India there was hairy-monster-making in the Ramsay brothers' **Dahshat**.

Graham Crowden was up to more mad science in another Lindsay Anderson picture in 1982, transplanting Malcolm McDowell's head so loosely it got pulled off courtesy of some fine Nick Maley effects in **Britannia Hospital**. That same year, Aaron Lipstadt's **Android** had Klaus Kinski creating robot Max 404 (Don Opper) on a remote space station. Carl Reiner directed Steve Martin as Dr. Michael Hfuhruhurr, otherwise

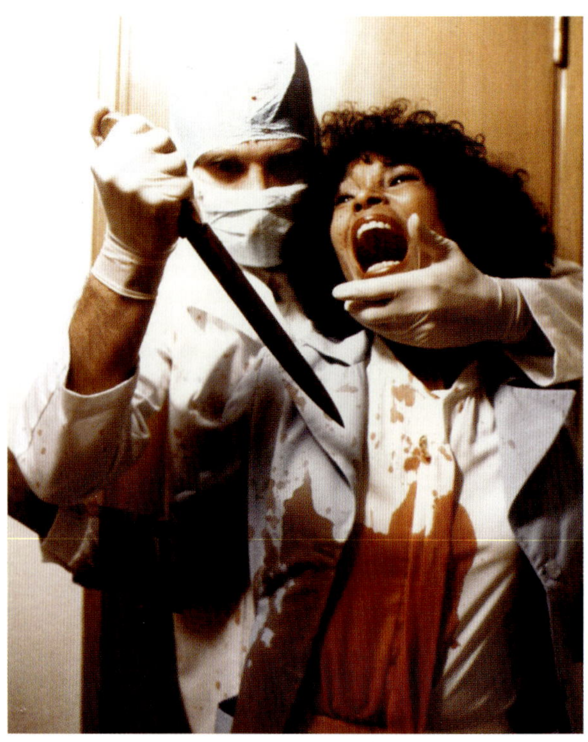

bottom right: **X-Ray** aka **Hospital Massacre** (1981).

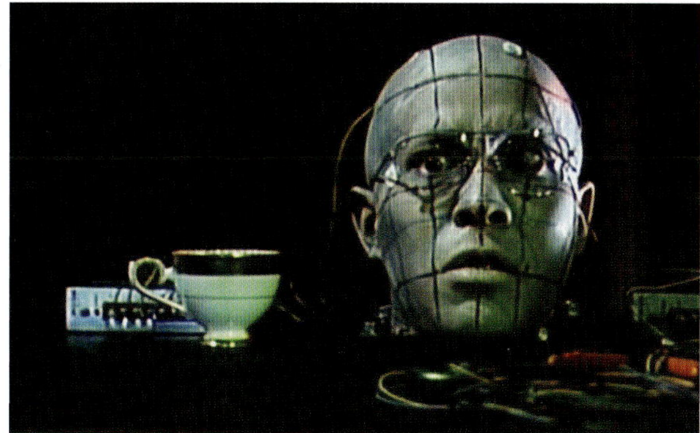

known as **The Man with Two Brains** in 1983. David Warner came along for the ride as Dr. Alfred Necessiter. 1984 proved the year of Frankenstein comedies with Alain Jessua's **Frankenstein 90** from France and Myron Gold's **Frankenstein's Great Aunt Tillie** from Mexico, the latter wasting an interesting cast including Donald Pleasence, Yvonne Furneaux, June Wilkinson, and Aldo Ray.

In 1985 Franc Roddam – best known for creating the BBC TV show *Masterchef* – directed an eclectic cast (including Sting and Jennifer Beals) in **The Bride**, a new version of James Whale's 1935 sequel to **Frankenstein**. It was the US that gave us 1985's best mad doctors, however, in the form of Richard Liberty's Logan, experimenting on the walking dead in his gore-splashed laboratory in George A. Romero's **Day of the Dead**, and Jeffrey Combs playing the title role of Herbert West in Stuart Gordon's adaptation of H.P. Lovecraft's **Re-Animator**. Gordon's film was a huge success, and another Lovecraft adaptation from the same team appeared the following year. **From Beyond** (1986) used the author's short story as its prologue before shooting off into its own decidedly kinky universe. The same year, David Cronenberg got mainstream mass audience acceptance without having to compromise a jot as he spliced Jeff Goldblum's Seth Brundle with *Musca domestica* in his superior remake of **The Fly**. Something far more bizarre came from Japan that year with **Devil Woman Doctor**, the fourth film in the controversial Guinea Pig series. The next, **Android of Notre Dame** (1989), also featured medical-based torture mayhem.

Jeffrey Obrow and Stephen Carpenter directed Rod Steiger as Dr. Lloyd in **The Kindred** (1987), which featured genetic experimentation and the creation of a monstrous 'baby brother'. Jess Franco was still busy, this time in France and with a budget that allowed him to cast stars Helmut Berger and Telly Savalas in **Faceless**, yet another take on Franju's film. Rather than accept the numerous Hollywood pictures offered to him on the back of **The Fly**'s success, David Cronenberg's next film was **Dead Ringers** (1988) in which twin gynaecologists played by Jeremy Irons became obsessed with patient Geneviève Bujold. Also from Canada, and released the same year, came **Pin**, in which an office anatomy model began to influence a doctor's family.

Kenneth Cranham was Dr. Channard, looking for a gateway to Hell (he found it) in Tony Randel's sequel to Clive Barker's original in the 1988 **Hellbound: Hellraiser II**. The following year another sequel to a milestone original saw Jeffrey Combs trying to recreate (or at least reanimate) the female of the species in Brian Yuzna's **Bride of Re-Animator**. Also from the US came Brett Leonard's entertainingly ambitious gore-splattered **The Dead Pit**, featuring an undead doctor and the patients he was buried with, while Stephen Sayadian's **Dr. Caligari** documented the activities of the grand-daughter of the character portrayed by Werner Krauss in the Robert Wiene original, offering audiences the kind of unique take one might expect from the director of 1982's **Cafe Flesh**. Back in India, heart transplants and a rampaging ghoul were some of the delights to be found in Mohan Bhakri's **Kabrastan**.

The 1990s opened with big-budget Hollywood mad doctor (or at least mad medical student) action, as Kiefer Sutherland led fellow brat packers Julia Roberts, Kevin Bacon, and William Baldwin

top left: Steve Martin is **The Man with Two Brains** in 1983.
top right: **Android of Notre Dame** (1989).

as the **Flatliners**, bringing themselves back from the brink of death, neuroses and all. If you preferred low-budget and sleazy then Hollywood could provide that as well in the form of Frank Henenlotter's **Frankenhooker**, in which student Jeffrey Franken (James Lorinz) loses his girlfriend in a tragic lawnmower accident but plans to bring her back with the aid of bits and pieces of prostitutes. Australia gave us Alec Mills' **Dead Sleep**, in which nurse Linda Blair investigated murders in a psychiatric unit.

Anthony Hopkins chilled audiences while winning an Oscar for his 1991 portrayal of Thomas Harris' psychopathic cannibal psychiatrist Hannibal Lecter in Jonathan Demme's **The Silence of the Lambs**, which also won four other major Academy Awards. David Cronenberg was back that year too, 'filming the unfilmable', in this case William Burroughs' book **Naked Lunch**, which featured Roy Scheider as Dr. Benway amongst its star turns in the drug-fuelled world of Interzone. Dr. Agatha Webb (Lindsay Duncan) gave Jeff Fahey the arm of a convicted murderer after he lost his own in a car accident in Eric Red's **Body Parts**, a movie that started off **Hands of Orlac** but quickly spiralled off into its own world of gleeful mad surgery. **Jenma Natchathiram** was an unofficial Tamil remake of Richard Donner's **The Omen**, where the birth of the Antichrist was coordinated by the evil Doctor Philips (V. Gopalakrishnan), while from India H.N. Singh's **Khatra** was another version of the Frankenstein tale.

Brian De Palma gave John Lithgow five starring roles – as a mad doctor and the results of his experimenting on his family – in 1992's **Raising Cain**. Also from the US came Larry Drake as **Dr. Giggles**, doing a Michael Myers by escaping from an asylum to terrorise the town where he was involved in a murder spree when he was younger. Danny Lee and Billy Tang's **Dr. Lamb** was allegedly based on the true story of a Hong Kong taxi driver serial killer. From the mind of Shinya Tsukamoto came **Tetsuo II: Body Hammer** which, in briefest and sanest terms, was about a mad scientist creating cyborg warriors. The sequel **Tetsuo: The Bullet Man**, followed in 2009.

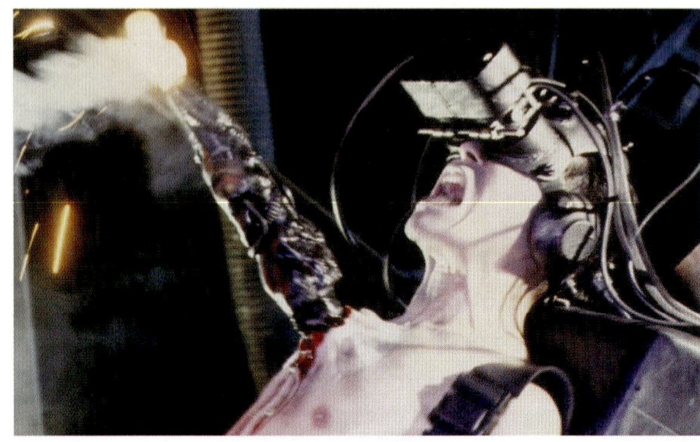

top: James Lorinz stars in **Frankenhooker** (1990).
lower right: Japanese body horror in **Tetsuo II: Body Hammer** (1992).

The middle segment of Brian Yuzna's Lovecraft anthology movie **Necronomicon** (1993) was an adaptation of the author's 'Cool Air' featuring David Warner as the medic who can only remain alive at low temperatures. Perhaps inspired by the success of Francis Ford Coppola's **Bram Stoker's Dracula** the previous year, in 1994 Kenneth Branagh directed **Mary Shelley's Frankenstein**, also casting himself in the lead, opposite Robert De Niro as his creation.

In 1996 New Line Cinema finally released their troubled adaptation of **The Island of Dr. Moreau**. It starred Marlon Brando and Val Kilmer, and was initially directed by Richard Stanley, who was then replaced by John Frankenheimer, with a lot of tearing out of hair in between. Michael Apted directed and Elizabeth Hurley produced **Extreme Measures**, in which junior doctor Hugh Grant found himself trying to find out why derelicts and vagrants keep disappearing from the streets close to the hospital of the famous Dr. Lawrence Myrick (Gene Hackman). Also that year, Corbin Bernsen was **The Dentist**, going insane after discovering his wife having an affair, and inflicting dental torture on all and sundry. (He was up to more illicit drilling and filling in the sequel **The Dentist 2** two years later.) Those looking for the more lunatic side of cinema in 1996 would have been well advised to turn their sights on Japan. Shozin Fukui's **Rubber's Lover** was 91 minutes of drug-crazed insanity filmed in black and white, with a grinding soundtrack to accompany all the screaming. Hisayasu Satô's **Naked Blood** was about a drug that turns pain into pleasure, and the three women to whom it is inadvertently administered, leading to deep fried hands and repetitive cutting and mutilation. Kei Fujiwara's **Organ** featured detectives on the trail of human organ traffickers, only for things to take a turn for the insanely splatter-filled.

Jess Franco cast his muse Lina Romay and US scream queen Michelle Bauer as creator and created respectively in 1998's **Lust for Frankenstein**. The following year saw Jeffrey Combs as the spectral but still mad Dr. Vannacutt, roaming the corridors with some of his patients/victims in William Malone's entertaining remake of **House on Haunted Hill**. Saffron Burrows was trying to cure dementia by performing brain surgery on sharks in Renny Harlin's decidedly potty 1999 movie **Deep Blue Sea**. From Japan, **Tetsuo** director Shinya Tsukamoto's **Gemini** was based on the Edogawa Rampo story 'The Twins', and concerned a doctor whose life is being destroyed by his avenging twin brother. Completing our line-up for 1999, in the Hong Kong film **Trust Me U Die** (aka **The New Dr. Lamb**), Simon Yam plays Dr. Greg Fong, who

top: Open wide! Corbin Bernsen is **The Dentist** (1996).

invents a super steroid that, amongst other things, turns his colleague and black market organ trafficker Dr. Mike (Mark Cheng) into a rapist.

The most financially successful film in Germany in 2000 was the country's home-produced **Anatomie**, in which **Run Lola Run**'s Franka Potente discovered a secret surgical society up to unethical practices. A sequel (**Anatomie 2**) followed in 2003. Viewers who wanted demented lunacy coupled with sub-par animation only needed to look once again to Japan to fry their brains with **Biohazard 4D-Executor**, a twenty-minute short about a squad sent into a city to find a medical researcher.

In 2001, Anthony Hopkins revisited the role that, after an already lengthy and respected career, had elevated him to megastar status. **Hannibal** saw him without director Jonathan Demme (Ridley Scott helmed) or co-star Jodie Foster (Julianne Moore played Clarice Starling). Gary Oldman, perhaps tired of being the actor with so many different faces, instead played someone without one at all as Lecter's nemesis Mason Verger. From France that year came Claire Denis' **Trouble Every Day**, which starred Vincent Gallo as the subject of an experiment that takes desire to its extremes.

More than ten years after we last saw him, it turned out Jeffery Combs' Herbert West had ended up in a Spanish prison, but was still busy continuing his experiments into conquering brain death in Brian Yuzna's **Beyond Re-Animator** (2003). Meanwhile, back in the US, Rob Zombie made his feature directorial debut with the sleazy grindhouse-style tale of the undead Dr. Satan, creator of the **House of a Thousand Corpses**.

Andreas Marschall's **Tears of Kali** was a 2004 German anthology picture with a framework that involved the Indian-based Taylor-Eriksson cult. Its middle story, 'Devi', concerned a doctor who has an unorthodox method for treating a socially dysfunctional hooligan. From Japan that year came Masayuki Ochiai's **Infection**, about evil on the prowl in an understaffed hospital. Nick Hamm's **Godsend**, which starred Greg Kinnear, Rebecca Romijn, and Robert De Niro, was a Canadian picture about the potential horrors of cloning. Meanwhile, Charles Band, head honcho at Empire and then Full Moon pictures, contributed his own version of the oft-adapted H.G. Wells novel with **Dr. Moreau's House of Pain**.

Mad veterinary science was then the order of the day in Ireland, creating monstrous bovine mutations on a grim and impoverish farm in Billy O'Brien's **Isolation** (2005). **Lunacy**, from the cult Czech director Jan Svankmajer, paid tribute to both Edgar Allan Poe and the Marquis de Sade in 2005, with its tale of Jean Berlot (Pavel Liska), confined to a lunatic asylum where he encounters a cavalcade of weirdness. The following year saw a US remake of Brian De Palma's **Sisters** with Stephen Rea as the doctor and Lou Doillon in

top left: Anthony Hopkins in **Hannibal** (2001).

Chill (2007) was an American adaptation of Lovecraft's 'Cool Air' by way of EuroTrash. Both doctor and patients burst into song in **Repo! The Genetic Opera** in 2008. Anthony Stewart Head plays the 'Repo Surgeon' whose job it is to repossess organs from patients who had missed payments in Darren Lynn Bousman's entertaining futuristic movie-cum-graphic novel. Also from the US that year was Adam Gierasch's **Autopsy**, featuring a nod to Burroughs with its villainous Dr. Benway (Robert Patrick). The UK had Lena Headey as a radiologist discovering people slowly being replaced by doppelgängers in Sean Ellis' **The Broken**. From Japan, Yoshihiro Nishimura's **Tokyo Gore Police** had its mad scientist creating weird, mutated creatures called 'Engineers' that had to be hunted down.

the dual role. Also from the US, John Stockwell's **Turistas** features a Brazilian transplant surgeon planning to harvest organs from American backpackers, including Melissa George. In 2007 there was more organ harvesting in **Sick Nurses** from Thailand, while Kôji Kawano's nudity-filled if rather incoherent Japanese film **The Girl Rebel Force of Competitive Swimmers** had a vaccine turning the cast into zombies.

Tom Six's Dutch shocker **The Human Centipede (First Sequence)** (2009) upset all kinds of people with its pulp horror plotline concerning mad Dr. Heiter, surgically joining people together mouth-to-anus. (Six told his funding source that it would be a film about a crazy doctor who sews people together but he left out the words 'mouth' and 'anus' because he knew he would never be given the money if he revealed this much detail!) That same year, Vincenzo Natali's **Splice** had scientists Adrien Brody and Sarah Polley creating a new organism they name Dren (Delphine Chanéac), in this Canadian-French co-production. Meanwhile, India came up with the giallo-esque **13B: Fear Has a New Address**, while Japan rounded out the decade with Kôji Shiraishi's **Grotesque**, which was 73 minutes of nihilistic torture nastiness wherein a surgeon tormented an unfortunate couple. Yoshihiro Nishimura and Naoyuki Tomomatsu's

top left: **Repo! The Genetic Opera** defied critics to become a cult hit. lower left: **Splice** (2009), lower right: **The Human Centipede** (2009).

Vampire Girl vs Frankenstein Girl was lighter in tone, though also completely barking mad. Panos Cosmatos (later to direct Nicolas Cage in **Mandy** in 2018) made his first feature in Canada in 2010. **Beyond the Black Rainbow** was the measured (and some would say ponderous) tale of bizarre happenings at a health institute. **The Sylvian Experiments** were in brain surgery and their subjects were teenagers in Japanese director Hiroshi Takahashi's tale of nightmarish research. Scott David Russell's **Exquisite Corpse** was a modern-day American tale of a young neuroscientist attempting to reanimate his dead bride to be.

From Spain, Pedro Almodóvar gave us his entry in the genre in 2011. Antonio Banderas plays a brilliant plastic surgeon with his fair share of secrets, including a beautiful girl he keeps locked up at his remote home in **The Skin I Live In**. Eron Sheean's **Errors of the Human Body** – a US-German co-production – didn't live up to its splendid title, but was still an interesting, chilly, Cronenbergian look at viral research. Much better was **Antiviral**, from David Cronenberg's son Brandon, in which fans could pay to be infected with viruses suffered by the rich and famous. Canada continued to give us that year's best mad doctor films with **American Mary**. 'Twisted Twins' Jen and Sylvia Soska directed this tale of down-on-her-luck medical student Katherine Isabelle, who resorts to taking a job as a body modification surgeon, before discovering she was actually very good at it. The Soskas returned to the world of science and surgery in 2019 with their remake of David Cronenberg's **Rabid**.

In the 2013 US film **The Harvest** (aka **Can't Come Out to Play**), surgeon Samantha Morton and husband Michael Shannon were keeping something in the basement. It was directed by John McNaughton, best known for his 1986 feature debut **Henry: Portrait of a Serial Killer**. Meanwhile, Dutch director Richard Raaphorst managed to combine World War II, found footage, a descendant of the dreaded Baron, and some cracking monsters in **Frankenstein's Army**.

above: Mad science in **Frankenstein's Army** (2013).
opposite lower left: **Frankenstein vs. the Mummy** (2015).

In Australia, Mark Hartley remade **Patrick** (2013), with Charles Dance in the mad scientist role and Sharni Vinson as the nurse the titular comatose patient develops a liking for. In 2014, Kevin Smith turned Justin Long into a walrus (or rather Michael Parks did) in **Tusk**. Ben Kingsley directed his slice of American Gothic, **Stonehearst Asylum** – Brad Anderson's adaptation of Poe's 'The System of Dr. Tarr and Professor Fether', starring Kate Beckinsale and Jim Sturgess. In the UK, the resurrected Hammer Films has Jared Harris performing paranormal experiments on Olivia Cooke in the early-1970s in **The Quiet Ones**. Ryan Bellgardt's 2014 American movie **Army of Frankensteins** combined time travel, parallel universes, numerous Frankenstein monsters, and the American Civil War. To say it was a bit of a mess would be an understatement.

Much better films to bear the name Frankenstein came out in 2015 from the US and the UK. Bernard Rose's **Frankenstein** was a modern-day Los Angeles-based remake with a touching lead performance from Xavier Samuel as the creation – it also features a turn from **Candyman** star Tony Todd as the blind man who befriends him. Far more irreverent (and deliciously so) was Paul McGuigan's period-set **Victor Frankenstein**, which told the tale from Igor's point of view. Daniel Radcliffe played the assistant with James McAvoy in the title role. Less accomplished was Damien Leone's **Frankenstein vs. the Mummy**, which pitted both scientist and monster against the mummy of an evil pharaoh.

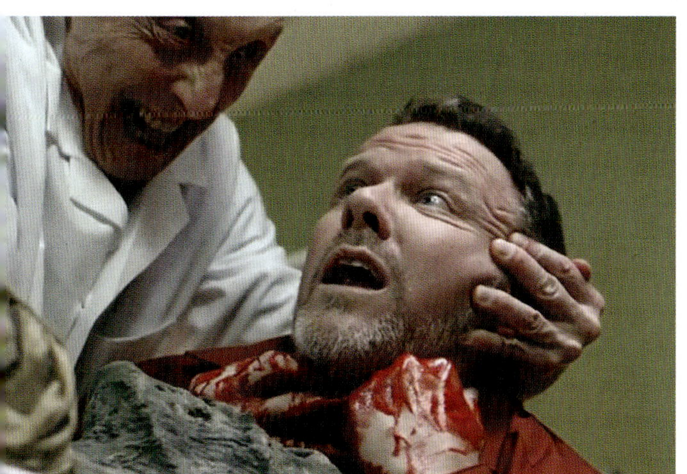

Gore Verbinski's **A Cure for Wellness** (2016) was a big-budget, glorious tribute to mad scientist movies of yesteryear and Hammer Films in particular. In it Dane DeHaan finds himself an unwilling patient at Jason Isaacs' exclusive and remote health spa in the Swiss Alps. That same year, Bobby Miller's US black comedy **The Cleanse** had scientists Oliver Platt and Anjelica Huston encouraging patients Johnny Galecki and Anne Friel to physicalise their neuroses as faecal creatures they would then expel from their bodies. Veterinary school in France proved to be quite the trial for Garance Marillier, who got to discover some disturbing truths about herself and her family in Julia Ducornau's **Raw**.

GRAND-GUIGNOL
LE SYSTÈME DU DOCTR. GOUDRON ET DU PROFR. PLUME
de ANDRÉ DE LORDE

Daniel Kaluuya found that wanting someone for their body took on a whole new meaning in Jordan Peele's Academy Award-winning **Get Out** (2017), while the US also offered us a remake of Joel Schumacher's **Flatliners**, and low-budget werefrog horror in Tim Reis' **Bad Blood: The Movie**. James Franco starred in and co-directed (with Pamela Romanowsky) **The Institute**, an American film so filled with cod psychology, lurid Sadean behaviour, and anachronistic nudity that it was almost as if Jess Franco (who had passed away in 2013) was back with us. From Hong Kong came Herman Yau's **The Sleep Curse**, which combined sleep research with over-the-top gore.

top right: 'The System of Dr. Tarr and Professor Fether', adapted for the Grand Guingol theatre, was filmed as **Stonehearst Asylum** (2014).

Leigh Whannell's Australia-shot **Upgrade** (2018) was a terrific tribute to 1980s science fiction, in which quadriplegic Logan Marshall-Green received a spinal implant that not only allowed him to walk again but also become a killing machine. The US offered more mad Nazis with Julius Avery's World War II-set **Overlord**, while Richard Chamberlain went plastic surgery mad in the Joe Dante-directed second story of the US anthology movie **Nightmare Cinema**. Tom Wilkinson turned Sam Worthington into **The Titan**, mankind's only hope of living on another planet in Lennart Ruff's Netflix science fiction picture.

Also in 2018, the US gave us Ciarán Hinds as the brilliant surgeon keeping new wife Abbey Lee confined to his remote mansion for reasons of mad surgery in Sebastien Gutierrez's **Elizabeth Harvest** and, in 2019, Larry Fessenden gave us his remake of Frankenstein, this time set in contemporary New York, with **Depraved**. Bringing it all back home, and proving the long-lasting appeal of the good old-fashioned mad doctor who just wants to transplant the severed head of his girlfriend onto a fresh body, 2020 saw Derek Carl's US remake of the 1962 film **The Brain That Wouldn't Die**, which appropriately enough received its UK premiere (as did **Depraved**) at FrightFest.

Mad doctor movies have been around almost as long as cinema itself, their exploits ranging from the believable, via the 'maybe it could happen', to the frankly outrageous. Thanks to the skill (or lack thereof) of the filmmakers involved, it's not always possible to tell how close to the real thing the exploits of some of these mad medical men has been. For those of you who have wondered whether it might be possible to turn a gorilla into a man, or just wanted to know which of cinema's Baron Frankensteins used the most accurate incisions, wonder no more. Before you lies a more detailed look at many of the films mentioned here, with careful attention paid to just how accurate (or not) some of the situations depicted are. Ready? Then roll up, roll up! Before we proceed to the main features, let's take a look at what's in store!

above: Boris Karloff, famous as Frankenstein's monster in the 1930s, became a favourite Hollywood mad scientist in subsequent decades.

We trust them with our lives and those of the ones we love, but what happens when doctors become mad and bad and dangerous to be around? What terrible things might occur when hospital doctors, general practitioners, and those who have been engaged solely in privately funded research, decide to go just that little bit too far to achieve their ends? Be it for personal gain, good old fashioned revenge, or that ultimate catch-all 'the good of mankind', the films on the following pages detail just some of the worst horrors the maddest doctors in movie history have brought about, including...

Full Moon Frog Murders...

Animals turned into human beings... but for how long?

Fiendish criminal masterminds with body counts to match their IQs!

Transplant terrors that cause murder sprees!

The health farm where human blood is the treatment!

Organ repossession – from recipients who are still alive!

The institutions where the insane are the ones in charge!

Doctors returned from the dead to prey on the living!

See a man turned into a gorilla! A woman into a snake!
A man, a woman and another woman into a centipede!

Psychopathic psychiatrists! Maniac medics! Devious dentists!
Psychotic surgeons! Secret surgical societies!

Experience terror sharper than a scalpel, more piercing than a spinal needle, more gut wrenching than major abdominal surgery as you turn the page and discover that the world of those entrusted with our well-being might just be awash with the blood and remains of those who were just as curious as you.

Trust me...

THE CABINET OF DR. CALIGARI

Germany, 1920
Director: Robert Wiene. Producers: Rudolf Meinert [uncredited], Erich Pommer [uncredited]. Screenplay: Carl Mayer, Hans Janowitz. Cinematography: Willy Hameister. Cast: Werner Krauss, Conrad Veidt, Lil Dagover, Friedrich Feher, Hans Heinrich von Twardowski, Rudolf Lettinger.

One of the most famous films of all time, considered by many to be the first feature length horror film, Robert Wiene's silent classic is a masterpiece of expressionism (a modern art form designed to express and create emotional mood rather than reproduce physical reality). Lead actors Werner Krauss (as Caligari) and Conrad Veidt (as the somnambulist assassin Cesare) had previously worked with Austrian born expressionist theatre producer Max Reinhardt and their acting style is in keeping with the weird, twisted sets, hand painted onto canvas in the cubist style. Wiene intended to remake the film with sound, acquiring the rights in 1934 but failing to get the project up and running before his death in 1938. Further attempts were made through the 1940s but in the end it wasn't until Robert Lippert (producer of 1958's **The Fly** and its two sequels) got hold of the rights that a new film entitled **The Cabinet of Caligari** (1962) appeared. Sadly, that version has very little to do with the original, the title instead being foisted onto a Robert Bloch screenplay that hadn't been written with that intention. The only thing in common with Wiene's version is the 'twist' at the end. A new version of Wiene's original was made in 2005, with Doug Jones starring as Cesare in front of the sets from the original film projected onto a green screen.

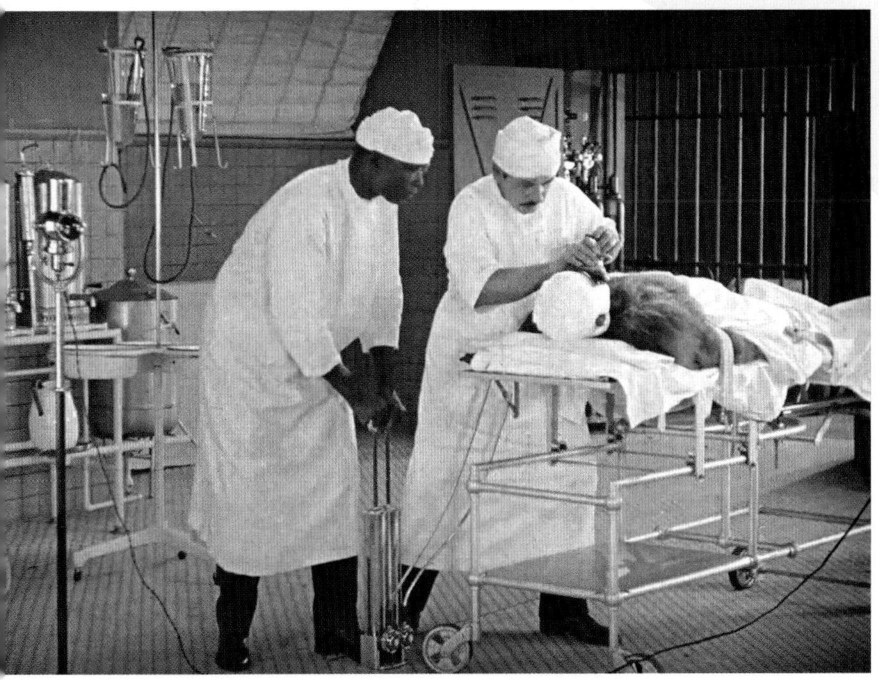

GO AND GET IT

USA, 1920
Directors: Marshall Neilan, Henry Roberts Symonds. Producer: Marshall Neilan. Screenplay: Marion Fairfax, Frances Marion. Cinematography: David Kesson.
Cast: Pat O'Malley, Wesley Barry, Agnes Ayres, J. Barney Sherry, Charles Hill Mailes, Bull Montana, Noah Beery Sr.

Two years before Lon Chaney Sr. played a scientifically created ape-man in the (now lost) **A Blind Bargain**, before 1932's **Island of Lost Souls** and way before the likes of Universal's **Captive Wild Woman** (1943), Noah Beery Sr. played Dr. Ord, transplanting the brain of an executed murderer into a gorilla. The gorilla, both pre- and post-transplant, is played by Bull Montana and unlike later movies his appearance is achieved with make-up instead of just putting him in a suit. The ape-monster's subsequent antics, in which he kills Dr. Ord and then goes on a rampage of revenge against those who convicted him, are unfortunately only shown as newspaper headlines. That's because these events, enough to form the meat of any other pulp thriller, are only incidental to the main plot of **Go and Get It**, which is all about rival newspapers. This brisk 70-minute feature, co-directed by Marshall Neilan and Henry Roberts Symonds was thought lost until recently, when an Italian version surfaced under the title **Le avventure di un reporter** and was screened by London's Gothique Film Society in early 2023. So hope still remains that the likes of **A Blind Bargain** may turn up sometime as well.

DR. JEKYLL AND MR. HYDE

USA, 1931
Director: Rouben Mamoulian. Producer: Rouben Mamoulian.
Screenplay: Samuel Hoffenstein, Percy Heath. Cinematography: Karl Struss.
Cast: Fredric March, Miriam Hopkins, Rose Hobart, Holmes Herbert, Halliwell Hobbes, Edgar Norton.

One of the best and most memorable versions of Robert Louis Stevenson's famous novella, Paramount's adaptation was originally intended to star John Barrymore (who had played the role in the studio's 1920 silent version). But, when it turned out he was now under contract to MGM, Fredric March was recruited instead, under the direction of Rouben Mamoulian. It was Mamoulian who eventually revealed, many years later, how the film's remarkable (for its time) transformation effect was achieved, using different coloured filters to reveal different levels of March's make-up. It was apparently quite uncomfortable for the actor to wear, but March won an Academy Award for his pains. However, when MGM decided to remake the property ten years later in a lavish version with Spencer Tracy in the lead and Victor Fleming (**Gone with the Wind**, **The Wizard of Oz**) directing, the company bought the rights to both the 1920 and 1931 Paramount versions with the intention of destroying all copies. For many years the film was believed lost. That, plus its six minutes of scandalous 'pre-Code' content – much of it featuring Miriam Hopkins' character of Ivy Pearson which had to be cut for its 1936 re-release – meant the film acquired quite the reputation, one that it more than lived up to when prints were eventually rediscovered.

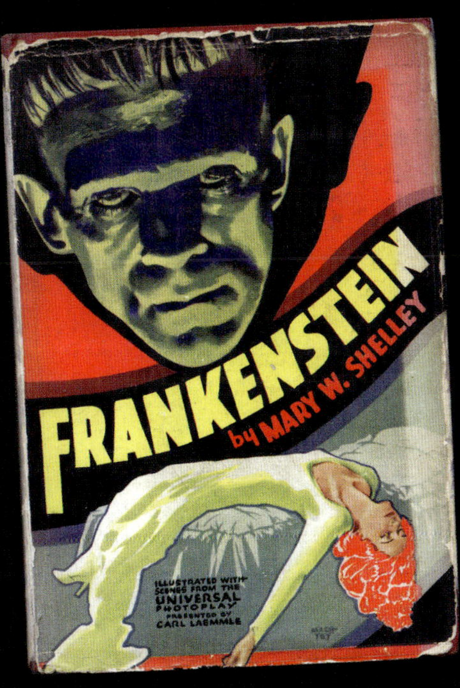

FRANKENSTEIN

USA, 1931
Director: James Whale. Producer: Carl Laemmle Jr.
Screenplay: Garrett Fort, Francis Edward Faragoh.
Music: Bernard Kaun [uncredited], Giuseppe Becce [uncredited].
Cinematography: Arthur Edeson, Paul Ivano [uncredited].
Cast: Colin Clive, Mae Clarke, John Boles, Boris Karloff, Dwight Frye, Edward Van Sloan.

A film that still stands as one of the best, most famous, and most influential horror films ever made, James Whale's version of Mary Shelley's novel was given the green light by Carl Laemmle Jr, Universal's 23-year-old head of production, following the enormous success of the studio's **Dracula** in February 1931. Whale's **Frankenstein** has become so iconic, that it's hard to credit how much our popular conception of the story owes to his film rather than Shelley's book. Kenneth Strickfaden's crackling laboratory equipment which harnesses lightning to animate the Monster (apparently including one Tesla coil constructed by Tesla himself), the torch-wielding mob fuelled by alcohol provided by the Frankenstein family to celebrate the wedding, the hunchbacked assistant Fritz (played by Dwight Frye), and above all the Monster himself. Jack Pierce provided the make-up but Boris Karloff gave the Monster his heart and soul in a career-making performance. Often overshadowed by its admittedly superior 1935 sequel **Bride of Frankenstein**, the original film remains a remarkable, revolutionary piece of work that wastes no time in its tale of the obsessed Henry Frankenstein (the intense Colin Clive) robbing graves and cutting bodies from the gibbet to obtain specimens for his experiments. His creation went on to feature in seven direct sequels made by Universal, the final film finding the Monster (now played by Glenn Strange) co-starring with comedy double act Abbott and Costello.

DOCTOR X

USA, 1932
Director: Michael Curtiz.
Screenplay: Robert Tasker, Earl Baldwin.
Cinematography: Ray Rennahan.
Cast: Lionel Atwill, Preston Foster,
Fay Wray, Lee Tracy, John Wray,
Harry Beresford.

A few years before directing Errol Flynn in **The Adventures of Robin Hood** (1938) and Humphrey Bogart in **Casablanca** (1942), Michael Curtiz made two pre-Code horrors starring Lionel Atwill and Fay Wray, both filmed in two-colour Technicolor, a process that involved exposing black and white film behind red and green filters. The pre-Code status of **Doctor X** means it's a no holds barred tale of the 'full moon murders', committed by a disfigured killer who indulges in cannibalism, using a scalpel from the institution run by Doctor Xavier (Atwill) to cut up the bodies. Rape, perversion, voyeurism, and the use of human flesh to create a new synthetic type are all packed into 76 minutes, climaxing at Atwill's old dark beach house where all the suspect doctors have been gathered. Now 90 years old, it's understandably a little creaky, especially the inclusion of the wisecracking reporter character played by Lee Tracy. Nevertheless, the scenes of the killer (you'll have to watch it to find out who) coating himself with his synthetic flesh is still the stuff of two-colour Technicolor nightmares. We're lucky to still be able to see them in that form. At the time of **Doctor X**'s release, the colour prints only went to major cities with everywhere else having to make do with an alternate black and white version shot at the same time. For many years the Technicolor version was thought lost until a copy was found in Jack Warner's archive after his death.

ISLAND OF LOST SOULS

USA, 1932
Director: Erle C. Kenton.
Screenplay: Waldemar Young, Philip Wylie.
Cinematography: Karl Struss.
Cast: Charles Laughton, Bela Lugosi, Richard Arlen, Stanley Fields, Leila Hyams, Kathleen Burke.

After a couple of silent film adaptations (the French **L'île d'épouvante** aka **The Island of Terror** from 1911, and 1921's unauthorised German adaptation **Die Insel der Verschollenen** aka **The Island of the Lost**) this Paramount Pictures adaptation remains the best version of the H.G. Wells novel. Erle C. Kenton directs Charles Laughton as the definitive Dr. Moreau, psychopathic in his detachment from suffering, childish in his glee at the potential success of his research. Bela Lugosi makes a memorable Sayer of the Law and Kathleen Burke is a remarkable Panther Woman. The lighting, photography (courtesy of Karl Struss) and make-up (by Charles Gemora and Wally Westmore) all combine to make Moreau's island less a tropical paradise and more something from the depths of nightmare. Evolutionary biologist (and eugenicist) Sir Julian Huxley was brought on board to ensure scientific accuracy and the script just about stands up to careful listening, although Laughton does rather allow Moreau's 'explanatory' speech about "germplasm" to tail off into mutters. Two American remakes followed, a 1977 version that is not too bad, and John Frankenheimer's 1996 near disaster which you can read about later on.

THE MASK OF FU MANCHU

USA, 1932
Directors: Charles Brabin, Charles Vidor [uncredited].
Screenplay: Irene Kuhn, Edgar Allan Woolf, John Willard.
Music: William Axt [uncredited].
Cinematography: Tony Gaudio.
Cast: Boris Karloff, Lewis Stone, Karen Morley, Myrna Loy, Charles Starrett, Jean Hersholt.

Sax Rohmer's 'diabolical mastermind' is one of only two iconic super villains who star in their own series of highly successful novels (the other being Hannibal Lecter), and are also actually medically qualified. Rohmer's creation was the subject of this lavish adaptation from MGM, and while Warner Oland had played Manchu in previous early talkies for Paramount, here the title role is taken by Boris Karloff. It's a film that is conspicuously from another age. One when cultural appropriation, casual racism, and the plundering of foreign countries for artefacts to put in the British Museum 'so English tourists can see them on holiday', could easily feature without comment. In fairness, the film was considered controversial at the time, both for the aforesaid racist overtones and the levels of pre-Code violence. There are indeed some splendidly elaborate torture contraptions on display here, the best of which is probably the crocodile seesaw. The Mongolian Emperor mask of the title looks a bit like a Carmen Miranda affair but with fluffy bobbles on it instead of fruit. Presumably viewers were too mortified by what had gone before to wonder what sort of parties Genghis Khan might have worn it to. (Or too titillated – allegedly the whipping scenes had to be reshot because actor Charles Starrett looked as if he was enjoying the beating too much.) All this, Myrna Loy as Fu's "ugly and insignificant daughter" and a spectacular climax where Fu's hordes are mown down by a laser cannon, make **The Mask of Fu Manchu** one of the most over the top (and therefore must see) pictures of the early-1930s.

MURDERS IN THE RUE MORGUE

USA, 1932
Director: Robert Florey.
Producer: Carl Laemmle
Jr. Screenplay: Tom Reed,
Dale Van Every, John Huston.
Cinematography: Karl Freund.
Cast: Bela Lugosi, Sidney Fox,
Leon Ames, Bert Roach,
Brandon Hurst, Noble Johnson.

Robert Florey directs this very loose adaptation of the Edgar Allan Poe story, starring Bela Lugosi as Dr. Mirakle who, in a plot device more worthy of the shudder pulps than Poe, is abducting young women and injecting them with ape blood. His reason? He wants a mate for his carnival sideshow ape Erik. Poe's detective C. Auguste Dupin (Leon Ames) is retained from the story and solves the murders prior to a climactic rooftop chase. Camille, the girl Mirakle and Erik set their sights on, is played by Sidney Fox. (Bette Davis was apparently originally up for the role but was rejected by studio head Carl Laemmle Jr. for not being sexy enough.) Florey is best known to horror fans these days for his adaptation of another famous short story, William Fryer Harvey's **The Beast with Five Fingers**. **Murders in the Rue Morgue** did not do well and it was over twenty years before Hollywood tried again, with even less fidelity to Poe. This time Roy Del Ruth directed Karl Malden as Dr. Marais in colour in **Phantom of the Rue Morgue** (1954), dropping the character of Dupin but retaining the mad doctor theme.

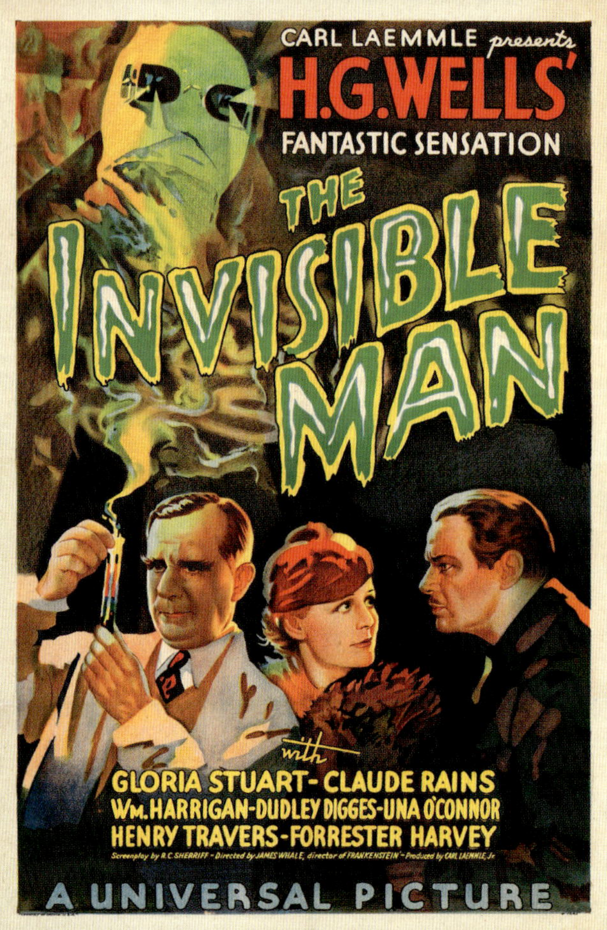

THE INVISIBLE MAN

USA, 1933
Director: James Whale. Producer: Carl Laemmle Jr. Screenplay: R.C. Sherriff, Preston Sturges [uncredited]. Music: Heinz Roemheld [uncredited]. Cinematography: Arthur Edeson.
Cast: Claude Rains, Gloria Stuart, Henry Travers, William Harrigan, Una O'Connor, Forrester Harvey.

Is this the first mainstream Hollywood film to feature full frontal male nudity? Admittedly the male in question is invisible but we are undoubtedly aware, once trousers et al have been doffed, that it's there. Something of a change of style for director James Whale after the Gothic trappings of both **Frankenstein** (1931) and **The Old Dark House** (1932), **The Invisible Man** has a lot more daylight scenes including, significantly, the initial 'reveal' of its title character. It also benefits from a sense of humour lacking from the H.G. Wells novel – although less screeching and gurning from Una O'Connor would make modern viewings of the film's opening act a little more bearable. Claude Rains as Dr. Jack Griffin, iconic in bandages and steampunk-style goggles, uses his voice to riveting effect, and Griffin's invisible rampage through the pub (and subsequent chaos-causing) was no doubt a show-stopping audience-pleasing special effects showcase in its day. Gloria Stuart from **The Old Dark House** (now perhaps most famous for her role in James Cameron's 1997 **Titanic**) is Griffin's girlfriend, and watch out for an uncredited but always unmissable Dwight Frye as a reporter. **The Invisible Man** enjoyed the best reviews of Universal's initial run of horror films, and five sequels followed between 1940 and 1951, the last being an outing for Abbott and Costello. The theme was never revisited during the golden era of Hammer remakes, but writer-director Leigh Whannell's 2020 version, minus the mad doctor but rather focused on Elisabeth Moss as the victim of the title creation's attentions, proved a resounding success both critically and financially, with its only misstep being that H.G. Wells doesn't get a credit.

THE VAMPIRE BAT

USA, 1933
Director: Frank Strayer. Producer: Phil Goldstone.
Screenplay: Edward T. Lowe.
Cinematography: Ira Morgan.
Cast: Lionel Atwill, Melvyn Douglas, Fay Wray, Dwight Frye, Maude Eburne, George E. Stone.

Combining elements from Universal's hits **Dracula** and **Frankenstein**, Frank Strayer's brisk B-movie was a success for the tiny low-budget outfit Majestic Pictures. This was in part thanks to the casting of the stars of Michael Curtiz's **Doctor X** – Fay Wray and Lionel Atwill – who were also due to appear in the same director's highly-publicised (and forthcoming) **Mystery of the Wax Museum** for Warner Bros. Shot at night on sets left over from two James Whale movies (**The Old Dark House** and **Frankenstein**), the plot of **The Vampire Bat** pits superstition against reason in its story of 'vampire murders' that turn out to be the work of Dr. Otto von Niemann (Atwill) who has created new life in his laboratory and needs blood for it to thrive. Niemann himself is one of the propagators of the vampire myth to the susceptible villagers on whom he is preying. Some atmospheric dialogue-free sequences, an angry mob chase through L.A.'s Bronson Canyon complete with red-tinted torch flames, and Fay Wray gagged and tied to a chair at the climax, are all highlights in one of the earliest examples of filmmakers cherry-picking elements from recent successes, then combining them to produce something that turns out slightly different and considerably more interesting than intended.

THE BLACK CAT

USA, 1934
Director: Edgar G. Ulmer. Producer: Carl Laemmle Jr. [uncredited].
Screenplay: Peter Ruric, Tom Kilpatrick [uncredited].
Music: Heinz Roemheld [uncredited]. Cinematography: John J. Mescall.
Cast: Boris Karloff, Bela Lugosi, Julie Bishop, David Manners, Lucille Lund.

Of all the films bearing this title and claiming to be based, however loosely, on the Edgar Allan Poe story of the same name, this is arguably both the least faithful and the best. Director Edgar G. Ulmer grabbed the opportunity he was given by Universal with both hands, delivering a film top-lining Boris Karloff as Hjalmar Poelzig, a mad architect and head of a sect of devil-worshippers, living in a mansion he designed himself that's built on a mass grave. Bela Lugosi is Dr. Vitus Werdegast, out for revenge against Poelzig for betraying soldiers during the war, and for stealing Werdegast's wife, and then when she died, marrying his daughter. David Manners and Julie Bishop are the unfortunate honeymooning couple who get caught in the middle of it all. It was Universal's biggest financial hit of that year. The production design is unforgettable, the second movement of Beethoven's Seventh Symphony is used to great effect, Karloff and Lugosi were never better, and the film also provides its fair share of pre-Code eroticism. By the time Karloff is strung up and about to be flayed alive by the now-insane Lugosi, you'll probably have forgotten there was even a cat in it.

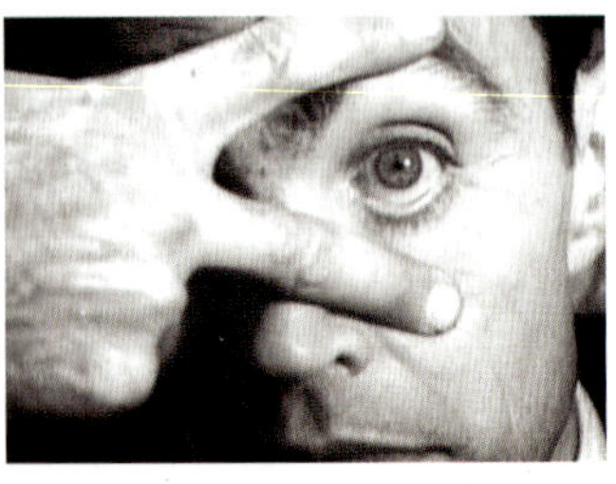

MANIAC

USA, 1934
Director: Dwain Esper. Producers: Dwain Esper [uncredited], Louis Sonney [uncredited], Hildegarde Stadie [uncredited]. Screenplay: Hildegarde Stadie.
Cinematography: William C. Thompson.
Cast: Bill Woods, Horace B. Carpenter, Ted Edwards, Phyllis Diller, Thea Ramsey, Jenny Dark.

This brief (51 minutes), lurid low-rent melodrama was the brainchild of exploitation huckster Dwain Esper, director of **Marihuana** (1936) and **How to Undress in Front of Your Husband** (1937). Mad Dr. Meirschultz with his stick-on beard (and likely stick-on eyebrows as well) suffers such an extreme bout of terrible overacting that his assistant, former vaudeville impersonator Don Maxwell (Bill Woods), shoots him. Through his skill with a comb and stick-on hairpieces Don assumes the doctor's persona, quickly going insane himself in the process. Even less coherent than the above might suggest, highlights of **Maniac** include a man who thinks he's the murdering ape from **Murders in the Rue Morgue** attacking the reanimated corpse of a girl and tearing all her clothes off; ladies conversing while wearing very little; a bobbing heart in a jar; and some kind of weird cat farm. The film also tries to riff on Poe's 'The Black Cat', with the dead doctor bricked up as incompetently as this film is made. Every now and then a card pops up with a completely inaccurate definition-cum-explanation of a particular psychiatric condition. Fascinating as it stands, insufferable if it were to be any longer, there has never been anything else quite like it.

BRIDE OF FRANKENSTEIN

USA, 1935
Director: James Whale. Producer: Carl Laemmle Jr.
Screenplay: William Hurlbut. Music: Franz Waxman.
Cinematography: John J. Mescall.
Cast: Boris Karloff, Colin Clive, Valerie Hobson, Elsa Lanchester, Ernest Thesiger, O.P. Heggie.

Horror cinema, indeed cinema as a whole, took one giant asphalt-spreader's booted foot forwards in 1935 with the release of Universal's sequel to their 1931 hit. The reputation of James Whale's **Bride of Frankenstein** overshadows its already impressive predecessor in a rare case of bigger actually meaning better – bigger budget, bigger sets, and in some cases bigger acting (and good for you Ernest Thesiger, creating one of the most iconic performances of all time). But most of all the success is down to Whale himself, given full permission to think bigger and to pepper the film with endearing quirks that range from the humorous to the morbid. Colin Clive returns as Frankenstein but he's overshadowed by Thesiger's Dr. Pretorius (it would be difficult not to be). Boris Karloff is once again the Monster, enjoying a cigar and uttering a few lines of dialogue (the actor himself was not best pleased with this development). Valerie Hobson replaces Mae Clarke as Elizabeth, Henry Frankenstein's actual wife, not that you'd know it from the posters. Here began Universal's practice of associating the Frankenstein name with the creation rather the creator, which proved so influential that it remains a cultural misconception to this day. Elsa Lanchester plays Mary Shelley in the prologue, and only gets to appear as the Bride of the Monster for a few brief minutes. Yet this, too, is such an iconic scene in a film stuffed with them that the Bride's image also indelibly entered the public consciousness. Horror fell out of favour in Hollywood for a few years thereafter, and so despite this being a big hit for Universal, it would be 1939 before the monster returned in **Son of Frankenstein**.

MAD LOVE

USA, 1935
Director: Karl Freund.
Producer: John W. Considine Jr.
Screenplay: P.J. Wolfson, John L. Balderston, Edgar Allan Woolf [uncredited], Leon Wolfson [uncredited]. Music: Dimitri Tiomkin.
Cinematography: Chester A. Lyons, Gregg Toland.
Cast: Peter Lorre, Frances Drake, Colin Clive, Ted Healy, Sara Haden, Edward Brophy.

Few today have heard of the 1920 novel *Les mains d'Orlac* by French author Maurice Renard despite it having been filmed four times – in 1924 in Austria, by MGM in 1935, as a French-British co-production starring Mel Ferrer and Christopher Lee from **Beat Girl** director Edmond T. Gréville in 1960, and as **Hands of a Stranger** from Allied Artists in 1962. Of this quartet, three can only be recommended to Orlac obsessives, but everyone should see **Mad Love**, German director Karl Freund's stylish and unsettling take on Renard's tale. **Frankenstein**'s Colin Clive is Orlac the pianist who loses his hands in a train crash. Brilliant transplant surgeon Dr. Gogol (Peter Lorre, apparently encouraged to reproduce his Fritz Lang's **M** look) gives Orlac the hands of a recently-executed knife-thrower called Rollo, and the pianist suddenly acquires the ability to accurately aim sharp objects. Gogol is obsessed with Orlac's wife Yvonne (Frances Drake) to the point of owning a life-size wax figure of her. The standout scene in a movie filled with memorable moments is when Gogol visits Orlac claiming to be Rollo. The mad surgeon claims he has transplanted the executed murderer's head onto a new donor body, his hands heavy steel claws. The shot of Peter Lorre pretending to be the guillotined knife-thrower, with his head strapped back on using a leather harness is a brilliant, unsettling image which has helped earn the film the fame it deserves. Sadly, **Mad Love** was not a success at the time, and turned out to be Freund's final feature as director, although he continued to be much in demand in Hollywood as a director of photography for many years.

THE RAVEN

USA, 1935
Director: Louis Friedlander [Lew Landers].
Screenplay: David Boehm. Music: Clifford Vaughan [uncredited].
Cinematography: Charles J. Stumar.
Cast: Boris Karloff, Bela Lugosi, Irene Ware, Lester Matthews, Samuel S. Hinds, Inez Courtney.

Still arguably the best film to boast that title, this bears little relation to Edgar Allan Poe's poem but it does star Bela Lugosi and Boris Karloff, in a mashup of a macabre conte cruel story and a Broadway old dark house mystery. Lugosi is brilliant surgeon and Poe obsessive Dr. Vollin, who saves the life of the brain-damaged Jean (Irene Ware). Vollin becomes obsessed with the girl and invites her family and friends to his mansion, plotting to torture and kill them. Karloff is convicted murderer Edmond Bateman, who needs his face changed. Vollin obliges by cutting the man's right facial nerve (this bit is possible), turning that side of his face into a wrinkled monstrosity that's revealed in the cruellest and most dramatic way imaginable before a wall of mirrors. Vollin promises to restore Bateman's face (this bit is not) if he helps him. The climax involves a swinging pendulum blade, crushing walls, impossibly moving rooms, and Lugosi getting to say "Poe you are avenged!" before laughing maniacally and being dragged into a crusher by Karloff, who then drops dead from the bullet wounds inflicted on him by the mad doctor. **The Raven**'s running time is only an hour but it's a glorious, incident-packed over-the-top hour with two riveting central performances, and brisk (because it had to be) direction from Louis Friedlander (later Lew Landers).

THE WALKING DEAD

USA, 1936
Director: Michael Curtiz. Producer: Louis F. Edelman [uncredited]. Screenplay: Ewart Adamson, Peter Milne, Robert Hardy Andrews, Lillie Hayward. Music: Bernhard Kaun [uncredited]. Cinematography: Hal Mohr.
Cast: Boris Karloff, Edmund Gwenn, Marguerite Churchill, Ricardo Cortez, Barton MacLane, Warren Hull.

After directing Errol Flynn as **Captain Blood** (1935), Michael Curtiz returned to horror after a three year break with this restrained tale of revenge from beyond the grave. Boris Karloff is concert pianist John Ellman, framed by racketeers for murdering a judge. Executed by electric chair, he's brought back to life by Dr. Beaumont (Edmund Gwenn). As well as making use of the (by now) standard mad scientist scientific equipment, the reanimation sequence also drew on a contemporary medical breakthrough in the form of the Lindbergh heart. This was a device invented by the famous American aviator in association with Nobel prizewinner Alexis Carrel and consisted of a Pyrex glass pump that could keep the organ going outside the body. The heart you see in the film apparently belonged to a chicken. There's also use of tilt tables inspired by the work of Dr. Robert Cornish who at the time had allegedly brought a dead dog back to life using the technique. (Cornish's account had also been used as inspiration for the previous year's **Life Returns**, in which Onslow Stevens attempted to do the same thing.) Ellman returns from the grave with the knowledge of those who framed him and, in the film's most impressive sequence, picks them out from an audience assembled by Beaumont to listen to Ellman's piano playing. Now unkillable, he pursues them until they have all met their doom, after which he dies once again.

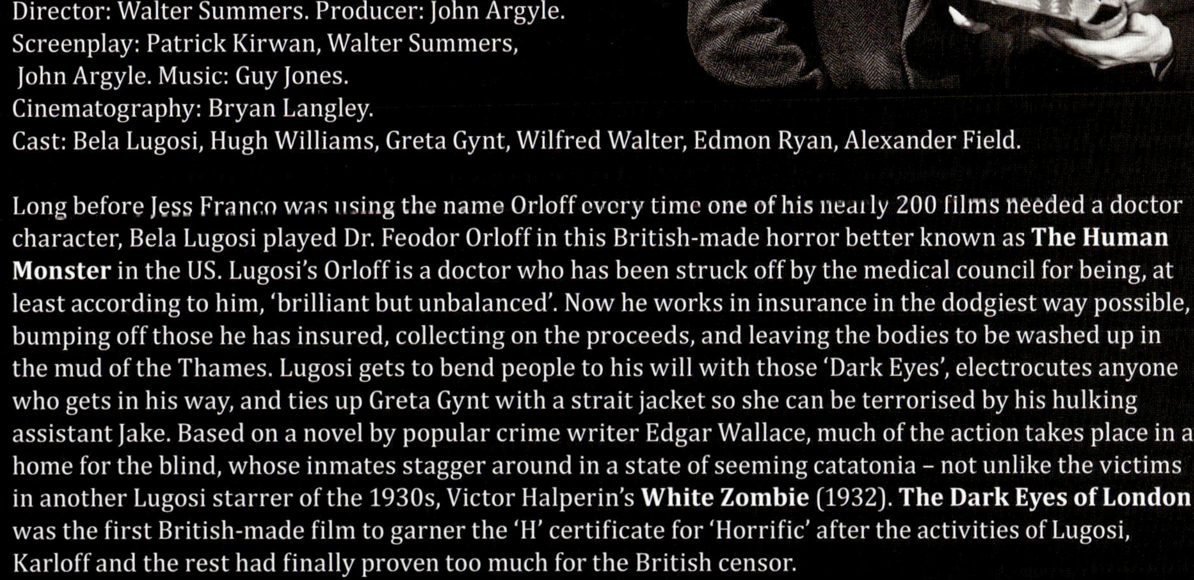

THE DARK EYES OF LONDON

UK, 1939
Director: Walter Summers. Producer: John Argyle.
Screenplay: Patrick Kirwan, Walter Summers, John Argyle. Music: Guy Jones.
Cinematography: Bryan Langley.
Cast: Bela Lugosi, Hugh Williams, Greta Gynt, Wilfred Walter, Edmon Ryan, Alexander Field.

Long before Jess Franco was using the name Orloff every time one of his nearly 200 films needed a doctor character, Bela Lugosi played Dr. Feodor Orloff in this British-made horror better known as **The Human Monster** in the US. Lugosi's Orloff is a doctor who has been struck off by the medical council for being, at least according to him, 'brilliant but unbalanced'. Now he works in insurance in the dodgiest way possible, bumping off those he has insured, collecting on the proceeds, and leaving the bodies to be washed up in the mud of the Thames. Lugosi gets to bend people to his will with those 'Dark Eyes', electrocutes anyone who gets in his way, and ties up Greta Gynt with a strait jacket so she can be terrorised by his hulking assistant Jake. Based on a novel by popular crime writer Edgar Wallace, much of the action takes place in a home for the blind, whose inmates stagger around in a state of seeming catatonia – not unlike the victims in another Lugosi starrer of the 1930s, Victor Halperin's **White Zombie** (1932). **The Dark Eyes of London** was the first British-made film to garner the 'H' certificate for 'Horrific' after the activities of Lugosi, Karloff and the rest had finally proven too much for the British censor.

THE MAN THEY COULD NOT HANG

USA, 1939
Director: Nick Grindé. Producer: Wallace MacDonald [uncredited]. Screenplay: Karl Brown. Cinematography: Benjamin H. Kline. Cast: Boris Karloff, Lorna Gray, Robert Wilcox, Roger Pryor, Don Beddoe, Ann Doran, Byron Foulger.

In 1939 Boris Karloff signed a contract with Columbia Pictures to make three mad doctor films with director Nick Grindé. He actually ended up making five, the final two with other directors. This is the best of all of them. Karloff is Dr. Henryk Savaard, who has designed a cardiac bypass machine that will work on a human being, more than a decade before the process was shown to work in real life. Unfortunately, his nurse alerts the police when the doctor uses her boyfriend as a subject, and they stop Savaard from reviving the boy. Found guilty of murder, Savaard is hanged but returns, thanks to his associate Lang (Byron Foulger), who knows how to use his machine. Savaard then proceeds to bump off the members of the jury who convicted him. The 64-minute running time doesn't really do justice to the plot, with a delicious final act that promises to develop along **Abominable Dr. Phibes / Saw** lines, with the final nine victims trapped in Savaard's house and sentenced to die at fifteen minutes intervals.

It's still a delight, thanks mainly to Karloff's performance and the ripe dialogue he's given to say from Karl Brown's screenplay. Brown would also script the following two Karloff Grindé pictures.

THE RETURN OF DOCTOR X

USA, 1939
Director: Vincent Sherman. Screenplay: Lee Katz. Music: Bernhard Kaun [uncredited]. Cinematography: Sidney Hickox. Cast: Humphrey Bogart, Rosemary Lane, Dennis Morgan, John Litel, Huntz Hall, Wayne Morris.

1932's **Doctor X** gave us synthetic flesh while seven years later we got synthetic blood in 1939's **The Return of Doctor X**, a film that has nothing to do with its predecessor despite both movies being made by Warner Bros. Humphrey Bogart stars in what he considered to be one of his worst films. He's Dr. Maurice Xavier, back from the dead after going to the electric chair because he "wanted to see how long a baby could go without eating for". He's hardly the genius surgeon – there must have been far better, more exotic and lurid ways to end up executed, even post-Code, and I bet Lionel Atwill would have known what they were. Xavier duly comes back to life as a result of blood transfusions and needs more of the stuff to keep him going. (The lecture we get on blood groups is as if Karl Landsteiner, the world-famous scientist who found out all about them back in 1900, never existed.) Bogie's back from the dead just long enough to take a pretty nurse off to his matte painting of an old shack in the swamp, where he promptly ends up shot, uttering a last line that's obviously meant to sound important but just isn't. By 1939 the Hays Code, brought in to protect a sensitive American public from the more extreme subjects cinema was edging into including excessive violence, sex, and good old deviant behaviour, was in full swing. While it no doubt affected the quality of some of the horror product of the time, all it likely did with minor movies like **The Return of Doctor X** was prevent such daft 'B' programmers from adding unpleasant cruelty to their already ludicrous, incomprehensible, and badly-researched plot lines.

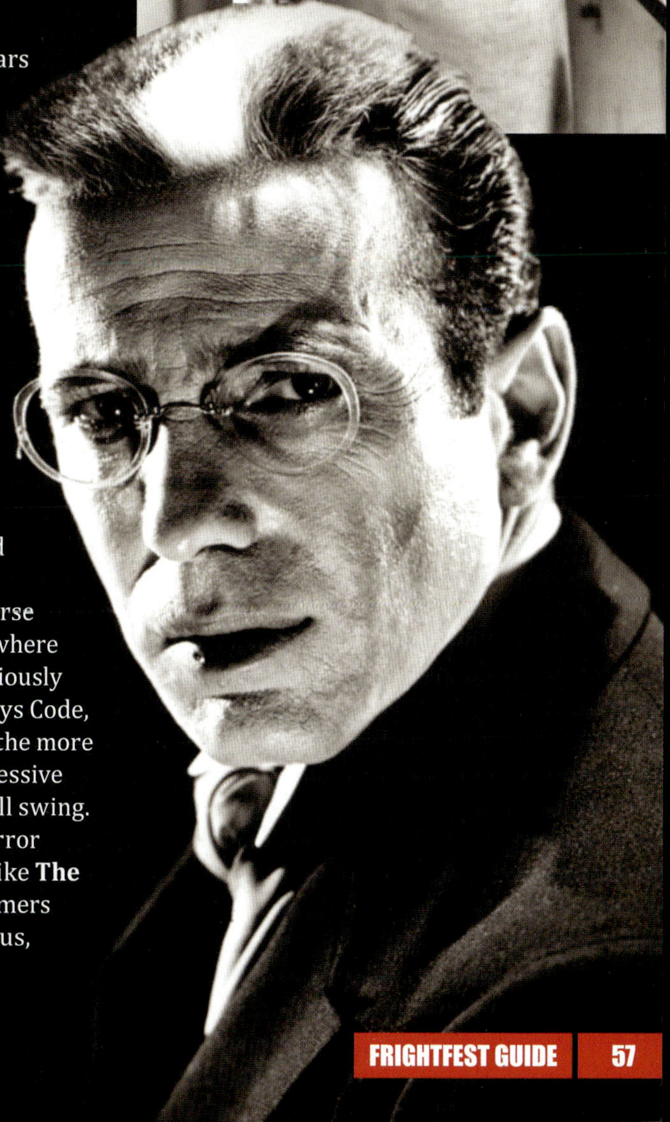

SON OF FRANKENSTEIN

USA, 1939
Director: Rowland V. Lee.
Producer: Rowland V. Lee.
Screenplay: Wyllis Cooper.
Music: Frank Skinner.
Cinematography: George Robinson.
Cast: Basil Rathbone, Boris Karloff, Bela Lugosi, Lionel Atwill, Josephine Hutchinson.

The second phase of classic Universal monster movies started here. After a phenomenally successful re-release of **Dracula** and **Frankenstein,** producer and director Rowland V. Lee got the job of bringing back Boris Karloff as the Monster, playing the character for the final time in a feature film. After talking in **Bride of Frankenstein**, this time the monster is mute but that's okay, because Bela Lugosi is on hand as broken-necked Ygor, the man they could hang but he survived anyway, and he never stops talking. Basil Rathbone is the titular son of the Baron, bringing his wife and annoying son – who gets far too much screen time – to his father's castle (which has undergone yet another Universal rebuild) where he finds the Monster ready to be reawoken. Lionel Atwill's memorable one-armed police inspector was one of the many elements of these classic movies parodied by Mel Brooks in 1974's **Young Frankenstein**. Some stunning sequences – the opening train journey through wind-blasted countryside, the Gothic interiors of castle Frankenstein, the sulphur pit – and fine performances all round ensured the quality of Universal's first two Frankensteins was maintained. It also ensured the success of the film, meaning yet another sequel was just around the corner.

BEFORE I HANG

USA, 1940
Director: Nick Grindé. Producer: Wallace MacDonald [uncredited].
Screenplay: Robert Hardy Andrews. Cinematography: Benjamin H. Kline.
Cast: Boris Karloff, Evelyn Keyes, Bruce Bennett, Edward Van Sloan, Ben Taggart, Pedro de Cordoba.

The third mad doctor movie collaboration between star Boris Karloff and director Nick Grindé for Columbia Pictures tells the story of Dr. John Garth. Sentenced to hang in a month for performing euthanasia, Garth spends his time in prison researching an anti-aging serum with the help of Edward Van Sloan (Universal's Van Helsing). He tries the serum on himself and it works, but has the inconvenient side-effect of turning him into a strangler. Pardoned and released, Garth tries to convince his elderly colleagues they should try his serum before he pulls on his black gloves (sometimes) and kills them. This one boasts a tighter narrative than the previous two films, aided by more than a few newspaper headlines to push the story along. Karloff is his usual riveting self, and this one's so well-paced that you don't even realise you've spent five minutes listening to Chopin's Étude No.12 in C Minor towards the end. Different directors would take over for Karloff's final two Columbia mad doctor pictures, **The Devil Commands** and **The Boogie Man Will Get You**, with noticeable stylistic differences in the results.

THE DEVIL BAT

USA, 1940
Director: Jean Yarbrough.
Producer: Jack Gallagher.
Screenplay: John T. Neville.
Cinematography: Arthur Martinelli.
Cast: Bela Lugosi, Suzanne Kaaren, Dave O'Brien, Guy Usher, Yolande Mallott [Yolande Donlan], Donald Kerr.

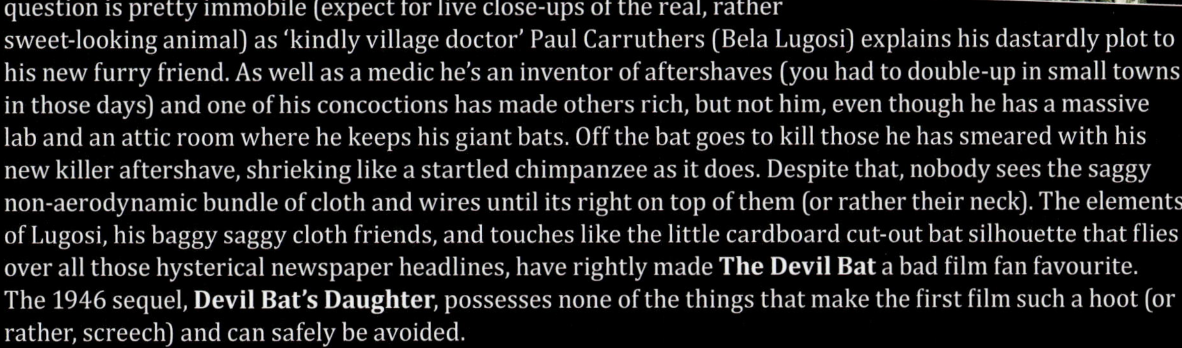

From bottom of the barrel PRC comes a quickie in all respects of the term. It even dispenses entirely with a first act (instead we get a 'Foreword') and plunges us straight into giant bat action. Though the giant bat in question is pretty immobile (expect for live close-ups of the real, rather sweet-looking animal) as 'kindly village doctor' Paul Carruthers (Bela Lugosi) explains his dastardly plot to his new furry friend. As well as a medic he's an inventor of aftershaves (you had to double-up in small towns in those days) and one of his concoctions has made others rich, but not him, even though he has a massive lab and an attic room where he keeps his giant bats. Off the bat goes to kill those he has smeared with his new killer aftershave, shrieking like a startled chimpanzee as it does. Despite that, nobody sees the saggy non-aerodynamic bundle of cloth and wires until its right on top of them (or rather their neck). The elements of Lugosi, his baggy saggy cloth friends, and touches like the little cardboard cut-out bat silhouette that flies over all those hysterical newspaper headlines, have rightly made **The Devil Bat** a bad film fan favourite. The 1946 sequel, **Devil Bat's Daughter**, possesses none of the things that make the first film such a hoot (or rather, screech) and can safely be avoided.

DR. CYCLOPS

USA, 1940

Director: Ernest B. Schoedsack. Producers: Dale Van Every, Merian C. Cooper [uncredited].
Screenplay: Tom Kilpatrick, Malcolm Stuart Boylan [uncredited].
Music: Gerard Carbonara, Albert Hay Malotte, Ernst Toch. Cinematography: Henry Sharp.
Cast: Albert Dekker, Thomas Coley, Janice Logan, Victor Kilian, Charles Halton, Frank Reicher.

While Michael Curtiz had directed both **Doctor X** (1932) and **Mystery of the Wax Museum** (1933) in two-colour Technicolor for Warner Bros, and Tod Browning had given us 1936's **The Devil-Doll** – the story of Lionel Barrymore's cross-dressing escaped criminal miniaturising those who had framed him – at MGM, it took **King Kong** co-director Ernest B. Schoedsack to give audiences the first American horror film in three-strip Technicolor that also featured the miniaturisation plot device. Albert Dekker (giving by far the best performance in the film) is bald bespectacled Dr. Thorkel, busy experimenting with radioisotopes in the depths of the Peruvian jungle. Like Charles Laughton's Dr. Moreau in Erle C. Kenton's 1932 **Island of Lost Souls**, the results of Thorkel's researches are less science gone wrong and rather science gone right for the purposes of just being evil and wanting a bit of entertainment. He's not above fudging his results, either – once he realises his miniaturised subjects are starting to grow in size, he kills one and sets off to hunt the others down. The themes of creating tiny people (human or otherwise) would be seen again in the works of the likes of Bert I. Gordon in1958's **Attack of the Puppet People** and producer Charles Band, who created an entire subgenre of 'tiny people movies' in the 1980s and 1990s, including the **Dollman** and seemingly endless series of **Puppet Master** movies.

THE MAN WITH NINE LIVES

USA, 1940
Director: Nick Grindé. Producer: Wallace MacDonald [uncredited].
Screenplay: Karl Brown. Cinematography: Benjamin H. Kline.
Cast: Boris Karloff, Roger Pryor, Jo Ann Sayers, Stanley Brown, Byron Foulger, Hal Taliaferro.

Star Boris Karloff and director Nick Grindé's second mad doctor picture for Columbia uses another widely reported medical advance for its subject. Whereas Karloff's Dr. Savaard in 1939's **Man They Could Not Hang** had made an artificial heart, here he's Dr. Kravaal (screenwriter Karl Brown must have liked his double vowel surnames), who has perfected a system of cryogenic freezing. Unfortunately, he's frozen himself and four others for ten years and when he wakes up, can't remember the formula. Cue experiments on those whom he has imprisoned. The scientific basis for the plot certainly exists – nowadays kidneys are kept cold for surgery that requires stopping the blood supply to the organ, or if they are needed for transplant. (The rule is one hour of 'cold ischaemia time' will result in the same necrosis as one minute at normal temperature). But most of this is pretty daft – in the first few minutes of the film a patient who's been frozen for five days is resuscitated by the administration of coffee via gravy boat. **The Man with Nine Lives** lacks the pulp vitality of its predecessor, and is all a bit stagey. Still, Karloff's ice room, with its occupants frozen within, is a well-rendered highlight that will make the film worth watching for many.

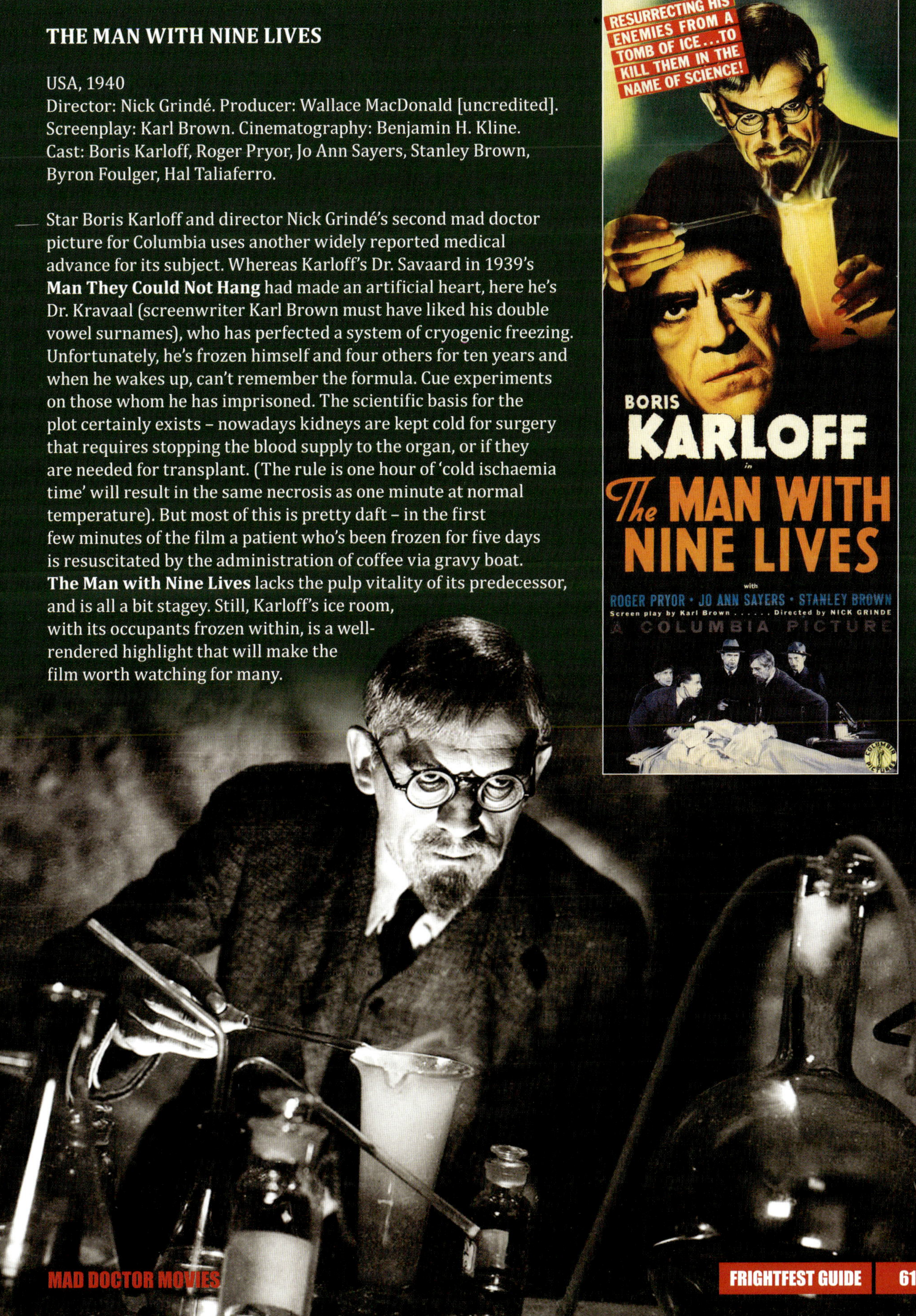

THE DEVIL COMMANDS

USA, 1941
Director: Edward Dmytryk. Producer: Wallace MacDonald. Screenplay: Robert Hardy Andrews, Milton Gunzburg.
Cinematography: Allen G. Siegler.
Cast: Boris Karloff, Richard Fiske, Amanda Duff, Anne Revere, Ralph Penney, Dorothy Adams.

William Sloane's excellent Nigel Kneale-style cosmic horror novel *The Edge of Running Water*, in which a scientist ends up using physics to explain the supernatural only to make it even scarier, provides the basis for this Columbia B-movie. Boris Karloff is Dr. Julian Blair, whose research into recording brain wave patterns takes a macabre bent when his wife is killed, and he begins to believe that she is trying to contact him through his machine. He employs a medium (Anne Revere) and becomes a recluse in order to 'pierce the veil' and see what lies beyond death. The disquieting possibilities inherent in such a storyline are all fumbled a bit by director Edward Dmytryk (of **Captive Wild Woman** and Richard Burton-starrer **Bluebeard** fame). There's a bland voice-over narration from Amanda Duff as Blair's daughter to paper over the cracks, which, combined with Anne Revere going full Mrs. Danvers, suggests that someone thought it would be a good idea for this one to emulate Alfred Hitchcock's **Rebecca**, released the previous year. Nevertheless, the scene of Karloff's top floor laboratory in his gloomy Gothic windswept beach house, with its grave-robbed corpses strapped into his spacesuit style brainwave-reading machines, is the stuff of mad doctor marvellousness and will be worth the price of admission for many.

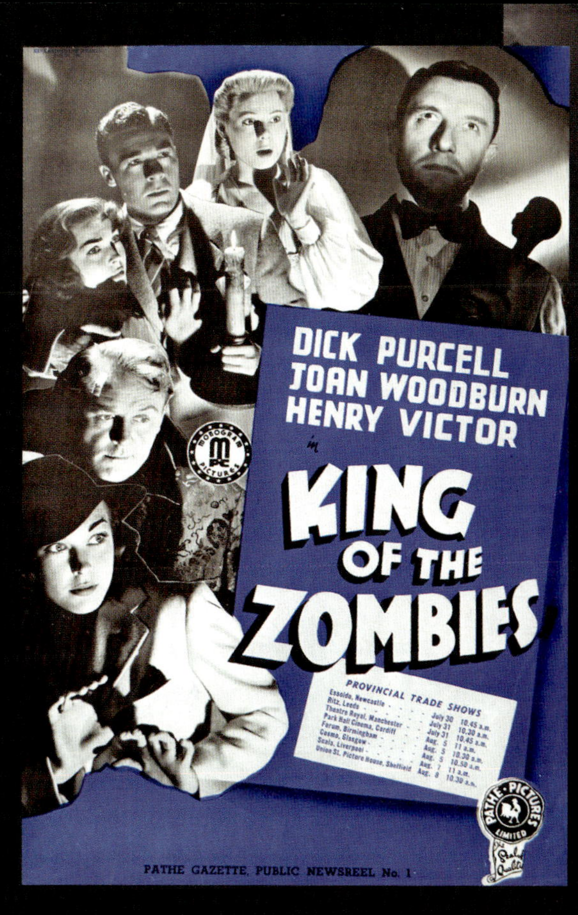

KING OF THE ZOMBIES

USA, 1941
Director: Jean Yarbrough. Producer: Lindsley Parsons.
Screenplay: Edmond Kelso. Music: Edward J. Kay.
Cinematography: Mack Stengler.
Cast: Dick Purcell, Joan Woodbury, Mantan Moreland, Henry Victor, John Archer, Patricia Stacey.

After making his previous mad doctor movie **The Devil Bat** for PRC, Jean Yarbrough moved to equally low-rent production company Monogram (later to become Allied Artists), where instead of devil bats and Bela Lugosi, he gives us zombies and... Henry Victor. Victor is Austrian scientist Dr. Sangre, dabbling in voodoo to allow him to hypnotise kidnapped US military officers and gain valuable information about the war effort for his superiors. Despite cramming a plane crash, Nazis, hypnotism, multiple zombies, and a fire and ritual fuelled climax into the running time, this is a terribly dull and stilted affair, where Victor seems to be reading from cue cards. When you consider that Bela Lugosi does a better job with a similar storyline in the pretty execrable 1945 film **Zombies on Broadway** that hopefully gives you an idea of how forgettable this is. Of the cast only Mantan Moreland (memorable for his role in Jack Hill's 1967 **Spider Baby**) emerges with any credit, giving the only performance with any genuine presence or charisma. In fact, he carries the film and is the sole reason to watch this, making **King of the Zombies** a rare case of a film from this era where the comic relief actually lives up to its name, with the emphasis very much on the relief.

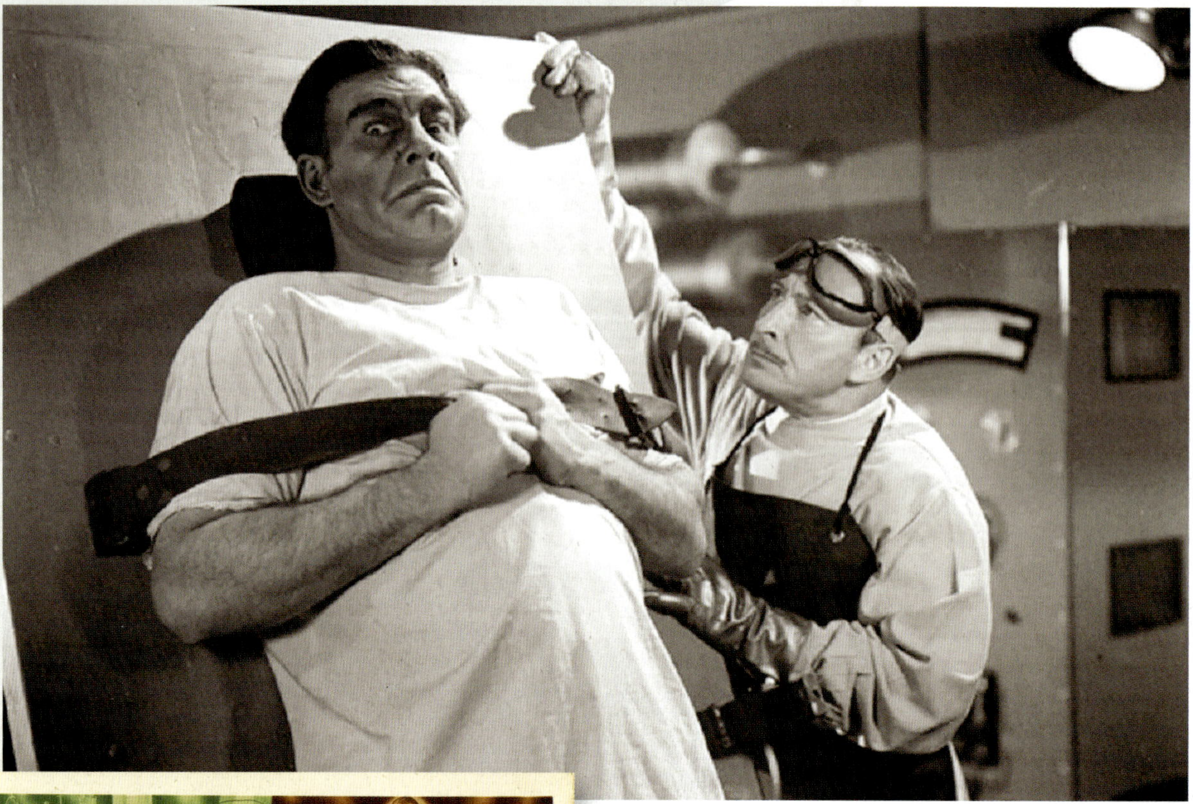

MAN MADE MONSTER

USA, 1941
Director: George Waggner. Screenplay: Joseph West [George Waggner]. Music: Hans J. Salter [uncredited]. Cinematography: Elwood Bredell. Cast: Lionel Atwill, Lon Chaney Jr., Frank Albertson, Anne Nagel, Samuel S. Hinds, William B. Davidson.

The script for a man turned into a killing machine by being supercharged with electricity had been kicking around Universal since the mid-1930s, first as a vehicle for Bela Lugosi and then for Boris Karloff, when it was deemed too similar to 1936's **The Invisible Ray**. It finally went before the cameras in 1940, with Lon Chaney Jr. in his first Universal starring role (a contract and **The Wolf Man** were still a year away). George Waggner directs from his own script (writing as 'Joseph West') based on a story written in part by Harry **Creature from the Black Lagoon** Essex. Chaney Jr. gives a sympathetic performance as Dynamo Dan 'The Electric Man' (the film's UK title as they disapproved of the word monster), who has the uncanny ability to survive being given large doses of electricity. Nice doctor Samuel S. Hinds wants to study him but Lionel Atwill, here playing mad Dr. Paul Rigas (yet another shooting title for this was The Mysterious Dr. R) wants to overdose Dan and turn him into the first of an electrically-charged super-race that will do his bidding. As a result, Dan glows in the dark and his touch becomes death, until he is foiled by a barbed wire fence. Universal's horror movie music scores were frequently a mishmash of work by different composers and of note here is a snippet that would turn up years later in Tim Burton's **Ed Wood** (1994).

THE CORPSE VANISHES

USA, 1942
Director: Wallace Fox. Producer: Jack Dietz, Sam Katzman.
Screenplay: Harvey Gates. Cinematography: Arthur Reed.
Cast: Bela Lugosi, Luana Walters, Tristram Coffin, Elizabeth Russell, Minerva Urecal, Angelo Rossitto.

We open at a wedding where the groom keeps looking at the camera rather than at the vicar. The bride collapses and is declared dead. Her body is loaded into an ambulance, which is actually grinning mad scientist Bela Lugosi's corpse-smuggling vehicle. All this happens in the first three minutes of this breezy and supremely entertaining Monogram quickie from co-producer Sam Katzman (who also brought us the massive chicken-vulture horror of 1957's **The Giant Claw**). Lugosi needs to extract something from dead brides to inject into his awful ancient wife to keep her young. So far, four brides have dropped dead at the altar, with the police baffled (and obviously very poor at their job) and that swirling headline machine beloved of low-budget 1940s programmers has gone into overdrive. Lugosi and his wife sleep in coffins. (Lugosi comments at one point how comfortable his casket is when all fans of Tim Burton's **Ed Wood** want him to say is that it's "Too constricting!") In his matte painting of a house on the hill, Lugosi is assisted in his bride-draining by diminutive exploitation legend Angelo Rossitto, and eye-rolling doom-laden Minerva Urecal, whose son has a hair fetish. Sassy reporter (there are a lot of them in movies of this period) Luana Walters helps set a trap for him. There's all this and more packed into just over an hour. Sheer class.

DR. RENAULT'S SECRET

USA, 1942
Director: Harry Lachman. Producer: Sol M. Wurtzel. Screenplay: William Bruckner, Robert F. Metzler.
Music: Emil Newman, David Raksin. Cinematography: Virgil Miller.
Cast: J. Carrol Naish, Shepperd Strudwick, Lynne Roberts, George Zucco, Bert Roach, Jack Norton.

A rare(ish) foray into horror for Twentieth Century-Fox, who made this as the B feature to their werewolf picture **The Undying Monster**. The secret of the title, revealed close to the end of the film although we've all guessed it way in advance, is that Renault (George Zucco in yet another ape brain surgery picture after 1941's **The Monster and the Girl**) has captured an ape in the jungles of Java, and used 'gland injections and brain surgery' to turn it into Noel (J. Carrol Naish, just prior to his Oscar-nominated role in 1943's **Sahara**). There are some attempts at moody lighting in an opening murder scene and for Renault's dungeon laboratory (a nice set, by the way), but otherwise the somewhat stately approach of the rest of the film gives it more of a mystery thriller feel (we even get a hand holding a knife emerging from a secret sliding panel) than a horror film. The film was loosely based on the 1911 novel *Balaoo* by Gaston Leroux, a prolific author mainly remembered today for *The Phantom of the Opera*. The book had been filmed previously as **The Wizard** (1927 and now lost) in which, not content with just the brain, a mad scientist transplants an entire human head onto the body of a gorilla.

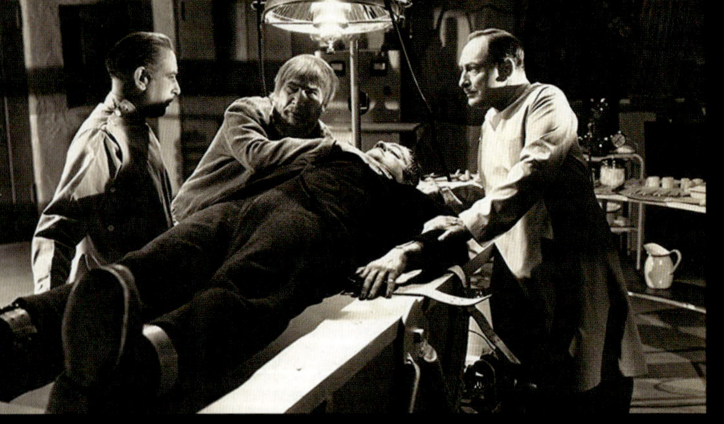

THE GHOST OF FRANKENSTEIN

USA, 1942
Director: Erle C. Kenton.
Producer: George Waggner. Screenplay: Scott Darling. Music: Hans J. Salter. Cinematography: Elwood Bredell, Milton R. Krasner.
Cast: Cedric Hardwicke, Lon Chaney Jr., Evelyn Ankers, Lionel Atwill, Ralph Bellamy, Bela Lugosi, Michael Mark, Lionel Belmore.

Universal's Castle Frankenstein was a little bit like Jason Voorhees of the **Friday the 13th** movies fame, having a completely different look from film to film and surviving more or less intact despite having been burned / blown up / flooded etc. at the end of the previous one. Continuity was never Universal's strong point. In fact, two burghers who appear in the opening scene of this fourth entry (played by Michael Mark and Lionel Belmore) were killed by the monster in the preceding film but don't seem any the worse for it here. For a change, the castle gets destroyed at the beginning, allowing the release of the Monster (played by Lon Chaney Jr.) from the sulphur pit it was knocked into by Basil Rathbone. Accompanied by Bela Lugosi's Ygor, they find Frankenstein's other son Ludwig, played by baggy of eye and limited of expression Sir Cedric Hardwicke, who doesn't look happy to be in this film at all. He runs the Frankenstein Institute for Diseases of the Mind, which seems to require him to have an old dungeon under his house equipped with prison cells and 'soporific gas'. Lugosi and Lionel Atwill, on hand to cause trouble again, keep things interesting from the acting point of view, and director Erle C. Kenton manages a few nice shots, including the lightning bolts hitting the Monster and some nice framing of Lugosi in the propped open lid of a grand piano.

THE MAD DOCTOR OF MARKET STREET

USA, 1942
Director: Joseph H. Lewis. Screenplay: Al Martin.
Cinematography: Jerome Ash.
Cast: Lionel Atwill, Una Merkel, Nat Pendleton, Claire Dodd, Richard Davies, Hardie Albright.

Lionel Atwill's Dr. Benson doesn't actually spend very long at Market Street in this tiny-budgeted Universal quickie, because his research into killing people and then bringing them back to life has so far only been fifty per cent successful. Soon he's on the run from the police and on the high seas. Unfortunately the boat catches fire and Atwill finds himself on a tropical island, where he is proclaimed God of Life by the natives after he resuscitates a woman who has had a heart attack. What mad doctor wouldn't love that? Director Joseph H. Lewis was a prolific B-movie director, directing Bela Lugosi in one of the better Monograms (**Invisible Ghost**) the previous year. He moved to Columbia, and got better and better with pictures like **My Name Is Julia Ross** (1945) and 1946's **So Dark the Night**, a forerunner of the giallo murder mystery popularised by Italian filmmakers a couple of decades later. Here, using South Sea Island sets left over from Abbott and Costello's 1942 comedy **Pardon My Sarong**, Lewis is lucky to have Atwill's electric performance to save the tatty everything-but-the-kitchen-sink script. Originally billed with Universal's far more respectable **The Wolf Man** and certainly best viewed with the prospect of something better to follow.

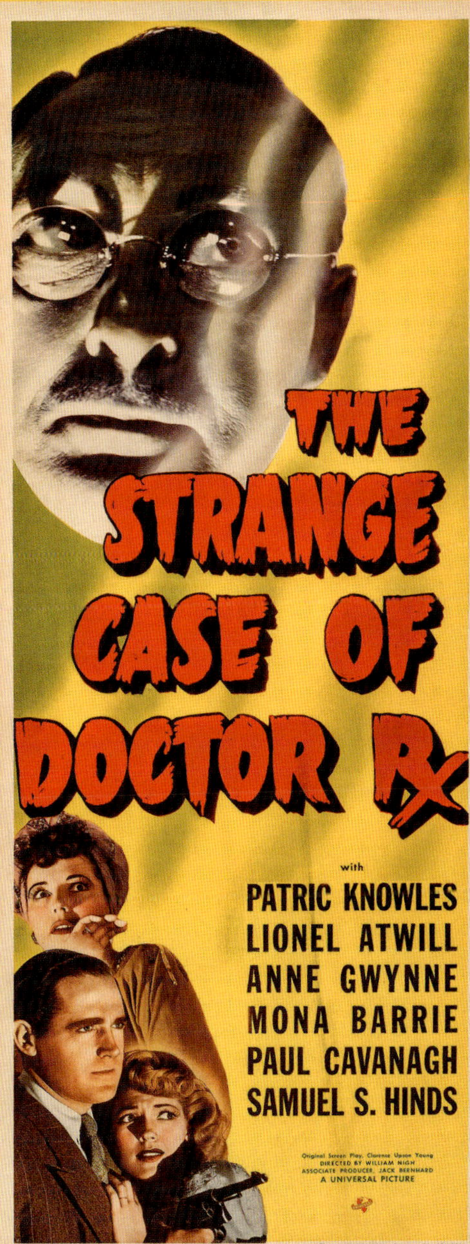

THE STRANGE CASE OF DOCTOR RX

USA, 1942
Director: William Nigh. Screenplay: Clarence Upson Young. Music: Hans J. Salter [uncredited], Frank Skinner [uncredited]. Cinematography: Elwood Bredell.
Cast: Patric Knowles, Anne Gwynne, Lionel Atwill, Mona Barrie, Shemp Howard, Samuel S. Hinds.

'Rx' used to be a commonly used medical abbreviation for a doctor's prescription (it's actually short for the Latin *Recipe*, meaning 'Takest thou'). Here the Dr. Rx of the title is a shadowy vigilante, bumping off criminals who have escaped lengthy sentences due to the efforts of defence lawyer Dudley Crispin (Samuel S. Hinds). It's more a detective mystery than a horror film, except for five minutes near the end when the masked Dr. Rx threatens hero Patric Knowles with having his brain transplanted into Nbongo the Gorilla (played by Ray 'Crash' Corrigan of **It! The Terror from Beyond Space** fame). Shemp Howard of Three Stooges and later 'Fake Shemp' fame (movie parlance for when an actor has to be replaced by someone else, coined from the situation when Howard died of a heart attack and had to have someone else complete his roles in unfinished shorts), is also in the cast. Much of the dialogue was apparently improvised, the comic relief is prolonged and painful, and even though Lionel Atwill is in it, he turns out to be one of the good guys, delivering a **Psycho**-style finale explanation of who Dr. Rx was, and why. It wasn't the gorilla with a new brain, which is a shame.

THE APE MAN

USA, 1943
Director: William Beaudine. Producer: Jack Dietz, Sam Katzman.
Screenplay: Barney A. Sarecky. Cinematography: Mack Stengler.
Cast: Bela Lugosi, Louise Currie, Wallace Ford, Henry Hall,
Minerva Urecal, Ralph Littlefield.

In this zero-budget Monogram quickie from director William Beaudine, Bela Lugosi stars as Dr. James Brewster who, in his bargain basement laboratory, has caused himself to become part ape. The reason for this transformation is never adequately explained but he needs fresh human cerebro-spinal fluid to reverse the process. Even in his semi-simian state he makes the aspiration of this tissue fluid look a lot easier than that process actually is. Karl Brown, who provided the original story for **The Ape Man**, also contributed writing duties on three of Boris Karloff's mad doctor pictures for Columbia, and this film's plot similarities to 1940's **The Ape**, also starring Karloff, has led researchers to suggest this project was also originally intended as a Columbia Karloff vehicle. Aside from Lugosi's frequent tiffs with his gorilla companion and his now-and-again loping gait, the oddest thing about the movie is the intermittent appearance of a character called Zippo (Ralph Littlefield) who points characters in the right direction, helps move the plot along, and at one point even saves a potential victim. At the end he breaks the fourth wall and claims to be 'the author of the story', making **The Ape Man** a curiously metatextual piece of no-budget silliness. The spelling of clue as 'clew' on a headline is actually correct for the period, by the way. But did journalists really refer to a photographer's camera as his 'one-eyed monster' back then?

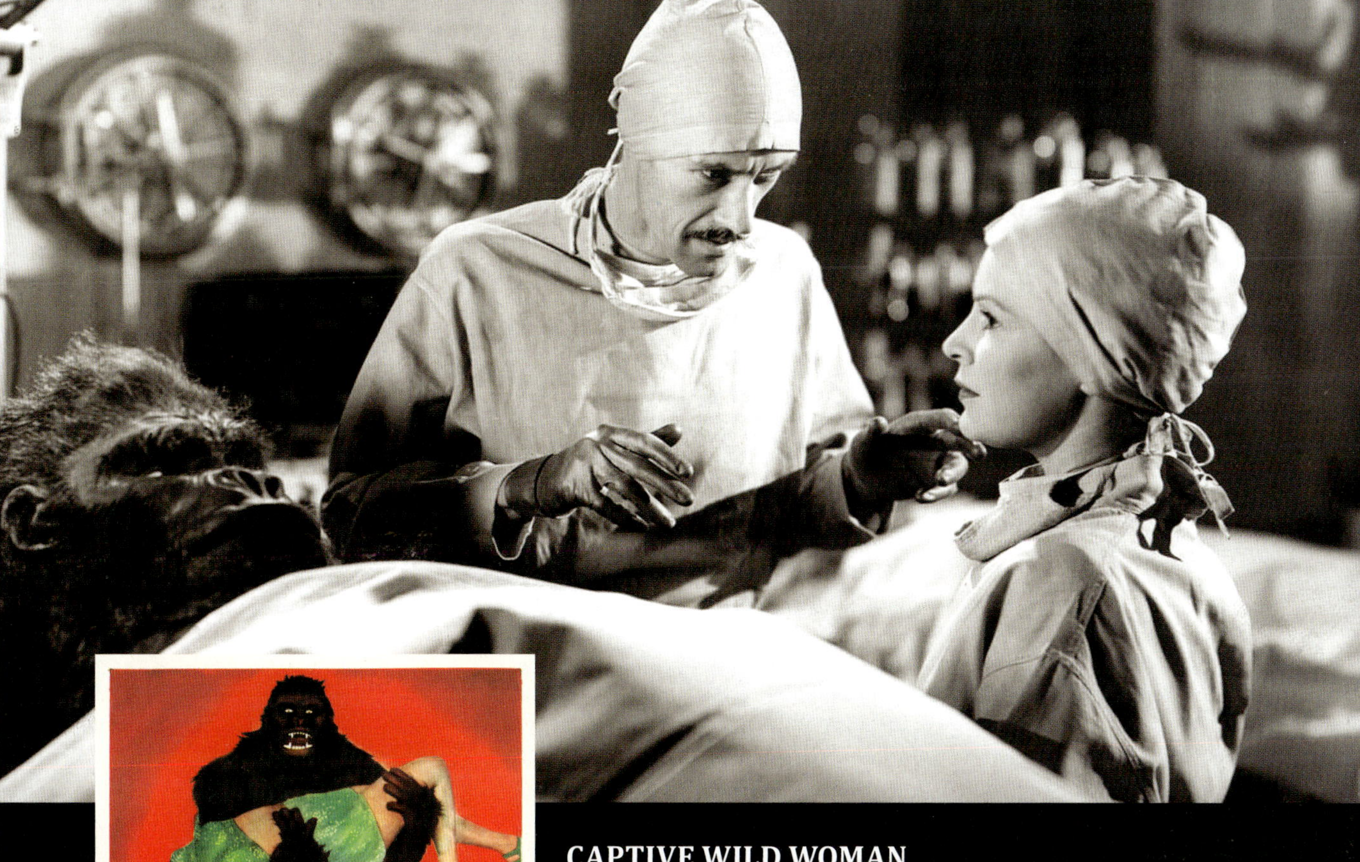

CAPTIVE WILD WOMAN

USA, 1943
Director: Edward Dmytryk. Screenplay: Griffin Jay, Henry Sucher. Cinematography: George Robinson.
Cast: Evelyn Ankers, Acquanetta, John Carradine, Martha Vickers, Milburn Stone, Lloyd Corrigan.

Apparently conceived as Universal's answer to RKO's elegant **Cat People**, **Captive Wild Woman** lives up to its less than subtle title by being something written by people who wouldn't recognise subtlety if it ran over them with a bus (that one for the Lewton fans). Circus animal tamer Milburn Stone returns from a ludicrous round the world trip, where he seems to have done his best to bring about some kind of global extinction plan, filling his ship with lions, tigers, and a man in a gorilla suit. Meanwhile, Evelyn Ankers has taken her friend Dorothy to a splendidly gloomy and windswept sanatorium run by John Carradine, here playing mad glandular specialist Dr. Sigmund Walters. Somehow Carradine realises that a man in a gorilla suit is just what he needs for his Experiments to Benefit Mankind. "You and I are very alike," he tells circus performer Ankers, "You use animals to entertain people, I do experiments on them." He kidnaps a gorilla, hooks it up to Dorothy, and then when his nurse objects he transplants her brain into the gorilla, which turns into a girl called Paula (Acquanetta). The ending sees Paula on a tiny rampage, turning back into a man in a gorilla suit, killing Carradine, and then executing the best sideways fall in response to a shot from a policeman's gun you will see in a movie of this type. Two sequels followed (1944's **Jungle Woman** with J. Carrol Naish and 1945's **The Jungle Captive** with Vicki Lane replacing Acquanetta). Neither are as deliriously entertaining as the film that spawned them.

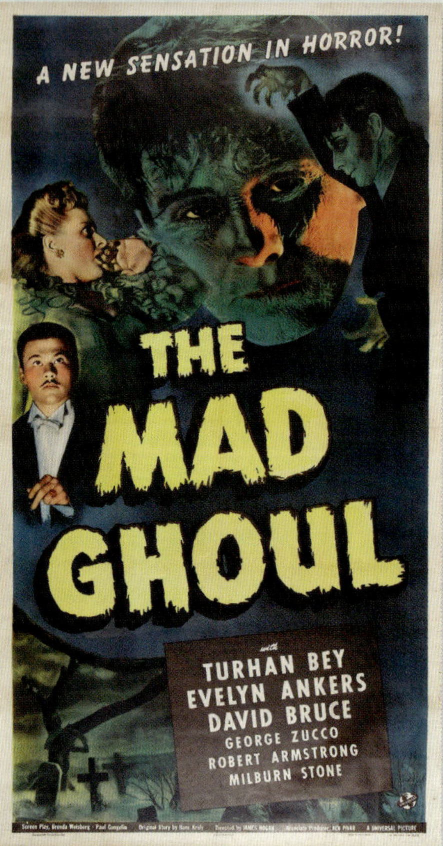

THE MAD GHOUL

USA, 1943
Director: James P. Hogan. Screenplay: Brenda Weisberg, Paul Gangelin. Cinematography: Milton R. Krasn. Cast: David Bruce, Evelyn Ankers, George Zucco, Robert Armstrong, Turhan Bey, Milburn Stone.

"Our students will detect a remarkably advanced cardiectomy technique" says mad chemistry professor George Zucco, pointing to a slide of an ancient wall painting where a heart is being ripped out by a method even goresploitation pioneer Herschell Gordon Lewis might have considered crude. In his home laboratory, Zucco turns student David Bruce into a zombie, and Bruce then has to keep obtaining fresh human hearts so the extracts can be used to keep him alive. **The Mad Ghoul** also features more piano playing by more Universal contract players than any other of the company's B-movies, as well as enough love confusion to keep fans of Shakespearean comedy busy. Evelyn Ankers is Bruce's girlfriend and a singer. She's accompanied on the piano in her performances by Turhan Bey (1942's **The Mummy's Tomb**). While Bruce mixes drinks at Zucco's house Ankers plays the piano, then it's Zucco's turn to tickle the ivories while Bruce is gassed to death in the room next door. Bruce is in love with Ankers who is in love with Bey, but Zucco thinks she's in love with him. Add in some funeral parlour comedy and a showdown at a music hall performance as a finale, and while some may complain that Brenda Weisberg and Paul Gangelin's script is daft (and it very much is), you can't help but applaud them for fitting all that into 65 minutes.

THE MONSTER MAKER

USA, 1944
Director: Sam Newfield. Producer: Sigmund Neufeld. Screenplay: Pierre Gendron, Martin Mooney.
Music: Albert Glasser. Cinematography: Robert E. Cline [uncredited].
Cast: J. Carrol Naish, Ralph Morgan, Wanda McKay, Terry Frost, Tala Birell, Glenn Strange.

From low rent outfit PRC comes the tale of Dr. Igor Markoff (J. Carrol Naish) who has a receptionist and obviously sees patients, but nevertheless also keeps a gorilla in a cage in his consulting room, an Alsatian dog to keep it quiet, and a pig he has been experimenting on as well. See what we might be risking if we lose the NHS? At least he has a tarpaulin to cover the gorilla's cage, presumably for the more delicate and harder of hearing cases. He fancies Patricia (Wanda McKay). Her concert pianist father Anthony (Ralph Morgan, also in Universal's 1942 **Night Monster**) tells him to back off, so Markoff injects him with acromegaly. This is as daft as injecting someone with 'high blood pressure' or 'diabetes' as such things cannot be found in a jar, no matter how much this film may seek to claim otherwise. Acromegaly is due to excessive growth hormone production in an adult (Ian Bannen's explanation in Tigon's 1972 film of **Doomwatch** is better), causing certain physical signs that are never like the ones we see in horror cinema, and certainly not here. Though it's worth pointing out that the make-up job on Morgan is remarkably good for a PRC film. Glenn Strange, Universal's Frankenstein Monster for their final three films, is on hand as Markoff's assistant.

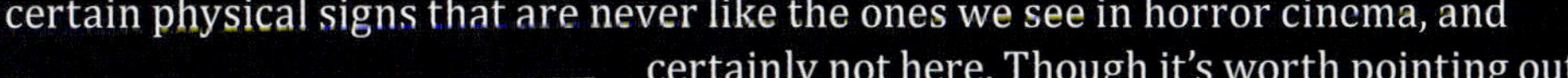

RETURN OF THE APE MAN

USA, 1944
Director: Phil Rosen. Producers: Jack Dietz, Sam Katzman.
Screenplay: Robert Charles.
Cinematography: Marcel Le Picard.
Cast: Bela Lugosi, John Carradine, Frank Moran, Judith Gibson [Teala Loring], Michael Ames [Tod Andrews], Mary Currier.

It's an indication of Monogram's throw-it-together attitude to film production that **Return of the Ape Man** has nothing to do with the same company's **The Ape Man** made the year before, even though it once again top-lines Bela Lugosi who again plays a mad scientist, this time assisted by fellow researcher John Carradine. After their tramp freezing experiment is a success, the natural next step (for them, at least) is to set off for the Arctic to find a prehistoric man frozen in a glacier. Their find was intended to be played by George Zucco but is actually Frank Moran. Both are credited. Different explanations exist as to why the refined, older Zucco left a role in which he was required to wear a stick-on beard, grunt, and risk his underpants being on display but the official line is that he became ill. Lugosi's next daft idea is to perform half a brain transplant, which he achieves without any cranial shaving whatsoever, and the caveman acquires Carradine's ability to play the piano. The finale is probably the best 'police carrying actual flaming torches chasing a prehistoric man around a theatre filled with flammable objects before himself causing an electrical fire' ever filmed, and if all this makes **Return of the Ape Man** sound as if it's worth watching then that's because it is.

VOODOO MAN

USA, 1944
Director: William Beaudine. Producers: Jack Dietz, Sam Katzman. Screenplay: Robert Charles.
Cinematography: Marcel Le Picard.
Cast: Bela Lugosi, John Carradine, George Zucco, Michael Ames [Tod Andrews], Wanda McKay, Louise Currie.

"She's not here! She must be somewhere else!" **Voodoo Man** is arguably the best of the infamous nine films Bela Lugosi made for the ultra-low-budget outfit Monogram Pictures in the 1940s. George Zucco runs a remote petrol station. When solitary young lady drivers ask for directions, he sends them to the house of Dr. Richard Marlowe (Lugosi), who is trying to resurrect his wife, who died 22 years ago, using 'exotic voodoo rituals'. So far they haven't worked, leading to four zombie women in the cellar and a baffled local police force of two. When Stella Saunders (Louise Currie) goes missing, it's up to our screenwriter hero Ralph (Tod Andrews here acting under the name Michael Ames) to solve the mystery and prevent his own wife-to-be from falling into Dr. Marlowe's clutches. **Voodoo Man** only lasts an hour and was directed by William 'One Shot' Beaudine (there'll be more from him later). One can sense a certain breathless urgency to get the film finished in time here, with occasional flubbed lines and missed cues all being retained. But it's not the mistakes in **Voodoo Man** that make it the enjoyable piece of cinema that it very much is. It's a script filled with lines like "Fetch my dead wife!" and "She deserves a good paddling!" combined with enthusiastic performances from Lugosi, Zucco, and John Carradine (giving us an essay in sleazy dysfunctionalism that must surely have influenced David Hess's role as Krug in Wes Craven's 1972 **The Last House on the Left**) that are the reasons to watch this. The story is ridiculous and the sets are flaky, but there's a vigour to the enterprise, combined with a cheery amateur dramatics feel that makes the whole thing utterly charming.

ZOMBIES ON BROADWAY

USA, 1945
Director: Gordon Douglas.
Producer: Benjamin Stoloff.
Screenplay: Lawrence Kimble. Music: Roy Webb. Cinematography: Jack MacKenzie.
Cast: Wally Brown, Alan Carney, Bela Lugosi, Anne Jeffreys, Sheldon Leonard, Darby Jones.

What does this film have in common with 1989's **Friday the 13th Part VIII: Jason Takes Manhattan**? That's right! Very little of this low rent RKO horror comedy takes place on Broadway, and we only get zombies in the closing shot. The rest of the time this is a fairly decent romp around the island of San Sebastian (actually sets from the RKO Tarzan films). The double act of Alan Carney and Wally Brown – RKO's answer to Universal's Abbott and Costello and Paramount's Bob Hope and Bing Crosby – play terrible press agents, who encounter mad doctor Bela Lugosi, who's been busy creating zombies. Surprisingly entertaining, with likeable leads, it's still hard to believe that in a few years director Gordon Douglas would be handling giant ants for Warner Bros. in **Them!** (1954). Val Lewton's regular composer Roy Webb provides the score. The island of 'San Sebastian' is also the setting for Lewton's 1943 **The Ghost Ship**, directed by Mark Robson, and more significantly and from the same year, the Jacques Tourneur-directed **I Walked with a Zombie**. Darby Jones appears in both zombie films as one of the walking dead, as does Sir Lancelot (Lancelot Victor Edward Pinard) as a calypso singer. If you're planning a double bill, **Zombies on Broadway** should probably go first.

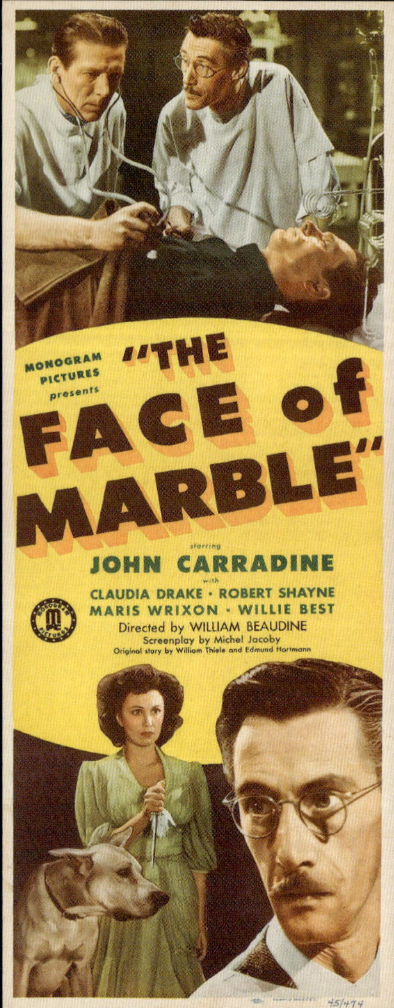

THE FACE OF MARBLE

USA, 1946
Director: William Beaudine. Producer: Jeffrey Bernerd.
Screenplay: Michel Jacoby. Music: Edward J. Kay [uncredited].
Cinematography: Harry Neumann.
Cast: John Carradine, Claudia Drake, Robert Shayne, Maris Wrixon, Willie Best, Thomas E. Jackson, Rosa Rey.

The final horror film from Z-movie specialists Monogram, once again directed by 'old reliable' William 'One Shot' Beaudine, offers perhaps the most incoherent and thrown together plot of the lot. The elements include a mad doctor (John Carradine) trying to bring back the dead, the doctor's wife (Claudia Drake) who has the hots for his assistant (Robert Shayne), his assistant's girlfriend (Maris Wrixon), an evil housekeeper (Rosa Rey) who practices voodoo and is an expert at falling down flights of stairs, and best of all Brutus the Great Dane who is killed, brought back to life, shot dead, turned into a vampire ghost dog and eventually commits suicide by walking into the sea alongside his now undead mistress. The opening scene of Carradine's wife being woken by the housekeeper beside a blazing fire is a direct copy of the opening scene from Twentieth Century-Fox's **The Undying Monster** (1942). Both films were written by Michel Jacoby. Carradine gives a remarkably restrained performance for such a terrible film, which also includes a voodoo doll boiled in acid, an undead fisherman dumped back on the beach when the reanimation process stops working, and implied illicit sexual shenanigans over the breakfast table. If all the above makes you want to watch this one be warned – most prints are of terrible quality as the Criterion Collection hasn't quite got round to picking this one up and restoring it. Yet.

BELA LUGOSI MEETS A BROOKLYN GORILLA

USA, 1952
Director: William Beaudine. Producer: Maurice Duke. Screenplay: Tim Ryan. Music: Richard Hazard. Cinematography: Charles Van Enger. Cast: Bela Lugosi, Duke Mitchell, Sammy Petrillo, Muriel Landers, Charlita, Al Kikume.

A unique title courtesy of associate producer Herman Cohen (who would go on to give us other memorably titled movies like **I Was a Teenage Frankenstein**, **Berserk**, and **Trog** in 1957, 1967, and 1970 respectively) for a uniquely terrible film courtesy of director William Beaudine. Dean Martin and Jerry Lewis rip-off act Duke Mitchell (who sings) and Sammy Petrillo (the other one) find themselves marooned at the island laboratory of Dr. Zabor (Lugosi). Zabor turns Mitchell into a man in a gorilla suit. Who sings. Shot in six days but looking like it took less than that, this is a banal, brain-numbing combination of stock footage, unfunny jokes and painful 'comedy' routines. The entire endeavour is cringeworthy and worse than anything Ed Wood ever made. Only Lugosi emerges with any dignity intact and the next best actor is Ramona the chimpanzee. Bad film enthusiasts may wish to view it for the sight of Lugosi in hunting regalia in pursuit of two men in gorilla suits. But the rest of the film, combined with an ending that's a slap in the face for any viewer who has managed the stamina to get through this, mean the only real reason for its inclusion in this volume is to warn off anyone who might consider giving it a chance. The first of a projected series of films that thankfully never happened and yes, Dean Martin and Jerry Lewis were unimpressed to the point of threatening legal action.

MESA OF LOST WOMEN

USA, 1953
Directors: Ron Ormond, Herbert Tevos. Producers: Melvin Gordon, William Perkins. Screenplay: Herbert Tevos. Music: Hoyt Curtin. Cinematography: Karl Struss, Gilbert Warrenton. Cast: Jackie Coogan, Allan Nixon, Richard Travis, Mary Hill, Robert Knapp, Tandra Quinn.

A film so truly terrible, incoherent, pointless, and confusing it's not surprising it took two people to direct it, **Mesa of Lost Women** is told mainly in flashback by someone who didn't witness most of what they are telling us. The jumbled (that's being kind) narrative (that's being very kind) features a lengthy silly dance, a mad doctor, and a giant spider that is utterly brilliant in its total awfulness, especially the bit where it gets thrown at someone. But so riveting are the 69 minutes of this strange mixture of random bits of dialogue and odd happenings, that the viewer may begin to wonder if the nightmare worlds of a young David Lynch might have been inspired by an early viewing of this bizarre offering. Former child star and **The Addams Family**'s Uncle Fester Jackie Coogan plays Dr. Aranya, doing his best with very limited resources somewhere in Mexico to create an army of dwarves, spiders, and superwomen. I think. The icing on this particularly cruddy cake is the music score, consisting of a repetitive guitar riff so irritating that it's hard to believe Ed Wood used it a couple of years later. Or maybe it isn't.

THE BLACK SLEEP

USA, 1956
Director: Reginald Le Borg. Producer: Howard W. Koch. Screenplay: John C. Higgins. Music: Les Baxter. Cinematography: Gordon Avil.
Cast: Basil Rathbone, Akim Tamiroff, Lon Chaney Jr., John Carradine, Bela Lugosi, Tor Johnson.

On the East Coast of England in 1872, eminent surgeon Dr. Joel Cadman (Basil Rathbone) is using a drug called Nind Andhera (which actually is Hindi for 'Black Sleep') to anaesthetise his patients so he can map areas of the brain and create a cellar-full of poster-worthy monsters at the same time. His aim is to cure his wife of a deep-seated brain tumour. The best production from Bel-Air, a low-rent outfit who also made **Voodoo Island** (which is eminently missable) and **Pharaoh's Curse** (which features an Egyptian mummy in pyjamas and is therefore quite the opposite) around the same time, **The Black Sleep** scores points for getting the order of the meninges covering the brain right (dura mater on the outside, arachnoid, and then pia mater as you go in) and for having one of the most interesting casts in a 1950s horror film. Bela Lugosi looks horribly frail as the mute butler. Lon Chaney Jr. looks healthier but is given little to do but lumber around. John Carradine pops up at the last minute, with a massive beard and his restraint switch firmly off. And while Rathbone is excellent, the most magnetic and entertaining performance is Akim Tamiroff's bodysnatching gypsy Odo. You can feel the unease of some of the other cast members at having to bounce off his undoubtedly improvised dialogue.

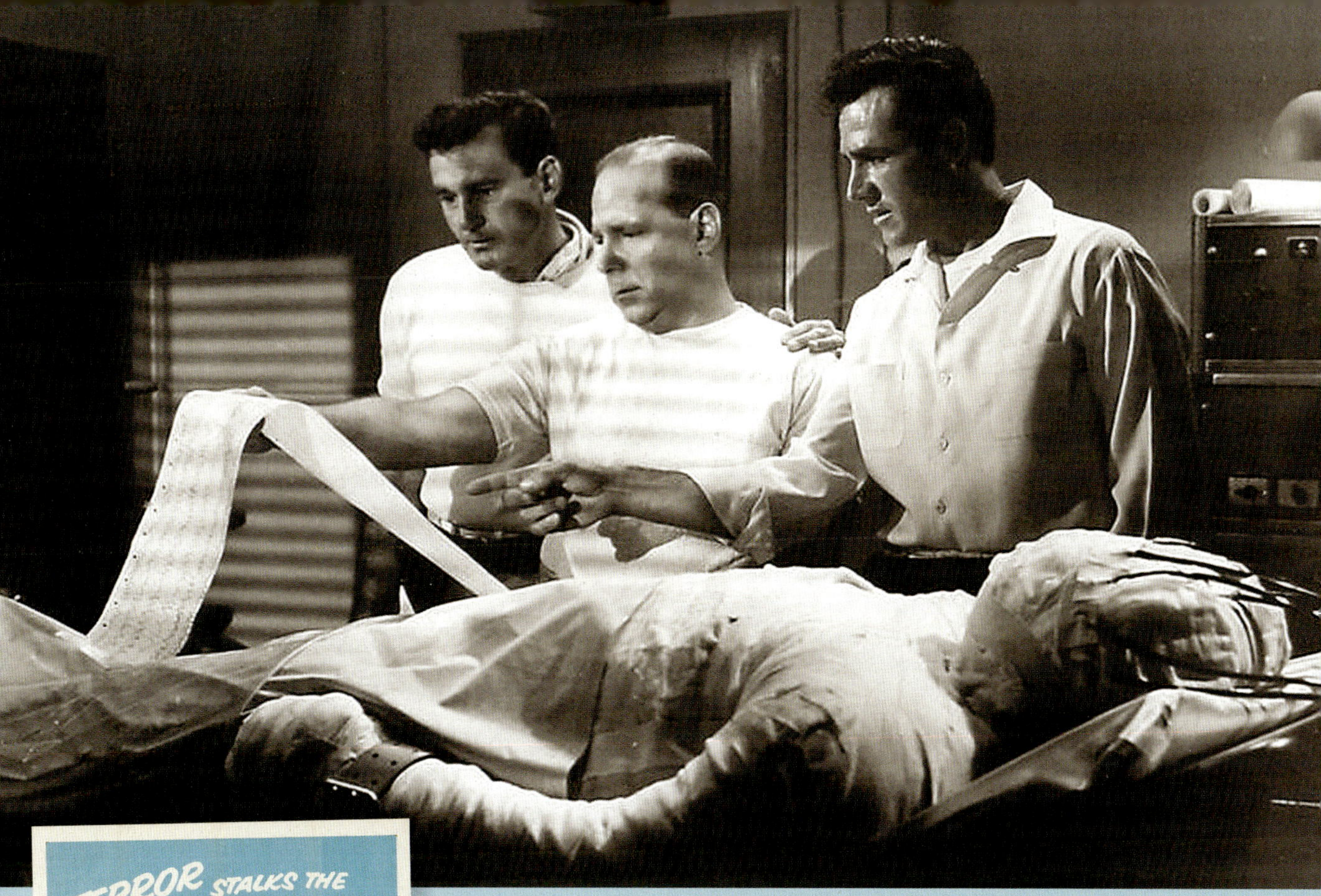

THE CREATURE WALKS AMONG US

USA, 1956
Director: John Sherwood. Producer: William Alland. Screenplay: Arthur A. Ross. Music: Irving Gertz [uncredited], Henry Mancini [uncredited], Heinz Roemheld [uncredited]. Cinematography: Maury Gertsman. Cast: Jeff Morrow, Rex Reason, Leigh Snowden, Gregg Palmer, Maurice Manson, James Rawley.

The third in Universal's series featuring the Gill-man after **Creature from the Black Lagoon** (1954) and **Revenge of the Creature** (1955). For a low-budget entry in a 1950s monster movie series it's actually hard to think of a bigger downer than **The Creature Walks Among Us**, a film where pretty much no one is likeable and nothing much happens except squabbling and pointless experiments on nature to no good whatsoever. In fact its nihilism makes it feel as if it should have been made 15 years later. A group of mad and also quite ghastly scientists journey upriver to catch the Gill-man. They set him on fire, cover him in bandages, give him a tracheotomy, and change him into a far cheaper and tattier looking monster altogether. Is it any wonder he's the only character in this to elicit sympathy? Not content with being the most despicable and miserable bunch of characters ever to grace a Universal monster movie, our band of bastards take the Gill-man to San Francisco. Well not San Francisco exactly, but the removal van that takes all their stuff to a house in the middle of nowhere has San Francisco written on the side, allowing Universal to put the Golden Gate Bridge on the poster when it has no involvement in the film whatsoever. Close to the end someone asks "Where's the Gill-man gone?" "Oh probably to kill himself" is the gist of the reply. We see the Gill-man walking along the beach and staring at the sea. He looks very sad indeed. We know exactly how he feels.

INDESTRUCTIBLE MAN

USA, 1956
Director: Jack Pollexfen.
Producer: Jack Pollexfen.
Screenplay: Vy Russell,
Sue Bradford [Sue Dwiggins].
Music: Albert Glasser [uncredited].
Cinematography: John L. Russell.
Cast: Lon Chaney Jr., Marian Carr,
Casey Adams [Max Showalter],
Ross Elliott, Stuart Randall, Robert Shayne.

From Allied Artists, or Monogram Pictures that was, comes this very Monogram-style ultra-low-budget quickie from producer-director Jack Pollexfen. Lon Chaney Jr. is Charles 'Butcher' Benton, sentenced to the gas chamber in the kind of set-up where twenty years earlier Boris Karloff would have been playing the role. He goes to his death swearing vengeance on the men who turned him in. After death his body is taken to the laboratory of Dr. Bradshaw (Robert Shayne), who is trying to cure cancer and needs the body for his experiments. Butcher is brought back to life but is now mute, reducing the need for synchronous sound. Oh yes, there's an awful lot of voice-over in this, all from police Lieutenant Dick Chasen (Max Showalter) whose name sounds like a British sex film character before his time. We can tell Dr. Bradshaw is a bit loopy when he starts talking to Butcher's chest X-ray, especially when he doesn't spot it's the wrong way around. This is the common mistake I mentioned in this book's intro. As you look at it, the shadow of the heart's left ventricle should be pointing to your right, so it's as if the patient is facing you. Lots of films get it wrong, so now see how many you can spot.

THE CURSE OF FRANKENSTEIN

UK, 1957
Director: Terence Fisher. Producer: Anthony Hinds. Screenplay: Jimmy Sangster. Music: James Bernard. Cinematography: Jack Asher. Cast: Peter Cushing, Christopher Lee, Hazel Court, Robert Urquhart, Valerie Gaunt, Paul Hardtmuth.

Doing for the horror genre what **Star Wars** would do for the science fiction spectacular twenty years later, it's difficult nowadays for most people to appreciate just what an impact Hammer's first colour horror film had on cinema-going audiences back in the day. So ingrained has Hammer become in modern parlance as a byword for a specific type of horror that it's hard to believe that up until this, pretty much every adaptation, spin-off, rip-off, and imitation of Mary Shelley's source novel had been given a contemporary setting. Thanks to the skill of all involved (and not least Jimmy Sangster's screenplay) Hammer's film cleverly avoids anything that Universal (or rather Universal's lawyers) might have considered a steal from their 1931 version (or its sequels) by setting the story in period, omitting any torch-wielding mobs, and having a laboratory set that feels cramped and realistic, the coloured fluids an added touch of gloriousness for the Eastmancolor it was photographed in by Jack Asher. Composer James Bernard provides what was to become the sound of British Gothic, Peter Cushing's status as a world star was confirmed (with Christopher Lee just behind him), while Terence Fisher, for so long one of the great unsung heroes of British cinema, pulls everything together with skill and passion and just the right degree of unrestraint to upset the critics and delight and thrill audiences everywhere. One of the most important British films ever made.

I WAS A TEENAGE FRANKENSTEIN

USA, 1957
Director: Herbert L. Strock. Producer: Herman Cohen.
Screenplay: Kenneth Langtry [Herman Cohen and Aben Kandel]. Music: Paul Dunlap.
Cinematography: Lothrop B. Worth.
Cast: Whit Bissell, Gary Conway, Phyllis Coates, Robert Burton, Marshall Bradford, George Lynn.

Before he came to England to make a series of pictures for Anglo-Amalgamated and AIP, producer (and often co-writer with Aben Kandel, this time under their pseudonym of Kenneth Langtry) Herman Cohen hit it big stateside in 1957 with a trio of movies aimed squarely at the youth market. Namely **I Was a Teenage Werewolf**, **Blood of Dracula**, and this, sandwiched between the two, and retitled simply **Teenage Frankenstein** in the UK. Whit Bissell is Frankenstein with Gary Conway as his muscular creation, with a face that looks like it's been put through a mangle. Shot in black and white, there was just enough money for the final few seconds to be in colour. So despite Conway's monster having a handsome new head (Conway's own) at this point, Cohen knew what his audiences wanted, and we get another look (this time in full colour) at that mashed-up face before the fade out. Conway returned the following year when AIP made a meta sequel to their 'Teenage' monster movies, **How to Make a Monster**, where a disaffected make-up artist takes revenge on the studio for cancelling their horror output in favour of making rock 'n' roll pictures.

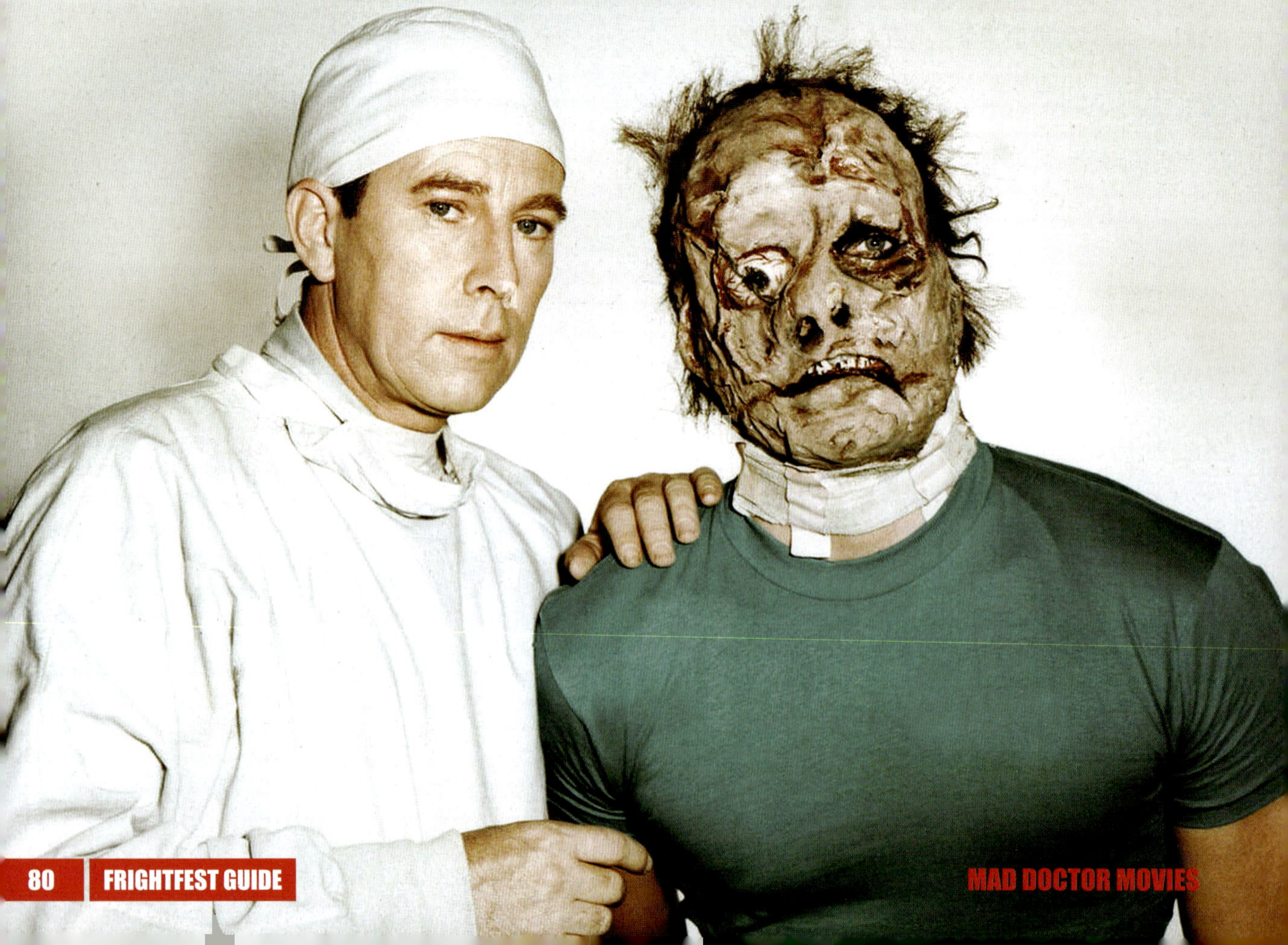

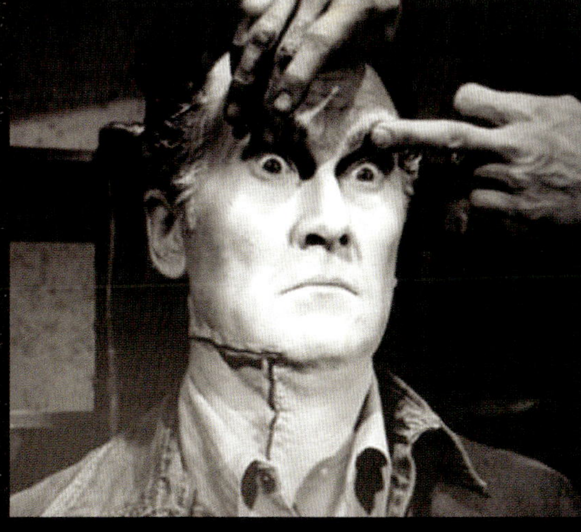

THE UNEARTHLY

USA, 1957
Director: Brooke L. Peters [Boris Petroff].
Producer: Brooke L. Peters [Boris Petroff].
Screenplay: Geoffrey Dennis [John D.F. Black], Jane Mann.
Music: Henry Vars. Cinematography: W. Merle Connell.
Cast: John Carradine, Allison Hayes, Myron Healey, Sally Todd, Marilyn Buferd, Tor Johnson.

In this low-budget B-movie quickie (shot in about five days, apparently) directed by 'Brooke L. Peters' (actually Boris Petroff) John Carradine is Dr. Conway. He runs a psychiatric hospital (i.e. a small house – remember that budget) where the regularly prescribed treatment for all his patients seems to be Nothing At All. Conway claims to have created a 'new gland' that is the secret of eternal youth and beauty. So far he has used it to create Tor Johnson, suggesting something of a yawning gulf between his ambitions and the results. Pretty Sally Todd, who would get her head pulled off in Richard E. Cunha's **Frankenstein's Daughter** the following year, is here subjected to Dr. Conway putting his pulsating gland inside her. After many running time-padding shots of surgery and fiddling with a big machine with knobs on, Sally ends up just looking shrivelled. Conway is eventually stabbed by someone who looks as if they've been forced to sit through this film, and the police discover a cellar full of Dr. Moreau-style rejects. Allison Hayes, the fifty-foot woman herself, manages to escape in the company of Myron Healy, best known to trash fans for playing the general in Bill Sachs' 1978 **The Incredible Melting Man**. It's all too brightly lit, too silly, and too long even at 73 minutes.

THE COLOSSUS OF NEW YORK

USA, 1958
Director: Eugène Lourié. Producer: William Alland.
Screenplay: Thelma Schnee. Music: Van Cleave. Cinematography: John F. Warren.
Cast: John Baragrey, Mala Powers, Otto Kruger, Robert Hutton, Ross Martin, Charles Herbert.

What are you to do if your brilliant son is run over just as he's about to win the 'International Peace Prize'? If you're mad scientist Otto Kruger, you get your other son, who happens to be an expert in robot engineering, to create a huge clanking body you can transplant your son's still-living brain into. Unfortunately, you can't always reckon with the side effects of such a procedure, which in this case include acquiring mind control, becoming a member of the far right (the food project he's been working on is now considered 'wasted on the slum people of the world'), and developing a death ray that the Colossus can shoot from his eyes. It doesn't help things when his brother falls in love with his (ex)wife. Eugène Lourié directed a couple of other movies to feature larger than life monsters, including 1953's **The Beast from 20,000 Fathoms**, **The Giant Behemoth** (1959) and **Gorgo** (1961). In fact, **The Colossus of New York** was his only directorial credit not to feature dinosaurs. Otto Kruger's filmography was vast, but today he's probably best known to horror fans for playing the hero in Lambert Hillyer's Universal sequel **Dracula's Daughter** (1936).

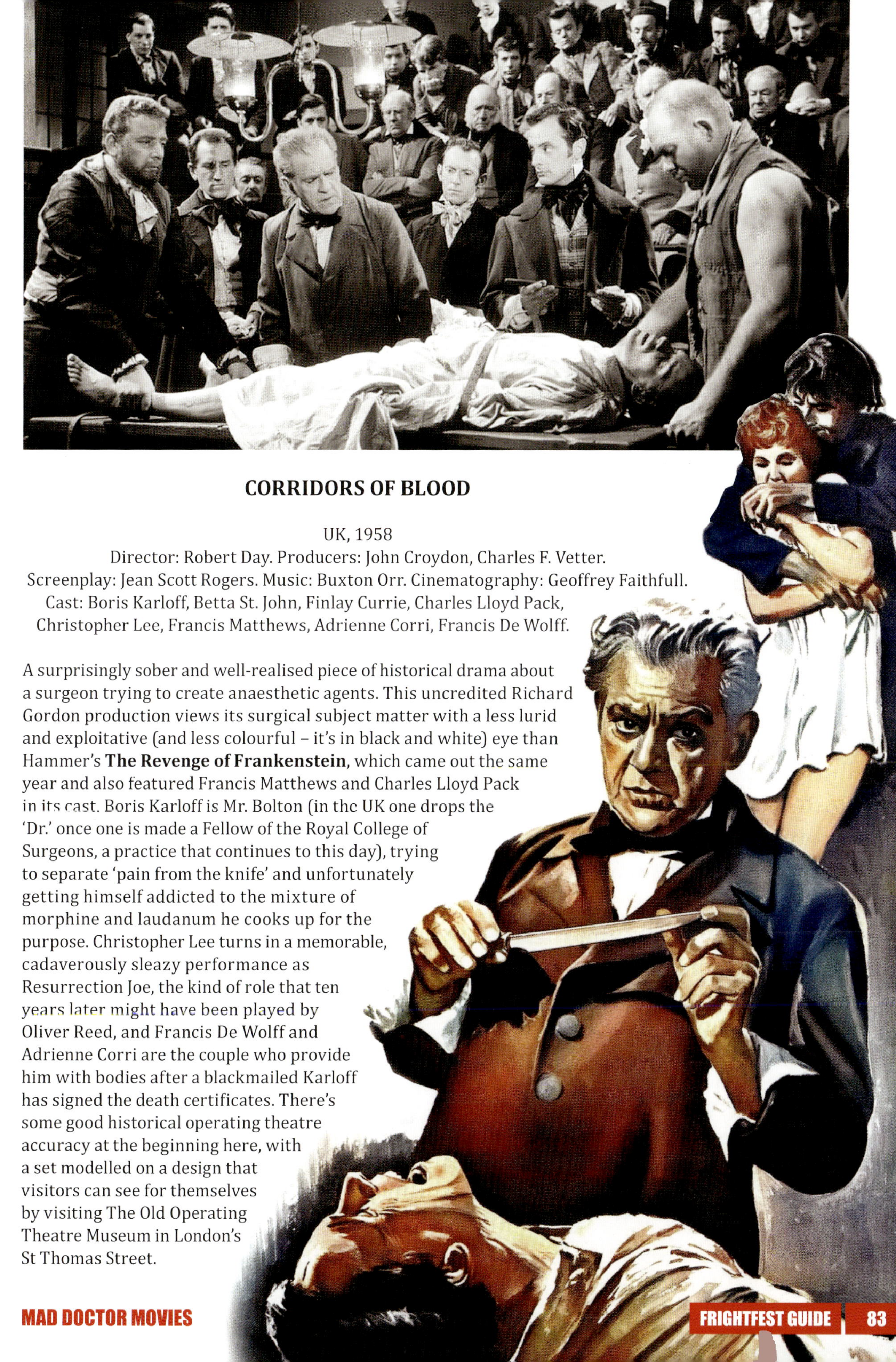

CORRIDORS OF BLOOD

UK, 1958
Director: Robert Day. Producers: John Croydon, Charles F. Vetter.
Screenplay: Jean Scott Rogers. Music: Buxton Orr. Cinematography: Geoffrey Faithfull.
Cast: Boris Karloff, Betta St. John, Finlay Currie, Charles Lloyd Pack,
Christopher Lee, Francis Matthews, Adrienne Corri, Francis De Wolff.

A surprisingly sober and well-realised piece of historical drama about a surgeon trying to create anaesthetic agents. This uncredited Richard Gordon production views its surgical subject matter with a less lurid and exploitative (and less colourful – it's in black and white) eye than Hammer's **The Revenge of Frankenstein**, which came out the same year and also featured Francis Matthews and Charles Lloyd Pack in its cast. Boris Karloff is Mr. Bolton (in the UK one drops the 'Dr.' once one is made a Fellow of the Royal College of Surgeons, a practice that continues to this day), trying to separate 'pain from the knife' and unfortunately getting himself addicted to the mixture of morphine and laudanum he cooks up for the purpose. Christopher Lee turns in a memorable, cadaverously sleazy performance as Resurrection Joe, the kind of role that ten years later might have been played by Oliver Reed, and Francis De Wolff and Adrienne Corri are the couple who provide him with bodies after a blackmailed Karloff has signed the death certificates. There's some good historical operating theatre accuracy at the beginning here, with a set modelled on a design that visitors can see for themselves by visiting The Old Operating Theatre Museum in London's St Thomas Street.

THE FLY

USA, 1958
Director: Kurt Neumann. Producers: Kurt Neumann, Robert L. Lippert [uncredited].
Screenplay: James Clavell. Music: Paul Sawtell.
Cinematography: Karl Struss.
Cast: David Hedison, Patricia Owens, Vincent Price, Herbert Marshall, Kathleen Freeman, Betty Lou Gerson.

The concept of a scientist who inadvertently swaps body parts or genetic material with another creature during matter transmission is now part of popular culture, and in major part it's due to this. Kurt Neumann's surprisingly faithful adaptation of George Langelaan's short story (adapted by James Clavell) was a huge hit for Twentieth Century-Fox on its original release (double billed with **The Alligator People**), spawning two direct sequels of which the second, Don Sharp's 1965 **Curse of the Fly**, is the more interesting. It was also remade in 1986 by David Cronenberg, and is on many people's lists of film sequels that are better than the originals. But Neumann's film is actually a very different beast, with its own individual strengths that justify it as a classic in its own right, concentrating more on the character of Helene (the scientist's wife) and the horrors she has had to witness. What the 1958 version also achieves superbly is the too seldom seen 'making a mundane everyday activity everyone can relate to into a scene of genuine suspense', in this case the catching of a house fly. Played as a mystery for much of its running time, it's late in the day when David Hedison as the Andre Delambre human-fly hybrid is finally revealed. The scene is built up so well and executed so superbly that it rightly entered the popular consciousness.

FRANKENSTEIN 1970

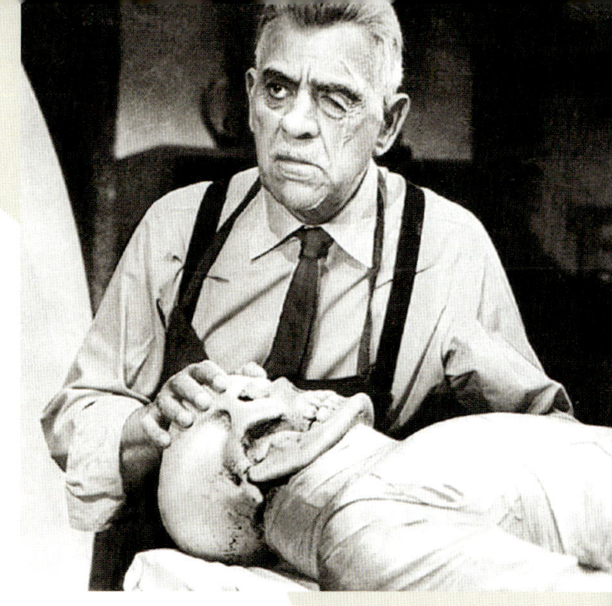

USA, 1958
Director: Howard W. Koch. Producer: Aubrey Schenck.
Screenplay: Richard H. Landau, George Worthing Yates.
Music: Paul Dunlap.
Cinematography: Carl E. Guthrie.
Cast: Boris Karloff, Tom Duggan, Jana Lund, Donald Barry, Charlotte Austin, Irwin Berke.

Frankenstein 1970, despite its 'futuristic' title, begins with a distinctly retro feel as a girl is chased through swampland by a faceless, hook-clawed monster. This effective and creepy opening is sadly just a gag, staged by a television crew who are in Germany to film the history of the Frankensteins. The only Frankenstein still living is concentration camp survivor Boris Karloff. Fortunately, his castle has fared rather better than he has and betrays none of the damage the fiery climax of numerous Universal and other pictures should have caused it by now. Boris has agreed to the TV crew coming because the money will help power his basement atomic reactor. Boris hypnotises his manservant with a pair of scissors and then takes the man's heart out to help create one of the cheapest, tattiest-looking monsters in Frankenstein history, who wanders around the castle looking like a half-hearted Michelin man in his head-to-toe bandage costume with eye holes punched in it. The Monster eventually gets some eyes. The underwhelming ending involves a cloud of radioactive steam killing both Monster and creator. A delicious lead performance and some nice Cinemascope framing (especially that opening sequence) are the only good reasons to watch this.

FRANKENSTEIN'S DAUGHTER

USA, 1958
Director: Richard E. Cunha.
Producers: George F. Foley Jr., Marc Frederic. Screenplay: H.E. Barrie. Music: Nicholas Carras.
Cinematography: Meredith M. Nicholson.
Cast: John Ashley, Sandra Knight, Donald Murphy, Sally Todd, Harold Lloyd Jr., Felix Locher.

In easily the best of director Richard E. Cunha's quartet of late-1950s exploitation pictures, Sandra Knight acquires Duane Dibbley teeth and googly eyes and goes on the rampage in her nightie. Meanwhile, sexy *Playboy* model Sally Todd gets run over, set on fire, and has her head knocked off and stitched onto the body of what looks like a biker. The result has a face that schoolboys of yesteryear would have described as a squashed tomato. It's doubtful that Mr. Cunha was going for verisimilitude here but the tatty falling-apart strapped-together creature we get in this is probably the best someone – in this case Frankenstein descendant 'Oliver Frank' (Donald Murphy) – could hope to come up with operating out of an ordinary house in late-1950s suburban America. Watch out for nominal lead John Ashley, future star of the **Blood Island** series of pictures and the man behind TV show *The A-Team*. Apparently make-up artist Harry Thomas didn't know the monster was supposed to be a woman and added last-minute lipstick to the actor (Harry Wilson) playing it, in a bid to prevent director Cunha from bursting into tears. It didn't work.

THE REVENGE OF FRANKENSTEIN

UK, 1958
Director: Terence Fisher. Producer: Anthony Hinds.
Screenplay: Jimmy Sangster. Music: Leonard Salzedo. Cinematography: Jack Asher.
Cast: Peter Cushing, Eunice Gayson, Francis Matthews, Michael Gwynn, John Welsh, Lionel Jeffries.

With the massive worldwide success of **The Curse of Frankenstein** it was inevitable that, as well as putting **Dracula** into production, Britain's Hammer Films were also going to be quick off the mark making a sequel to their first Gothic money-spinner. Maintaining an admirable sense of continuity that sadly was not to last (Hammer managed it a bit better with their Dracula series), this one kicks off with the Baron about to be guillotined. He escapes and is soon back to work, this time as 'Dr. Stein'. Screenwriter Jimmy Sangster has a lot of fun making digs at Victorian society, both at the level of the pompous medical council and with the inmates laid up at the forerunner of the NHS hospital which the Baron uses to get any spare parts he needs. The climactic appearance of Michael Gwynn's creature at a posh dinner party, brain transplanted and now tending to cannibalism, is a deliciously anarchic kick in the etiquettes, and while the Baron's subsequent destruction and resurrection feels like the stuff of screenwriter desperation, the final shot, of the Baron now as 'Dr. Victor', established in his Harley Street practice, is filled with potential that sadly was never fulfilled.

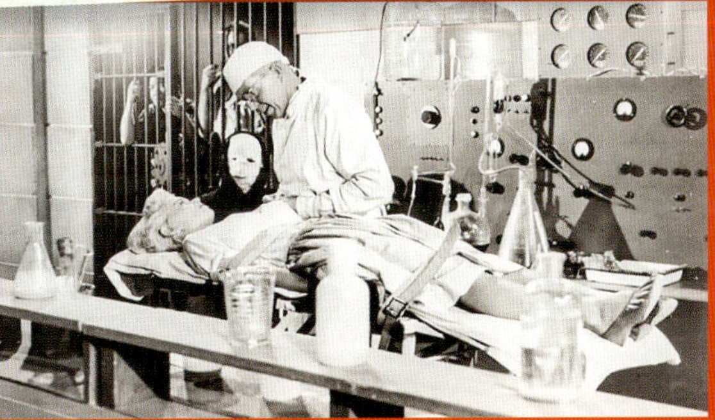

SHE DEMONS

USA, 1958
Director: Richard E. Cunha.
Producer: Arthur A. Jacobs.
Screenplay: Richard E. Cunha, H.E. Barrie.
Music: Nicholas Carras.
Cinematography: Meredith M. Nicholson.
Cast: Irish McCalla, Tod Griffin, Victor Sen Yung, Rudolph Anders, Gene Roth, Leni Tana.

Director Richard E. Cunha made four tiny-budget exploitation pictures in the late-1950s of which this is the most entertaining. Castaways Fred the explorer, spoilt rich girl Jerrie, and crewmen Sammy and Kris end up on a remote island, where they encounter a very poorly choreographed troupe of 'native women', who go on to perform their thigh-slapping dance of death. After this, our motley group is rounded up by Nazis. One poor girl gets flogged to such an extent that when she falls over, a bra miraculously appears on her as if from nowhere. Others are taken to the lab of mad concentration camp doctor Karl 'The Butcher' Osler (Rudolph Anders) who is trying to restore the scarred face of his wife. His laboratory is powered by lava. For some reason that is never adequately explained, there is a chicken in it. Osler's 'scientific' explanations for what is going on are so protracted and ridiculous they deserve some sort of award. The climax includes a reveal of the mad doctor's hideously-scarred wife (anything less would have been impolite) and the best 'dummy in a Nazi uniform thrown off a cliff' sequence you may ever see.

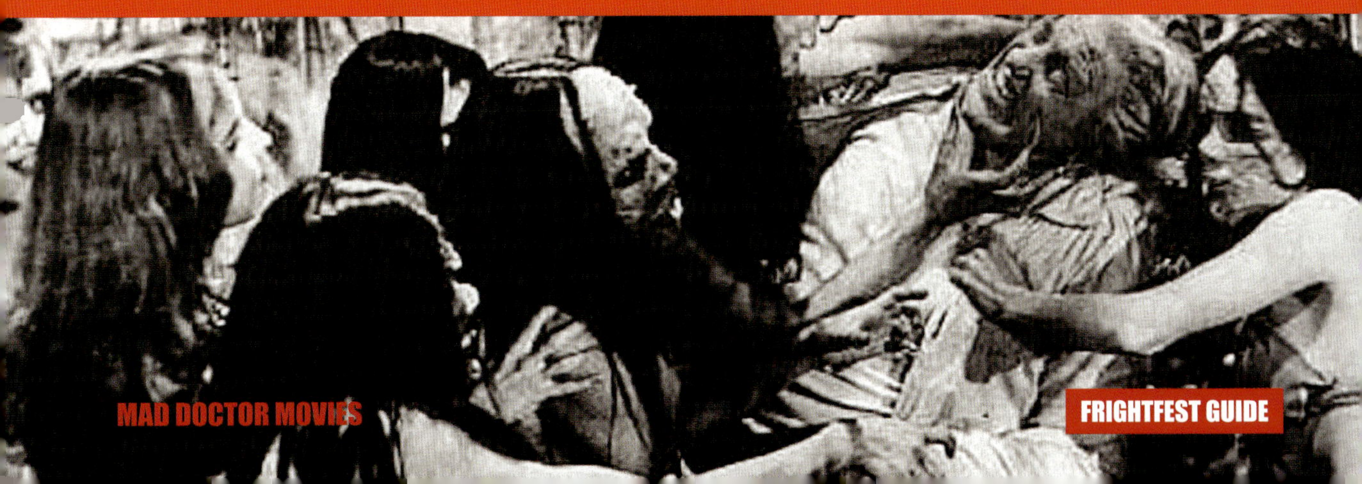

WOMANEATER

UK, 1958
Director: Charles Saunders. Producer: Guido Coen.
Screenplay: Brandon Fleming. Music: Edwin Astley.
Cinematography: Ernest Palmer.
Cast: George Coulouris, Vera Day, Peter Wayn [Peter Forbes-Robertson], Joyce Gregg, Joy Webster, Jimmy Vaughn.

From its 'Explorers Club' opening we're firmly in B-movie programmer territory here. George Coulouris, making a bid to be the Lionel Atwill of 1950s UK cinema, travels up the Amazon to discover a modestly budgeted Twickenham Studios temple set complete with the titular rubbery plant. Once the plant has had its dinner it produces a substance capable of reanimating the dead. Five years later, George has somehow got it past customs and it lives in his cellar, where he feeds it scantily clad (for 1958) glamour models. Exotic dancer Vera Day is probably the best advert for Kia-Ora it ever had, and if nothing else director Charles Saunders knows how to frame her bosom. Despite quite a bit of woman-eating there's precious little bringing back from the dead (it's saved for the end), making **Womaneater** a film with more ideas than it knows what to do with. A scene where Coulouris stalks a potential victim (Joy Webster) through London streets at night appears to have been shot *cinéma vérité* style and provides an interesting snapshot of the city at the time. When filming the 'Checkmate' episode of Patrick McGoohan's TV series *The Prisoner* Coulouris allegedly complained that all anyone wanted to ask him about was **Citizen Kane**. It's hard to believe not a single fan wanted to ask him about this one.

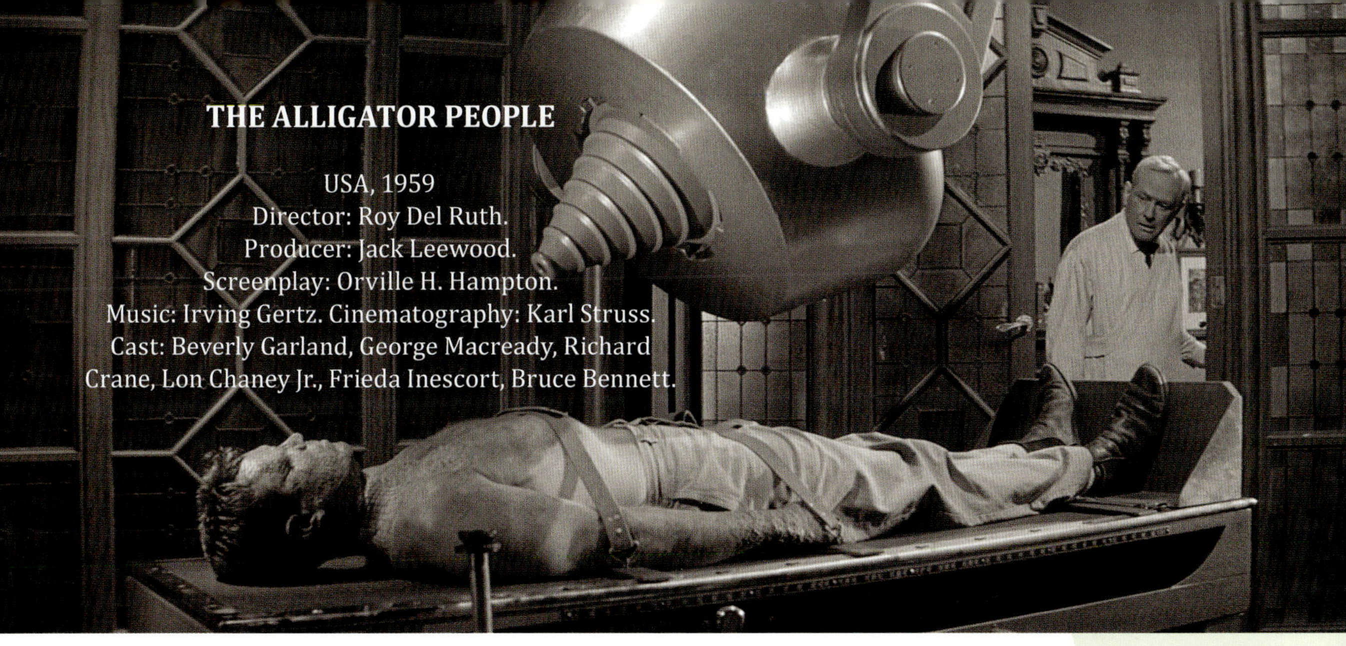

THE ALLIGATOR PEOPLE

USA, 1959
Director: Roy Del Ruth.
Producer: Jack Leewood.
Screenplay: Orville H. Hampton.
Music: Irving Gertz. Cinematography: Karl Struss.
Cast: Beverly Garland, George Macready, Richard Crane, Lon Chaney Jr., Frieda Inescort, Bruce Bennett.

Deep in the heart of Louisiana swamp country George Macready has been injecting accident victims with a serum from alligators that allows them to grow new limbs. It also makes them go all scaly and turn green (probably – this one's in black and white). George has a cobalt bomb and he means to use it. It's a complex looking piece of equipment that must have cost a bit, as it gets demonstrated frequently during the film's brief running time of 74 minutes. Because men turning into alligators and the constant threat of radiation poisoning isn't enough, Lon Chaney Jr. is also here, stumbling around in a torn seersucker suit, and boasting a hook instead of a right hand due to a previous alligator attack, allowing him to wax lyrical at length about how much he hates them 'gators and would spend the rest of his life killing them if he could. Heroine Beverly Garland manages to lose most of her skirt as she follows her snouty-faced fiancé into the swamp at the climax. Director Roy Del Ruth manages a few nice moments, including Garland's arrival at a deserted Louisiana railway station, while Irving Gertz provides a creepy score, with a splendid piano solo played in the dark by our near-alligator man at one point. The combination of Twentieth Century-Fox, Cinemascope, and mad science yielded **The Fly** as this film's 'A' feature on double bills. **The Alligator People** isn't in the same league, but it's rarely dull and displays great creativity in turning the few medical facts we get to hear into a movie of reptilian mayhem.

AFB

BLACK PIT OF DR. M

Mexico, 1959
Director: Fernando Méndez. Producer: Alfredo Ripstein Jr.
Screenplay: Ramón Obón. Music: Gustavo César Carrión.
Cinematography: Víctor Herrera.
Cast: Gastón Santos, Rafael Bertrand, Mapita Cortés, Carlos Ancira, Carolina Barret, Luis Aragón.

An exemplary Gothic, **Misterios de ultratumba** ('Mysteries from Beyond the Grave' to give this Mexican production its original title) begins with the death of one of two doctors who have been researching the afterlife. The attempts of Dr. Mazali (Rafael Betrand) to contact his now-deceased colleague via a seance are successful but only lead to tragedy as 'Dr. M' finds himself, first metaphorically and then literally in the pit of the title. The full-blooded script by Ramón Obón gives Dr. M a day job running the local lunatic asylum, calming down his most aggressive female patient with a music box before she throws acid in the face of one of his staff. (Why do psychiatrists keep acid lying around in easy-to-throw bottles? Twenty years later they still hadn't learned – Patrick Macnee's Dr. Waggner had one that Dee Wallace threw at a transforming Eddie Quist in **The Howling**.) The story builds in its complexity, so that by the time there's a body clawing its way out of a grave the horrific implications are far greater than it being a mere corpse on the rampage. Production design and photography under the skilful direction of Fernando Méndez are reminiscent of the best classic Universal horrors, making this the ideal place to start for those unfamiliar with Mexican horror cinema.

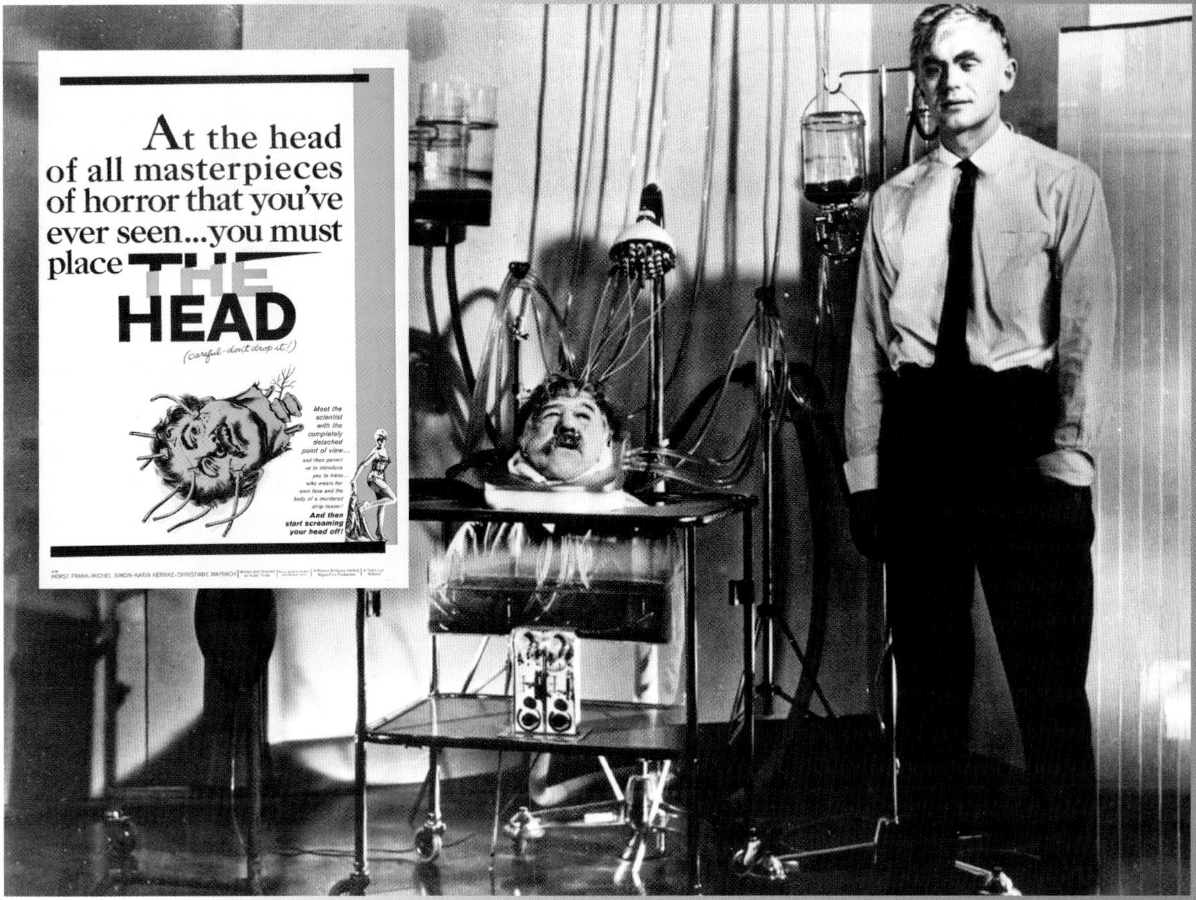

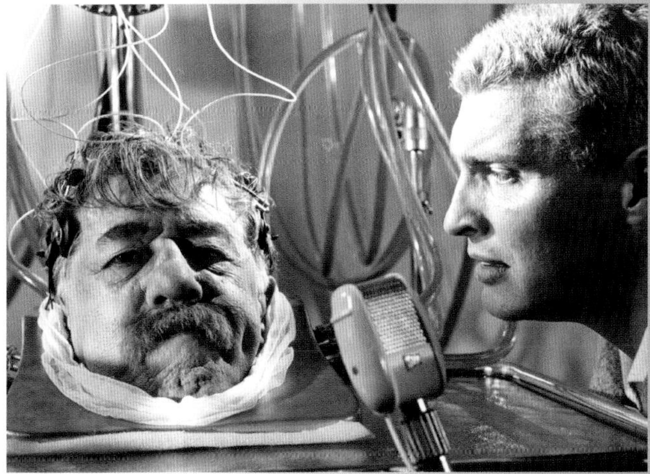

THE HEAD

West Germany, 1959
Director: Victor Trivas. Producer: Wolf C. Hartwig. Screenplay: Victor Trivas. Music: Willy Mattes, Jacques Lasry. Cinematography: Georg Krause.
Cast: Horst Frank, Michel Simon, Karin Kernke, Helmut Schmid, Paul Dahlke, Dieter Eppler, Kurt Müller-Graf.

This German entry in the head transplant subgenre stars prolific actor Horst Frank (Jeremy Summers' 1967 **The Vengeance of Fu Manchu**, Dario Argento's **The Cat O'Nine Tails** from 1971) as Dr. Ood, who possesses the most amazing eyebrows that resemble Conrad Veidt's eye make-up from **The Cabinet of Dr. Caligari** but upside down. He removes the head of Professor Abel (Michel Simon), keeping it alive for advice on how to transplant the head of the severely scoliotic nurse he fancies onto the body of a stripper, thus creating the naked woman of the original German title **Die Nackte und der Satan**. Nobody ever explains in these films how a severed head, bereft of vocal cords (which are further down) or lungs (further down still) to provide air to blow through them, can talk. Even Joe Pilato in George Romero's 1985 **Day of the Dead** is able to keep chatting while his head is wrenched off. But we'll forgive **The Head** if only because about fourteen minutes in there's an excellent chest X-ray on display that shows severe disruption of the thoracic spinal column. If it really is Professor Abel's (as he claims) then he shouldn't be standing as straight as he is, or at all, in fact.

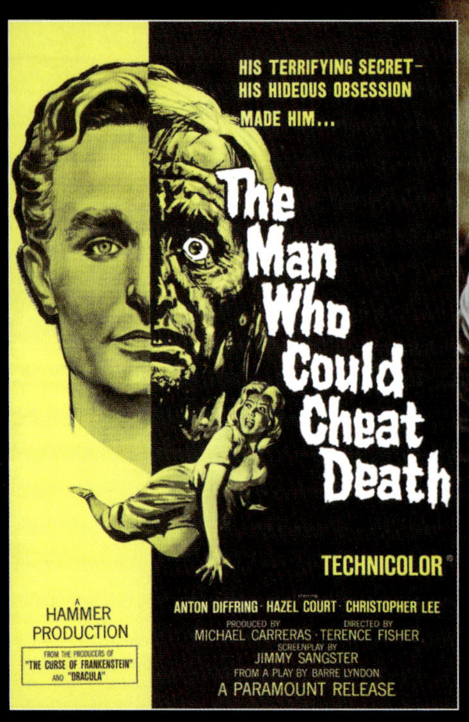

THE MAN WHO COULD CHEAT DEATH

UK, 1959
Director: Terence Fisher. Producer: Michael Carreras.
Screenplay: Jimmy Sangster. Music: Richard Rodney Bennett.
Cinematography: Jack Asher.
Cast: Anton Diffring, Hazel Court, Christopher Lee, Arnold Marlé, Delphi Lawrence, Francis De Wolff.

After a string of remakes of famous properties including **The Curse of Frankenstein**, **Dracula** and most recently **The Hound of the Baskervilles**, Hammer chose as their next project for the same treatment the 1945 MGM production **The Man in Half Moon Street**, based on a Barré Lyndon play about a doctor who needs regular surgery to prolong his life. Peter Cushing was slated to star but cried off, claiming understandable exhaustion having just completed Hammer's Sherlock Holmes **Hound** picture. Instead the lead went to Anton Diffring, whose acting style in this tends towards delivering his most impassioned speeches to the stalls rather than the actor standing next to him. Christopher Lee is also in it, as a doctor who might be able to perform the life-saving operation, and Hazel Court is Diffring's nude sculpting interest. Talk of this apparently now lost footage often predominates in discussions of this one, which just demonstrates how unmemorable the rest of it is. Even director Terence Fisher couldn't wring much life out of it, although the climactic ageing sequence is staged with the usual lascivious aplomb. Hammer would have been better off remaking Albert Lewin's **The Picture of Dorian Gray** (1945) – we had to wait until 2009 for Oliver Parker's version to see a modern British adaptation of Oscar Wilde's decadent 1890 novel.

TERROR IS A MAN

Philippines, 1959
Directors: Gerardo de Leon, Eddie Romero [uncredited].
Producers: Kane W. Lynn, Eddie Romero.
Screenplay: Paul Harber. Music: Ariston Avelino.
Cinematography: Emmanuel I. Rojas.
Cast: Francis Lederer, Greta Thyssen, Richard Derr, Oscar Keesee, Lilia Duran, Flory Carlos.

H.G. Wells' novel *The Island of Dr. Moreau* provided the unofficial inspiration for a number of Philippines-produced horror films including Eddie Romero's **The Twilight People** (featuring Pam Grier as the Panther Woman) and George Schenck's **Superbeast** (both 1972). Before those, however, Gerardo de Leon directed the tale of shipwrecked Richard Derr finding himself rescued by Dr. Girard (Francis Lederer from Paul Landres' 1958 **The Return of Dracula**). He then witnesses Girard's attempts to turn a panther into a human being, aided by his improbably blonde and busty wife (Greta Thyssen). The opening act is a little slow, but **Terror Is a Man** does an excellent job of evoking sympathy for the doctor's creation, with an atmospherically lit climax that even suggests an escape for the bandage-swathed panther man. Picked up by Sam Sherman for US distribution nearly ten years after it was made and retitled **Blood Creature** as part of a double bill, **Terror Is a Man** was such a hit it led to a string of horror movies being shot in the Philippines by Hemisphere Productions (essentially producers Irwin Pizor and ex US Navy pilot Kane Lynn along with local filmmaker Eddie Romero). They were all set on the same location of Blood Island (called Isla de Sangre in this) and followed much the same basic template. **Brides of Blood** (1968) had a man turning into a monster due to radiation exposure, **Mad Doctor of Blood Island** (1969 and covered in the *FrightFest Guide to Monster Movies*) had Dr. Lorca (Ronald Remy) trying to cure cancer but creating chlorophyll creatures instead, and **Beast of Blood** (1970) followed directly on from the end of its predecessor.

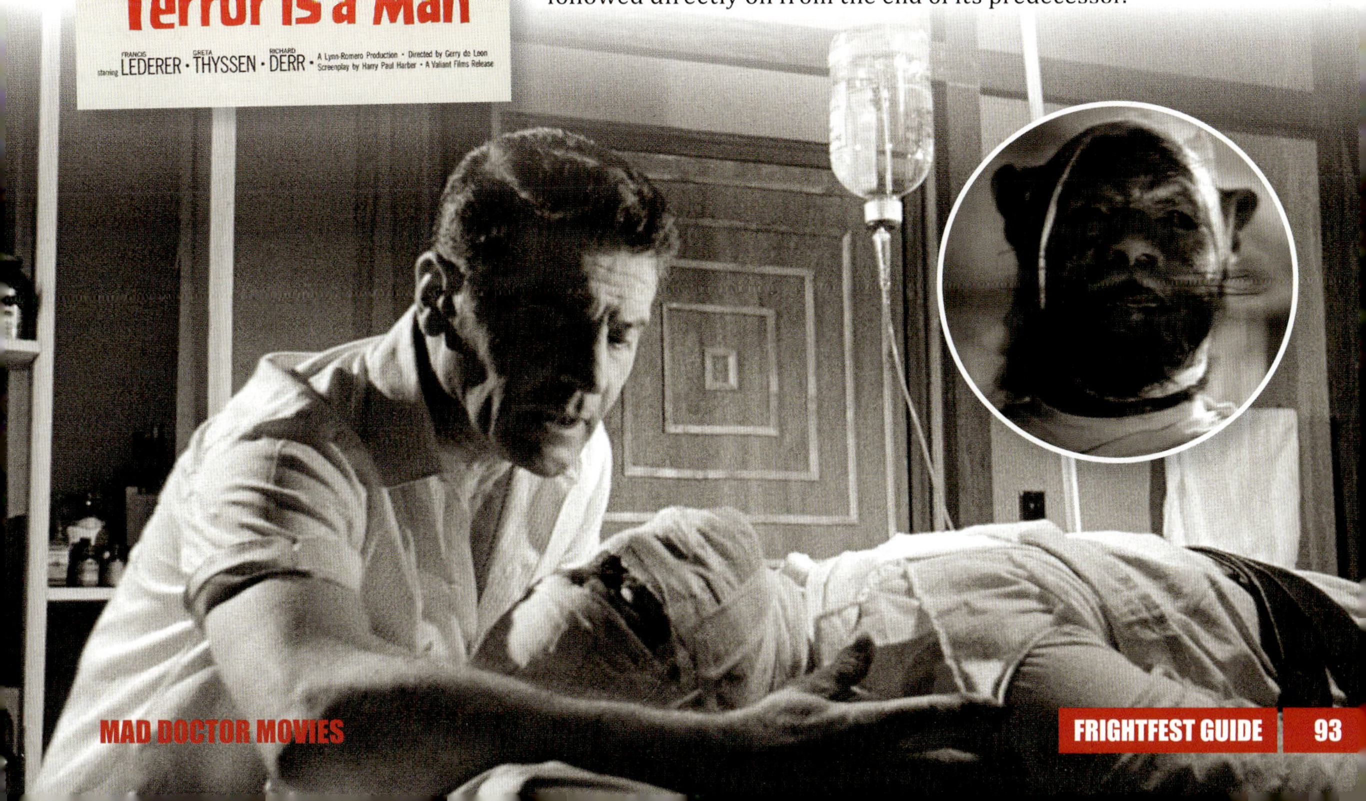

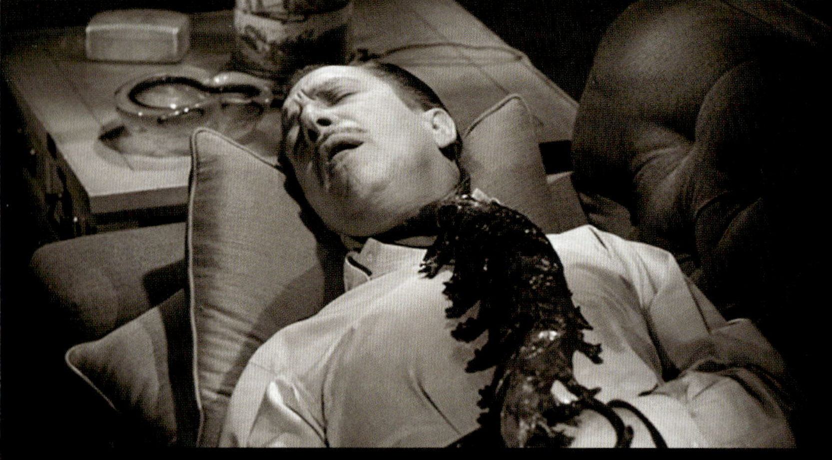

THE TINGLER

USA, 1959
Director: William Castle. Producer: William Castle. Screenplay: Robb White. Music: Von Dexter. Cinematography: Wilfred M. Cline. Cast: Vincent Price, Judith Evelyn, Darryl Hickman, Patricia Cutts, Pamela Lincoln, Philip Coolidge.

Producer-director William Castle, the 'king of the gimmicks' came up with arguably his best in this literal shocker (or at least it was if you were sat in one of his specially wired cinema seats). Vincent Price discovers that a centipede-like creature materialises on your spinal column at moments of extreme fear, and if you don't scream it crushes your vertebrae and kills you. One of the more original movie monsters, the tingler made manifest is actually more of a cute rubber toy dragged along with a wire, but the basic concept remains rather horrific. Copying a move producer Herman Cohen used a couple of times, Castle includes colour at a judicious point in his otherwise black and white film to show a bloody hand rising from a bath to induce terror in a victim incapable of the necessary utterance to free her of the tingler's spinal embrace. The sequence everyone remembers is when the tingler gets loose in a movie theatre and Price encourages the audience to scream for their lives. It was the cue for the projectionist to switch on the electric motors wired under cinema seats. This particular page of the volume you are currently reading was supposed to be implanted with tiny electrodes to reproduce the experience but costs proved too prohibitive. Or did they? You'd better scream now, just to be on the safe side.

CIRCUS OF HORRORS

UK, 1960
Director: Sidney Hayers. Producers: Samuel Z. Arkoff, Leslie Parkyn, Julian Wintle. Screenplay: George Baxt. Music: Muir Mathieson, Franz Reizenstein. Cinematography: Douglas Slocombe.
Cast: Anton Diffring, Donald Pleasence, Yvonne Monlaur, Erika Remberg, Jane Hylton, Kenneth Griffith, Yvonne Romain.

The third of Anglo-Amalgamated's 'Sadean Trilogy' – the other two being the Herman Cohen-produced **Horrors of the Black Museum** (1959) and Michael Powell's **Peeping Tom** (1960) and – takes the concept of the mad plastic surgeon and gives it a twist. Dr. Bernard Schüler (Anton Diffring) performs surgery that goes horribly wrong at the beginning of the film, which necessitates him going on the run from the law. Unlike some of his fellow mad doctors, Schüler obviously learns from his mistakes, as his subsequent efforts are masterpieces (Yvonne Romain can certainly be described thusly). Screenwriter George Baxt was asked for a horror film set in a circus and came up with the idea of Schüler transforming wanted criminals who would then be indebted to him and recruited to join the circus he ends up owning through murder. The icing on this particular bloodstained cake is that when members of his villainous troupe want to leave, they meet their end in various creatively engineered 'accidents', predating (and possibly even inspiring) both the **Dr. Phibes** and **Saw** series of films. It was directed by Sidney Hayers, who worked with George Baxt again shortly after on the classic **Night of the Eagle** (1962). Baxt also provided the original stories for Hammer's **Vampire Circus** and Richard Gordon's **Tower of Evil** (both 1972).

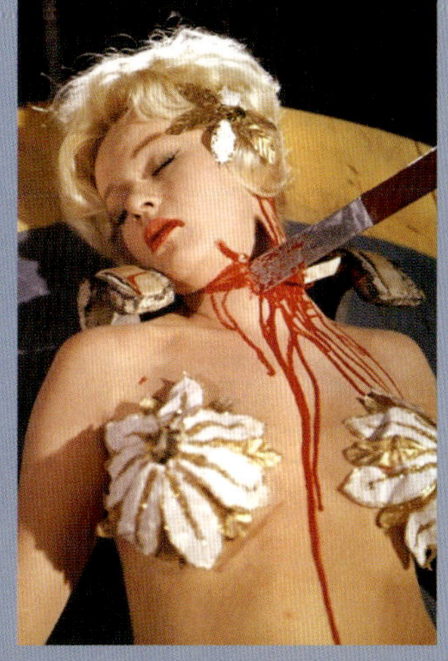

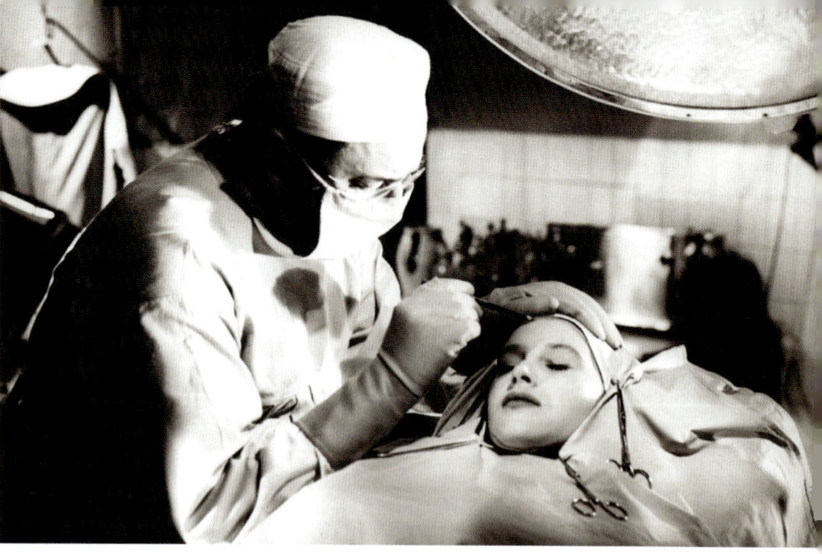

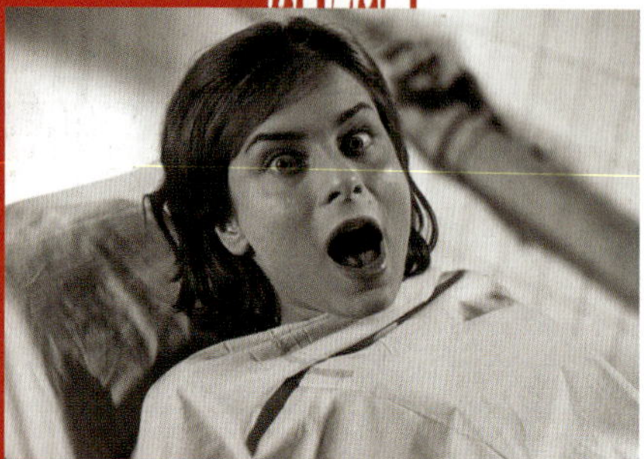

EYES WITHOUT A FACE

France/Italy, 1960
Director: Georges Franju. Producers: Jules Borkon, Riccardo Gualino [uncredited]. Screenplay: Pierre Boileau, Thomas Narcejac, Jean Redon, Claude Sautet. Music: Maurice Jarre. Cinematography: Eugen Schüfftan.
Cast: Pierre Brasseur, Alida Valli, Juliette Mayniel, Edith Scob, Béatrice Altariba, François Guérin.

Plastic surgeon Dr. Génessier (Pierre Brasseur) has, through his careless driving, caused extensive damage to the face of his daughter Christianne (Edith Scob). Unfortunately Génessier hasn't heard of trying to take skin grafts from elsewhere on Christianne's body to try and improve her appearance, even though he gives a lecture on the subject at the start of the film. But why should he when he lives so near Paris and there's a bevy of beautiful women whom he can kidnap and graphically remove the faces of in increasingly desperate acts of transplantation? With its *Grand Guignol* gruesomeness it's not surprising that Georges Franju's film kick-started a subgenre of horror cinema that concentrated on the lurid rather than the lyrical aspects of his movie. The tale of the surgeon responsible for destroying his own daughter's face and willing to do anything to repair his actions is the stuff of pulp paperback grotesquerie, but Franju skilfully elevates it way above its penny dreadful potential, making as fine a horror film as one could hope for with the material. Apart from the nasty bits, there's a pervasive gloom to the film that serves to augment the desperate situation of its central character, wandering her father's isolated country mansion, a literally faceless wraith assumed dead by the rest of the world. One imagines the city-set scenes at the police station and its environs would be grey even if the picture were in colour, and it never seems to stop raining. Almost from the beginning there is no suggestion that the film is going to end anything other than badly, which is possibly why the final scene is all the more moving, leaving us with an image that simultaneously suggests both freedom and utter loneliness.

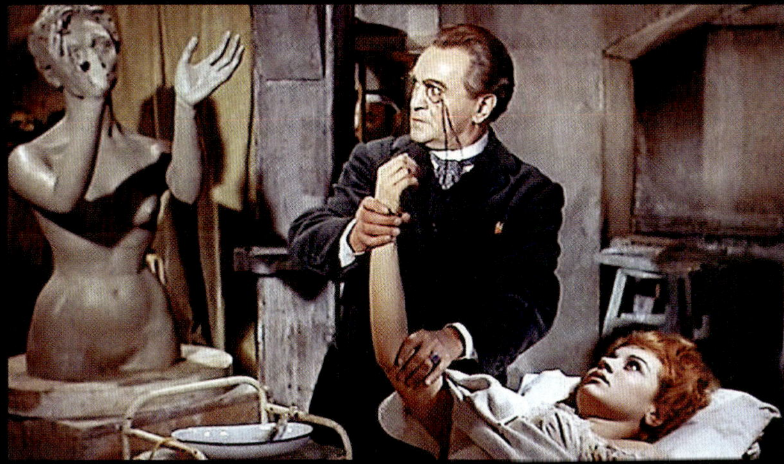

MILL OF THE STONE WOMEN

Italy/France, 1960
Director: Giorgio Ferroni. Producer: Giampaolo Bigazzi.
Screenplay: Giorgio Ferroni [uncredited], Ugo Liberatore [uncredited], Giorgio Stegani [uncredited].
Music: Carlo Innocenzi. Cinematography: Pier Ludovico Pavoni.
Cast: Pierre Brice, Scilla Gabel, Dany Carrel, Wolfgang Preiss, Herbert Boehme, Marco Guglielmi.

The first Italian horror film to be shot in colour mixes themes strongly resonant of Poe (catalepsy and necrophilia) overlaying a mad science plot. It's highly likely that Giorgio Ferroni's film influenced the later Gothics of Italian directors like Mario Bava and Riccardo Freda who went on to become much better known, as well as anticipating some of the more fetishistic imagery seen in the work of Jess Franco. An art professor's daughter suffers from a rare blood disease that means he has to arrange for women to be abducted so she can receive blood transfusions. The donors die and are turned into statues, which are then exhibited in the professor's windmill as part of a bizarre carousel. Parts of this, especially a dream sequence where the hero encounters the 'undead' daughter, feel like scenes from a Roger Corman Gothic That Never Was, and its influence might even have been so far reaching that one wonders if Talbot Rothwell was thinking of this when he was writing the women-into-mannequins bit in **Carry On Screaming!** We shall likely never know. Despite being an Italian film, it was shot on location in Holland, where the gloomy weather adds immensely to the atmosphere. There aren't enough horror films set in windmills.

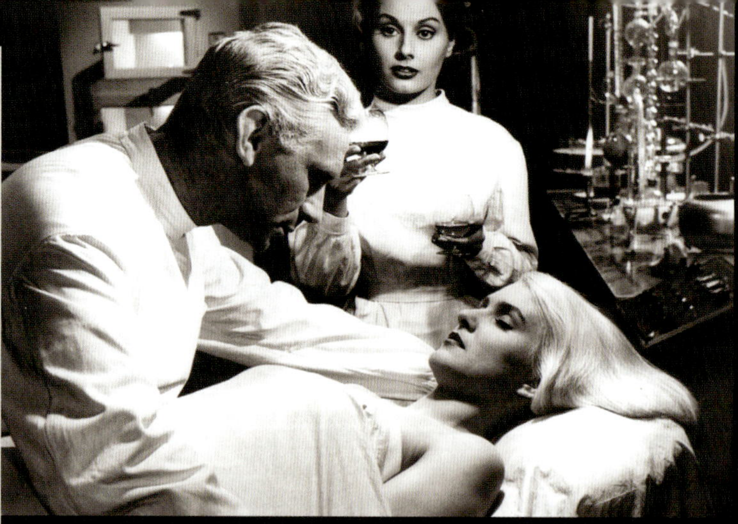

SEDDOK

Italy, 1960
Director: Anton Giulio Majano. Producer: Mario Fava [Elio Ippolito Mellino]. Screenplay: Gino De Santis, Alberto Bevilacqua, Anton Giulio Majano. Music: Armando Trovajoli. Cinematography: Aldo Giordani.
Cast: Alberto Lupo, Susanne Loret, Sergio Fantoni, Franca Parisi, Ivo Garrani, Andrea Scotti.

Seddok is the UK title of this Italian film, the titular monster being named by a drunk lady in a bar in one scene. Who knows, perhaps that's how they came up with the name in real life as well. The US title is **Atom Age Vampire** but there's no vampire here, despite an awkward line of dialogue in the dubbed version to justify it, and the US print should be avoided anyway. You can tell we're in EuroHorror territory because Monique, the mad doctor's sexy lab assistant, is so besotted with him she mutilates herself so he can use her as a test subject for his new skin restorer – and it works! Unfortunately, car crash victim Jeanette the Stripper, with whom the doctor falls in love, doesn't have so much luck with her face, which keeps scarring up. The solution? The doctor ingests his mutilating agent, lap dissolves into a Mr. Hyde-like warty monster, and sets off to abduct women so he can obtain the necessary 'glandular tissue' (always a good mad doctor plot standby) to cure her... again. Producer 'Mario Fava' was actually Elio Ippolito Mellino. Perhaps the credits cost by the letter. Be warned that the public domain print in circulation for this one is thirty minutes shorter than the Italian version, shorn of 'sophisticated dance routines', monster action, and some dialogue US censor boards were presumably keen to protect 1960s audiences from.

THE THOUSAND EYES OF DR. MABUSE

West Germany/Italy/France, 1960
Director: Fritz Lang. Producers: Artur Brauner, Fritz Lang [uncredited], Sandro Pallavicini [uncredited].
Screenplay: Fritz Lang, Heinz Oskar Wuttig.
Music: Gerhard Becker. Cinematography: Karl Löb.
Cast: Dawn Addams, Peter van Eyck, Gert Fröbe, Wolfgang Preiss, Werner Peters, Andrea Checchi, Howard Vernon.

The third and final Mabuse film to be directed by Fritz Lang gives us a brief summary of the first two (1922's **Dr. Mabuse the Gambler** and 1933's **The Testament of Dr. Mabuse**) culminating in a shot of the infamous doctor's gravestone, all this coming after the killing of a journalist by hitman Howard Vernon using a high-tech needle gun. Criminal mastermind Dr. Mabuse may be dead, but his spirit lives on in what feels like a James Bond film before such a thing existed. Made in 1960, it anticipates the spy thrillers of the forthcoming decade(s) with its weird gadgets, surveillance cameras, and a master villain intent on ruling the world. Fritz Lang later admired Gordon Hessler's **Scream and Scream Again** (1970) and it's not difficult to see why. The excellent climactic car chase is similar to that in Hessler's film and Gert Fröbe's Inspector Kras – the man who finds himself in a strange world of insurance salesmen who rely on astrology, a blind man who can predict the future, the suicidal Marion Menil (Dawn Addams), and rich industrialist Henry Travers (Peter van Eyck of Hammer's **The Snorkel**) – was the likely inspiration for Alfred Marks' Inspector Bellaver, hunting down Vincent Price's synthetic humanoids in one of the most Mabuse-like movies not to bear the name. The success of Lang's film led to a number of sequels made by German producer Artur Brauner.

DR. BLOOD'S COFFIN

UK, 1961
Director: Sidney J. Furie.
Producer: George Fowler.
Screenplay: Jerry Juran [Nathan Juran].
Music: Buxton Orr. Cinematography: Stephen Dade.
Cast: Kieron Moore, Hazel Court, Ian Hunter,
Kenneth J. Warren, Fred Johnson, Paul Hardtmuth.

Dr. Peter Blood (Kieron Moore) is thrown out of Vienna and reduced to paralysing Cornish villagers to further his heart transplant research. He uses curare, a nicotinic acetylcholine receptor blocker which will indeed produce that effect, although you can't bring them back to life or do open heart surgery on them while they look at you. Curare should not be confused with tetrodotoxin, which is a sodium channel blocker and is the drug used to create zombies in Wes Craven's **The Serpent and the Rainbow** (1988). The climactic surgery sequence (performed in the depths of a tin mine – the 'coffin' of the title where little Dr. Blood used to imagine he was a buried Egyptian pharaoh amongst other things) boasts a rather floppy heart, that once transplanted revives a fairly decent if briefly seen zombie. Directed by Sidney J. Furie from a script by Nathan (credited as Jerry) Juran and filmed in authentic Cornish locations (the village of Portcarron where the action takes place is fictional, though), the most shocking thing for today's viewers will be how nice the weather stays for the entire film. Composer Buxton Orr (the man who took over from Sir Malcolm Arnold on 1959's **Suddenly Last Summer** after Arnold left in disgust on learning of the subject matter) helps bring life to several lengthy dialogue free sequences, and Hazel Court as a nurse also makes the film more watchable.

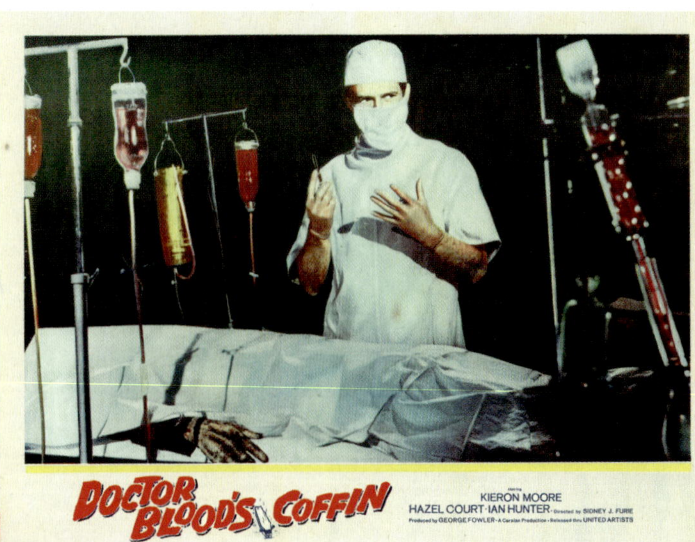

THE SNAKE WOMAN

UK, 1961
Director: Sidney J. Furie. Producer: George Fowler.
Screenplay: Orville H. Hampton.
Music: Buxton Orr. Cinematography: Stephen Dade.
Cast: John McCarthy, Susan Travers, Geoffrey Denton, Elsie Wagstaff, Arnold Marlé, John Cazabon.

One hopes the writer of this one didn't spend more than a weekend on the script as it's mainly people sitting and telling us things we already know, then telling us again and again. And that's a shame because **The Snake Woman** is filled with so much appealing daftness it's a pity a better job wasn't made of it. A Victorian scientist has been injecting his wife with cobra venom to 'keep her sane'. She gives birth to a 'cold baby' who grows into a sexy girl who turns feral and lives in the Northumberland countryside, biting some poor chap to death once a month (not the same one, obviously). She sheds her skin, five years before Hammer used the same idea in their (considerably superior) **The Reptile**. There's a disgruntled low-budget Northumberland mob! (The budget can only stretch to four torches.) There's a mad old lady! Voodoo! Cobras happily living in the North of England! Would this film have us believe it was a lot warmer in Victorian times? Susan Travers is the snake girl and is probably best known for playing Nurse Travers, smeared in sprout juice and eaten by locusts a few years later in Robert Fuest's **The Abominable Dr. Phibes**. Director Sidney J. Furie eventually moved on to **The Ipcress File** (1965). One presumes he never reconsidered remaking this.

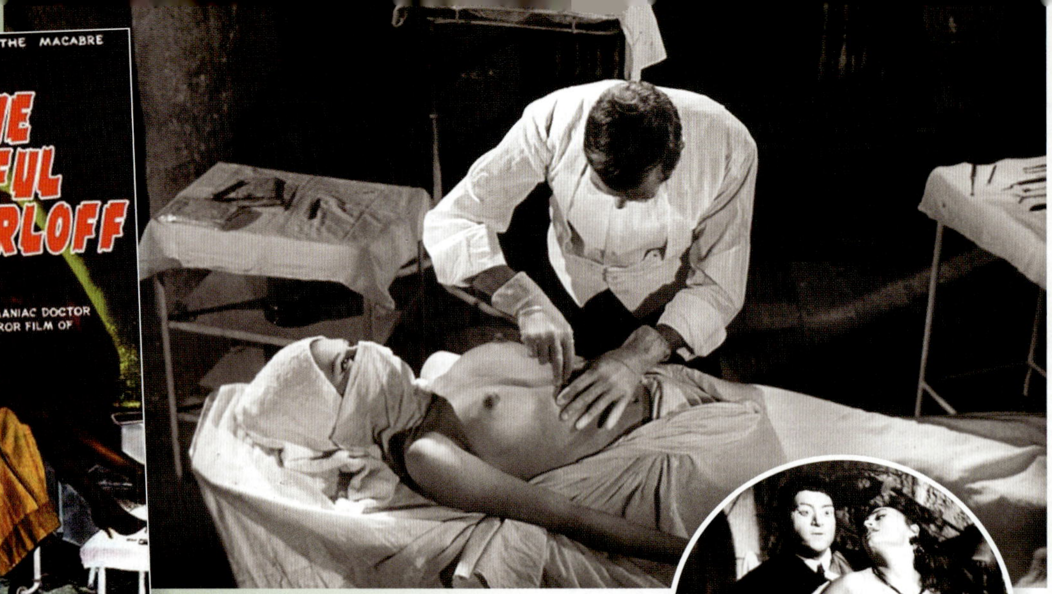

THE AWFUL DR. ORLOF

Spain/France, 1962
Director: Jess Franco.
Producers: María Ángel Coma Borrás, Leo Lax, Marius Lesoeur.
Screenplay: Jess Franco.
Music: José Pagán, Antonio Ramírez Ángel. Cinematography: Godofredo Pacheco.
Cast: Howard Vernon, Conrado San Martin, Diana Lorys, Perla Cristal, Ricardo Valle, María Silva.

Known as **The Demon Doctor** in the UK and **Gritos en la noche** in its country of origin, anyone who wants to understand the lengthy and frequently challenging filmography of director Jess Franco (or show an example of his work to a friend who will stay a friend) should start here. Despite taking plenty of its ideas from other sources: including a surgeon trying to restore the face of his daughter (Franco claimed he had never seen Franju's **Les yeux sans visage** prior to making the film, and that in fact the inspiration to make a horror film was Hammer's 1960 **The Brides of Dracula**); the name Orlof (originally from Edgar Wallace's 1924 novel *The Dark Eyes of London* minus an 'f'); the assistant who is both blind and mute (any number of US B-movie programmers); who knows where to go from the tapping of Orlof's cane (**The Cabinet of Caligari**); and the cloaked abductor of 'harlots' (sundry Jack the Ripper media). Despite all of these inspirations, Franco imbues this morbid, erotic, sadistic movie with a style all his own, introducing themes that would recur throughout his immense body of work of around 200 films as director. The names Orloff (in subsequent films it would get the extra 'f' back), Morpho (the assistant), the pairing of lovers as detectives, the innovative and effective use of avant-garde music scores, and a fixation with eroticism and obsession that threatened to destroy all concerned, would recur again and again in films where conventional filmmaking techniques (very much in evidence here so don't let that put you off) would be routinely abandoned. His films divide viewers into those who find his oeuvre fascinating and those who would rather run for the hills than have to sit through another one. If you don't yet know which category you fall into, then you could be denying yourselves the cinematic journey of a lifetime. And this is where it all begins...

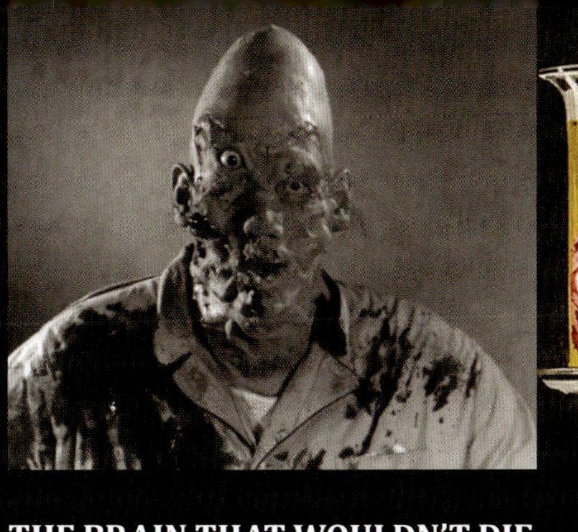

THE BRAIN THAT WOULDN'T DIE

USA, 1962
Director: Joseph Green. Producer: Rex Carlton.
Screenplay: Joseph Green. Cinematography: Stephen Hajnal.
Cast: Virginia Leith, Herb Evers [Jason Evers], Adele Lamont, Bruce Brighton, Doris Brent, Leslie Daniel [Anthony La Penna].

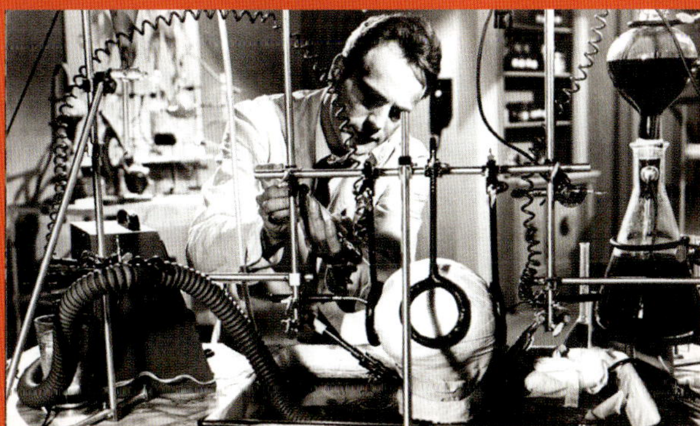

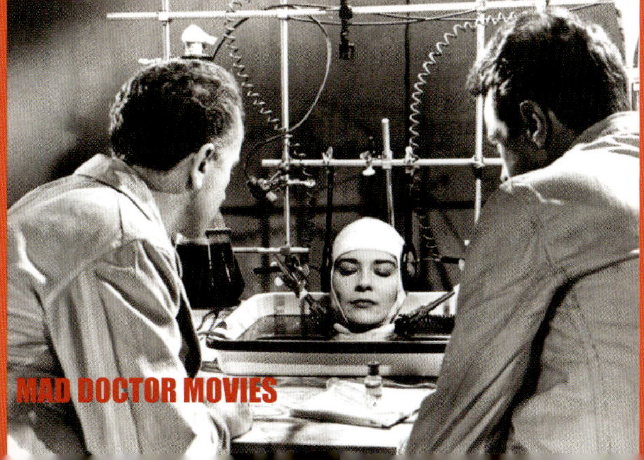

Or even **The Head That Wouldn't Die** according to this film's end title card (perhaps it couldn't make its mind up), this one's rather more gruesome and explicit than most US horror fare made around this time. It has more in common with the UK's Sadean pictures of the era (Michael Powell's **Peeping Tom**, Sidney Hayers' **Circus of Horrors**, both 1960) or even foreshadows themes to be seen in the European cinema of Jess Franco. Dr. Bill Cortner (Jason Evers) has been doing transplant experiments with "those limbs from the amputee operations". In a bit of a rush one day, he crashes his car, causing the removal of the head of his girlfriend Jan (Virginia Leith, who apparently in the 1940s was arrested for slashing her roommates's face with a razor causing 40 stitches' worth of real-life surgery). Much of the rest of the film involves Bill visiting strip clubs and a 'camera club' session (this bit shot twice, once with actress Adele Lamont in skimpy clothes, the other with her wearing pretty much nothing at all) in the search for a new body for Jan. He also has a deformed monster literally in his closet. Leith's severed head begging to be killed also prefigures the final shot of Herbert J. Leder's 1966 **The Frozen Dead.** The film itself was the subject of a scene-for-scene period-faithful colour remake in 2020, but we all know the best talking-head-in-a-tray film remains Stuart Gordon's 1985 **Re-Animator**.

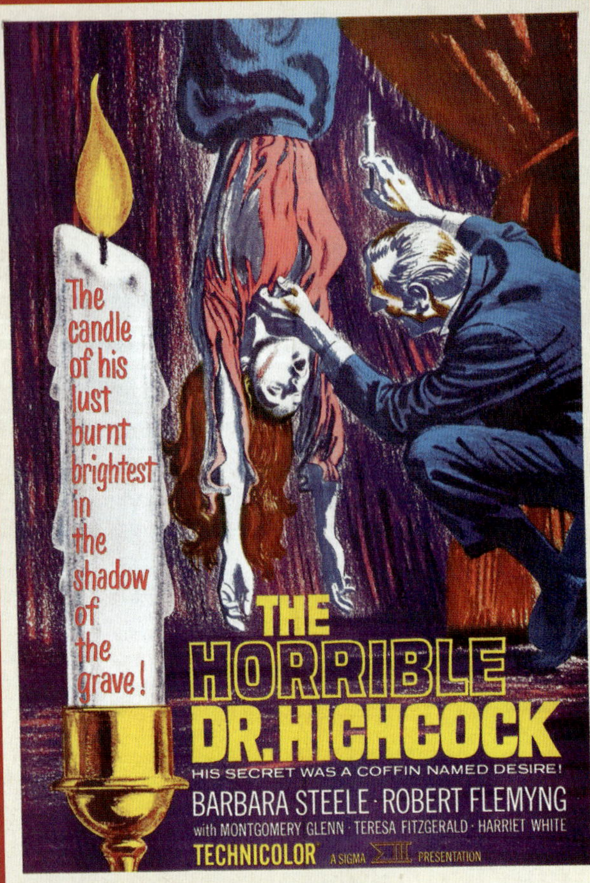

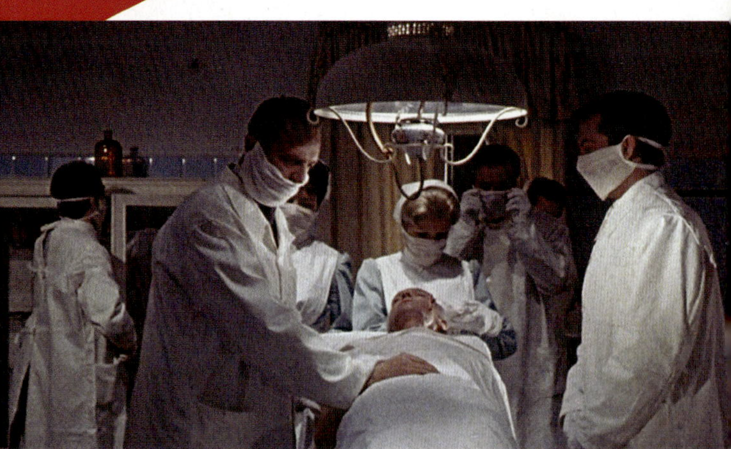

THE HORRIBLE DR. HICHCOCK

Italy, 1962
Director: Robert Hampton [Riccardo Freda]. Producers: Louis Mann [Luigi Carpentieri & Ermanno Donati]. Screenplay: Julyan Perry [Ernesto Gastaldi]. Music: Roman Vlad. Cinematography: Donald Green [Raffaele Masciocchi].
Cast: Robert Flemyng, Barbara Steele, Teresa Fitzgerald [Maria Teresa Vianello], Harriet White [Harriet Medin], Montgomery Glenn [Silvano Tranquilli], Spencer Williams.

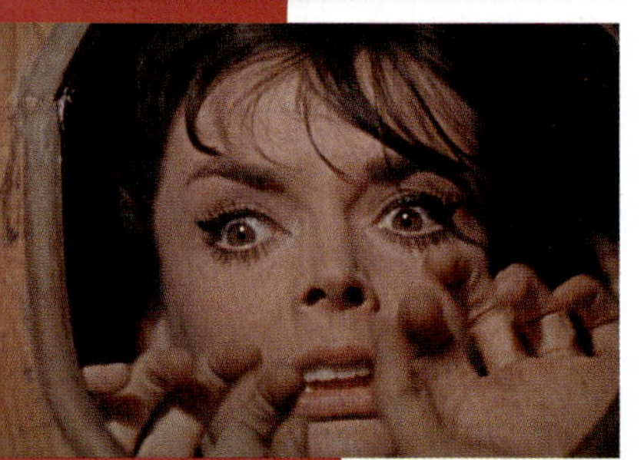

Director Riccardo Freda's sumptuous full-blooded Italian Gothic has plenty of other titles (the screenplay started out as **Raptus** and that can still be found on some prints) but the above is probably how it's best known, with the 't' deliberately removed from the name to avoid any issues with a certain director. Robert Flemyng is the title character, who likes nothing more than to sedate his wife to the point of death so he can have sex with her. Twelve years after she has seemingly died after one of these bouts of near-necrophilia, he returns to his extremely Italianate-looking 'London' house with his new wife Cinzia. Cinzia is played by Barbara Steele, which means it's the cue for her to be haunted, spooked, buried alive, and generally put through anything that will evoke the wide-eyed vulnerability that contributed to her becoming a cultural icon. The story has all the twists and turns of a typical screenplay by another icon of Italian cinema, Ernesto Gastaldi, but what makes the film so memorable is the considerable degree of panache with which Freda pulls everything off, making this movie a landmark in the genre, one which established Freda, along with colleague Mario Bava (they directed the Lovecraftian **Caltiki the Immortal Monster** together in 1959) as one of the leading auteurs of Italian horror cinema.

THE WITCH'S MIRROR

Mexico, 1962
Director: Chano Urueta. Producer: Abel Salazar.
Screenplay: Alfredo Ruanova, Carlos Enrique Taboada.
Music: Gustavo César Carrión. Cinematography: Jorge Stahl Jr.
Cast: Armando Calvo, Rosita Arenas, Isabela Corona, Dina de Marco, Carlos Nieto, Alfredo Wally Barrón.

This Mexican take on the 'surgeon tries to restore wife's burned hands and face' subgenre starts off as a supernatural Gothic, with Elena being warned by her devil-worshiping godmother-cum-housekeeper that her doctor husband intends to kill her. When Elena dies she rises from the grave, causing the doctor's new wife to end up horribly burned, and so the morgue raiding and grave digging for beautiful young women (of which there always seem to be so many handily available although those were harder times) begins. The same producer (Abel Salazar) and director (Chano Urueta) team would go onto make the same year's markedly different and considerably sillier **El barón del terror** aka **The Brainiac**. Here the piling on of the horror elements is played straight, culminating in the transplant of the first wife's ghost hands onto the second wife who then goes on the rampage. Director Urueta had been making movies since 1928, later in his career demonstrating a penchant for the weird, including the above, along with two Blue Demon wrestling pictures (**Blue Demon El Demonio Azul** and **Blue Demon vs. the Satanic Power**) he made a few years later. His intermittent sideline career as an actor means you can see him in Sam Peckinpah's **The Wild Bunch** (1969) and **Bring Me the Head of Alfredo Garcia** (1974) amongst others.

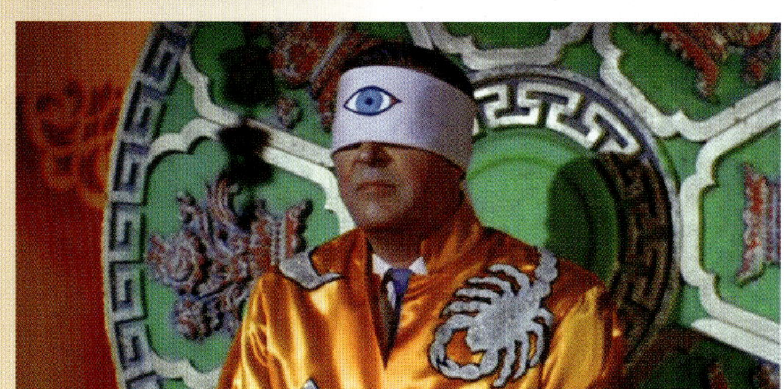

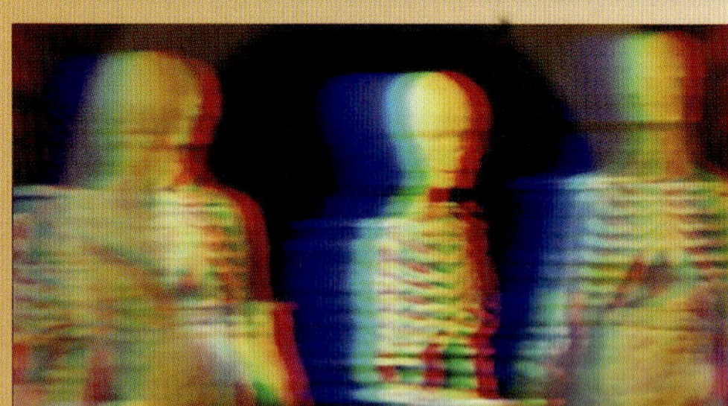

THE MAN WITH THE X-RAY EYES

USA, 1963
Director: Roger Corman. Producer: Roger Corman.
Screenplay: Robert Dillon, Ray Russell. Music: Les Baxter.
Cinematography: Floyd Crosby.
Cast: Ray Milland, Diana van der Vlis, Harold J. Stone, John Hoyt, Don Rickles, John Dierkes [uncredited].

Right in the middle of his series of Edgar Allan Poe adaptations for AIP, Roger Corman made this contemporary science fiction picture that adds in more than a hint of cosmic horror. Having had Richard Matheson write the screenplay for the previous Poe pictures, and with Charles Beaumont due to get screenplay duties on a couple that were to come, Corman completed a hat trick of working with three of the greatest contemporary US writers of the fantastique by having Ray Russell (whose **Sardonicus** had been filmed by William Castle in 1961) provide the original story and co-write the screenplay for this one. Ray Milland (the Vincent Price substitute for Corman's initially non-AIP 1962 **The Premature Burial**) plays Dr. Xavier, using himself as a guinea pig for a solution he has developed that allows him to see through things – paper, peoples' clothes, and soon flesh itself. But then things go further than that. The idea that Xavier ends up tormented by the horrors he can see lurking at the edges of the universe has its roots in Lovecraft, but Corman's no-nonsense direction keeps it all very sober until that final, classic, scene which I will leave you to discover for yourselves if you haven't already.

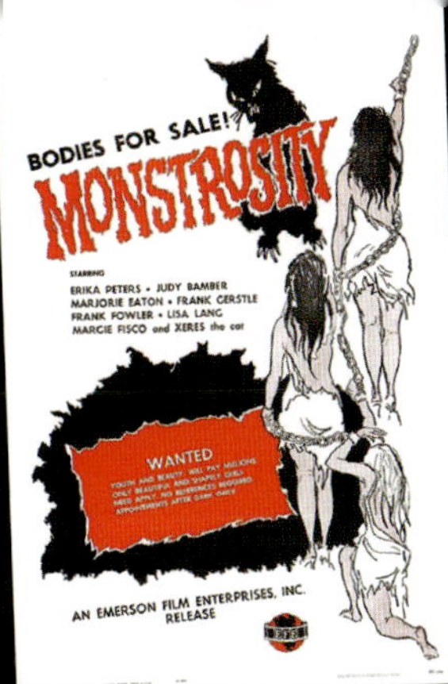

MONSTROSITY

USA, 1963
Directors: Joseph Mascelli, Jack Pollexfen [uncredited].
Producers: Dean Dillman Jr., Jack Pollexfen.
Screenplay: Vy Russell, Sue Dwiggins, Dean Dillman Jr., Jack Pollexfen [uncredited].
Music: Gene Kauer. Cinematography: Alfred Taylor.
Cast: Frank Gerstle, Erika Peters, Judy Bamber, Marjorie Eaton, Frank Fowler, Lisa Lang.

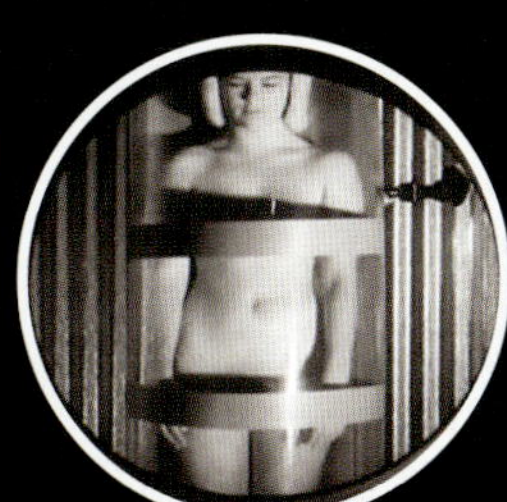

The rampant xylophone glissando is perhaps not the best musical way of impressing on an audience the idea that a girl is sexy but that doesn't stop the makers of this one having a jolly good try. A piece of low rent tat that barely stretches to an hour and has voiceovers at points where either it was considered helpful or they'd forgotten to record the sound, **Monstrosity** is directed by Joseph Mascelli. It's his only directorial credit and he was more prolific as a director of photography for Ray Dennis Steckler. Apparently, co-writer and co-producer Jack Pollexfen (1956's **Indestructible Man**) helped him tell the tale of the basement transplant experiments of Dr. Frank, who is trying to perfect the technique and get a new body to serve as a vehicle for the brain of his ageing sponsor, mad old Mrs. March (Marjorie Eaton, who plays the Emperor in **The Empire Strikes Back**. Yes that's right). He transplants the brain of 'his favourite cat' (thanks voiceover!) into one of the home helps and she develops a predilection for eating mice and climbing on the roof. The ending almost makes the rest of the film worth sitting through, defying as it does all laws of anatomical proportion and cognitive ability and yes it does involve the cat. Best watched at 3am when it will feel like a transmission from some David Lynch-style parallel universe.

DR. ORLOFF'S MONSTER

Spain/Austria/France, 1964
Director: Jess Franco. Producer: Marius Lesoeur. Screenplay: Jess Franco.
Music: Fernando García Morcillo, Daniel White. Cinematography: Alfonso Nieva.
Cast: Agnès Spaak, José Rubio [Pepe Rubio], Perla Cristal, Javier de Rivera, Hugh White [Hugo Blanco], Marcelo Arroita-Jáuregui, Luisa Sala.

Jess Franco's follow-up to 1962's **The Awful Dr. Orlof** isn't a sequel – the Dr. Orloff in this one has an extra 'f' and is only glimpsed briefly in a couple of scenes. The film was released as **Dr. Jekyll's Mistresses** in the UK but you'll only find a Dr. Jekyll in one of the English dubs of this Spanish picture. Marcelo Arroita-Jáuregui is Professor Conrad Fisherman, who walked in on his brother Andros (Hugo Blanco) having sex with Conrad's wife Inglud (Luisa Sala). Conrad killed Andros and with information gleaned from a Dr. Orloff (Javier de Rivera) brought Andros back to life as a murderous automaton, whom Conrad then uses to murder the nightclub dancers Conrad has dalliances with. Then Andros's daughter Melissa turns up, and sets in motion a tale of melancholy ripe with incest as she exhibits a not-entirely daughterly fascination with her Cesare/Caligari-like father, still in his twenties when he was murdered. This is another film that lays the groundwork for what Franco would be exploring more fully over the next ten years. Often treated as a footnote to his previous mad doctor picture, **Dr. Orloff's Monster** actually stands up perfectly well on its own, and that final scene is a heartbreaker.

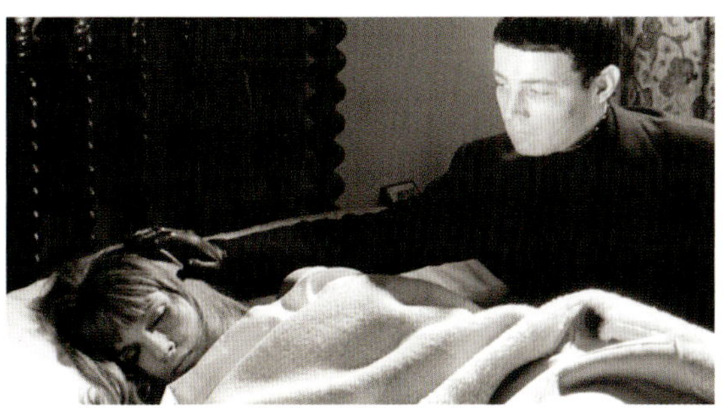

THE EVIL OF FRANKENSTEIN

UK, 1964
Director: Freddie Francis. Producer: Anthony Hinds.
Screenplay: John Elder [Anthony Hinds].
Music: Don Banks. Cinematography: John Wilcox.
Cast: Peter Cushing, Peter Woodthorpe, Duncan Lamont, Sandor Elès, Kiwi Kingston, Katy Wild.

In modern film parlance Hammer's third Frankenstein film is something of a reboot, rejecting the fascinating premise set up at the end of Terence Fisher's **The Revenge of Frankenstein** and instead moving the action (and Peter Cushing's Baron) from London's Harley Street back to the 'Hammerland' we all know and love, located in the never never land of somewhere in middle Europe. Anthony Hinds' script is a by the numbers revenge plot which is far less interesting than the films that preceded it. The monster this time is a box-headed creation found frozen in ice (ideas pillaged from Universal). After Christopher Lee and Michael Gwynn's complex, nuanced interpretations of the Cushing Frankenstein creations, it's a bit unfair to compare New Zealand wrestler Kiwi Kingston's performance as he stomps around, but it all adds to the general feeling of 'never mind the quality, just get the film made'. Highlights include Cushing (as always), and Peter Woodthorpe (memorably sleazy in Amicus's **The Skull** the following year) as an evil hypnotist the Baron employs to control the monster. Cardiff born Katy Wild, who plays the mute beggar girl, would go on to play Valda in 1965's **Dr. Terror's House of Horrors** before facing Amicus's **The Deadly Bees** (all for director Freddie Francis) in 1966.

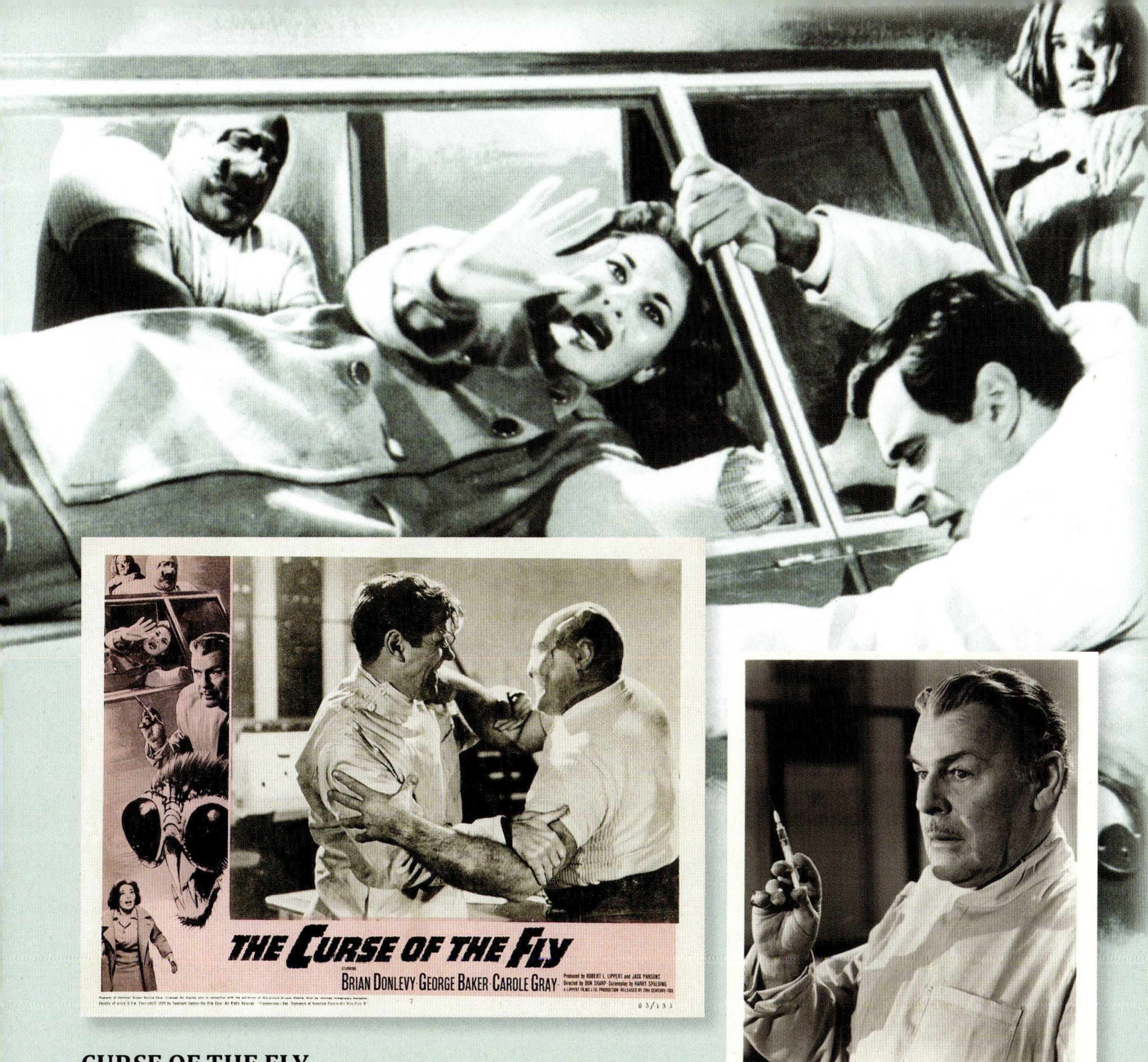

CURSE OF THE FLY

UK, 1965
Director: Don Sharp. Producers: Robert L. Lippert, Jack Parsons. Screenplay: Harry Spalding.
Music: Bert Shefter. Cinematography: Basil Emmott.
Cast: Brian Donlevy, George Baker, Carole Gray, Yvette Rees, Michael Graham, Rachel Kempson.

The final film in Twentieth Century-Fox's original **The Fly** trilogy is arguably the best and certainly the most atmospheric and strange. A group of British character actors do their best to pretend they're in Montreal, except for Carole Gray who escapes from an asylum during the credits clad only in her underwear. She's meant to be mad so presumably that's why she's allowed to keep her English accent. George Baker veers between cod-American and English while mad scientist, nominal star and well-known alcoholic Brian Donlevy just veers. The stylish and often dreamlike feel can be credited to Don Sharp (just coming off some second unit work and willing to 'do anything' to get directing again) and the excellent, crisp black and white photography deftly shows off the few sets and the country locations. One of a number of effective scenes has Baker's wife, on whom he has experimented, trying to play the piano and all we hear is the music – the right hand perfect and the left hand a mess, reflecting her actual physical state. The stables, with their mutated inhabitants – failed results of the matter transmission experiments – are appropriately unsettling, and the ending is as grim as they come.

THE FACE OF FU MANCHU

UK/West Germany, 1965
Director: Don Sharp. Producer: Harry Alan Towers.
Screenplay: Peter Welbeck [Harry Alan Towers].
Music: Christopher Whelen. Cinematography: Ernest Steward.
Cast: Christopher Lee, Nigel Green, Joachim Fuchsberger, Karin Dor, Tsai Chin, James Robertson Justice.

As well as being the definitive Count Dracula for a generation, Christopher Lee became the face of Sax Rohmer's diabolical villain for schoolboys everywhere when he starred in this, the first of five feature films all produced by Harry Alan Towers, in which Lee played Dr. Fu Manchu. Aside from Lee, the only actors to appear in every film in the series were Tsai Chin as Fu Manchu's daughter, Lin Tang, and Howard Marion Crawford as Dr. Petrie, the sidekick to Fu's indomitable Scotland Yard nemesis Nayland Smith, played here by Nigel Green.

After an atmospheric opening in which we apparently see Fu Manchu executed in China (actually Kilmainham Jail in Dublin, Ireland) the plot involves the actually-not-dead doctor planning to hold the world to ransom with poison gas. What makes the film really work is the dashing, action-packed style given the whole enterprise by director Don Sharp, who refused to allow producer Towers to cut budgetary corners with the costumes and production design. The best scene, apart from the opening beheading, is set in an English village where the poison gas has been released and everyone has been killed. "The world will hear from me again" promises Fu as the heroes blow up his Tibetan monastery retreat, and indeed audiences did. A few too many times, in fact.

THE BRIDES OF FU MANCHU

UK/West Germany, 1966
Director: Don Sharp.
Producers: David Henley, Harry Alan Towers.
Screenplay: Peter Welbeck [Harry Alan Towers]. Music: Bruce Montgomery.
Cinematography: Ernest Steward.
Cast: Christopher Lee, Douglas Wilmer, Marie Versini, Heinz Drache, Howard Marion Crawford.

The second of producer Harry Alan Towers' five Sax Rohmer adaptations starring Christopher Lee as the titular diabolical mastermind maintains the high standards set by the first. A major reason for this is undoubtedly the crisp direction by returning director Don Sharp, who wrings as much action as possible out of Towers' script (writing as always under his pseudonym Peter Welbeck). Dr. Fu needs to build a radio telescope so he can once again hold the world to ransom. All the top scientists who can help him just happen to have wives or daughters in their late-teens and early-twenties who look good tied up in their lingerie, so they end up as prisoners in his underground lair. Douglas Wilmer is Fu's arch nemesis Nayland Smith, replacing Nigel Green from 1965's **The Face of Fu Manchu**. Wilmer would repeat the role in the next film, **The Vengeance of Fu Manchu** (1967), directed by Jeremy Summers and a considerably duller film than its two predecessors. The true nadir of the series however, both in terms of tattiness of presentation and daftness of plots, was the final two movies, 1968's **The Blood of Fu Manchu** and the following year's **The Castle of Fu Manchu** (a film which managed to include footage not just from **The Brides of Fu Manchu**, but also Roy Ward Baker's British Titanic movie **A Night to Remember** (1958) at the start and the Dirk Bogarde-starrer **Campbell's Kingdom** (1957) at the end). Both final Fus were directed by Jess Franco, whom producer Towers later allegedly accused of doing something no one else had previously been able to achieve, namely killing Fu Manchu.

CARRY ON SCREAMING!

UK, 1966
Director: Gerald Thomas. Producer: Peter Rogers. Screenplay: Talbot Rothwell. Music: Eric Rogers. Cinematography: Alan Hume.
Cast: Harry H. Corbett, Kenneth Williams, Jim Dale, Joan Sims, Charles Hawtrey, Fenella Fielding.

Made at a time when both the Carry Ons and Hammer Films were at their peak, in terms of popularity and also the skill with which they were being made, this is the twelfth in the popular UK comedy series (of 31). Director Gerald Thomas and screenwriter Talbot Rothwell, along with the usual cast (and Harry H. Corbett standing in for Sid James, who was persona non grata for this one apparently) expertly carry off the difficult job of spoofing Hammer and Universal, while still making something that's uniquely their own. Many of their targets are obvious – **Dr. Jekyll and Mr. Hyde**, **The Mummy**, and **The Old Dark House**. Kenneth Williams is the Frankenstein-like Dr. Watt (undead for good measure), reanimating hairy primordial men to kidnap women so they can be turned into mannequins in a touch possibly inspired by Giorgio Ferroni's **Mill of the Stone Women** (which came out in the UK in 1963). Charles Hawtrey was also out of favour but was incorporated at the last minute, replacing Sydney Bromley in the role of Dan Dann, the lavatory attendant who dies as he lived, with his head down the loo. Some of the jokes are understandably dated now – there probably aren't too many of us who will appreciate composer Eric Rogers' skill at incorporating the theme for *Z Cars* into his bouncy police theme – but it's still lots of knockabout, silly fun, managing to satirise the Gothic horror genre surprisingly well.

THE DIABOLICAL DR. Z

Spain/France, 1966
Director: Henri Baum [Jess Franco]. Producers: Michel Safra, Serge Silberman. Screenplay: Jean-Claude Carrière. Music: Daniel White. Cinematography: Alejandro Ulloa. Cast: Mabel Karr, Fernando Montes, Marcelo Arroita-Jáuregui, Estella Blain, Howard Vernon, Guy Mairesse.

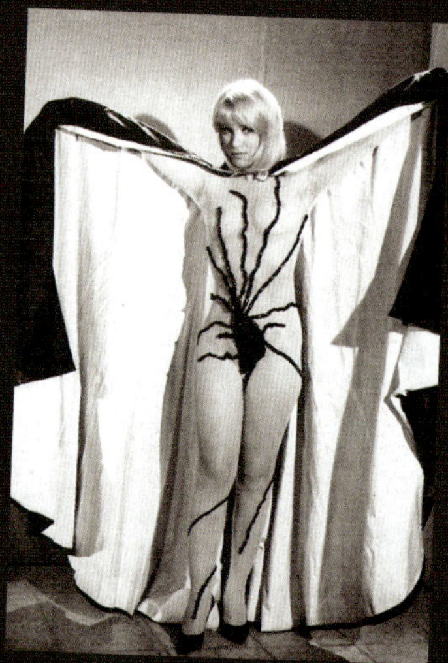

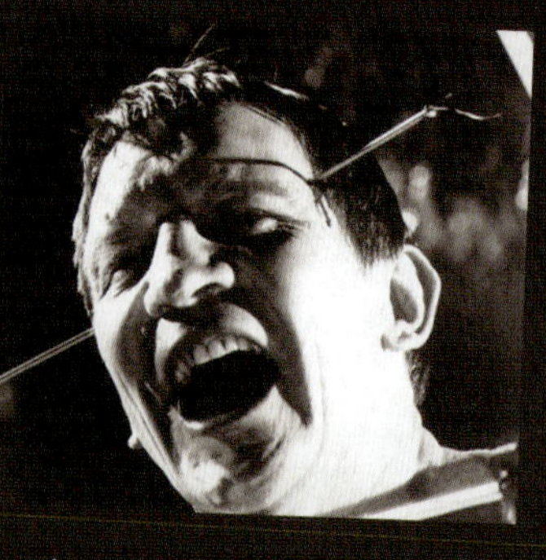

Jess Franco strikes again with this slick, beautifully shot, perfectly realised science fiction, pulp horror thriller. Dr. Zimmer (Antonio Giménez Escribano) has developed a technique for drilling into the brains of criminals and removing their ability to be evil, turning them into placid subservients. Zimmer's research presentation is laughed out of a meeting with his colleagues and he dies from a heart attack as a result. His daughter Irma (Mabel Karr) is also a doctor (so this could have been called 'The Diabolical Dr. Zs') and decides to take revenge on the three doctors she holds most responsible for her father's death. To effect this, Irma uses the brain-drilling machine and a kidnapped nightclub dancer with poisoned fingernails. For anyone claiming Franco was a shoddy filmmaker (as opposed to making some shoddy films, which he certainly did), **The Diabolical Dr. Z** is one to show them. The black and white photography is sharp, the lighting carefully considered, and the opening scenes of the Woodside Strangler escaping from prison could look at home in a classic film noir. The plot is crazy but in the best way, and while there's not a lot of subtext, Franco can't help but include some of his recurring obsessions, the poisoned 'Miss Death' aka Nadia (Estella Blain) among them.

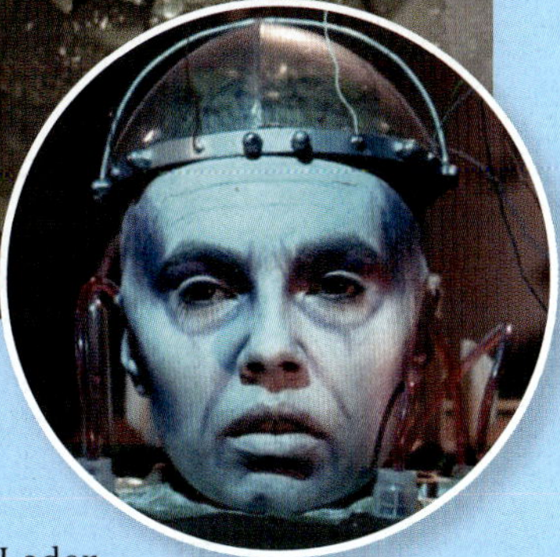

THE FROZEN DEAD

UK, 1966
Director: Herbert J. Leder. Producer: Herbert J. Leder.
Screenplay: Herbert J. Leder. Music: Don Banks.
Cinematography: Davis Boulton.
Cast: Dana Andrews, Anna Palk, Philip Gilbert, Karel Stepanek, Kathleen Breck, Alan Tilvern, Edward Fox.

In this co-feature to the same writer-producer-director's **It!**, Dana Andrews stars as Dr. Norberg, trying to thaw out Nazi soldiers frozen at the end of the Second World War (all while still wearing their uniforms, presumably because the only thing worse than a Nazi is a nude Nazi). So far, his results have not been good. One Nazi soldier does nothing but repetitively bounce an imaginary ball, one does nothing but comb his hair all day, and one is Edward Fox. Herbert J. Leder's directorial technique tends towards covering everything in master shots and he was obviously a graduate of the 'one take' school of filmmaking. The sound isn't very good either, which is surprising considering the boom mike has been brought so close to the actors in some scenes that you can actually see it. In amongst all this there is some pleasingly weird imagery that more than makes up for any incompetence. There's a wall of severed arms that can still move, a mysterious old lady in the village who wears a rubber mask, and best of all, the severed head of a green-faced girl kept in a box with her brain exposed and pulsating. Then of course there's the kind of dialogue that would have brought a tear to the eye of Ed Wood. "That head will destroy us all!" "It can't do that – it's only a head." Actors stumble over their lines, Dana goes to put his glass down before the butler gets there with the tray for him to put it on, and the ending is so completely crazy, with the severed head taking control of the wall of arms, that it has to be seen to be believed. You think this can't be topped but it is, with a final shot that's genuinely unnerving and a very strange way to end a mid-'60s horror film.

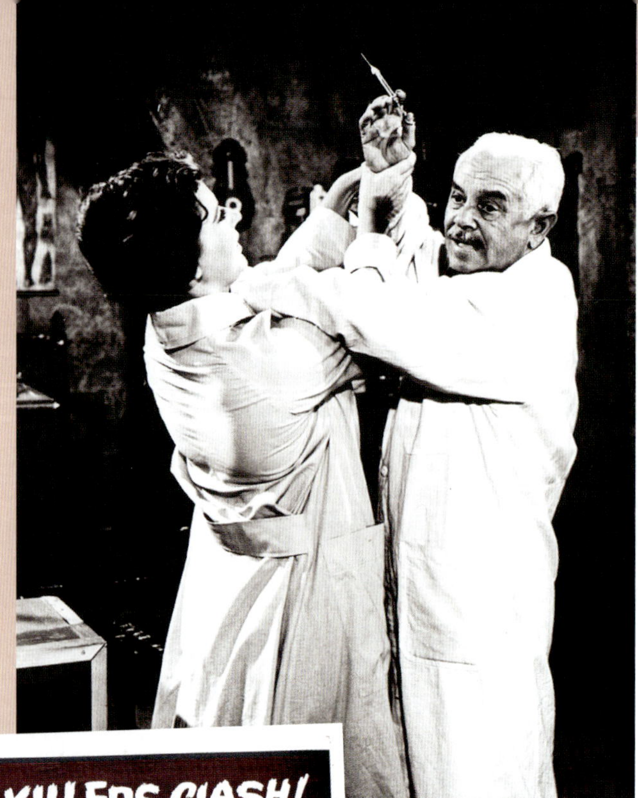

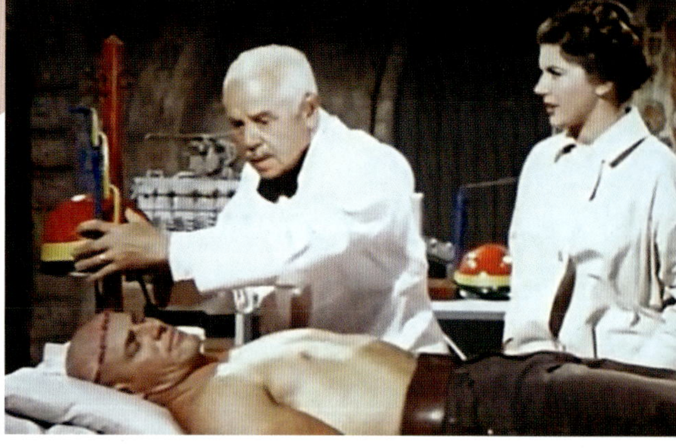

JESSE JAMES MEETS FRANKENSTEIN'S DAUGHTER

USA, 1966
Director: William Beaudine.
Producer: Carroll Case. Screenplay: Carl K. Hittleman. Music: Raoul Kraushaar. Cinematography: Lothrop B. Worth.
Cast: John Lupton, Cal Bolder, Estelita [Estelita Rodriguez], Narda Onyx, Steven Geray, Rayford Barnes.

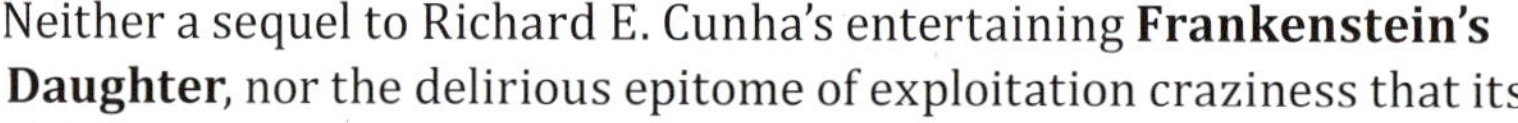

Neither a sequel to Richard E. Cunha's entertaining **Frankenstein's Daughter**, nor the delirious epitome of exploitation craziness that its title may suggest, one of the final films by director William 'One-Shot' Beaudine welds together the Western and horror genres with all the have-a-go attitude of the man who also gave us **Billy the Kid Versus Dracula**. Maria Frankenstein (Narda Onyx) and her brother Rudolph (Steven Geray) have escaped to the Wild West to continue the family's brain transplant experiments. With his brightly striped army helmet and combat trousers, their initial experiment looks more like the first LGBTQ Vietnam veteran than the creation of mad science, so when he dies it's back to the drawing board. Jesse James (John Lupton) arrives at their 'castle' with wounded musclebound sidekick Hank (Cal Bolder – really?) and Maria decides the bodybuilder has all the right attributes to be laid out on her operating table so she can turn him into Igor with the Synthetic Brain. Stilted acting and cheap TV comedy sketch sets abound in a film that also packs in a low-budget **Wild Bunch** (there are three of them) amidst the thunder, lightning, and matte paintings. Those with minimal expectations will be best rewarded.

THE MURDER CLINIC

Italy/France, 1966
Directors: Michael Hamilton [Elio Scardamaglia], Lionello De Felice [uncredited]. Producer: Michael Hamilton [Elio Scardamaglia]. Screenplay: Julian Berry [Ernesto Gastaldi], Martin Hardy [Luciano Martino]. Music: Frank Mason [Francesco De Masi]. Cinematography: Marc Lane [Marcello Masciocchi]. Cast: William Berger, Françoise Prévost, Mary Young, Barbara Wilson, Harriet White [Harriet Medin], Max Dean [Massimo Righi].

According to **The Murder Clinic**'s opening caption it's 'About 1870' and we're in Norfolk. However, the mountainous forest-filled countryside and Italianate architecture on display are less suggestive of Norwich and its environs and more of a country considerably further south (and a bit east as well). A hooded and cloaked figure stalks the corridors of an isolated asylum run by Dr. Vance (William Berger) that's filled with the kind of inmates that only exist in Italian horror films, including an old lady whose best friend is her stuffed cat, and a young man called Fred who has violent tendencies and should have been played by Klaus Kinski but sadly isn't. Both inmates and staff are being bumped off and it soon becomes apparent that while the trappings are Gothic and the style is giallo, screenwriters Ernesto Gastaldi and Luciano Martino have also decided to mix in a goodly dollop of **Eyes Without a Face**. The mysterious figure is Dr. Vance's sister-in-law Laura, whom he believes he caused to fall into a lime pit. Now he spends his days skin-grafting guinea pigs and keeping his fingers crossed that his housekeeper Harriet White Medin (Italy's Sheila Keith) won't tell people why he spends so much time shaving them. The climax has the traditional crazy Italian twist ending, where it turns out quite a bit wasn't what it seemed (including the flashback detailing the Laura-in-lime tragedy) and with nearly everyone dead by the time we get to the fadeout to Francesco De Masi's main theme.

THE PROJECTED MAN

UK, 1966
Directors: Ian Curteis, John Croydon [uncredited]. Producers: John Croydon, Maurice Foster, Richard Gordon [uncredited]. Screenplay: John C. Cooper [John Croydon], Peter Bryan.
Music: Kenneth V. Jones. Cinematography: Stanley Pavey.
Cast: Bryant Halliday, Mary Peach, Norman Wooland, Ronald Allen, Derek Farr, Tracey Crisp.

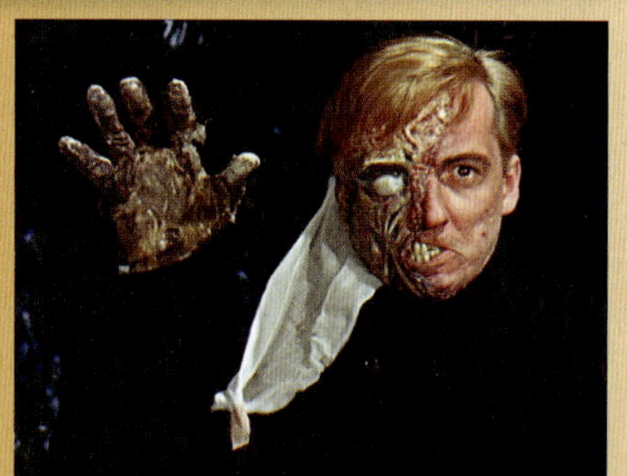

"No wonder that guinea pig died!" Oh yes, in **The Projected Man** the experiments of Dr. Paul Steiner (Bryant Haliday, whose penultimate film as an actor this was, the last being 1972's **Tower of Evil**) in turning things inside-out might have some use for those underpants that have just come out of the washing machine, but he really should stay away from living tissue. Meanwhile sidekick Ronald Allen (of *Crossroads* 'fame') utters every line of dialogue in a restrained whisper as if he's in terrible and imminent danger of breaking an especially raucous amount of wind. Despite that he seems to be quite the ladies' man. "You're better than beer and a pork pie down the pub" he tells Mary Peach in probably the most romantic chat-up line to feature in a 1966 British film. **The Projected Man** had all kinds of problems, including needing some sequences reshot and, according to credited director Ian Curteis, having its UK premiere in the wrong aspect ratio. From the legendary (and frequently uncredited) producer Richard Gordon, the film probably works best if watched as the opening half of its original US double bill, when it was paired with another Gordon production, the superior (and supremely entertaining) Terence Fisher-directed **Island of Terror**.

FRANKENSTEIN CREATED WOMAN

UK, 1967
Director: Terence Fisher.
Producer: Anthony Nelson Keys.
Screenplay: John Elder [Anthony Hinds].
Music: James Bernard.
Cinematography: Arthur Grant.
Cast: Peter Cushing, Susan Denberg, Thorley Walters, Robert Morris, Duncan Lamont, Peter Blythe.

Hammer's fourth Frankenstein film sees the return of both director Terence Fisher and composer James Bernard to aid Peter Cushing's Baron in his latest project. It was originally conceived to follow 1958's **The Revenge of Frankenstein** while cashing in on the success of Roger Vadim's 1956 Brigitte Bardot-starrer **And God Created Woman**. As in his previous script for **The Evil of Frankenstein**, producer Anthony Hinds' screenplay once again goes the revenge route, but at least Frankenstein has a more interesting experiment on the go here to kick start everything. Taking the dead body of suicide Christina (Susan Denberg), the Baron somehow manages not just to bring her back to life and cure her facial disfigurement, but somehow transplants the soul of her executed boyfriend Hans (Robert Morris) into the mix. The idea of a beautiful woman possessed by a vengeful spirit takes this one into European folk tale territory, and in this respect the casting of Denberg (an actress long believed dead but actually alive and well and living in Vienna) is spot on, evoking the fairytale beauty with murder in her heart. Bernard's score augments the underlying tragic nature of the whole affair beautifully, and Cushing's expression as he views where his creation has met its demise is perfect.

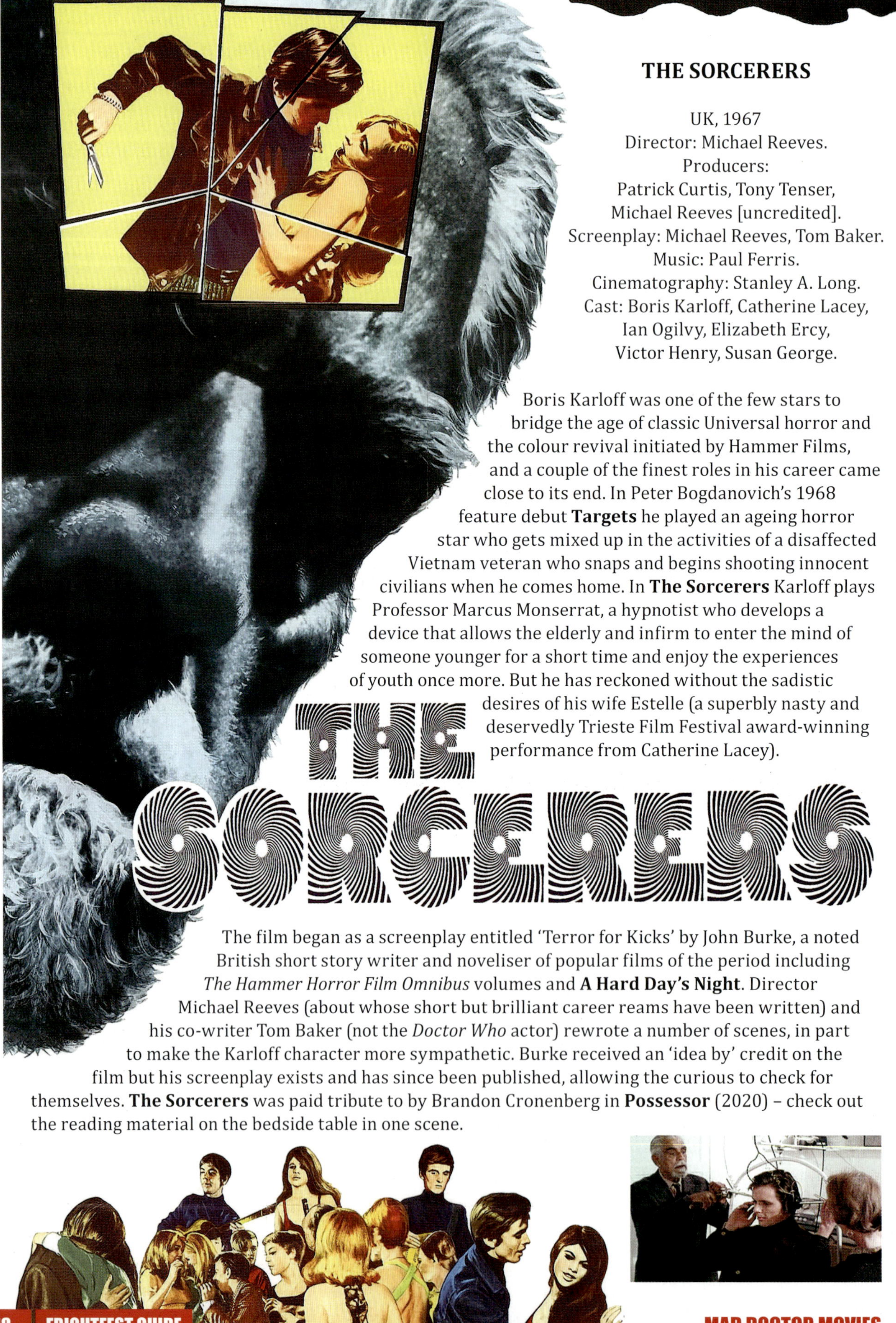

THE SORCERERS

UK, 1967
Director: Michael Reeves.
Producers:
Patrick Curtis, Tony Tenser,
Michael Reeves [uncredited].
Screenplay: Michael Reeves, Tom Baker.
Music: Paul Ferris.
Cinematography: Stanley A. Long.
Cast: Boris Karloff, Catherine Lacey,
Ian Ogilvy, Elizabeth Ercy,
Victor Henry, Susan George.

Boris Karloff was one of the few stars to bridge the age of classic Universal horror and the colour revival initiated by Hammer Films, and a couple of the finest roles in his career came close to its end. In Peter Bogdanovich's 1968 feature debut **Targets** he played an ageing horror star who gets mixed up in the activities of a disaffected Vietnam veteran who snaps and begins shooting innocent civilians when he comes home. In **The Sorcerers** Karloff plays Professor Marcus Monserrat, a hypnotist who develops a device that allows the elderly and infirm to enter the mind of someone younger for a short time and enjoy the experiences of youth once more. But he has reckoned without the sadistic desires of his wife Estelle (a superbly nasty and deservedly Trieste Film Festival award-winning performance from Catherine Lacey).

The film began as a screenplay entitled 'Terror for Kicks' by John Burke, a noted British short story writer and noveliser of popular films of the period including *The Hammer Horror Film Omnibus* volumes and **A Hard Day's Night**. Director Michael Reeves (about whose short but brilliant career reams have been written) and his co-writer Tom Baker (not the *Doctor Who* actor) rewrote a number of scenes, in part to make the Karloff character more sympathetic. Burke received an 'idea by' credit on the film but his screenplay exists and has since been published, allowing the curious to check for themselves. **The Sorcerers** was paid tribute to by Brandon Cronenberg in **Possessor** (2020) – check out the reading material on the bedside table in one scene.

THE BLOOD BEAST TERROR

UK, 1968
Director: Vernon Sewell. Producer: Arnold L. Miller. Screenplay: Peter Bryan. Music: Paul Ferris. Cinematography: Stanley A. Long.
Cast: Peter Cushing, Robert Flemyng, Wanda Ventham, Vanessa Howard, Roy Hudd, David Griffin.

Released in the US as **The Vampire Beast Craves Blood**, giving us two title options that, despite their drive-in connotations, are still far better than this film deserves. Poor old Peter Cushing is Inspector Quennell, on the trail of vampire-like murders caused by the results of the experiments of Dr. Mallinger (played by Robert Flemyng, looking quite uncomfortable, probably partly because he was filling in for Basil Rathbone at the last minute but mainly because this film is quite terrible). Dr. Mallinger has succeeded in turning his daughter (Wanda Ventham) into a moth. There is no good reason for him to have done this, not even that producer Tony Tenser had been given a moth costume and a gap in Peter Cushing's schedule and saw dollar signs light up. There's a pointless prologue that goes on and on that, in a rare case of it being justifiable, tended to get cut from TV showings. The moth creature is a terrible, flappy thing that looks like it couldn't get off the ground never mind flutter. When the best thing about a Gothic film from the golden age of British horror is Roy Hudd you know you're in trouble. Possibly worth watching for perky Vanessa Howard and a score from composer Paul Ferris, using what sounds like the same mix of instruments he put together for the same year's **Witchfinder General**, otherwise more fun can be had from reading this film's reviews than watching it.

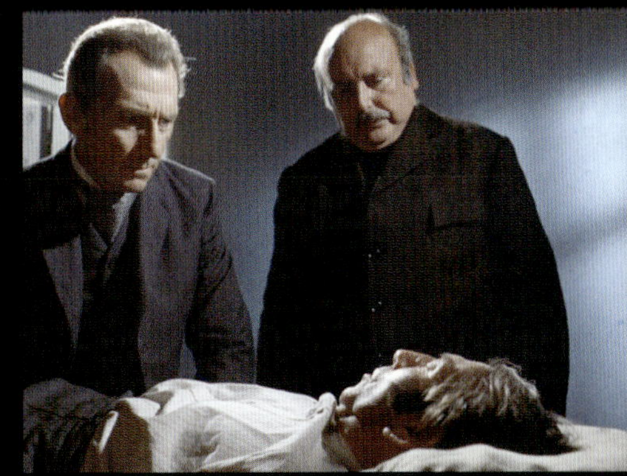

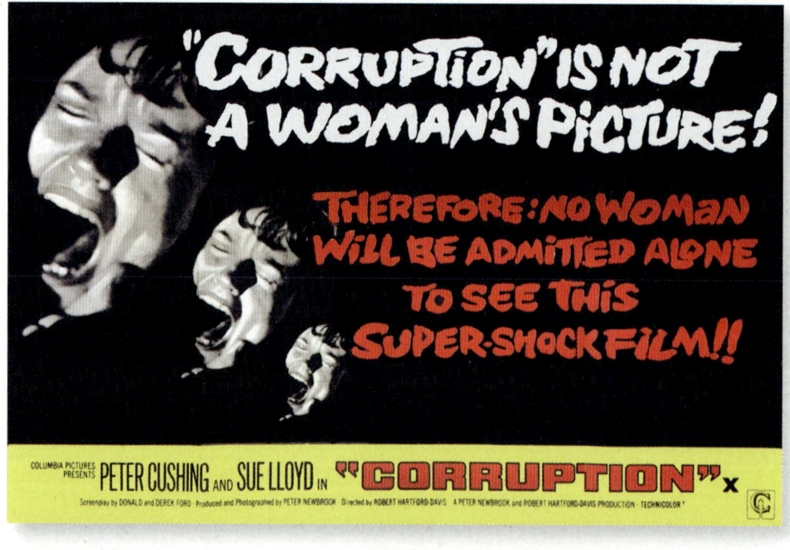

CORRUPTION

UK, 1968
Director: Robert Hartford-Davis. Producer: Peter Newbrook.
Screenplay: Donald Ford, Derek Ford. Music: Bill McGuffie.
Cinematography: Peter Newbrook.
Cast: Peter Cushing, Sue Lloyd, Noel Trevarthen, Kate O'Mara, David Lodge, Anthony Booth, Vanessa Howard.

Who would have guessed that the British would come up with the silliest, sleaziest, nastiest version of Franju's **Les yeux sans visage**? Peter Cushing is the surgeon who wears horrible caps and cravats on his days off, while Sue Lloyd is his waspish, increasingly insane girlfriend, who he facially scars before working out how to make her better. For a bit. The process involves cutting out girls' pituitary glands. The real pituitary is the size of a pinhead. The one we see in this film looks like a small cauliflower. Ably assisted by Bill McGuffie's truly horrible jazz score, director Robert Hartford-Davis ensures that every murder is milked for late-1960s maximum need-a-bath-afterwards potential. **Corruption** gives the impression that nobody had any idea how to end it – in case you're wondering, all that stuff with the massive laser going haywire actually is in the screenplay by Donald and Derek Ford. The film also features a tiny role for Vanessa Howard, who's always worth watching, and a larger more shouty one for Anthony Booth, who isn't.

THE CURIOUS DR. HUMPP

Argentina, 1969
Directors: Emilio Vieyra, Jerald Intrator (new footage) [uncredited]. Producers: Orestes Trucco, Emilio Vieyra [uncredited]. Screenplay: Emilio Vieyra. Music: Víctor Buchino. Cinematography: Aníbal González Paz.
Cast: Ricardo Bauleo, Gloria Prat, Aldo Barbero, Susana Beltrán, Justin Martin, Michel Angel.

A curious film indeed, this black and white Argentinean production was beefed up and lengthened by its American distributor by the insertion of more than 17 minutes of sex scenes. These sequences were edited into the main footage with all the finesse of the worst of Al Adamson's films. This does go someway to explaining why, fifteen minutes into the movie, many viewers will be wondering when something is going to actually happen. The plot involves a monster with a lumpy misshapen head abducting men and women so Dr. Humpp can perform sex experiments on them. The doctor is conducting his research at the behest of an Italian scientist who is nothing more than a pulsating brain in a jar. The copious nudity actually gets in the way of the more interesting aspects of this one. The doctor's house is guarded by rubber-faced automatons straight out of *Doctor Who* of the period, while the strangest scene of all shows the monster playing a guitar while the doctor's captive subjects wander around the gardens of his isolated mansion in a bizarre sexploitation version of Alain Resnais' 1961 surrealist landmark **Last Year in Marienbad**. If you can make it to the end the final five minutes are exploitation gold, featuring a stabbing, a melting corpse, and the Italian brain in a jar becoming so upset it explodes.

FRANKENSTEIN MUST BE DESTROYED

UK, 1969
Director: Terence Fisher. Producer: Anthony Nelson Keys. Screenplay: Bert Batt. Music: James Bernard. Cinematography: Arthur Grant.
Cast: Peter Cushing, Veronica Carlson, Simon Ward, Freddie Jones, Thorley Walters, Maxine Audley.

The Hammer Frankenstein series reaches its (arguable) peak with this brutal, cynical film appropriate to the changing times in which it was released. This one sets out its portrayal of the Baron in no uncertain terms from the beginning, as he chops off a head, having to destroy a body and flee a laboratory when he's discovered. That rotting-face mask he's first seen wearing is no coincidence, either. More driven, more ruthless, and more intolerant than we've ever seen him before, pity the poor fools who end up sharing a boarding house with Peter Cushing's Frankenstein. Like the hapless young lovers he blackmails into helping him. Or the poor couple whose lives he destroys by transplanting the husband's brain into another body – he then goes looking for his wife leading to nothing but tragedy. Nobody is spared and pretty much everyone is dead by the finale, which would have been the perfect point on which to end the series. Cushing is brilliant, director Terence Fisher is brilliant, James Bernard's score is great. Even though there would have been no long-term game plan, it feels as if all the other Frankenstein films (except perhaps **Evil**) were all leading up to this. If you only ever watch one Hammer Frankenstein, make it this.

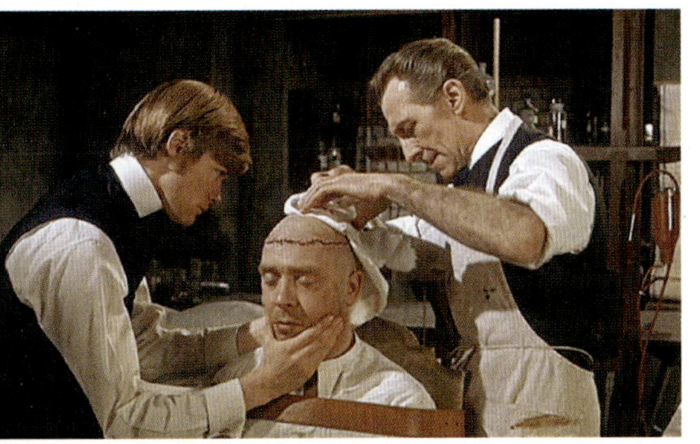

HORRORS OF MALFORMED MEN

Japan, 1969
Director: Teruo Ishii.
Screenplay: Teruo Ishii, Masahiro Kakefuda.
Music: Hajime Kaburagi.
Cinematography: Shigeru Akatsuka.
Cast: Teruo Yoshida, Minoru Ôki, Asao Koike, Yukie Kagawa, Mitsuko Aoi, Teruko Yumi.

Featuring a web-fingered mad surgeon who looks like Jesus and wears a dress, a Buddhist priest in an ill-fitting bald cap who can't lift anything on account of his appalling diarrhoea, a naked girl painted gold lying on a boat with her legs in the air, three naked girls painted silver and doing a funny dance with sparklers in their hair, a cross-dressing sadist, a woman eating the crabs that are at the same time devouring her husband's corpse, an unbelievable finale involving fireworks and exploding body parts, and some malformed men... Teruo Ishii's film is ostensibly based on the works of Japanese horror author Edogawa Rampo, and anyone familiar with Mr. Rampo's work will spot the scene based on his story 'The Chair', but otherwise this is quite the tenuous mishmash of an adaptation. Weird, depraved, nonsensical, screwed up, and utterly bonkers with dialogue to match ("I tore off his backside!"), the plot involves a medical student who travels to the island where all the above craziness takes place, in search of a man who seems to be the student's doppelganger. There are a few versions of H.G. Wells' *The Island of Dr. Moreau* out there, but this is the only one that tries to be the Japanese **El Topo** as well.

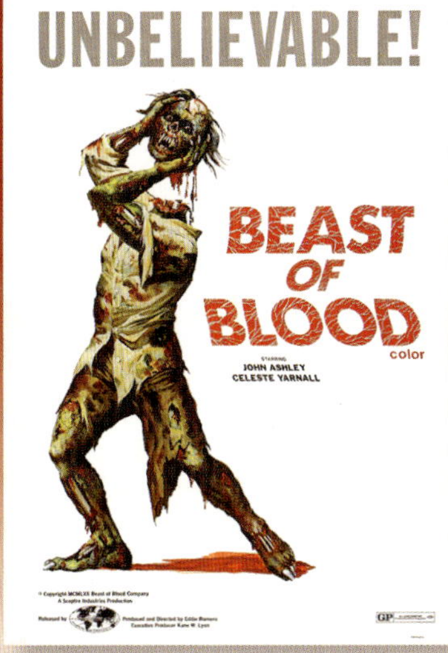

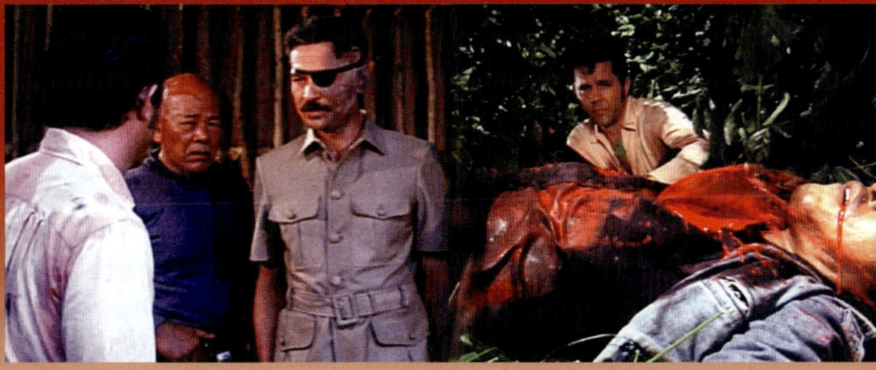

BEAST OF BLOOD

Philippines, 1970
Director: Eddie Romero. Producer: Eddie Romero.
Screenplay: Eddie Romero. Music: Tito Arevalo.
Cinematography: Justo Paulino.
Cast: John Ashley, Celeste Yarnall, Eddie Garcia, Liza Belmonte, Alfonso Carvajal, Bruno Punzalan.

After co-directing **Mad Doctor of Blood Island** (1969) with the prolific Gerardo de Leon, Hemisphere Pictures producer Eddie Romero performed solo duties on this follow-up. The chlorophyll creature (a wondrously nightmarish creation, stills of which deservedly graced many an early-1970s film publication) attacks Hemisphere star and future producer (and opening narrator) of TV's *The A-Team* John Ashley as he leaves Blood Island on a boat. The creature gets knocked off, is washed ashore, and ends up losing its head, or so it's implied by the animated opening credits. Meanwhile, not satisfied with having said goodbye to one *Star Trek* actress in the previous film ('The Gamesters of Triskelion's Angelique Pettyjohn), Mr. Ashley then hooks up with Celeste Yarnall (the *Star Trek* episode 'The Apple' and more importantly Stephanie Rothman's **The Velvet Vampire** the following year). Back they go to Blood Island where a scarred Dr. Lorca (played by the prolific – 659 IMDb credits – Eddie Garcia) has his very own talking head in a lab, fifteen years before David Gale's Dr. Hill would be immortalised in Stuart Gordon's **Re-Animator**. With its colourful gore, nudity, and ludicrous plot concerning reattaching the chlorophyll monster's head to its body, **Beast of Blood** is a world away from the film that started it all eleven years earlier (de Leon's rather more subtle **Terror Is a Man**). Although it's good to know that, according to the credits, this one did at least have a qualified MD on hand as medical advisor.

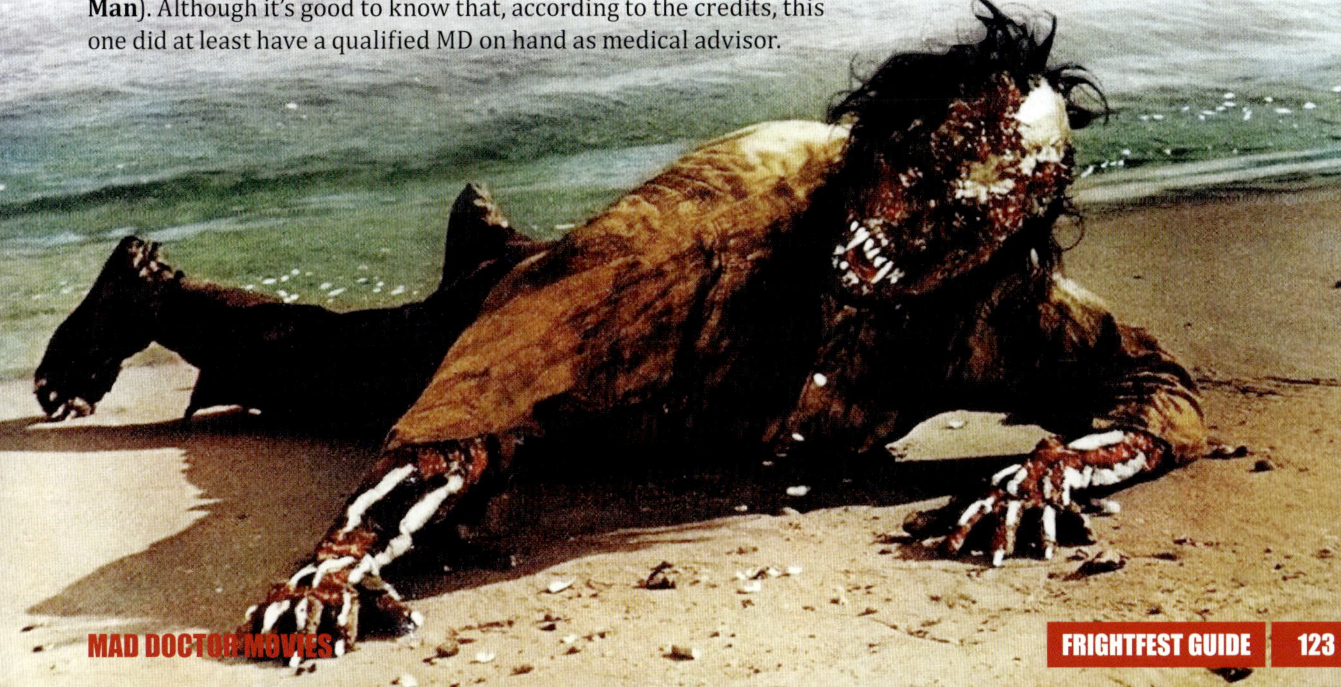

DR. FRANKENSTEIN ON CAMPUS

Canada, 1970
Director: Gilbert W. Taylor. Producer: Bill Marshall [William T. Marshall].
Screenplay: David Cobb, Bill Marshall [William T. Marshall], Gilbert W. Taylor.
Music: Paul Hoffert. Cinematography: Jackson Samuels.
Cast: Robin Ward, Kathleen Sawyer, Austin Willis, Sean Sullivan, Ty Haller, Tony Moffat-Lynch.

In this groovy if frequently stilted piece of contemporary exploitation from Canada, we kick off with a scene worthy of *The Avengers* TV series, with young Viktor Frankenstein being expelled from the German university where he is a student, for getting into a duel with sabres. He relocates to a 'North American' institution and instantly gets involved in its psychedelic happening scene, attending parties filled with drug taking, talk of astrology, love-ins, and a most peculiar use of a rowing machine. When he's not being interviewed by his frequently topless girlfriend to the accompaniment of awful lounge music, Frankenstein is asking questions in lectures about the possibility of remote-control brains, being mocked by a wind-up Boris Karloff Monster for his efforts. Meanwhile his student colleagues are involved in a major protest against technology. 'Computer Must Go' says one of the many badly worded placards we get to see being held aloft. Frankenstein eventually manages to create a remote-control cat and dog (it doesn't end well for one of them), then when he's involved in a drugs bust, he turns his friend Tony into a remote-controlled killing machine to take revenge on those who have got him expelled yet again. Foiled by a small boy, Frankenstein is chased up some stairs and falls off a balcony, only for his skin to split open, proving him to be a creation as well. The finale has the true mad scientist having what we presume is a Brian Donlevy Quatermass-style 'gonna start again' moment as he wanders away from the end credits. (Director Gilbert W. Taylor was no relation to Gilbert Taylor the BAFTA-nominated cinematographer of **Star Wars**, **The Omen**, and Polanski's **Repulsion**, just in case anyone was wondering.) The film is also known as **Flick**, apparently because the distributor hoped potential punters might misread its capitalised title on cinema marquees.

THE HORROR OF FRANKENSTEIN

UK, 1970
Director: Jimmy Sangster. Producer: Jimmy Sangster.
Screenplay: Jeremy Burnham, Jimmy Sangster.
Music: Malcolm Williamson. Cinematography: Moray Grant.
Cast: Ralph Bates, Kate O'Mara, Veronica Carlson, Dennis Price, Joan Rice, Bernard Archard, George Belbin, Jon Finch.

Rather than carry on from the high of the previous year's **Frankenstein Must Be Destroyed**, Hammer Films decided to reboot their franchise and go back to remaking the film that started it all, employing original screenwriter Jimmy Sangster to write (with Jeremy Burnham), produce, and direct. The result gives us a smarmy young Baron (Ralph Bates) whose drunken womanising git of a father (George Belbin) dies, allowing Frankenstein Junior to embark on a witless attempt to literally build a monster by numbers while seducing 1970s starlets. The result lumbers about for a bit before suffering an ignominious fate, leading to a final freeze frame shot of the Baron, who looks about as upset as someone who has just received an especially large and unexpected gas bill. The few joys to be found in this one are in the character roles. Dennis Price and Joan Rice are a delight as a grave robbing husband and wife team, and Jon Finch, inexplicably not cast as the Baron (now there would have been a Frankenstein for the 1970s) but in a far less interesting bit part as a policeman. Even composer James Bernard sat this one out (soon-to-be Master of the Queen's Music Malcolm Williamson stepped in instead). The one many Hammer fans hate and it's not difficult to see why.

ORLOFF AND THE INVISIBLE MAN

France/Spain, 1970
Director: Pierre Chevalier. Producer: Marius Lesoeur.
Screenplay: Pierre Chevalier, Juan Fortuny. Music: Camille Sauvage.
Cinematography: Raymond Heil, Juan Fortuny [uncredited].
Cast: Howard Vernon, Brigitte Carva, Fernando Sancho, Francisco Valladares, Isabel del Rio, Evane Hanska.

Pierre Chevalier's tatty, ramshackle, zoom-filled movie could easily be mistaken for the work of Jess Franco on a bad day (especially with that title). It's set in Eighteenth Century Europe (one presumes), in grim weather – usually due to actual rain but sometimes, in a rare and impressive attempt to provide some continuity, due to a watering can just out of shot being poured from above the camera. Putting an interesting spin on the proceedings (and they need it) is a somewhat peculiar jazz score that seems to consist of various instrumentalists plucking and blowing notes at random with little thought for what their colleagues are up to. Sometimes everyone just gives up and snaps their fingers, presumably to gain the attention of whoever was providing them with the hallucinogenic drugs that made them think what they were producing was actually music. Orloff is Howard Vernon (naturally) who creates an invisible man. Or does he? No spoilers here because any viewer sitting through the 76 minutes of this one deserves to be rewarded with a punchline so unremittingly daft it will at least wake them up. This invisible 'man' can serve drinks, bump into furniture, and is also capable of chasing serving girls around, tearing all their clothes off, and ravishing them in a scene which begs for use of the fast forward button. At the end the now visible 'man' is bonked on the head, the castle burns, and something happens that is best not questioned. Now you know if you want to watch this.

LA ROSE ECORCHÉE

France, 1970
Director: Claude Mulot. Producers: Raymond Hébert, Edgar Oppenheimer. Screenplay: Claude Mulot, Jean Larriaga, Edgar Oppenheimer. Music: Jean-Pierre Dorsay.
Cinematography: Roger Fellous.
Cast: Philippe Lemaire, Anny Duperey, Howard Vernon, Elizabeth Teissier, Olivia Robin, Michèle Perello.

France's horror heritage doesn't quite match up to the quality and sheer quantity of Spain and Italy, but for burned faces and lustful revenge as a consequence it's hard to beat, be it in literature (Maurice Level) or movies (**Les yeux sans visage**). Director Claude Mulot's stylish, bawdy, and energetic take on the theme (the title translates as **The Blood Rose**) gives us the story as a sexy neo-Gothic fairytale, in which famous artist Frédéric (Philippe Lemaire) holds a fancy dress party at his crumbling castle to celebrate his engagement to Anne (Anny Duperey). Frédéric's ex Moira (Elizabeth Teissier) isn't invited but comes anyway, dressed as the evil red queen and causing Anne to fall into a bonfire. Luckily Professor Römer, who works at Frédéric's botanical institute sideline, is played by Howard Vernon and happens to be a disgraced plastic surgeon, dressed in black and every inch the court physician or alchemist of myth. The fairytale element is further embellished by Frédéric's two dwarf servants, Igor and Olaf, who also have a role to play in the splendidly weird and atmospheric necrophile lesbian scene that pops up halfway through, as well as helping to have the film climax on a dwarf fight. Not enough films end using this device.

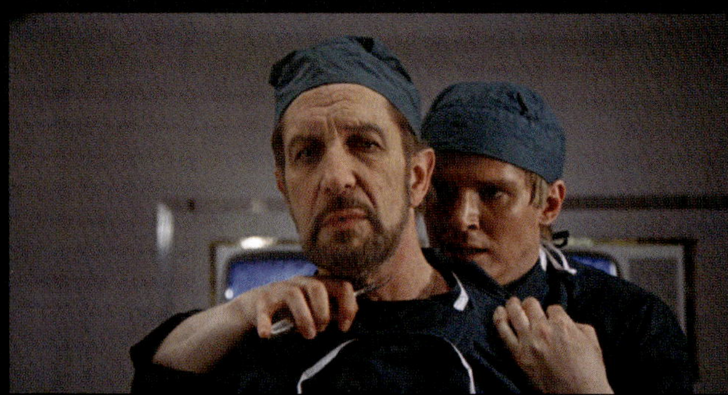

SCREAM AND SCREAM AGAIN

UK, 1970
Director: Gordon Hessler. Producers: Max Rosenberg, Milton Subotsky. Screenplay: Christopher Wicking. Music: David Whitaker. Cinematography: John Coquillon.
Cast: Vincent Price, Christopher Lee, Peter Cushing, Alfred Marks, Anthony Newlands, Peter Sallis, Michael Gothard.

Best known for uniting three major stars of the horror genre (Vincent Price, Christopher Lee, and Peter Cushing) but only having Lee and Price meet, and in the final scene at that. It's peculiarly apt that a film about synthetic humans with different aliases should have been based on a book by a man who didn't exist. 'Peter Saxon' who wrote *The Disorientated Man* was a house pseudonym for various authors, at least two of whom (Stephen Frances and W. Howard Baker) worked on the book, undoubtedly contributing to the fragmented feel of the narrative retained by Christopher Wicking for his screenplay. However, Wicking sensibly rejected several of the novel's plotlines – including aliens being behind a series of vampire-like killings in London, a fascist takeover in Eastern Europe, and a man repeatedly waking to find new parts of his body have been removed – and replaced them with something far more political and far more interesting. Director Gordon Hessler (it's his best film) uses *cinéma vérité* techniques to make scenes at a British police station more involving, there's a great car chase, and fine performances from Michael Gothard ("not today, lady") as the vampire synthetic, and Alfred Marks as the policeman in charge of the investigation.
David Whitaker provides an off-kilter jazz score that was unavailable for many years due to rights issues (Kendall Schmidt provided a new score for video that's actually not that bad) but the original music is now all back in place, Amen Corner song and all.

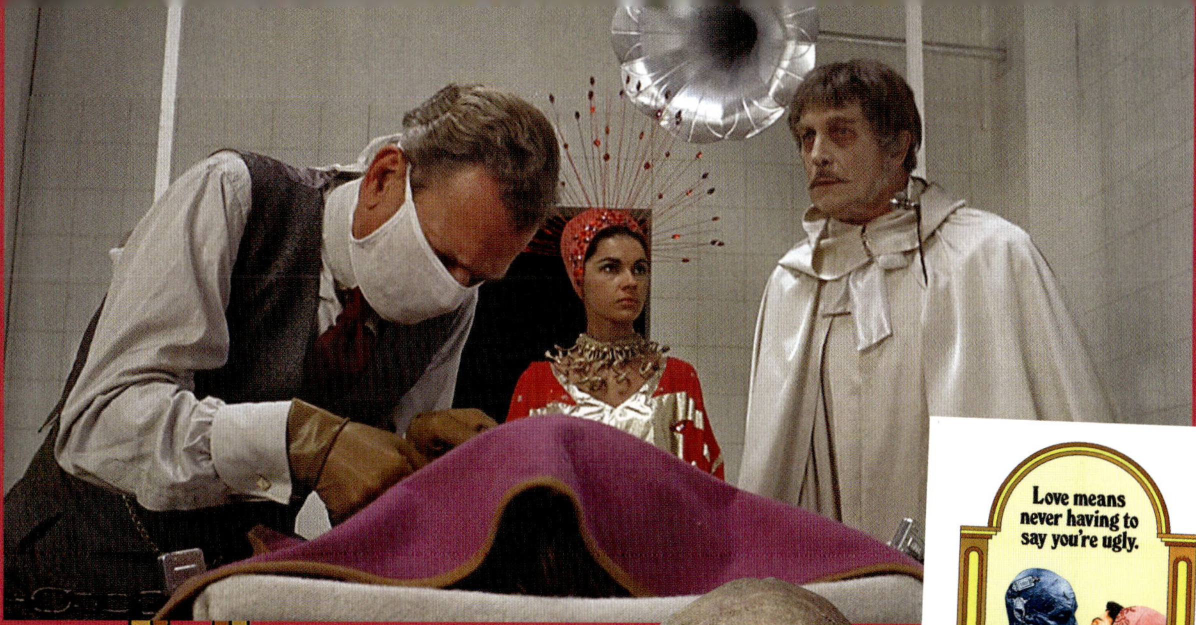

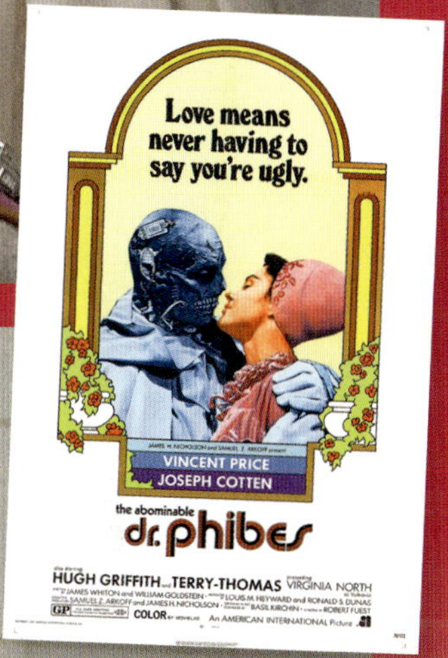

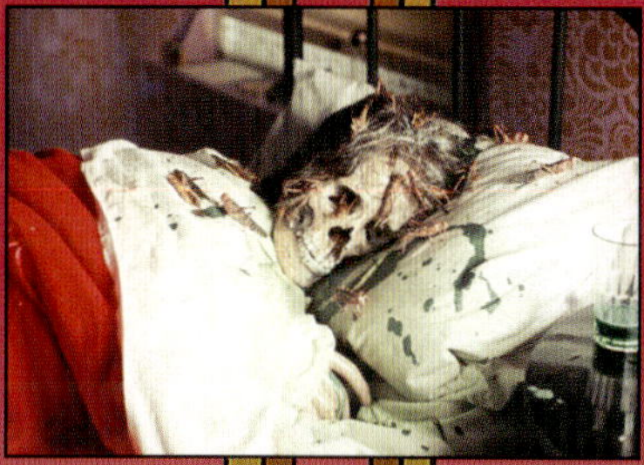

THE ABOMINABLE DR. PHIBES

UK, 1971
Director: Robert Fuest. Producers: Ronald Dunas, Louis M. Heyward.
Screenplay: James Whiton, William Goldstein. Music: Basil Kirchin.
Cinematography: Norman Warwick.
Cast: Vincent Price, Joseph Cotten, Hugh Griffith, Terry-Thomas, Virginia North, Aubrey Woods.

The cinema of the Gothic that had been such a success in the 1960s for the UK (Hammer et al), the US (Roger Corman's Poe pictures), and Italy (Mario Bava, Riccardo Freda, et al) was on the decline in the 1970s. But period horror still had at least one more delicious trick up its sleeve as the UK arm of American International Pictures joined forces with director Robert Fuest, dusted off a script by James Whiton and William Goldstein, and rewrote the ending with the uncredited aid of Brian Clemens. They then set the whole thing in the 1920s and cast Vincent Price in the title role of a man bumping off the doctors whom he believed responsible for the death of his wife (Caroline Munro in pictures). Even all that doesn't go halfway to explaining why this film is so well loved. The murders are themed to emulate the ten biblical plagues! They're explained by a Rabbi played by electrifying Welshman Hugh Griffith! Dr. Phibes has life-sized clockwork musicians that play Basil Kirchin jazz! Fuest wasn't completely happy with the score and got his friend John Gale to write the theme for Phibes' assistant Vulnavia (Virginia North), giving full scoring duties to Gale for the follow up. Fifty years later and everything about this film still feels very special, from the sets to the costumes to the array of character actors who play Phibes' victims. A gem.

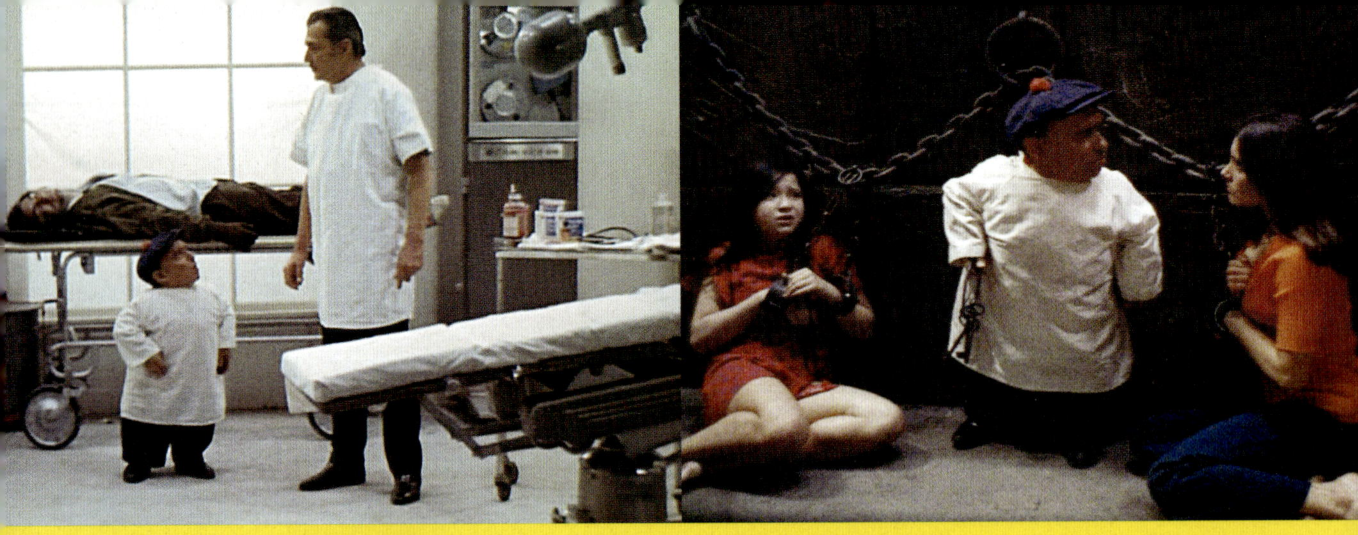

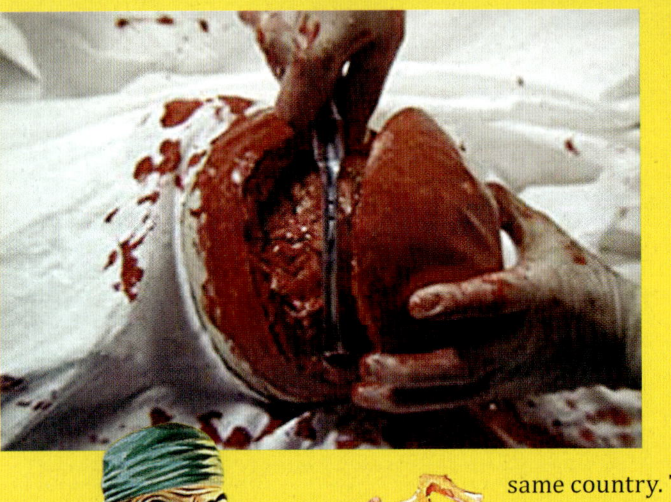

BRAIN OF BLOOD

USA/Philippines, 1971
Director: Al Adamson. Producers: Al Adamson, Samuel M. Sherman. Screenplay: Joe Van Rodgers. Cinematography: Louis Horvath.
Cast: Kent Taylor, Grant Williams, Regina Carroll, Angelo Rossitto, John Bloom, Reed Hadley.

After the tremendous success of the Philippines-set Blood Island series of movies, Hemisphere Pictures tasked producer Sam Sherman and director Al Adamson with making a film in Los Angeles that looked as if it had been shot in the same country. The result was **Brain of Blood**, in which the body of the recently deceased president of the made-up Middle Eastern country of Kalid (depicted by a still photograph of the Taj Mahal) is wrapped in tinfoil and brought to the US where Dr. Trenton (Kent Taylor from Hemisphere's **Brides of Blood** and a host of Adamson-directed movies of this period) can transplant his brain into a new living subject. Angelo Rossitto (star of everything from Tod Browning's **Freaks** in 1932 to 1985's **Mad Max Beyond Thunderdome**) helps him out, as does **The Incredible Shrinking Man**'s Grant Williams. The brain transplant scene (described as 'a fistful of cerebellum' in a 1980s *Fangoria* magazine article) is probably the best they could do with a mannikin and what looks like sheep's brains. It goes on for over ten minutes (which might be a record) and that's just to put it in a jar because the donor body hasn't turned up yet. It never does and the poor old brain ends up in a body only fans of director Adamson's movies could truly love.

DR. JEKYLL AND SISTER HYDE

UK, 1971
Director: Roy Ward Baker.
Producers: Brian Clemens, Albert Fennell.
Screenplay: Brian Clemens. Music: David Whitaker.
Cinematography: Norman Warwick.
Cast: Ralph Bates, Martine Beswick, Gerald Sim, Lewis Fiander, Dorothy Alison, Neil Wilson.

Never make a joke in a studio canteen said screenwriter Curt Siodmak in an interview once. It caused him to end up writing **Frankenstein Meets the Wolf Man** and nearly sixty years later it resulted in Brian Clemens coming up with the screenplay for this, Hammer's best and most interesting stab at adapting the Robert Louis Stevenson story. Allowed the opportunity to write a Victorian Gothic, Clemens did go a bit mad, cramming in Burke and Hare and Jack the Ripper for good measure, and giving Ralph Bates's Jekyll the search for an elixir of life (so he has the time to cure all known diseases) as the reason for his transformation into Martine Beswick. But in all honesty who cares? This is great stuff, well directed by Roy Ward Baker, whose record with the Gothic could be decidedly patchy (the sex comedy stylings of 1970's **Scars of Dracula**, the dirge-like **And Now the Screaming Starts!** for Amicus in 1973). The casting of Jekyll and Hyde looks like result of the meticulous and lengthy efforts of a casting director but apparently that wasn't the case at all. Sometimes you just get happy accidents. David Whitaker did the music to this one and it's just lovely.

HANDS OF THE RIPPER

UK, 1971
Director: Peter Sasdy. Producer: Aida Young. Screenplay: Lewis Davidson. Music: Christopher Gunning. Cinematography: Kenneth Talbot. Cast: Eric Porter, Angharad Rees, Jane Merrow, Keith Bell, Derek Godfrey, Dora Bryan.

One of the best films Hammer ever made, and arguably the best not to star either Peter Cushing or Christopher Lee (or both of them together), **Hands of the Ripper**'s original sleazy double bill poster art belies the fact that it's actually a fascinating, gorgeous, and superbly made mixture of tragic love story and gory slasher picture that borders on the giallo. Eric Porter is splendid as John Pritchard, the movie's mad doctor where in this case the science is psychology rather than any physical discipline. At the climax, Porter makes the scene of him wrenching a sword from his abdomen so agonising as to be one of the most painful scenes in cinema of the period. Angharad Rees is tiny, delicate, and yet somehow believable as both the helpless Anna and as someone possessed by the murderous the spirit of Jack the Ripper, slashing his way through Victorian London. It's impossible to believe that any other actress could have done a better job. The production design and locations are sumptuous and superb for a low-budget film – the result apparently of Peter Sasdy pulling in numerous favours from his television directing days. Christopher Gunning's music plays up to the film's emotional core, and this could quite possibly be director Peter Sasdy's best film. All this and Dora Bryan getting skewered with a poker once we're barely past the credits – what more could you want?

I, MONSTER

UK, 1971
Director: Stephen Weeks. Producers: Max Rosenberg, Milton Subotsky. Screenplay: Milton Subotsky. Music: Carl Davis. Cinematography: Moray Grant.
Cast: Christopher Lee, Peter Cushing, Mike Raven, Richard Hurndall, George Merritt, Kenneth J. Warren.

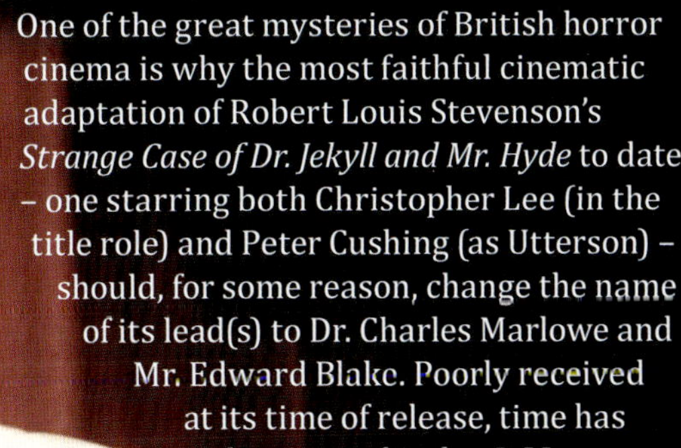

One of the great mysteries of British horror cinema is why the most faithful cinematic adaptation of Robert Louis Stevenson's *Strange Case of Dr. Jekyll and Mr. Hyde* to date – one starring both Christopher Lee (in the title role) and Peter Cushing (as Utterson) – should, for some reason, change the name of its lead(s) to Dr. Charles Marlowe and Mr. Edward Blake. Poorly received at its time of release, time has been very kind to **I, Monster,** especially considering its troubled production history. Peter Duffell (Amicus's 1971 **The House That Dripped Blood**) was originally slated to direct, but was replaced by first-timer Stephen Weeks, who had trouble getting respect from technicians who had sons older than him. It was originally intended to be shot in 3D using the Pulfrich effect, which involves covering one eye with a dark lens. The process required the camera to be moved in a certain way, which is why the film has some rather peculiar tracking shots where you would swear they'd set up the dolly rails at right angles to where they should be. **I, Monster** also boasts an early music score from renowned composer Carl Davis, which also helps to offset any failings the film may be perceived to have.

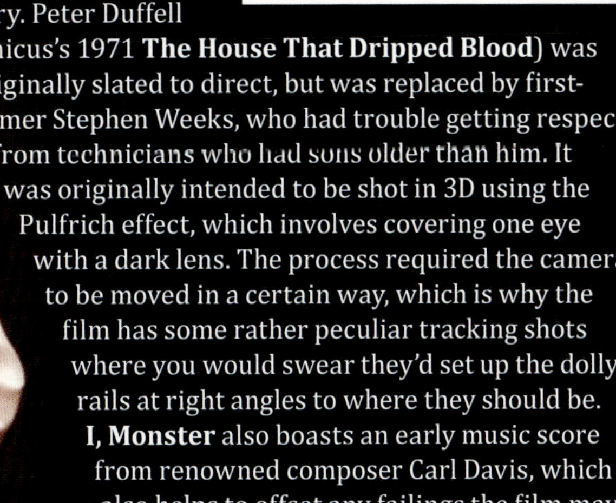

LADY FRANKENSTEIN

Italy, 1971
Director: Mel Welles. Producers: Mel Welles, Egidio Gelso [uncredited], Roger Corman [uncredited]. Screenplay: Edward Di Lorenzo, Mel Welles, Umberto Borsato, Egidio Gelso, Aureliano Luppi.
Music: Alessandro Alessandroni.
Cinematography: Richard Pallotin [Riccardo Pallottini].
Cast: Joseph Cotten, Sara Bey [Rosalba Neri], Mickey Hargitay, Herbert Fux, Paul Muller, Peter Whiteman [Riccardo Pizzuti].

A rare directorial outing (at least compared with the rest of his career) for Mel Welles, who was better known as an actor (1960's **The Little Shop of Horrors** and many others) and dubbing editor (apparently over 800 films). It features the always-welcome presence of Rosalba Neri in the title role, initially helping her father (Joseph Cotten) create a bulbous-headed googly-eyed monster that then kills the Baron and swiftly escapes. After burying her father, our heroine makes another creature to 'satisfy her strange desires' as the poster proclaimed. In fairness, what she actually wants is a clever brain in a perfect male body, and just happens to know how to bring it about, even if the whole thing ends in a pool of blood. (One of the scenes cut from some prints – until recently **Lady Frankenstein** had always been a notoriously difficult film to find in its complete form.) EuroHorror standbys Paul Muller, Herbert Fux, and Mickey Hargitay fill out the cast, and the buzzy, string-plucky score is by Alessandro Alessandroni. Neri (often credited as 'Sara Bey' in US prints) is extremely capable in the lead, the sets and locations are decent, and despite the ludicrous goings-on Welles keeps a firm hand on proceedings. This results in one of the better European Gothic horrors of the era – certainly much more effective than Hammer's then-current offering of **The Horror of Frankenstein**.

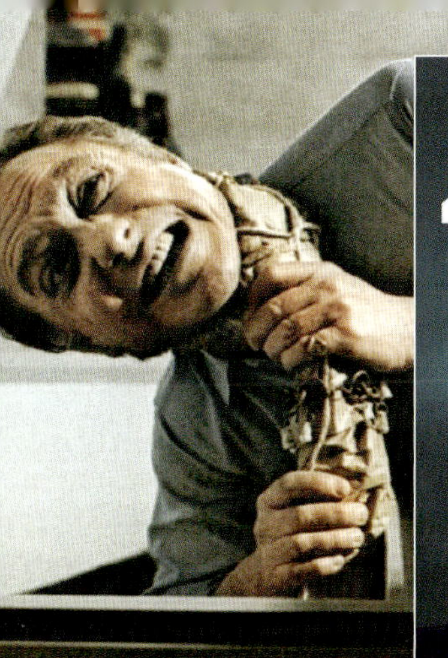

ASYLUM

UK, 1972
Director: Roy Ward Baker. Producers: Max Rosenberg, Milton Subotsky. Screenplay: Robert Bloch. Music: Douglas Gamley. Cinematography: Denys N. Coop.
Cast: Barbara Parkins, Richard Todd, Sylvia Syms, Peter Cushing, Barry Morse, Britt Ekland, Robert Powell, Charlotte Rampling, Herbert Lom.

Nearly everyone we encounter is mad, in one of the best Amicus portmanteau pictures. In order to secure the job of senior house officer Robert Powell has to guess which of the patients he is shown is Dr. B. Starr, the former head of the institution and now an inmate. Is it Bonnie (Barbara Parkins) whose lover chopped up his wife and put her in the freezer only for her to return from the dead thanks to voodoo? Bruno (Barry Morse) a tailor who brought a mannequin to life? Barbara (Charlotte Rampling) whose imaginary friend drives her to murder? Or Byron (Herbert Lom) who believes he can breathe life into the little models of humans he's been making? Writer Robert Bloch will always be best remembered for **Psycho** but Amicus deserves credit for doing such a fine job filming many of his short stories. Working from four of them here, with the fourth turning out to be the framework ('Mannequins of Horror') director Roy Ward Baker makes good use of cramped sets, and a host of great British character actors with a couple of spare days in their schedule, to create a mounting atmosphere of claustrophobia and insanity, helped immensely by composer Douglas Gamley's bombastic use of Mussorgsky's *Night on the Bare Mountain* for the main titles, with the Russian composer's *Pictures at an Exhibition* peppered throughout.

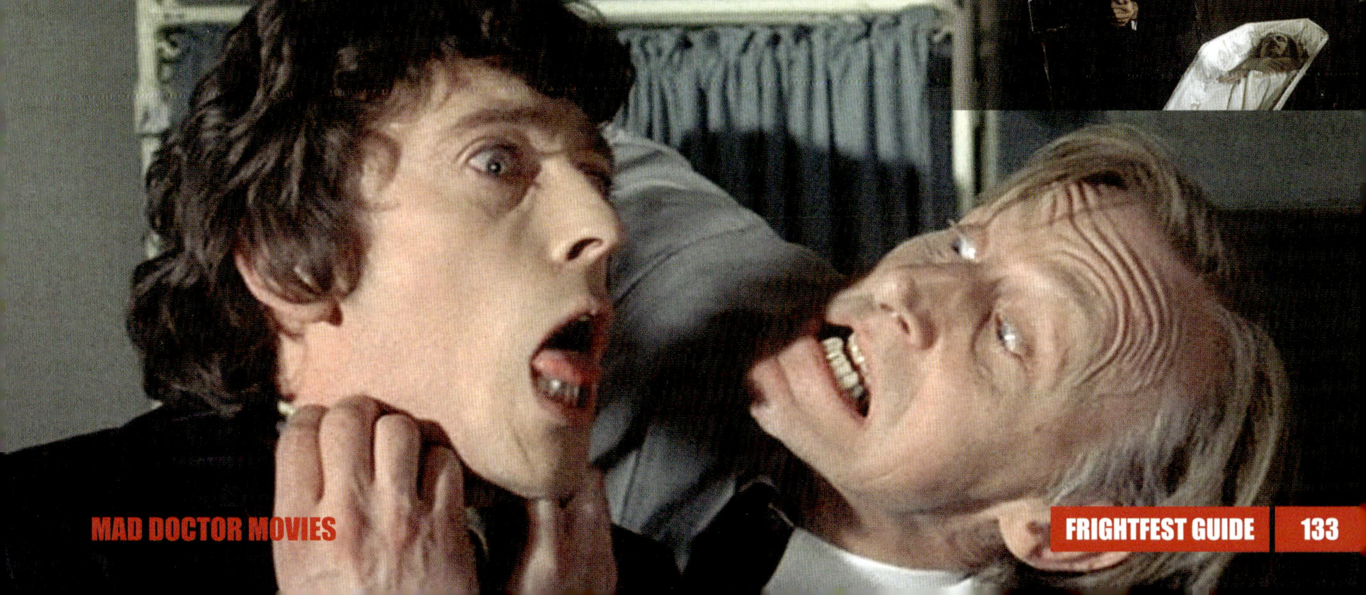

BLOOD OF GHASTLY HORROR

USA, 1972
Director: Al Adamson. Producer: Al Adamson. Screenplay: Dick Poston, Chris Martino, Mark Eden [uncredited]. Cinematography: Louis Horvath, William [Vilmos] Zsigmond. Cast: John Carradine, Kent Taylor, Tommy Kirk, Roy Morton, Regina Carrol, Richard Smedley.

An extreme example of the recycling machinations of exploitation filmmakers Al Adamson (as producer-director) and Sam Sherman (producer, co-screenwriter and distributor). **Blood of Ghastly Horror** started life as **Psycho A-Go-Go** (1965), a movie about a jewellery heist gone wrong and the subsequent attempts of the gang, especially the psychopathic Joe Corey (Roy Morton), to recover their loot. The film flopped, so Adamson shot an extra 13 minutes of footage with John Carradine as the mad Dr. Vanard, showing how Corey's character had been brought back from the dead with a brain implant. The result was retitled **Fiend with the Electronic Brain** (1967). But that was not the end. In 1971 Adamson shot yet more footage, this time with Kent Taylor as the mad scientist father of Corey's character, creating zombies by a technique he had learned 'in Jamaica and Haiti' to avenge the cops' killing of his son. This, then, became **Blood of Ghastly Horror**, incorporating all the new footage, all the Carradine-shot footage, and filling up the rest of its 84-minute running time with lengthy flashbacks to the 1965 original. As a piece of coherent narrative entertainment it's a mess, with footage shot by a pre-fame Vilmos Zsigmond (who won the Cinematography Oscar for **Close Encounters of the Third Kind**) for the first two versions clashing with the ugly amateurish photography of Louis Horvath for the third. Viewed alongside its predecessors, however, it's a fascinating insight into the thought processes of low-budget cinema's very own mad doctors of exploitation.

DOCTOR GORE

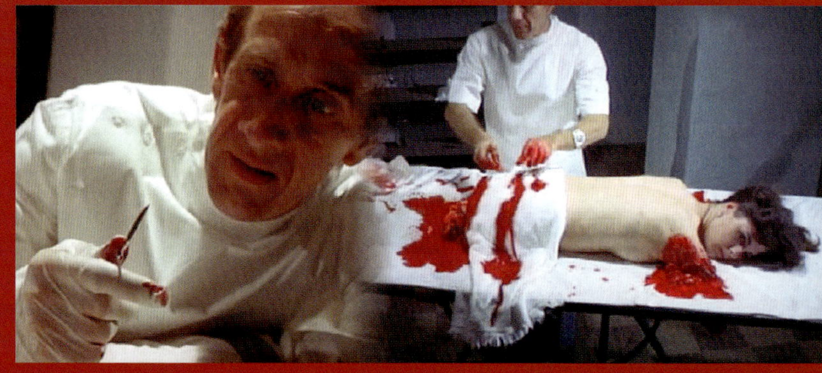

USA, 1972
Director: J.G. Patterson Jr. Producers: Jeffrey C. Hogue, J.G. Patterson Jr. Screenplay: J.G. Patterson Jr. Music: William Girdler. Cinematography: W. Martin Hill, Harry M. Joyner. Cast: Don Brandon [J.G. Patterson Jr.], Jenny Driggers, Roy Mehaffey, Linda Faile, Candy Furr, Bill Hicks.

Dr. Brandon's wife dies and so he decides to build himself a new one. His first try is a failure, most likely because he smokes in his operating room and cleans his fingernails with his scalpel, but possibly also because the reanimation of his creation involves the use of little other than tinfoil and gaffer tape, with sparklers being thrown into the frame for good measure. During all this the doctor's hunchbacked assistant Greg is constantly in danger of developing a case of workman's bottom. A later attempt involves some graphic gore effects that are rather better and more disturbing than those featured in H.G. Lewis's **The Gore Gore Girls** from the same year. The credits would have us believe Dr. Brandon is played by 'America's No.1 magician' Don Brandon but we know it's actually writer-producer-director J.G. Patterson Jr., whose acting capabilities are only slightly more restrained than Mal Arnold's Fuad Ramses in 1963's **Blood Feast**, especially during the hypnotism bits. This ramshackle affair also features the most stilted dinner conversation to take place while a magician plays with his balls in the background ever committed to celluloid. William Girdler (future director of 1978's **The Manitou**) supplied the music score. About halfway through a large man with a beard starts singing a Country and Western song entitled 'My Heart Has Just Died'. Anyone but the most devoted aficionado of trash cinema will know just how he feels.

DR. PHIBES RISES AGAIN

UK, 1972
Director: Robert Fuest. Producer: Louis M. Heyward.
Screenplay: Robert Fuest, Robert Blees.
Music: John Gale.
Cinematography: Alex Thomson.
Cast: Vincent Price, Robert Quarry, Valli Kemp, Fiona Lewis, Peter Cushing, Beryl Reid.

Of course it had to happen, and quite cleverly, too, considering we last saw Vincent Price's mad doctor being embalmed. A conjunction of the planets causes Phibes' resurrection so he can travel to Egypt to search for the River of Life. Vulnavia's along for the ride again, and the fact she's played by a different actress (Valli Kemp) seems somehow right seeing as the previous Vulnavia was dissolved in acid. Darius Biederbeck (Robert Quarry), desperately trying to cheat death, is also looking for the River, necessitating Phibes to once again employ all manner of creative methods to bump off his rival's assistants, who include a lineup of younger British character actors (John Thaw, Keith Buckley, Lewis Fiander) than the first film. The production design is once again fabulous, the music is better, and Price and Quarry make for very good adversaries, but somehow this doesn't have quite the zing of the first film. Getting Price to sing 'Somewhere Over the Rainbow' at the end is a masterstroke, although it represents so much of a full stop happy ending that it almost makes you glad the proposed third film, **Phibes Resurrectus** (still being announced as a go project five years after this) wasn't made.

SISTERS

USA, 1972
Director: Brian De Palma. Producer: Edward R. Pressman. Screenplay: Brian De Palma. Louisa Rose. Music: Bernard Herrmann. Cinematography: Gregory Sandor.
Cast: Margot Kidder, Jennifer Salt, Charles Durning, Bill Finley, Lisle Wilson, Barnard Hughes.

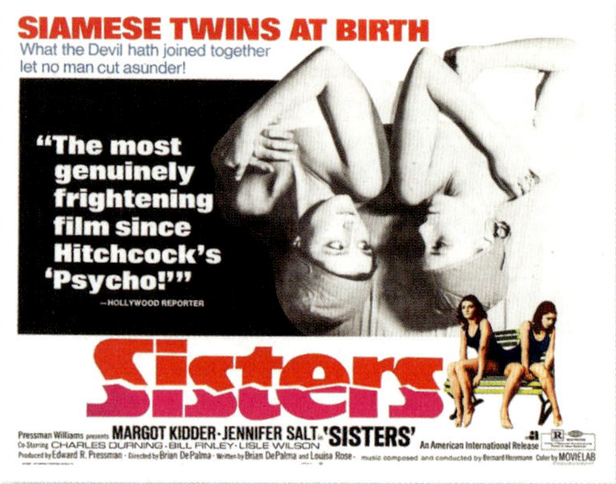

This early film from Brian De Palma gives us a brutal stabbing early on that now feels more as if it belongs in an Argento movie than anything from Hitchcock, who De Palma usually cites as his main influence. De Palma's screenplay (with Louisa Rose) feels more Italian as well, giving us the ludicrous story of Siamese twins, both Margot Kidder, one needing the other to stay sane, with the underlying suggestion that separating them may have caused one to become a psychotic killer. It's all daft as a brush but, like Argento's movies, if you don't think about it too much De Palma's style almost lets him get away with it. William Finley is the surgeon-psychiatrist (there should be more of those in movies – needless to say there aren't very many in real life), who runs a psychiatric institution and is also capable of performing the complex surgery required to separate the sisters. Or does he just use a meat cleaver, as the gloriously mad climactic dream sequence might suggest? Fans of the split screen technique De Palma uses here might want to check out Richard L. Bare's 1973 **Wicked, Wicked** which uses the effect for its entire running time. There aren't many conjoined twin movies out there (Keith Fulton and Louis Pepe's 2005 version of Brian Aldiss' novel **Brothers of the Head** comes to mind) but **Sisters** was itself remade in 2006 by Douglas Buck, starring Stephen Rea as the doctor and Lou Doillon as his patient(s).

SUPERBEAST

USA, 1972
Director: George Schenck. Producer: George Schenck. Screenplay: George Schenck.
Music: Richard LaSalle. Cinematography: Nonong Rasca.
Cast: Antoinette Bower, Craig Littler, Harry Lauter, Vic Diaz, Jose Romulo, John Garwood.

Inspired by the success of the Eddie Romero / Gerardo de Leon Blood Island pictures, American filmmakers George and Aubrey Schenck decided to make their own double bill of Philippines-set horror films. Hollingsworth Morse's **Daughters of Satan** gave Tom Selleck (*Magnum P.I.*) one of his first starring roles in a tale of witchcraft, while the supporting feature was yet another spin on the *Dr. Moreau* tale. This time Dr. Alix Pardee (Antoinette Bower, probably best known to genre fans for the 'Catspaw' episode of the original *Star Trek* series) travels deep into the jungle to find out why convicts are turning into primordial madmen. It's all the fault of Dr. Bill Fleming (Craig Littler) and his genetic experiments. When they go wrong, the results are released into the wild so financier Stewart Victor (Harry Lauter) can hunt them for sport. Stewart's obviously more of a fan of Richard Connell's story *The Most Dangerous Game* than *The Island of Dr. Moreau*. Using the then-popular exploitation movie trope of including real autopsy footage at the beginning to kick things off, **Superbeast**'s main claim to fame (and the reason to watch it) is because the make-up designs for the mutated animal-humans is by John Chambers, most famous for his work on the five original **Planet of the Apes** films.

BLACKENSTEIN

USA, 1973
Director: William A. Levey.
Producer: Frank R. Saletri. Screenplay: Frank R. Saletri. Music: Cardella Di Milo, Lou Frohman. Cinematography: Robert Caramico.
Cast: John Hart, Ivory Stone, Liz Renay, Joe De Sue, Andrea King, Nick Bolin.

During the 'blaxploitation' boom of the early-1970s, horror classics were considered fair game for reimagining with African American actors in the lead roles. William Marshall gave a fine lead performance as the vampire count in both William Crain's **Blacula** (1972) and Bob Kelljan's **Scream Blacula Scream** (1973). Crain also directed Bernie Casey in 1976's **Dr. Black, Mr. Hyde** while William Girdler gave the world a black exorcist in **Abby** (1974). Unfit to be mentioned in the same breath as those still immensely watchable and entertaining pieces of their time is director William A. Levey's woeful **Blackenstein**, disdainfully subtitled 'The Black Frankenstein', presumably because its makers felt their target audience might need that to be made clear. To pile on the cinematic insult, the 'Dr. Stein' character in this is actually white, creating a clodhopping black monster when a former student begs him to help her fiancé Eddie, who had his arms and legs blown off when he stepped on a landmine in Vietnam. Bad film aficionados will relish the terrible laboratory set that sounds as if it has an owl trapped in the roof, terrible dialogue (we are told Dr. Stein has just won the Nobel prize for solving the DNA genetic code, making him only eleven years behind actual winners Watson and Crick), and quite remarkable acting. Fans of ludicrous rambling monologues delivered by an angry nurse will find a cracking one just thirteen minutes in, while the most undignified scene of all is reserved for the monster, who meets his end during what looks like a proposed crossover with Byron Chudnow's 1972 **The Doberman Gang**.

THE CREEPING FLESH

UK, 1973
Director: Freddie Francis.
Producer: Michael P. Redbourn.
Screenplay: Peter Spenceley, Jonathan Rumbold.
Music: Paul Ferris.
Cinematography: Norman Warwick.
Cast: Christopher Lee, Peter Cushing, Lorna Heilbron, George Benson, Kenneth J. Warren, Duncan Lamont, Jenny Runacre.

Peter Cushing is mad Victorian anthropologist Dr. Emmanuel Hildern, who has brought back to England a massive skeleton he discovered on his travels in New Guinea. Christopher Lee is Emmanuel's brother Dr. James Hildern, who runs the local lunatic asylum where Emmanuel's mad wife (Jenny Runacre) spent her final days. Emmanuel wants to protect his daughter (Lorna Heilbron) so he injects her with blood from the giant's reconstituted phallic finger. She goes mad, while James steals the skeleton. It rains, the monster comes looking for its missing finger. The brainchild of former dubbing editor-turned producer Mike Redbourn, and one of director Freddie Francis' best films, **The Creeping Flesh** manages to cram in all sorts of interesting ideas as well as effectively satirising the hypocrisy of Victorian society without ever feeling jumbled or confusing. Credit is therefore also due to Peter Spenceley and Jonathan Rumbold who wrote the script. The whole thing is ludicrous (and the film basically tells you so at the end) but it's played with such conviction and sensitivity that, with the aid of Paul Ferris' effective score, it all works. One of the best British Gothic horrors and all the more surprising for appearing at the tail end of the British horror boom.

THE DOCTOR IN THE NUDE

France/Italy, 1973
Director: Alain Jessua. Producers: Raymond Danon, Jacques Dorfmann, Alain Jessua [uncredited]. Screenplay: Alain Jessua. Music: Alain Jessua, René Koering. Cinematography: Jacques Robin.
Cast: Alain Delon, Annie Girardot, Michel Duchaussoy, Robert Hirsch, Jean-François Calvé, Gabriel Cattand.

Alain Jessua's modern-day medical vampire tale is better known under the title **Shock Treatment** (not to be confused with Jim Sharman and Richard O'Brien's 1981 follow up to **The Rocky Horror Picture Show**). It was released in the UK by Antony Balch (director of **Horror Hospital**) under the remarkably misleading title **The Doctor in the Nude**, presumably to cash in on the sex appeal of its famous French star Alain Delon.

Annie Giradot plays 38-year-old Hélène who attends the health rejuvenation clinic of Dr. Devilers (Delon) only to discover that the treatment administered to its wealthy clients comes at a human cost. Delivering its message of the rich living off the poor with rather broad strokes, the film nevertheless provides some arresting imagery, especially when Hélène discovers the semi-gutted corpse of one of the clinic's porters in a laboratory, his remaining tissues still useful to the clients. Likely an influence on Gore Verbinski's 2016 **A Cure for Wellness**, the cold, metallic look of Dr. Devilers' clinic may well have influenced production design on some of David Cronenberg's early films as well. Jessua had previously worked as assistant director to Max Ophüls on 1955's **Lola Montès**. In 1984 he made **Frankenstein 90**, his comedy variation on Mary Shelley's novel, but the Jessua films most worth seeking out are 1967's **The Killing Game** in which a rich man acts out the plots of comic strips, and **The Dogs** (1979) with Gérard Depardieu.

DON'T LOOK IN THE BASEMENT

USA, 1973
Director: S.F. Brownrigg. Producer: S.F. Brownrigg.
Screenplay: Tim Pope, Thomas Pope [uncredited].
Music: Robert Farrar. Cinematography: Robert B. Alcott.
Cast: Bill McGee, Anne MacAdams [Annabelle Weenick], Rosie Holotik, Gene Ross, Jessie Lee Fulton, Camilla Carr.

The first and best of what became known as the 'Brownies' – four sweaty, grimy, backwoods American Gothics made by Texas-based independent producer-director S.F. (Sherald Fergus) Brownrigg over a four year period. The others being **Don't Open the Door** (girl menaced by an obscene phone caller), **Scum of the Earth** (redneck horrors) both made in 1974, followed by the poorest, **Keep My Grave Open** (troubled woman becomes increasingly so in her isolated house) in 1977. In **Don't Look in the Basement** a nurse comes to work at the kind of isolated exploitation movie mental hospital where therapy includes encouraging its most violent inmates to whack at things with an axe. Unfortunately, the head psychiatrist gets in the way during a session and it's not long before the inmates have taken over. The cast members revel in their full throttle depictions of the institute's patients, and the fact that many of the actors appeared in little else makes their performances all the more believable, and in some cases oddly affecting. Despite the sunshine and frequently brightly lit interiors, Brownrigg infuses the film with an all-pervading sense of claustrophobic bleakness and gloom. These elements, plus the ultimate hopelessness of the situations in which his lead characters find themselves, came to characterise his subsequent horror films.

THE EROTIC RITES OF FRANKENSTEIN

France/Spain, 1973
Director: Jess Franco.
Screenplay: Jess Franco.
Music: H. Tical [Armando Sciascia], Vincent Gemignani, Robert Hermel, Vladimir Cosma.
Cinematography: Raoul Artigot.
Cast: Howard Vernon, Alberto Dalbés, Dennis Price, Anne Libert, Britt Nichols [Carmen Yazalde], Luis Barboo.

In this follow-on to the previous year's **Dracula, Prisoner of Frankenstein**, Jess Franco continues his avant-garde and decidedly 1970s freewheeling approach to adapting the Gothic. In the first five minutes of **The Erotic Rites of Frankenstein** (the UK release title) the Baron (a rather wobbly Dennis Price) is murdered by a blind naked vampire bird woman (Anne Libert) after transplanting a human brain into his silver-skinned monster (Fernando Bilbao), assisted by the mute Morpho (blink and you'll miss him Franco himself). But no sooner has one mad doctor been despatched than the writer-director introduces another in the form of the immortal Cagliostro (Howard Vernon) who wants to create a race of women who look like Britt Nichols (an entirely acceptable aesthetic choice) with the help of Frankenstein's daughter Vera. The film boasts stunning locations and delirious stuff you will never see anywhere else – a unique and mesmerising performance from Anne Libert, the silver monster whipping a naked couple tied together to try and make them fall onto razor-sharp spikes. The 74 minute running time will breeze by if you're a Franco fan, as you forgive shots that are out of focus, the occasional modern car driving by, and the fact that Frankenstein is spelt wrong on the family crypt. It will feel like forever if you're not. Many will likely agree, however, that the 'music' used to score the climax sounds like an unsupervised hyperactive five-year-old has been let loose on a church organ.

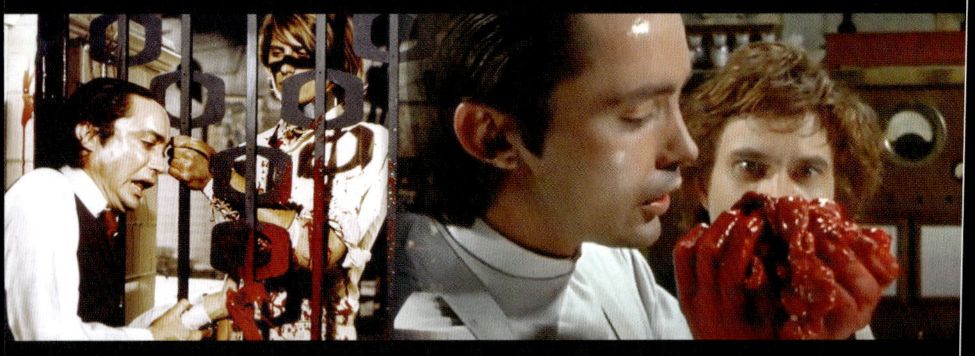

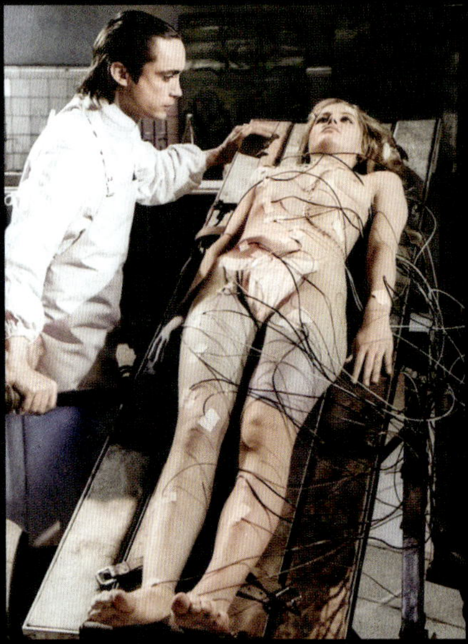

FLESH FOR FRANKENSTEIN

Italy/France, 1973
Director: Paul Morrissey. Producer: Andrew Braunsberg.
Screenplay: Paul Morrissey. Music: Claudio Gizzi.
Cinematography: Luigi Kuveiller.
Cast: Joe Dallesandro, Monique van Vooren, Udo Kier,
Arno Juerging, Dalila Di Lazzaro, Carla Mancini.

It's time to protect your gall bladders! Featuring not just one of the most iconic lines in horror but in cinema full stop, Andy Warhol's 'presentation' of Paul Morrissey's retelling of Mary Shelley's story is as entertainingly and deliriously unfaithful as the same team's subsequent effort to portray Bram Stoker's elegant count as a blood-vomiting, whining aristocrat in **Blood for Dracula** (1974). Udo Kier, the star of both, gives us an increasingly manic Baron, determined to create a 'zombie' (his own words) with the 'perfect nasum'. Quite why the nose is so important is never explained, but then the Baron is also obsessed with purity, being married to his own sister (Monique van Vooren) who spends her days carrying on with the handyman (Warhol alumnus Joe Dallesandro with the most New York-sounding Austrian accent even to grace a movie). Critics were so busy being outraged by the film's gory excesses (the film was cut by eight minutes for its UK release) that precious little praise was given to the amazing laboratory set (courtesy of production designer Enrico Job) or Claudio Gizzi's nuanced music (he also provided the score for **Blood for Dracula**). Carlo Rambaldi's effects, on the other hand, were too in your face not to notice, especially for audiences who saw this in its original anaglyph 3D presentation.

HORROR HOSPITAL

UK, 1973
Director: Antony Balch.
Producer: Richard Gordon. Screenplay:
Antony Balch, Alan Watson. Music: De Wolfe.
Cinematography: David McDonald.
Cast: Michael Gough, Robin Askwith, Skip Martin,
Vanessa Shaw, Ellen Pollock, Dennis Price.

From legendary producer Richard Gordon and exploitation entrepreneur Antony Balch, alternative titles for this include **Computer Killers** (not so good) and **Dr. Frankenstein's Horrorklinik** (now that's more like it). Song writer Robin Askwith embarks on a 'Hairy Holiday' at the 'health farm' (i.e. gloomy rambling country residence) of Dr. Storm (Michael Gough), only to discover that the seemingly wheelchair-bound leather glove and floppy hat-wearing doctor is more interested in operating on his guests' brains so he can control them. This one's got its tongue firmly in the cheek of its severed head, that was probably chopped off by the peculiar 'knife and basketball net' contraption the doctor has on his car. There's a bed filled with blood, leather-clad motorcycle henchmen, leery Dennis Price, pretty Vanessa Shaw (who appeared in very little else of note), diminutive Skip Martin (who seems to be well in on in the joke), a scene where Askwith stops to eat some quiche in the middle of a chase, and a gloopy monster at the climax. All of which add up to something rather different to your average early-1970s British horror film. Apparently, at the post-wrap party producer Gordon's potential future investors were unwittingly rendered unconscious by the hash cake Askwith's girlfriend had brought along.

THE MANSION OF MADNESS

Mexico, 1973
Director: Juan López Moctezuma. Producer: Roberto Viskin.
Screenplay: Carlos Illescas, Juan López Moctezuma. Music: Nacho Méndez.
Cinematography: Rafael Corkidi.
Cast: Claudio Brook, Arthur Hansel, Ellen Sherman, Martin LaSalle, David Silva, Pancho Córdova.

Before he made **Alucarda** (1977), the screamiest, bloodiest, nudiest film ever to be inspired by the works of J. Sheridan Le Fanu, Mexican director Juan López Moctezuma gave the world this loose adaptation of Poe's darkly comic tale 'The System of Dr. Tarr and Professor Fether'. In the early part of the Nineteenth Century, a journalist travels to a mental institution in the South of France, only to discover, in the denouement of the story, that before he arrived the inmates rebelled and took over the asylum, incarcerating the staff and assuming their roles. López Moctezuma's wild interpretation is filled with imagery reminiscent of the works of Alejandro Jodorowsky (especially 1970's **El Topo** and 1973's **The Holy Mountain**), Wojciech Has (1973's **The Hourglass Sanatorium**) and Fellini (1969's **Satyricon** and others). He had worked with Jodorowsky on both **El Topo** and the earlier **Fando and Lis** (1968). The horror genre appealed to Moctezuma because it allowed him to explore and express controversial political and religious statements under the guise of exploitation. The cavalcade of grotesque characters and peculiar, often playfully bizarre, situations presented in **The Mansion of Madness** also foreshadow elements to be found within the work of director Terry Gilliam. Poe's story has been adapted numerous times in various media, most recently by Brad Anderson as the film **Stonehearst Asylum** aka **Eliza Graves** (2014), starring Kate Beckinsale and Jim Sturgess, with Ben Kingsley as the asylum's 'director'. Anderson's version is fun but lacks the visceral oddness that permeates the entirety of Lopez Moctezuma's version.

THE SINISTER EYES OF DR. ORLOFF

Spain, 1973
Director: Jess Franco. Screenplay: Jess Franco.
Music: David Khunne [Jess Franco].
Cinematography: Antonio Millán.
Cast: Montserrat Prous, William Berger, Kali Hansa, Robert Woods, Edmund Purdom, Loreta Tovar.

Anyone familiar with the delirious fever-dream world of Jess Franco may be a bit disappointed with this, a far more straightforward thriller than one might expect from this period of the director's career. Pretty Melissa (Montserrat Prous) has been confined to a wheelchair all her life, except when she's hypnotised by the evil Dr. Orloff (William Berger), when she regains her ability to walk and starts bumping off her rich family one by one, starting with Franco himself who plays her father. It's all part of an inheritance plot that would have made a poor Hammer psycho-thriller and was released ten years after such things were popular. Allegedly set in the UK but filmed in the Canary Islands, which provides at least one element of Franco 'unrealism' (the pretty young things come home one night after partying with the Duke of Windsor) but this is still pretty basic, unambitious stuff. The 'jewel' here (because if one looks hard enough there's always one in a Franco film) is Prous' murder of her faithful manservant, shot in a dreamlike nightmare style that this film could have done with more of. Edmund Purdom is the police inspector who drinks 'Hindu tea' and has to come in at the end to sort it all out.

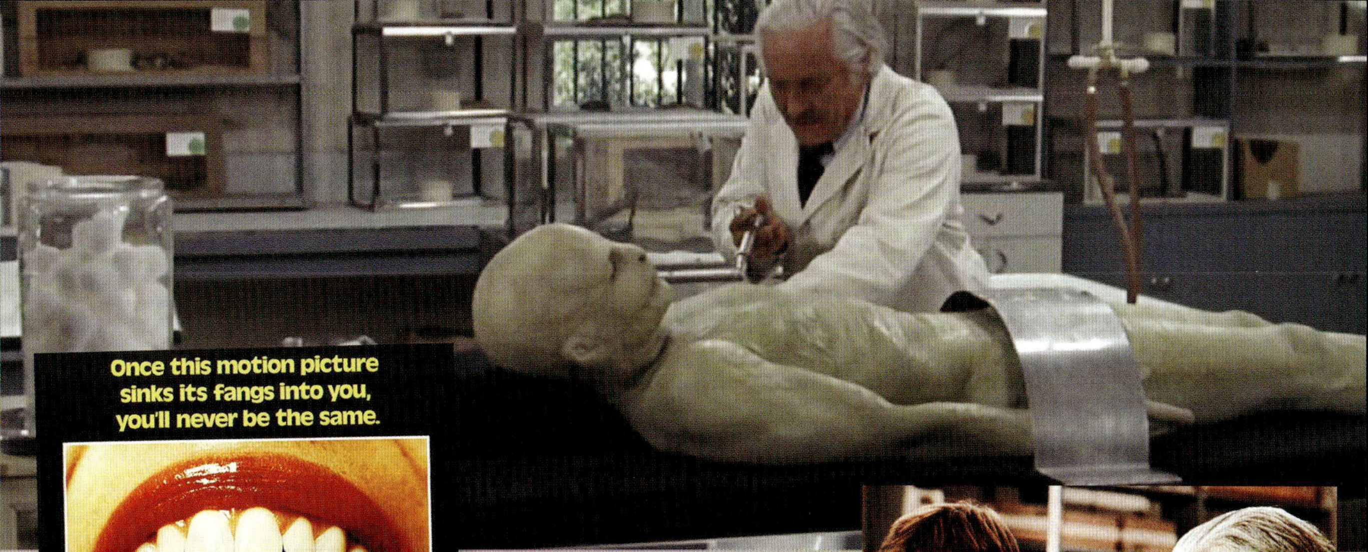

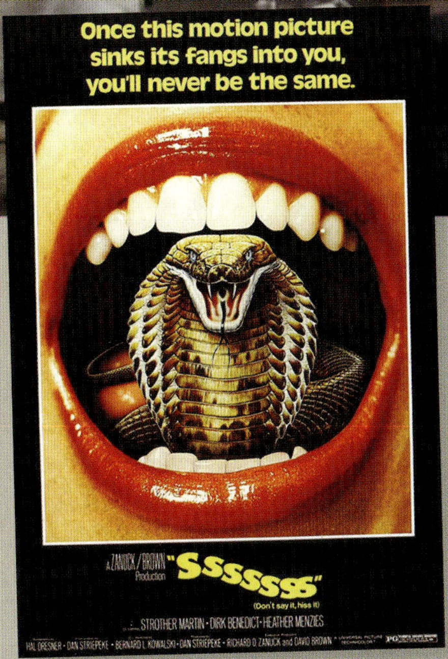

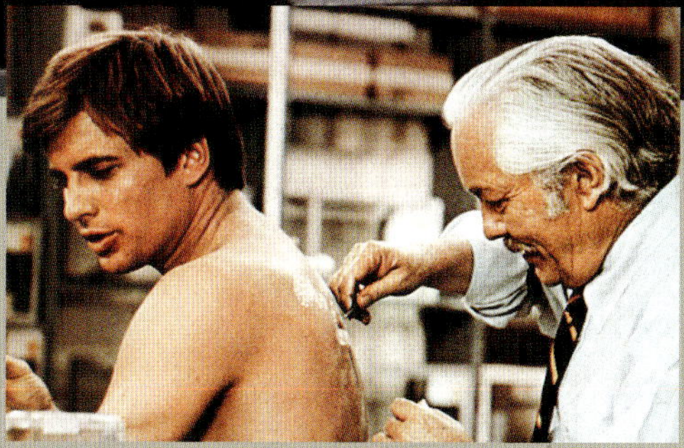

SSSSSSS

USA, 1973
Director: Bernard L. Kowalski.
Producer: Daniel C. Striepeke.
Screenplay: Hal Dresner.
Music: Patrick Williams.
Cinematography: Gerald Perry Finnerman.
Cast: Strother Martin, Dirk Benedict, Heather Menzies, Tim O'Connor, Richard B. Shull, Jack Ging, Reb Brown.

The only film whose title is a consonant repeated seven times (aka **SSSSnake**), Bernard L. Kowalski's film is **The Alligator People** for the 1970s. Kowalski substitutes snake venom for alligator serum, Strother Martin (as Dr. Stoner) for George Macready, Heather Menzies for Beverly Garland, and Dirk Benedict as the recipient of the serum that causes him to turn green and develop scales at the end of the film, thanks this time to make-up effects by John Chambers. Other highlights include Dr. Stoner's random babbling about the next stage of evolution, failed experiment Tim who now lives at the local sideshow, and Harry the python who gets a hangover and is fed Alka Seltzer by the doctor. Harry doesn't expand in the way one might expect a reptile with a simple digestive tract given large quantities of carbon-dioxide containing fizzy water to do (don't do this at home, kids) but that's because he has to be killed by evil soccer jock Reb Brown a little bit later on. Everything gets very silly by the end, including the audience needing to suspend their disbelief that a mongoose can pick a lock. Kowalski worked mainly in television, but he was also responsible for sweaty Deep South low-budget AIP picture **Attack of the Giant Leeches** (1959), a different kettle of wriggly things altogether.

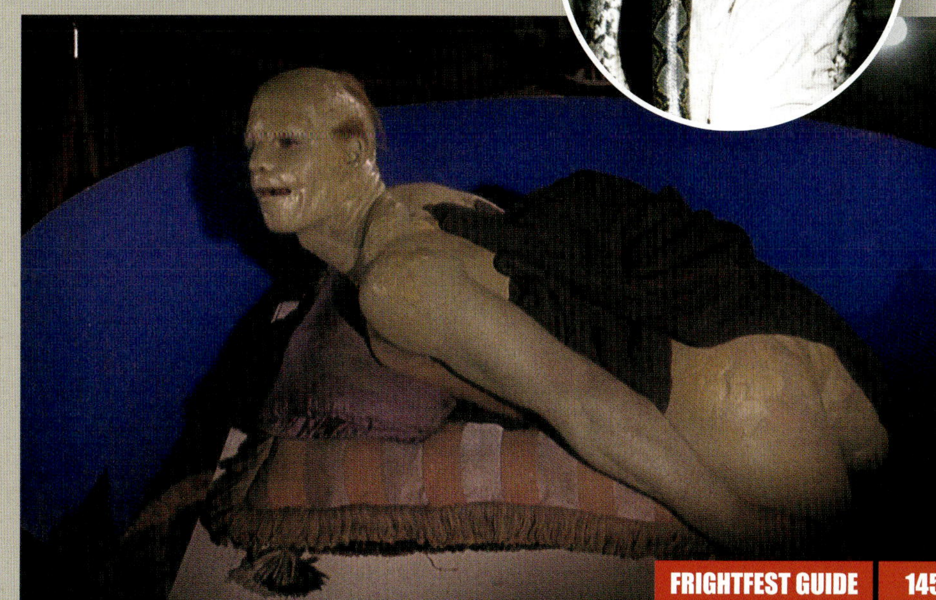

FRANKENSTEIN AND THE MONSTER FROM HELL

UK, 1974
Director: Terence Fisher.
Producer: Roy Skeggs.
Screenplay: John Elder [Anthony Hinds].
Music: James Bernard.
Cinematography: Brian Probyn.
Cast: Peter Cushing, Shane Briant, Madeline Smith, John Stratton, Bernard Lee, Clifford Mollison.

Hammer's longest-running franchise (starting with **The Curse of Frankenstein** back in 1957) bows out on a high, albeit a downbeat one. Director Terence Fisher returns to continue the story of Peter Cushing's Baron, now locked up in a mental institution and having had to fake his own death so he can carry on his experiments under the alias of Dr. Carl Victor. When Dr. Simon Helder (Shane Briant) is arrested for the possession of eyeballs and other body parts and gets sentenced to the same asylum for the same crime, the Baron has a fresh pair of hands to assist his own burned ones. He employs them in the creation of something sufficiently monstrous and primitive that it perfectly represents the Baron's own mental state – relentless, brutal, and slowly deteriorating. The over-the-top climax to this one (thunder, lightning, monster on the prowl, composer James Bernard giving his all) is a splendid last hurrah for British Gothic cinema, something that had enjoyed a long and prosperous run but was now being superseded by Hollywood blockbusters like William Friedkin's **The Exorcist,** which had shocked audiences the previous year then walked away with a brace of Oscars. Yet a strong supporting cast, featuring Patrick Troughton, Norman Mitchell, Madeline Smith, and Charles Lloyd Pack helped ensure that **Frankenstein and the Monster from Hell** represented a fitting ending to one of Hammer's (and especially Peter Cushing's) most endearing and enduring creations.

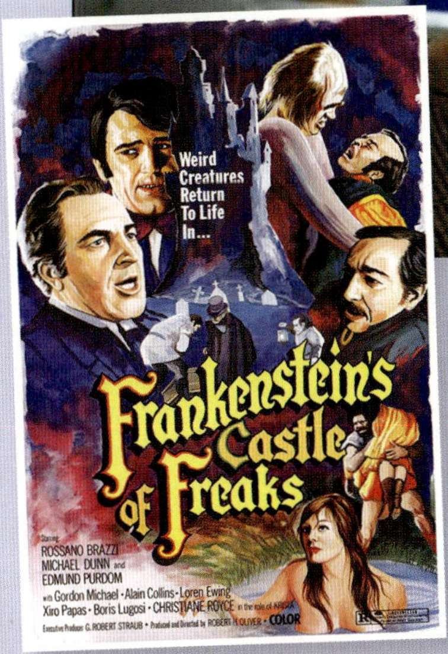

FRANKENSTEIN'S CASTLE OF FREAKS

Italy, 1974
Director: Robert H. Oliver [Dick Randall]. Producers: Robert H. Oliver [Dick Randall], Oscar Brazzi [uncredited]. Screenplay: Mark Smith, William Rose, Roberto Spano, Mario Francini [uncredited].
Music: Marcello Gigante. Cinematography: Mario Mancini.
Cast: Rossano Brazzi, Edmund Purdom, Michael Dunn, Gordon Mitchell, Christiane Royce [Christiane Rücker], Boris Lugosi [Salvatore Baccaro].

Who was responsible for this one, then? No one seems to be sure. The onscreen credit reads 'Produced and Directed by Robert H. Oliver', a pseudonym for Dick Randall (real name Irving Reuben) the exploitation specialist who brought us **For Y'ur Height Only** (1981), **Pieces** (1982), and **Don't Open Till Christmas** (1984). If this is true, that makes this his only directorial credit. It's also possible Randall left the shoot early and it was finished by director of photography Mario Mancini, but that information is also disputable. Not disputable is that the terrible music score is by Marcello Gigante and it's another reason to steer clear of this, a film in which the castle of Count Frankenstein (Rossano Brazzi, from 1958's **South Pacific**) seems to be situated near a colony of Neanderthals. Frankenstein kidnaps one. Another, Ook (played by 'Boris Lugosi' aka Salvatore Baccaro who would later pop up in **The Beast in Heat**) is befriended by Frankenstein's incompetent necrophilia-obsessed assistant Genz (Michael Dunn) who has been thrown out of the castle. None of what happens makes a lot of sense. Familiar face Luciano Pigozzi is on hand as another assistant. Less familiar starlets Simonetta Vitelli and Christiane Rücker play two well-to-do young ladies who need to take an awful lot of baths, during which the director (whoever they may be) engages in a shooting style pinched from the José Larraz school of voyeurism. It's all silly, slow-moving stuff. After this, Brazzi must have found taking on the Antichrist (in **The Final Conflict,** the third of the original **Omen** trilogy in 1981) a piece of cake.

The once-human horror waits in the attic ... for YOU to open the door!

HOUSE OF THE LIVING DEAD

Starring MARK BURNS · SHIRLEY ANNE FIELD DAVID OXLEY A PHILIP N. KRASNE production

HOUSE OF THE LIVING DEAD

South Africa, 1974
Director: Ray Austin. Producers: Matt Druker, Basil Rubin [Basil Rayburn].
Screenplay: Marc Marais. Music: Peter J. Elliott.
Cinematography: Lionel Friedberg.
Cast: Mark Burns, Shirley Anne Field, David Oxley, Margaret Inglis, Dia Sydow, Lynne Maree.

A rare attempt to film a 1960s Italian-style period Gothic on location in South Africa, starring Shirley Anne Field. She takes the Barbara Steele role as a bride-to-be who arrives at her intended's remote mansion only to find herself unwelcome, and faced by murder, voodoo, and a lunatic in the attic experimenting with trapping souls in jars. Director Ray Austin also made **Virgin Witch** (1971) for Tigon, and had a prolific career in television both as director and earlier on as stunt arranger, mainly on *The Avengers*. While he's no Riccardo Freda, Austin makes the most of the stunning locations and gets vigorous performances from his leads. Mark Burns, in a rare starring role among a lengthy career playing character parts, gives it his all. Especially during the full-on climax that comes complete with organ music playing, the keyboard soaked with blood, and lots and lots of screaming from Miss Field, who ends up being so suited to the material one wonders what Hammer could have done with her. Originally filmed as **Skaduwees Oor Brugplass (Shadows Over Bridge Place)**, the film is also known as **Doctor Maniac**, with its best-known title an obvious cash-in on George Romero's **Night of the Living Dead** (1968). There are no zombies but there is a murder committed by a ghost horse and that alone makes this one unmissable.

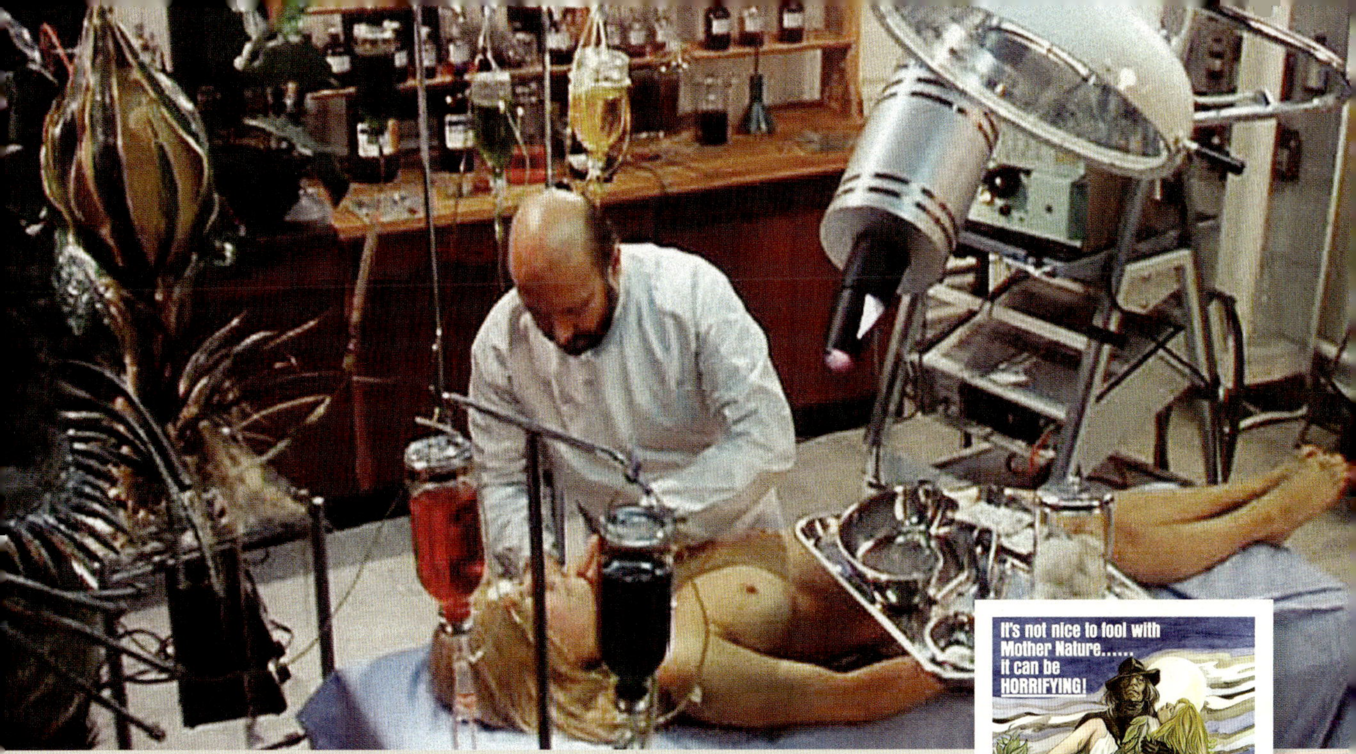

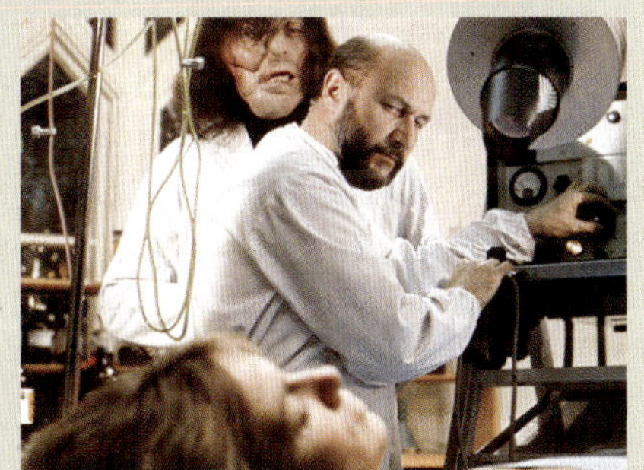

THE MUTATIONS

UK, 1974
Director: Jack Cardiff.
Producer: Robert D. Weinbach. Screenplay: Robert D. Weinbach, Edward Mann. Music: Basil Kirchin. Cinematography: Paul Beeson. Cast: Donald Pleasence, Tom Baker, Michael Dunn, Brad Harris, Julie Ege, Scott Antony.

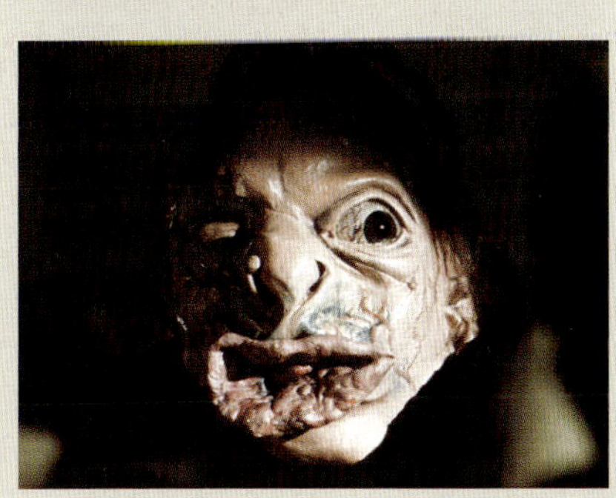

In the make-believe world of 1960s-1970s British horror, the imaginary landlord of Oakley Court must have made a fortune renting it out to mad scientists, sexy vampire ladies, and transsexual visitors from another planet, to name just a few. In 1974 it was the turn (for a couple of weeks at least) of Dr. Nolter (Donald Pleasence), university lecturer by day and converter of topless ladies and Scott Antony into vegetable monsters by night. He doesn't get his hands on Jill Haworth but he does manage to turn poor Olga Anthony into something green and rubbery. When he's not turning people into Venus fly traps for the usual misguided 'good of mankind' the doctor's feeding rabbits to something that looks like a tatty trial run for Audrey II in Frank Oz's **Little Shop of Horrors** (1986). Possibly inspired by somebody somewhere having a lot of time lapse photography of plants and the rights to some Basil Kirchin records (there's a lot of both in this). A fairground plays a large part and is just as grim and miserable as 1970s British fairgrounds tended to be. Tom Baker, just pre-*Doctor Who* and plastered in 'ugly' make-up, runs the fair with TV's *The Wild Wild West* star Michael Dunn (who died aged 38 after shooting his scenes for this). World famous, highly respected Oscar-winning cinematographer Jack Cardiff directed this grainy, sleazy mixture of Soho prostitutes, real circus freaks, and utterly daft science, which presumably must have made a nice change from working on all those Hollywood 'A' features.

YOUNG FRANKENSTEIN

USA, 1974
Director: Mel Brooks. Producer: Michael Gruskoff. Screenplay: Gene Wilder, Mel Brooks.
Music: John Morris. Cinematography: Gerald Hirschfeld.
Cast: Gene Wilder, Peter Boyle, Marty Feldman, Madeline Kahn, Cloris Leachman, Teri Garr.

Just as the original black and white series of Universal Horrors had petered out into Abbott and Costello comedies a couple of decades earlier, by 1974 the Gothic horror boom pioneered by Hammer and significantly contributed to by Roger Corman and AIP in the US and Mario Bava and Riccardo Freda in Italy, was coming to an end. Mel Brooks, on the other hand, was about to have arguably the best year of his career with **Blazing Saddles** and this, a film allegedly conceived over a cup of coffee with co-star Gene Wilder during the final days of shooting of his Western spoof. Filmed in black and white and utilising some of the original laboratory equipment designed by Kenneth Strickfaden for Universal's 1931 **Frankenstein**, Brooks' film is more an affectionate comedy tribute to the films of forty years earlier than a mickey take of the more recent Gothic resurgence. Wilder plays the Baron with Peter Boyle as the Monster. Add in a rendition of the song and dance number 'Puttin' on the Ritz' (Wilder's idea), and Marty Feldman as Igor (the role was especially written for him), and you have a film that's as funny as it is knowledgeable about classic movies as it was inspiring to some of those who viewed it. (Feldman's line "Walk this way" allegedly inspired the Aerosmith song after the band went to see the movie.) No wonder it was a huge success.

ILSA, SHE-WOLF OF THE SS

Canada, 1975
Director: Don Edmonds. Producer: Herman Traeger [David F. Friedman].
Screenplay: Jonah Royston [John Saxton]. Cinematography: Glen Rowland [Glenn Roland].
Cast: Dyanne Thorne, Sandy Richman, Jo Jo Deville, Gregory Knoph, Tony Mumolo, Wolfgang Roehm [Richard Kennedy].

And so it came to pass that a film from Canada became responsible for an entire genre commonly known as Nazisploitation and charitably described as 'in poor taste'. Most such movies combine elements of the women in prison genre popularised by the films of Roger Corman and Jack Hill (1971's **The Big Doll House** and 1972's **The Big Bird Cage**) with added scenes of torture and excess. **Ilsa**, produced by David F. Friedman (as Herman Traeger) and directed by Don Edmonds (who returned for the first of three sequels, 1976's **Isla, Harem Keeper of the Oil Sheiks**) stars Dyanne Thorne as the title character, in charge of torturing inmates of both sexes at a death camp conducting 'medical experiments', frequently having sex with the suitable male ones beforehand. Joe Blasco, who provided the special make-up effects for David Cronenberg's **Shivers** and **Rabid**, was on hand to make sure the results of Ilsa's handiwork was suitably stomach churning. Italian filmmakers leapt on the bandwagon of the film's success, resulting in such notorious titles as **The Beast in Heat** (1977) directed by 'Ivan Katansky' – actually Luigi Batzella of **The Devil's Wedding Night** (1973) and **Nude for Satan** (1974) fame – and Cesare Canevari's **The Gestapo's Last Orgy** (1977).

THE ROCKY HORROR PICTURE SHOW

UK/USA, 1975
Director: Jim Sharman. Producer: Michael White. Screenplay: Jim Sharman, Richard O'Brien. Music: Richard O'Brien, Richard Hartley. Cinematography: Peter Suschitzky. Cast: Tim Curry, Susan Sarandon, Barry Bostwick, Richard O'Brien, Jonathan Adams, Nell Campbell.

It's hard to believe now, but on its initial release **The Rocky Horror Picture Show** wasn't much of a success. Journals like *Cinefantastique* did praise the Ken Russell-style design of Frank N. Furter's laboratory (all pink bathroom tiling) and Tim Curry's performance, in which he effortlessly achieved the most abrupt and wildest swings from gentle femininity to full-on masculine bellowing, but it was some time before the film picked up a following on the midnight movie circuit. The combination of movie references, toe-tapping songs, and a cast of unknowns who looked born to play their roles (and for all audiences knew, behaved like that all the time anyway) meant that the film eventually gained a reputation for being a good night out, especially when the audience participation screenings kicked in. Coming at the very tail end of the British horror film boom (it was even filmed in part at Oakley Court), as a theatrical experience the film remains unique. Creator Richard O'Brien and co-writer and director Jim Sharman were unable to recapture any of its magic in their subsequent **Shock Treatment** (1981). Later O'Brien stated that this was due to Sharman having no interest in doing something similar, and especially not wanting to make **The Revenge of the Old Queen**, the direct sequel to **Rocky** that O'Brien had been preparing, which remains a tantalising 'what might have been'.

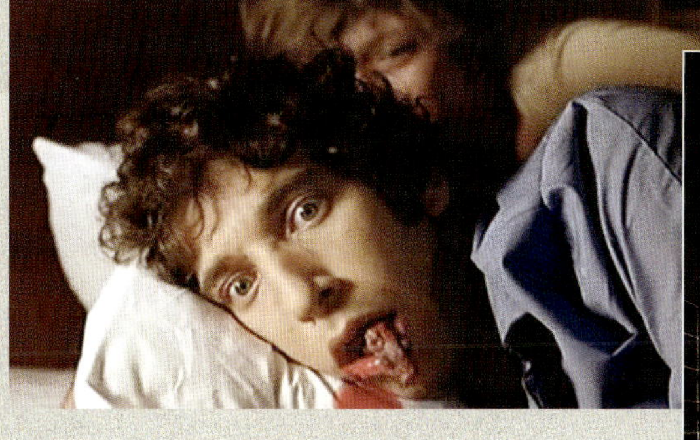

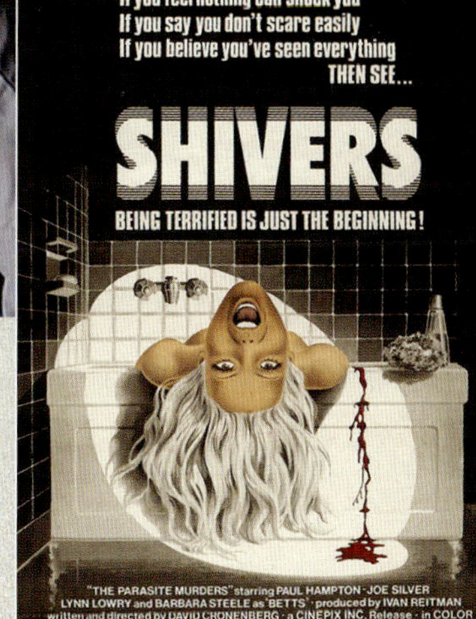

SHIVERS

Canada, 1975
Director: David Cronenberg.
Producer: Ivan Reitman. Screenplay: David Cronenberg. Cinematography: Robert Saad.
Cast: Paul Hampton, Joe Silver, Lynn Lowry, Allan Migicovsky [Allan Kolman], Susan Petrie, Barbara Steele.

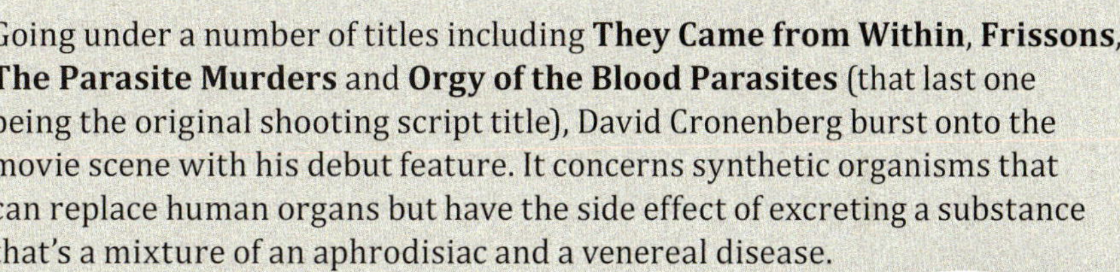

Going under a number of titles including **They Came from Within**, **Frissons**, **The Parasite Murders** and **Orgy of the Blood Parasites** (that last one being the original shooting script title), David Cronenberg burst onto the movie scene with his debut feature. It concerns synthetic organisms that can replace human organs but have the side effect of excreting a substance that's a mixture of an aphrodisiac and a venereal disease.

The parasites, rather uncomfortably resembling bowel movements, were created by special effects designer Joe Blasco, who also worked on two of the **Ilsa** movies as well as Cronenberg's 1977 follow-up **Rabid**. He animated them via a mixture of finger puppetry and running them along fishing line. Cronenberg based his screenplay on a dream he had. A problem with the film processing meant that rushes weren't available during the first few days of shooting, Despite having made short projects that approached feature length (**Stereo** in 1969 and **Crimes of the Future** in 1970) when Cronenberg eventually saw the first day's work he was hugely disappointed with the result, claiming that if the day two and three footage (which was better) hadn't been there it would have destroyed his confidence in directing the project. Future **Ghostbusters** director Ivan Reitman was one of the producers and also put together the 'needle drop' library scores for both **Shivers** and **Rabid**, which included composer David Lindup's famous 'Trap Door' cue, perhaps best known for heralding the arrival of *Monty Python*'s Spanish Inquisition.

EMBRYO

USA, 1976
Director: Ralph Nelson. Producers: Anita Doohan, Arnold H. Orgolini. Screenplay: Anita Doohan, Jack W. Thomas. Music: Gil Mellé.
Cinematography: Fred J. Koenekamp.
Cast: Rock Hudson, Diane Ladd, Barbara Carrera, Roddy McDowall, Anne Schedeen, John Elerick.

Modern cinema has a predilection for claiming its stories are 'based on true events', but even back in the 1970s one could come across the occasional opening caption claiming that 'this could really happen'. To open **Embryo** we have one from a Charles R. Brinkman III M.D. (who it turns out in the end credits is a UCLA gynaecologist). Rock Hudson's research doctor runs over a pregnant Doberman but is able to save one of her puppies, which demonstrates hugely accelerated growth as a result of his treatments. Instead of getting the incredibly well-trained adult dog to rob a bank à la Byron Chudnow's **The Doberman Gang,** he then creates Barbara Carrera in his lab using the same principles – human placental lactogen to speed up growth (which makes mad movie science sense) and methotrexate (a drug commonly used to treat rheumatoid arthritis) to slow it down (which is rather dafter but proves someone behind the scenes is at least thinking about what might actually work). Director Ralph Nelson is best known for the ultra-violent Western **Soldier Blue** (1970) and he delivers a slick, glossy, and entertaining potboiler, in which all the main participants (Roddy McDowall pops up to play chess, Diane Ladd's on hand to irritate Hudson's creation) are more famous for appearing in other movies.

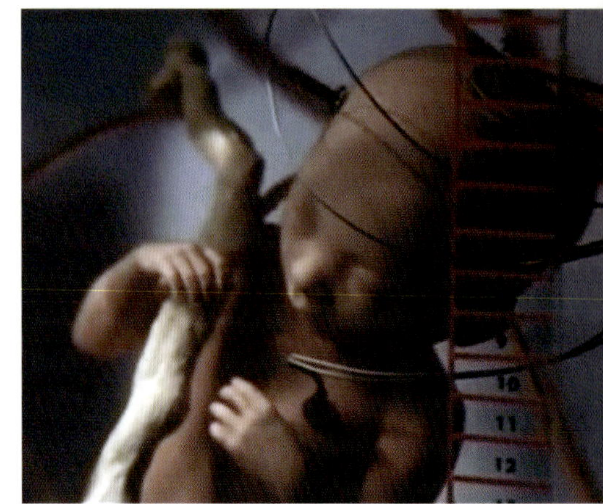

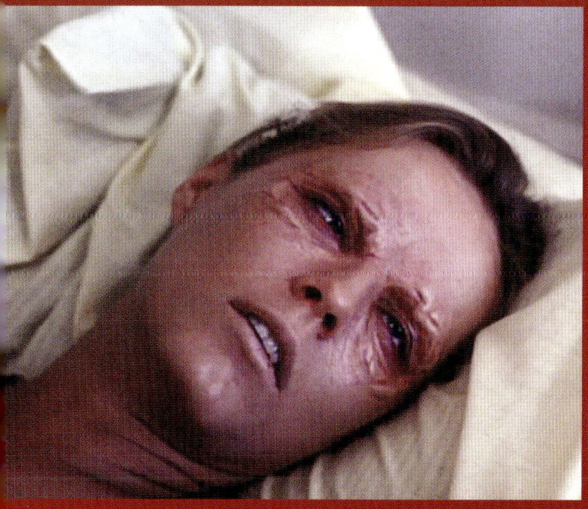

MANSION OF THE DOOMED

USA, 1976
Director: Michael Pataki.
Producer: Charles Band.
Screenplay: Frank Ray Perilli.
Music: Robert O. Ragland.
Cinematography: Andrew Davis.
Cast: Richard Basehart,
Trish Stewart, Gloria Grahame,
Lance Henriksen, Al Ferrara,
JoJo D'Amore.

This American exploitation take on Franju's **Les yeux sans visage** stars Richard Basehart a few years on from his most famous role as Admiral Nelson in the TV series *Voyage to the Bottom of the Sea*. Basehart plays Dr. Chaney (**The Terror of Dr. Chaney** was the film's UK title), a surgeon who has caused his daughter to lose her sight in a car accident. Now he kidnaps people and removes their eyeballs in the hope of effecting a successful transplant. The procedures work for a while but her sight inevitably then deteriorates. Eyeball removal is not a fatal operation and so Dr. Chaney also has a cellar full of blind victims that he has to keep locked up. Featuring an early role for Lance Henriksen as a doctor who is Chaney's assistant but ends up in the cellar anyway, the key personnel responsible behind the scenes have quite the exploitation pedigree. The producer was Charles Band, future Empire and Full Moon Pictures impresario. Screenwriter Frank Ray Perilli performed similar duties on 1977's **Zoltan... Hound of Dracula** which starred Michael Pataki, director of **Mansion of the Doomed** and better known as a character actor whose horror credits included 1972's **Grave of the Vampire,** and Gary Sherman's 1981 **Dead and Buried.**

SS EXPERIMENT CAMP

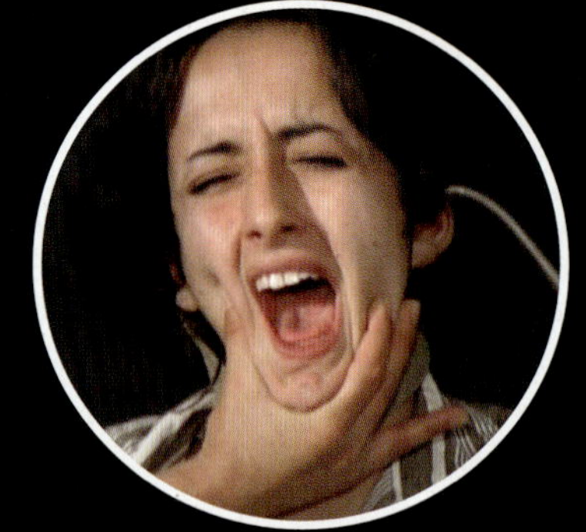

Italy, 1976
Director: Sergio Garrone. Screenplay: Sergio Garrone, Vinicio Marinucci. Music: Vasili Kojucharov, Roberto Pregadio. Cinematography: Maurizio Centini.
Cast: Paola Coruzzi, Mircha Carven, Giorgio Cerioni, Serafino Profumo, Patrizia Melega, Almina De Sanzio.

Among the most notorious of the Nazisploitation films kickstarted (presumably with a jackboot) by **Ilsa, She Wolf of the SS** the previous year, the video box cover art of Sergio Garrone's **SS Experiment Camp** added considerable fuel to the UK's video nasty outrage of the early-1980s. The plot concerns itself with sexual experimentation in a women's prison camp, while the colonel in charge is in need of a testicle transplant after he is subjected to a bilateral orchidectomy (that's the actual surgical term for having both one's testicles removed) by a Russian prisoner. Garrone's movie is in as poor taste as its colleagues in cinematic shame, with its scenes of women being incinerated perhaps the most laughable of its poorly rendered onscreen atrocities.

INFERNO CARNAL

Brazil, 1977
Director: José Mojica Marins. Producer: José Mojica Marins. Screenplay: Rubens Francisco Luchetti. Music: Solon Curvelo. Cinematography: Giorgio Attili.
Cast: José Mojica Marins, Luely Figueiró, Oswaldo De Souza, Helena Ramos, Lirio Bertelli, Mauro Russo.

A Brazilian oddity from the often strange and frequently unpleasant mind of writer producer, director, and actor José Mojica Marins (famous for his Ze Do Caixão, or Coffin Joe, series of sadistic melodramas in which he fulfils all the above roles). **Inferno carnal** takes us to a world of big-haired ladies and abysmally loud furniture to deliver Marins' version of a conte cruel. Marins is Dr. George Medeiros, a seemingly mild-mannered, cardigan-wearing pipe-smoking scientist whose wife Raquel is having an affair with his best friend Oliver. The two decide they can't be apart any longer, so rather than get a divorce Raquel throws acid in George's face and Oliver sets fire to George's laboratory. George gets taken to hospital where we are treated to some actual eye surgery (it looks as if they're removing a sliver of metal) in graphic detail. George is discharged from hospital with his face looking like a cross between Cropsy from **The Burning** and the scary mask used by Baird Stafford in Romano Scavolini's **Nightmares in a Damaged Brain** (both 1981 and both coincidentally prosecuted as 'video nasties' in the UK). Raquel, consumed by guilt, begs George to take her back, picks up a jar of acid that just happens to be sitting on the dining room table and empties it all over her own face. Off she goes to hospital for some plastic surgery that doesn't work at all. She is discharged and comes back to the family home, where the acid-scarred wife comes face to face with her acid-scarred husband. The best is yet to come. George isn't scarred at all! He's wearing a mask! "The acid you threw at me was much weaker than what you poured on yourself," he sneers as his beautiful girlfriend Virginia walks in. George embraces Virginia and, as the two of them prepare to go out to the theatre, he orders his acid-scarred wife to be thrown out onto the street. "What's the play about darling?" asks Virginia as the immaculately-attired couple prepare to leave. "Oh infidelity," he replies, "as so many stories are these days." Despite being a bit rough around the edges (the credits look like a five-year-old's school arts and crafts project) **Inferno carnal** does an excellent job of emulating the style of the conte cruel and serves as one of Marins' better, more watchable efforts.

THE ISLAND OF DR. MOREAU

USA, 1977
Director: Don Taylor.
Producers: Skip Steloff, John Temple-Smith.
Screenplay: Al Ramrus, John Herman Shaner,
Richard Alan Simmons [uncredited].
Music: Laurence Rosenthal. Cinematography: Gerry Fisher.
Cast: Burt Lancaster, Michael York, Nigel Davenport,
Barbara Carrera, Richard Basehart, Nick Cravat.

Here's a surprise – a late-1970s Samuel Z. Arkoff production that doesn't feature giant ants or enormous chickens. Destined to live forever sandwiched between the shadows of its marvellous predecessor (Erle Kenton's 1932 **Island of Lost Souls**) and the quite unbelievable 1996 Marlon Brando remake, yet Don Taylor's 1977 version of the H.G. Wells novel is actually perfectly respectable and, while it takes a few liberties with its source material, is never less than interesting to watch. The screenplay, by Taylor associates John Herman Shaner and Al Ramrus (they did uncredited rewrites on the script to the 1978 sequel **Damien: Omen II** for Taylor after he took over the project), dispenses with any shenanigans aboard the Lady Vain, and gets Michael York's character of Andrew Braddock to the island as soon as the credits are over. His shipwrecked companions are swiftly dispensed with, and Braddock finds himself being looked after in the jungle compound of Dr. Moreau (Burt Lancaster). Lancaster's interpretation of Moreau is radically different from Charles Laughton's but is no less fascinating. In fact, his low key softly-spoken demeanour is perhaps all the more terrifying because he seems such a nice and reasonable chap even though we know what he's doing is actually obscene. As versions go, this one's not bad, and stratospherically better than the Marlon Brando one. Even **Superbeast** is better than the Brando one.

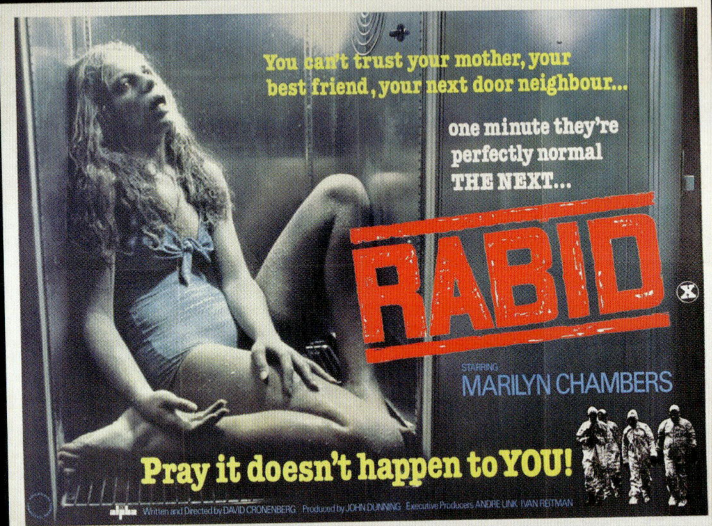

RABID

Canada, 1977
Director: David Cronenberg.
Producer: John Dunning. Screenplay: David Cronenberg. Cinematography: René Verzier.
Cast: Marilyn Chambers, Frank Moore, Joe Silver, Patricia Gage, Susan Roman, Howard Ryshpan.

When Rose (Marilyn Chambers) is injured in a motorcycle accident, her only chance for surviving lies with the only nearby hospital. Unfortunately, it's the David Cronenberg Keloid Plastic Surgery Clinic for Wildly New and Untested Techniques That Could Prove Disastrous. Rose's intestines have been mangled by the motorbike and skin grafts are taken from her thighs, denatured, and implanted within her, in an attempt to encourage them to grow as new bowel tissue. Sadly, the denatured tissue decides to do its own thing and causes a blood sucking proboscis (the original title was **Mosquito**) to develop in Rose's armpit and she becomes a science fiction vampire. The clothes and hairstyles are period mid-1970s, but Cronenberg's dead serious approach to the science gives **Rabid** a timelessness that means it still packs a punch today. Allowed a broader canvas on which to cause biological mayhem than in 1975's **Shivers**, **Rabid** is a grim and humourless experience, and it's a testament to Cronenberg's skills that a scene in which Dr. Keloid looks at porn star Marilyn Chambers' breasts and says "The grafts appear to have healed well" isn't in the slightest bit funny. And even now, after **Videodrome**, **Crash** and especially **Dead Ringers** (1983, 1996, and 1988 respectively), **Rabid** still boasts arguably the most depressing and heart-breaking ending of any Cronenberg film.

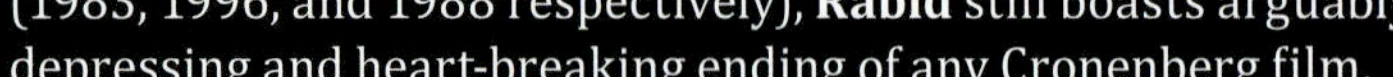

FEDORA

West Germany/France, 1978
Director: Billy Wilder. Producer: Billy Wilder.
Screenplay: Billy Wilder, I.A.L. Diamond.
Music: Miklós Rózsa. Cinematography: Gerry Fisher.
Cast: William Holden, Marthe Keller, José Ferrer, Frances Sternhagen, Mario Adorf, Stephen Collins.

It's likely that with **Fedora**, director Billy Wilder (with co-writer I.A.L. Diamond) was aiming for a commentary comparing Hollywood of the 1970s with 1940s Hollywood. While at the same time examining what a 'star' really is – a person or an elaborate construct that actually destroys lives? What he ended up with is something a little more lurid and unexpectedly entertaining for fans of 1970s European horror films. William Holden is on hand to give the film a **Sunset Boulevard** (1950) feel as he attends the funeral of movie star Fedora (Marthe Keller). He then narrates the events of the weeks leading up to it, when he travelled to Corfu to convince the reclusive star to appear in a new movie. It's there that the EuroHorror feel kicks in, with Fedora seemingly being kept prisoner in an isolated mansion by the kind of people usually seen in the more bonkers early-1970s Italian horrors. Even Fedora doesn't appear to be particularly sane, and may have been the subject of bizarre youth-enhancing experiments performed by disgraced Doctor Vando (José Ferrer, looking like he's having a lot more fun here than in the previous year's **Zoltan... Hound of Dracula**). Miklós Rózsa's score channels James Bernard, as the plot gets stranger and takes a right turn into **Les yeux sans visage** territory. Nowhere near as well-known as Wilder triumphs like 1960's **The Apartment** or 1970s' **The Private Life of Sherlock Holmes**, **Fedora** is worthy of equal attention if you're reading this book.

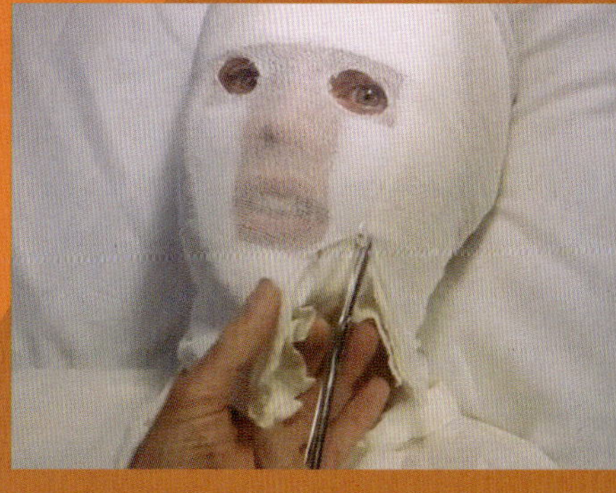

THE BROOD

Canada, 1979
Director: David Cronenberg.
Producer: Claude Héroux.
Screenplay: David Cronenberg.
Music: Howard Shore. Cinematography: Mark Irwin.
Cast: Oliver Reed, Samantha Eggar, Art Hindle, Cindy Hinds, Nuala Fitzgerald, Henry Beckman.

The film that David Cronenberg wrote as a reaction to his divorce is a cold, grim fascinating look at a broken family dynamic, while also further developing the unique themes of body horror the director had begun to explore with his previous two works, **Shivers** (1975) and **Rabid** (1977). It's a film in which the sun never shines – except ironically, so that father Frank (Art Hindle) can get a better look at the bruises on daughter Candice's (Cindy Hinds) back, after she has been beaten by the somatised products of his wife Nola's (Samantha Eggar's) rage. Oliver Reed is terrific in a restrained performance as mad scientist Dr. Raglan, who has developed the technique of psychoplasmics. He wasn't so restrained off set apparently, but then we wouldn't want to remember dear old Ollie any other way. **The Brood** also marked the first body horror collaboration between Cronenberg and many key personnel with whom he would work again, including director of photography Mark Irwin, art director Carol Spier and composer Howard Shore. The UK press book for **The Brood** tried to sell the film by including several blurry black and white photographs of audiences shocked reactions to the film, while also reminding distributors that the film came paired with British period Sadean co-feature **Cruel Passion**.

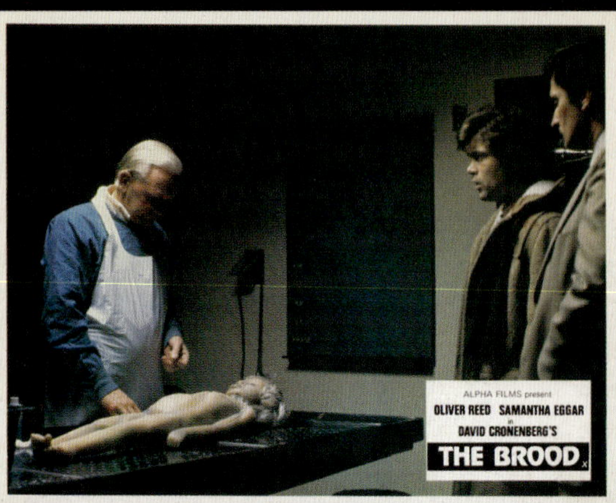

DR. JEKYLL'S DUNGEON OF DEATH

USA, 1979
Director: James Wood.
Producer: James Wood. Screenplay: James Mathers.
Music: Marty Allen. Cinematography: James Wood.
Cast: James Mathers, John F. Kearney, Dawn Carver Kelly, Nadine Kalmes, Jake Pearson, Tom Nicholson.

One of the darkest films you will ever see – quite literally. Indeed, even with the benefit of a 2K Blu-ray transfer it can be difficult at times to work out exactly what is going on, in this tale of a descendant of the original Dr. Jekyll living in San Francisco in 1959. This doctor is at work on an 'aggression' serum which he tests on the subjects that his Morpho-like henchman brings to the house. All of them seem to have been trained in martial arts and the interminably lengthy fighting sequences that ensue will try even the most patient of viewers. Jekyll has given his sister Hilda a lobotomy and the mute eye-rolling performance from the actress who plays her (Nadine Kalmes) is the most restrained in the picture. Little is known about producer, director, cinematographer, and editor 'James Wood'. Apparently, this is the only non 'X-rated' film he made. The room in which all the violence takes place will remind Cronenberg fans of the TV show set from **Videodrome**. Those concerned may wish to check their brain for tumours after watching this. Nice final shot, though. It's on the poster if you look hard enough so you still don't have to watch this.

TIME AFTER TIME

USA, 1979
Director: Nicholas Meyer.
Producer: Herb Jaffe. Screenplay: Nicholas Meyer.
Music: Miklós Rózsa. Cinematography: Paul Lohmann.
Cast: Malcolm McDowell, David Warner, Charles Cioffi, Mary Steenburgen, Kent Williams, Andonia Katsaros.

Malcolm McDowell, chilling out a little after appearing in Bob Guccione's **Caligula** (1979), takes the part of H.G. Wells. He's chasing David Warner's Jack the Ripper (aka Dr. John Stevenson) to the accompaniment of a lush Miklós Rózsa score, ending up in contemporary New York, in director Nicholas Meyer's time travel fantasy. Rarely has a film been so perfectly placed in a filmmaker's filmography, preceded as this one was by Herbert Ross' **The Seven-Per-Cent Solution** (1976), a Sherlock Holmes adventure for which Meyer wrote the screenplay, followed by scripting science fiction adventure **Star Trek II: The Wrath of Khan** (1982). It wasn't until director Leonard Nimoy's **Star Trek IV: The Voyage Home** (1986) that Meyer, called in to write the sequences set on earth, was once again afforded the opportunity to exercise the satirical wit about modern life that's also very much in evidence in **Time After Time**. McDowell plays the fish out of water hero with just the right mixture of confidence and sympathy, thankfully not emulating the speaking voice of the real H.G. Wells (apparently it was high-pitched and squeaky with a Southeast London accent). While David Warner – far more suitable to the role than studio's original preference Mick Jagger – is the perfect Victorian Gentleman Psychopath. A delight.

ALTERED STATES

USA, 1980
Director: Ken Russell. Producer: Howard Gottfried.
Screenplay: Sidney Aaron [Paddy Chayefsky].
Music: John Corigliano.
Cinematography: Jordan Cronenweth.
Cast: William Hurt, Blair Brown, Bob Balaban,
Charles Haid, Thaao Penghlis, Dori Brenner.

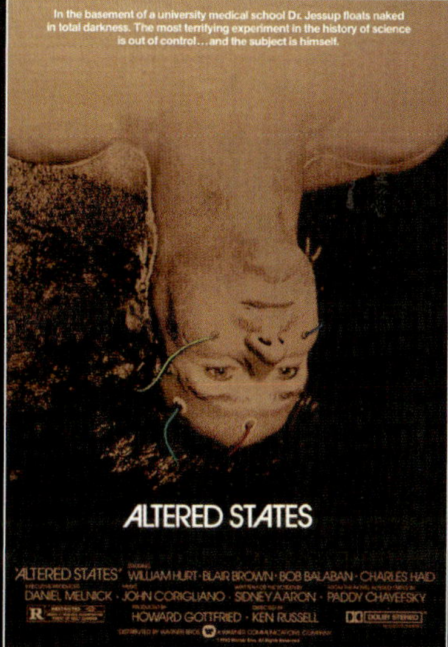

William Hurt's Dr. Edward Jessup uses a combination of sensory deprivation and a distillate of Mexican magic mushrooms in an attempt to awaken the more primitive parts of his DNA, in Ken Russell's adaptation of Paddy Chayefsky's novel of the same name. Mr. Chayefsky wasn't too happy with the end result, which is why the screenplay is credited to 'Sidney Aaron', a Chayefsky pseudonym. It's a shame he didn't like it because, for a modern science fiction twist on *Dr. Jekyll and Mr. Hyde*, Russell's film still holds up remarkably well. Largely thanks to the director's arresting and unique use of imagery, sensitive performances from Hurt and Blair Brown as his anthropologist wife, and special effects from Dick Smith, Carl Fullerton, and Craig Reardon. (Fullerton would go on to work very successfully with Smith on Tony Scott's 1983 cult flick **The Hunger**.) **Altered States** even steals a little from Hammer's 1961 **The Curse of the Werewolf** with its idea that as long as our metamorphosing central character is with the woman he loves, she can quell his transformation. The only real misstep is the ending. After Jessop has alluded repeatedly to how – Ray Milland **The Man with the X-Ray Eyes**-style – his experiments have allowed him to see the horror that lurks at the centre of the universe, and after all those wonderful fiery visuals (some of them footage from Henry Lachman's 1935 **Dante's Inferno**), the film more or less just stops. Mind you, we probably need more movies about how love can make mad scientists all better.

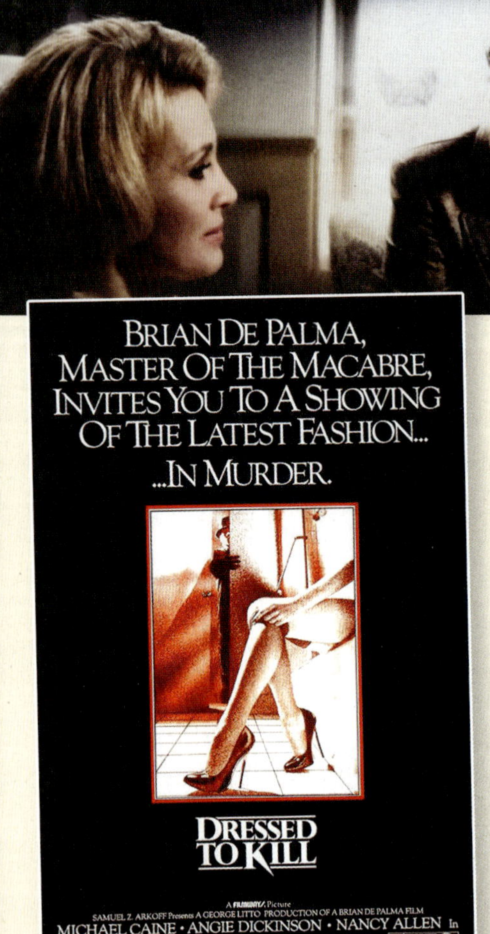

DRESSED TO KILL

USA, 1980
Director: Brian De Palma. Producer: George Litto.
Screenplay: Brian De Palma. Music: Pino Donaggio.
Cinematography: Ralf D. Bode.
Cast: Michael Caine, Angie Dickinson, Nancy Allen, Keith Gordon, Dennis Franz, David Margulies.

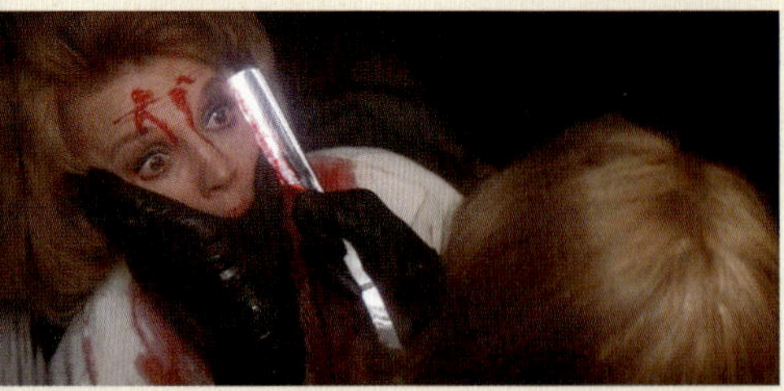

Brian De Palma's Hitchcock-fuelled cross-dressing psycho thriller was met with a lot of hate on its original release, with claims of misogyny being bandied about by critics of the time. Angie Dickinson's murder in the lift is supremely horrible – in fact it's one of the great operatic moments of horror cinema – and a major reason for this is because we've come to like and sympathise with her beforehand. In fact, if anything it's men who get a far rougher portrayal in this movie than the women. The male characters in the world of **Dressed to Kill** are either beer-swilling useless insensitive bores (poor old husband Ted), geeks (son Peter), STD-infected lotharios (the chap from the museum), or nutters (guess who). Today, as De Palma himself has acknowledged, the film would be more likely to be charged with being transphobic. But at the end of the day, in the unreal world of the giallo (because it is, come on, of course it is) the individual characters don't matter as much as the overall style of the piece. It's a testament to De Palma's skill as a filmmaker that **Dressed to Kill** doesn't stand up to repeat viewing from a logical viewpoint (the plot cheats all over the place, often so blatantly you can't help but see De Palma evincing a cheeky grin while filming it) but nevertheless it's a film you have to see several times to appreciate the sheer technical accomplishment of the piece, as well as the many subtleties that you may miss the first time around.

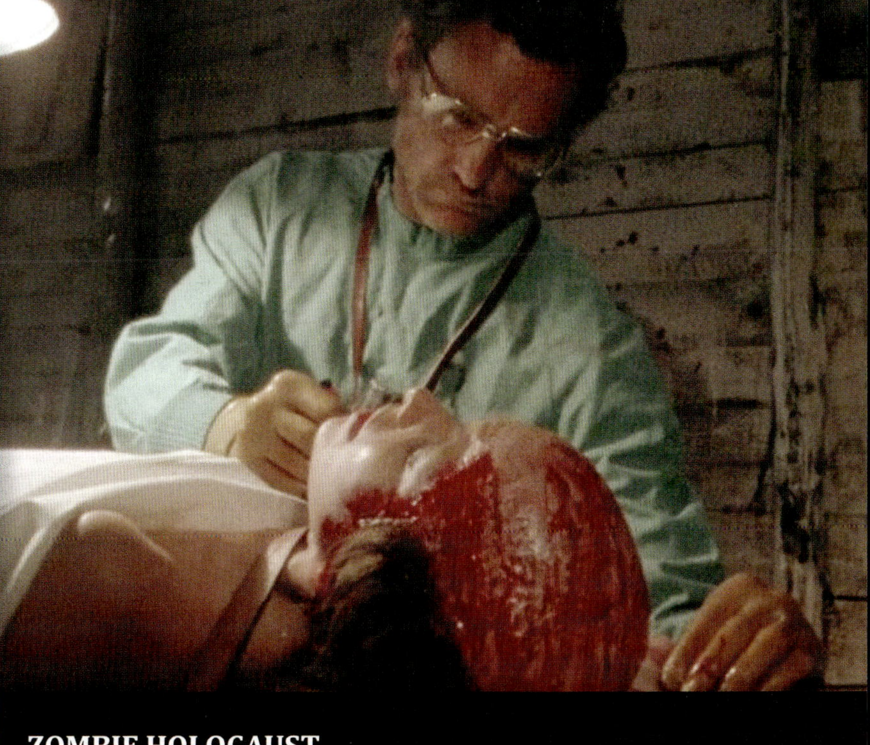

ZOMBIE HOLOCAUST

Italy, 1980
Director: Frank Martin [Marino Girolami]. Producers: Gianfranco Couyoumdjian, Fabrizio De Angelis. Screenplay: Romano Scandariato. Music: Nino Fidenco. Cinematography: Fausto Zuccoli. Cast: Ian McCulloch, Alexandra Delli Colli, Sherry Buchanan, Peter O'Neal, Donald O'Brien, Dakar.

Time to journey to the jolly, knockabout, randomly plotted world of the post-**Dawn of the Dead** (1978) and indeed post-**Zombie Flesh-Eaters** (1979) Italian zombie movie, with a film with its severed finger so on the pulse of current movie trends of the time that it was changed halfway through from being a cannibal movie to a zombie film, when the cinema-going public showed more of a predilection for the latter. Going out in the US under the title **Doctor Butcher M.D.** (helpfully subtitled 'Medical Deviate'), the plot sees one-time 'most banned man in Britain' (video cassette-wise at least, including this one) Ian McCulloch journeying once again to the back of the tropical beyond to discover why body parts are being stolen from a New York hospital. Mad doctor Donald O'Brien is conducting intricate brain surgery experiments in a ratty old shed, which might go some way to explaining why they're not working very well. Journalist Sherry Buchanan talks too much so the doctor severs her vocal cords. Shorn of its blood, guts, and nudity (including Alexandra Delli Colli being pronounced 'queen of the cannibals') Marino Girolami's film bears a considerable similarity to routine 1940s B-movie jungle adventure programmers. Thank heavens they put plenty of all those things in, then.

THE HOUSE BY THE CEMETERY

Italy, 1981
Director: Lucio Fulci. Producer: Fabrizio De Angelis.
Screenplay: Dardano Sacchetti, Giorgio Mariuzzo, Lucio Fulci.
Music: Walter Rizzati. Cinematography: Sergio Salvati.
Cast: Catriona MacColl, Giovanni De Nava, Paolo Malco, Giovanni Frezza, Silvia Collatina, Dagmar Lassander.

We knew we could rely on good old Lucio Fulci to give us not just a mad doctor but one who's also one of the living dead, creeping around his cellar doing truly horrible things, in what is also one of the best haunted house movies ever. Somehow Fulci manages to combine the ideas from Dan Curtis' **The Night Strangler** (1973) and the works of Henry James with extreme gore, and still ends up with a film that owes much of its effectiveness to its subtlety. Who is the insectoid Dr. Freudstein? How does he 'renew his cells' in that grim and grimy basement abattoir of his? Never mind because that's not important. Instead, sit back and allow this one's nightmarish atmosphere to work its insidious magic, worming its way into your mind like the damp and cold that infests the old Freudstein house. Fulci's regular team are at the top of their game here, and there's a splendid score that surprisingly benefits from using the work of two different composers (Walter Rizzati and Alessandro Blonksteiner). Does little Bob escape into the past or some parallel dimension at the end? Who knows? Endlessly watchable and a classic of Italian horror cinema.

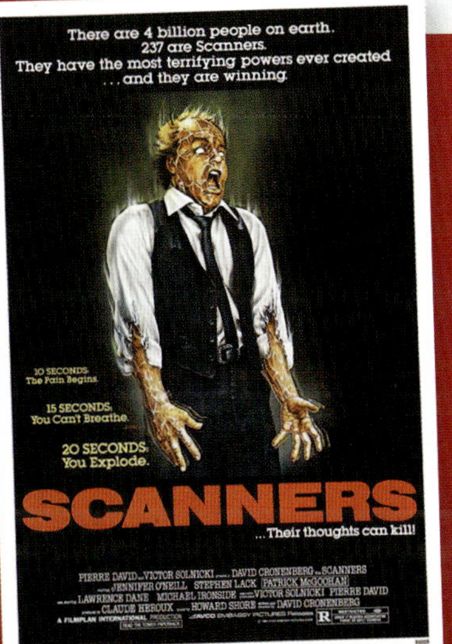

SCANNERS

Canada, 1981
Director: David Cronenberg. Producer: Claude Héroux.
Screenplay: David Cronenberg.
Music: Howard Shore. Cinematography: Mark Irwin.
Cast: Stephen Lack, Jennifer O'Neill, Michael Ironside, Patrick McGoohan, Lawrence Dane, Robert A. Silverman.

Famous as 'the exploding heads movie', with the first such scene originally planned to open the film. But director David Cronenberg moved the scene, in which the scanner underground lead Darryl Revok (Michael Ironside) causes a short-lived cast member's head to burst, further into the picture. Various reasons have been given for this, including to ensure late cinema attenders got to see it (IMDb), or because it was too much too early on and audiences would still be traumatised while important plot points were being delivered. Coping with his biggest budget to date, Cronenberg also had to deal with star Jennifer O'Neill (and her agent) threatening to leave because cinematographer Mark Irwin was allegedly filming her unflatteringly. Cronenberg stood by his DP. Meanwhile, producer Pierre David, who during **The Brood** (1979) had marvelled at Oliver Reed's ability to drink the equivalent of half an off licence during an all-nighter but still be word perfect next morning, now encountered the same thing on **Scanners** with Patrick McGoohan. The success of the film eventually led to several sequels: **Scanners II: The New Order** (1991), **Scanners III: The Takeover** (1992), **Scanner Cop** (1994) and **Scanner Cop II** (1995). Neither Cronenberg nor his principal cast were involved with any of them, although Stephen Lack and Jennifer O'Neill's characters are name-checked in the second. Producer Pierre David was the only person from the original involved with these, and he also wrote and directed **Scanner Cop**.

STRANGE BEHAVIOR

New Zealand/Australia, 1981
Director: Michael Laughlin.
Producers: John Barnett,
Antony I. Ginnane. Screenplay:
Bill Condon, Michael Laughlin.
Music: Tangerine Dream.
Cinematography: Louis Horvath.
Cast: Michael Murphy, Dan Shor,
Louise Fletcher, Fiona Lewis,
Arthur Dignam, Dey Young.

Teenagers from the Illinois town of Galesberg (actually Auckland in New Zealand) are being turned into murderers by Dr. Le Sange (Arthur Dignam), who has been experimenting with mind control. Director Michael Laughlin's film was intended as the first in a trilogy of movies with 'Strange' in the title, but this was abandoned when the second, 1983's **Strange Invaders** didn't do well. **Strange Behavior** subsequently underwent a number of retitlings, including **Dead Kids**, **Human Experiments**, and **Small Town Massacre**, all of which were used in the UK within just a couple of years of each other. Whatever it's called, it's a quirky little horror film with an interesting cast, including Fiona Lewis in spiked heels and dragon lady hairdo as Le Sange's assistant, Michael Murphy (everything from 1970s **Count Yorga, Vampire** to **X-Men: The Last Stand** in 2006), and Oscar winner Louise Fletcher. The film was co-written by Bill Condon, who appears in the film and would go on to write and direct 1998's **Gods and Monsters** about the life and career of **Frankenstein** director James Whale. To date Laughlin has only directed one more film, 1985's **Mesmerized** with Jodie Foster. He probably remains best known for producing Monte Hellman's 1971 road movie **Two-Lane Blacktop**.

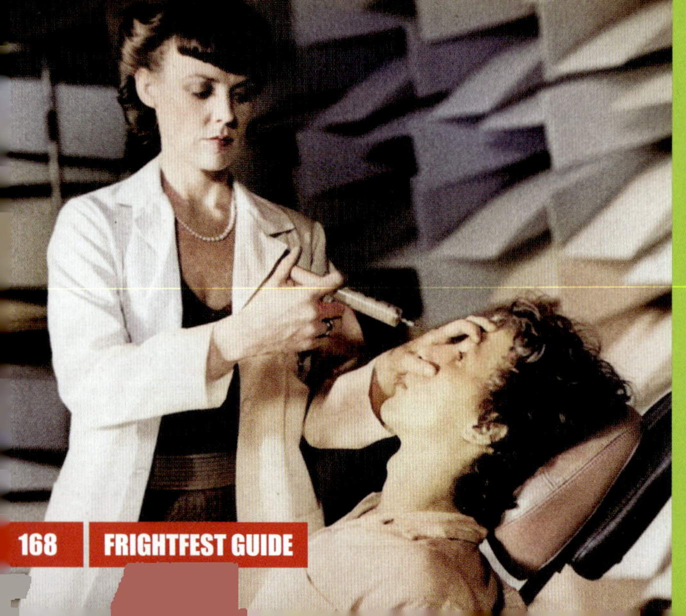

THE STRANGE CASE OF DR. JEKYLL AND MISS OSBOURNE

France, 1981
Director: Walerian Borowczyk. Producers: Robert Kuperberg, Jean-Pierre Labrande. Screenplay: Walerian Borowczyk. Music: Bernard Parmegiani. Cinematography: Noël Véry. Cast: Udo Kier, Marina Pierro, Patrick Magee, Gérard Zalcberg, Howard Vernon, Clément Harari.

In Victorian London guests converge at the house of Dr. Henry Jekyll (a thinner than thin Udo Kier) to celebrate his engagement to Fanny Osbourne (Marina Pierro, who looks as if she could quite comfortably put her screen fiancé under her arm and carry him off). The guests consist of, amongst others, a doctor (Jess Franco standby Howard Vernon), a military man (beautifully bonkers Patrick Magee, all in scarlet to match his face), and a priest. There are also various ladies who are due to end up in assorted states of undress and bloodedness. As the night goes on the house is invaded by the evil Mr. Hyde who proceeds to wreak havoc. Of course, we all know who this fellow actually is, so director Walerian Borowczyk sensibly doesn't waste time (or special effects) detailing Udo's transformation into an entirely different actor. As Dr. Jekyll's house guests end up the subjects of a catalogue of rape, flogging, and murder, the viewer is left to appreciate the renowned Polish director's singular take on the Dr. Jekyll tale, using it not only to trash Victorian society, but also suggesting that Mr. Hyde might actually be the hero of the tale (or at least the natural result of such repression), rather than the villain.

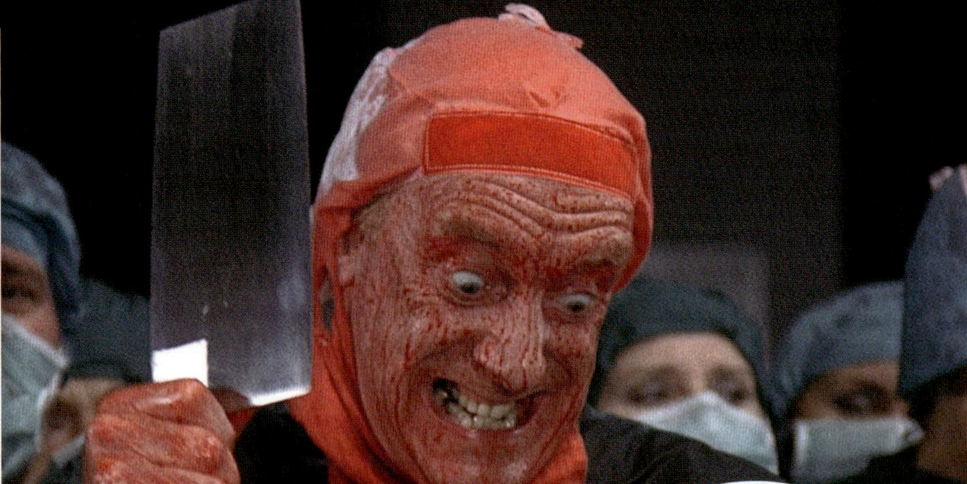

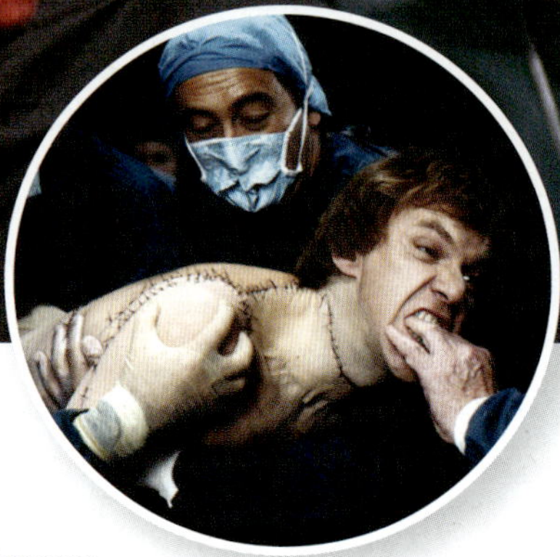

BRITANNIA HOSPITAL

UK, 1982
Director: Lindsay Anderson. Producers: Davina Belling, Clive Parsons. Screenplay: David Sherwin. Music: Alan Price. Cinematography: Mike Fash.
Cast: Leonard Rossiter, Graham Crowden, Malcolm McDowell, Joan Plowright, Jill Bennett, Marsha Hunt.

In one of the most memorable moments in **O Lucky Man!**, director Lindsay Anderson's 1973 odyssey through England, Mick Travis – Anderson's everyman character played by Malcolm McDowell – encountered the results of mad scientist Graham Crowden's experiments in the form of a huge human-guinea pig hybrid creature. Both Crowden and McDowell were back for **Britannia Hospital**, Anderson's next feature, with McDowell again playing Travis, and Crowden as a mad surgeon busy monster building (with the assistance of Jill Bennett) in the research wing of the NHS hospital that forms the main setting for this one. This time Travis is a television journalist whose head ends up on Crowden's Frankenstein-style creation. It's only on there for a few frames before it gets ripped off again courtesy of some fine Nick Maley (**Inseminoid** and **Lifeforce**) effects. The most overt scene of physical horror in a filmography known for its confrontational and satirical political comment, it's a shocking sequence in a film that, more than any of the movies made previously by its director, feels intended to rattle as many cages as possible. Anderson's final cinema feature film was the far gentler **The Whales of August** (1987), which starred Bette Davis and Lillian Gish and provided a fine supporting role for horror legend Vincent Price.

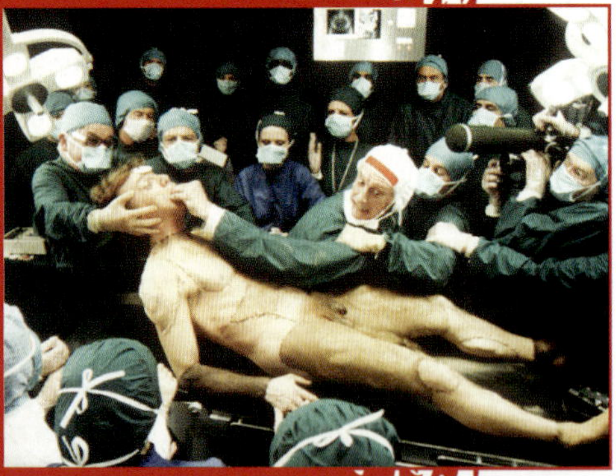

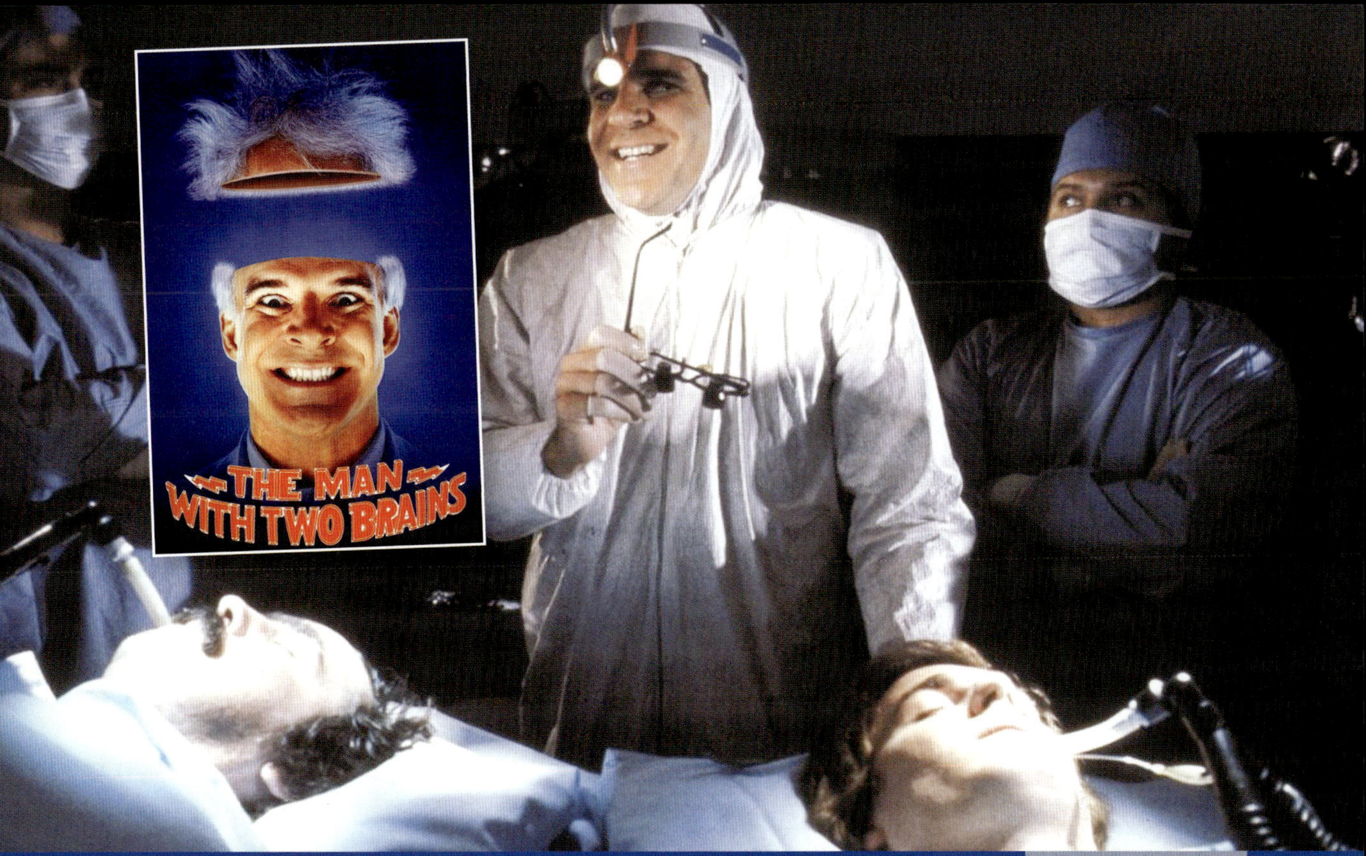

THE MAN WITH TWO BRAINS

USA, 1983
Director: Carl Reiner. Producers: William E. McEuen, David V. Picker.
Screenplay: George Gipe, Steve Martin, Carl Reiner.
Music: Joel Goldsmith. Cinematography: Michael Chapman.
Cast: Steve Martin, Kathleen Turner, David Warner, Paul Benedict, Richard Brestoff, James Cromwell.

By 1983, director Carl Reiner and star Steve Martin were on a roll, Reiner having directed Martin in the comedy actor's breakout movie **The Jerk** (1979), then following it up with 1982's **Dead Men Don't Wear Plaid**. The latter's a black and white film noir parody that intercut scenes from older movies, allowing Martin to 'interact' with classic stars of yesteryear such as Humphrey Bogart and Alan Ladd. Reiner and Martin's next feature was this, their brain transplant comedy in which Martin plays Dr. Michael Hfuhruhurr, who has pioneered the 'screw top' method of cranial surgery. After marrying gold-digging Kathleen Turner, he finds himself falling in love with the brain of Anne Uumellmahaye (voiced by an uncredited Sissy Spacek), currently resident in a jar. With a turn from David Warner as assistant Dr. Alfred Necessiter, a pre-**Re-Animator** Jeffrey Combs appearing way down the cast list, and a subplot involving elevator murders in Vienna, Reiner and Martin ensure the ensuing lunacy is kept under careful control. Most importantly they keep it funny, too. Their next combined effort, **All of Me** (1984) continued the fantastic flavour to their comedy, involving Lily Tomlin as a dying millionairess and Martin as her lawyer, with a plot concerning the (frequently accidental) transference of souls.

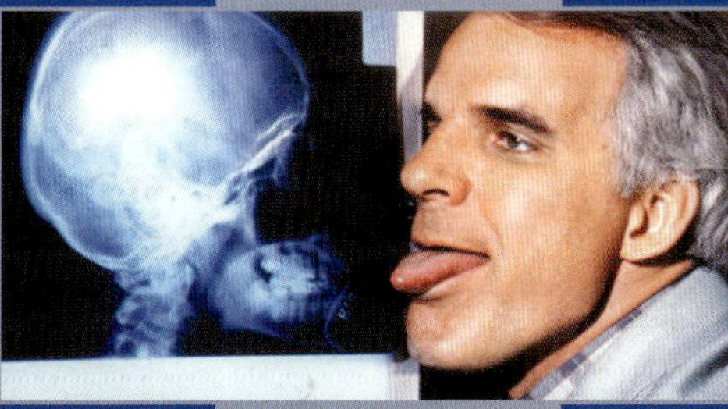

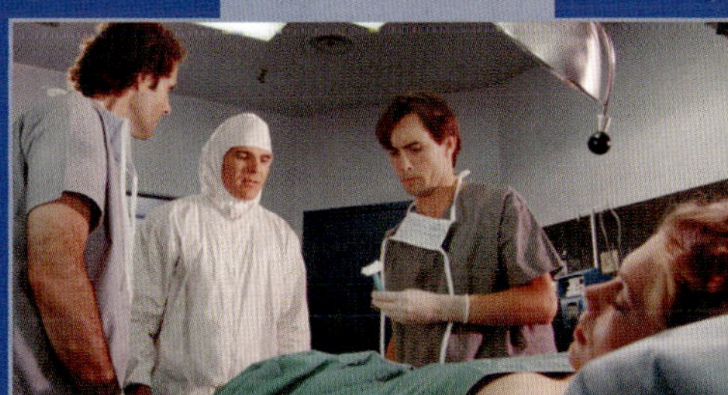

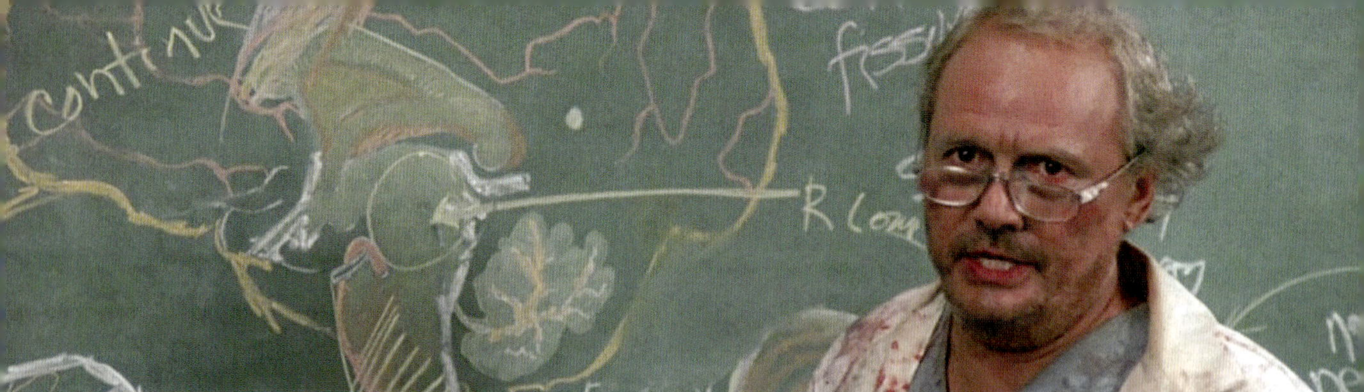

DAY OF THE DEAD

USA, 1985
Director: George A. Romero.
Producer: Richard P. Rubinstein. Screenplay: George A. Romero.
Music: John Harrison. Cinematography: Michael Gornick.
Cast: Lori Cardille, Terry Alexander, Joseph Pilato, Jarlath Conroy, Anthony Dileo Jr., Richard Liberty, Howard Sherman.

The third in director George A. Romero's 'Dead' series of zombie movies suffered from a severe reduction in budget just before shooting was due to begin. This was at least partly as a consequence of Romero's refusal to compromise with his initial investors, who demanded that the film he made have a sufficiently low quantity of splatter to allow it to qualify for the US 'R' rating. Romero stuck to his guns, rewrote the script, and as a result one of the things we get to see is the handiwork of post-apocalypse mad doctor Logan (Richard Liberty, who was also in Romero's 1973 germ warfare gone wrong picture **The Crazies**). He's dubbed 'Frankenstein' by the few military personnel left alive to guard the scientists researching the zombie plague in a government bunker. Logan's detailed dissections (shown in all their anatomical glory courtesy of Tom Savini's gloopily accurate effects) and attempts to psychologically 'rehabilitate' Bub (Howard Sherman) the zombie he is yet to take apart, all add to Romero's deadly serious approach to his subject matter. The confined setting and an excellent cast, playing characters who have all had enough of one another, ratchet up the tension to a prolonged and well-executed climax. **Day of the Dead** is a blood-splattered, gore-drenched thoughtful and thought-provoking horror classic, and arguably the best of Romero's zombie films.

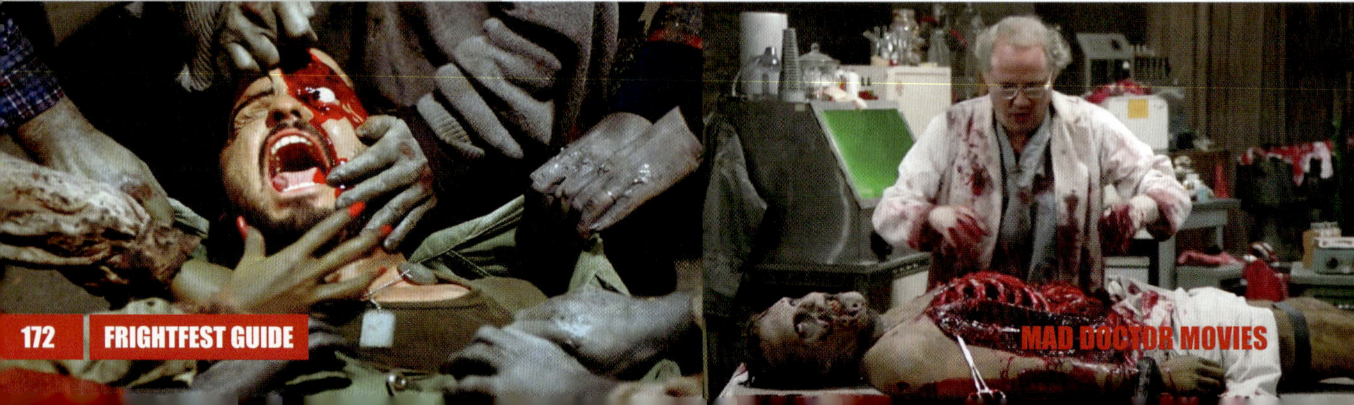

RE-ANIMATOR

USA, 1985
Director: Stuart Gordon. Producer: Brian Yuzna.
Screenplay: Dennis Paoli, William J. Norris, Stuart Gordon.
Music: Richard Band. Cinematography: Mac Ahlberg.
Cast: Jeffrey Combs, Bruce Abbott, Barbara Crampton, David Gale, Robert Sampson, Gerry Black.

A frenetic, frenzied approach to adapting Lovecraft that skilfully adds generous doses of humour and sex to produce a work of manic genius on a par with Herbert West himself, Stuart Gordon's **Re-Animator** made deserved instant stars (at least in the exploitation world) of some of its cast. Along with George A. Romero's contemporaneous **Day of the Dead** it also elevated the reputation of both mad scientist and zombie movies to new levels. The nifty screenplay takes the essence of Lovecraft's story (something Gordon and screenwriter Dennis Paoli would later do successfully with **Dagon**, their adaptation of *The Shadow Over Innsmouth*) and deftly turns something pretty turgid (try reading it) into one of the classics of the genre. Gordon works wonders with an obviously small budget (rehearsal time and Gordon's theatre experience helped) and credit should be given to Richard Band's score which, while derivative in places (especially that main title theme), hits just the right note of twinkle-in-the-eye 'you won't believe what's coming next' so many times that he can be forgiven the steals from Bernard Herrmann. But the film belongs to Jeffrey Combs, who in his performance as Herbert West created an icon of modern horror – one who refreshingly could talk, didn't solve all his problems with a machete, and had actually been to university. Even if he had been thrown out for making his professor's eyeballs explode.

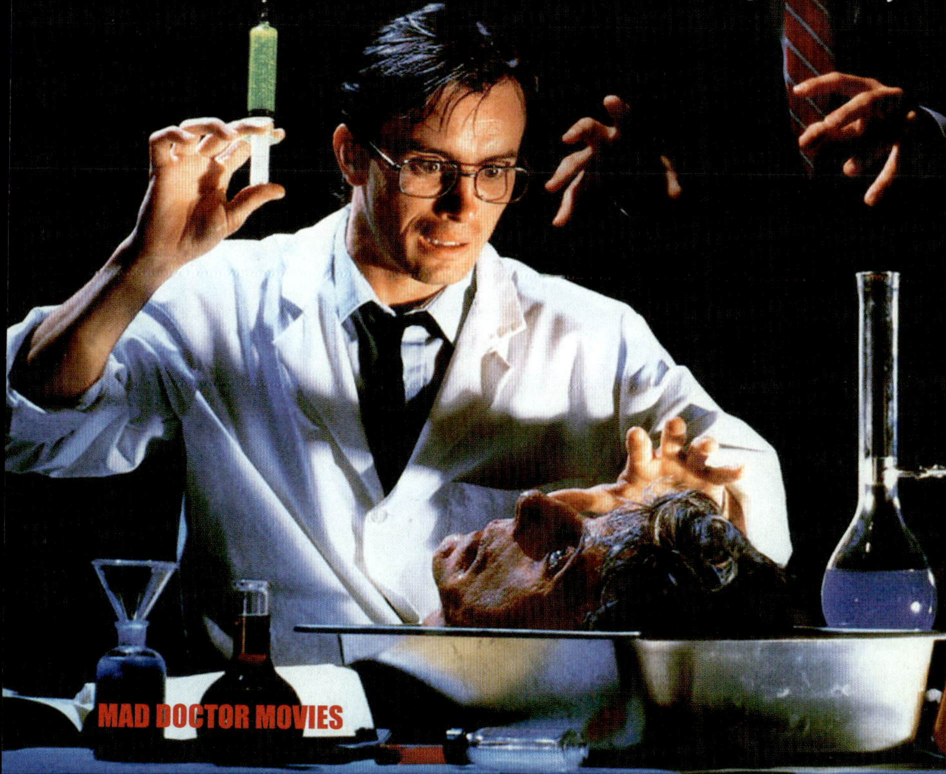

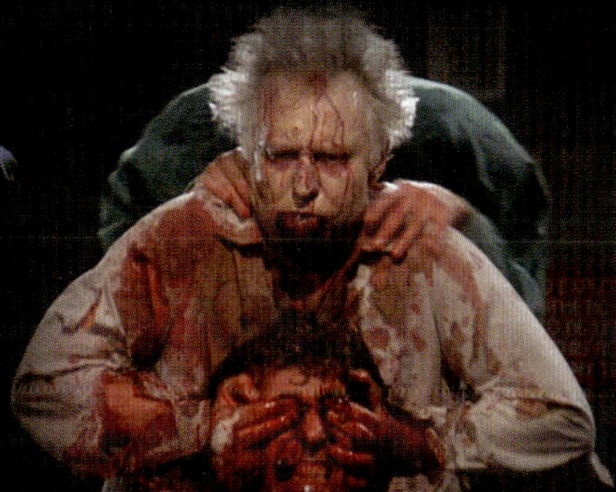

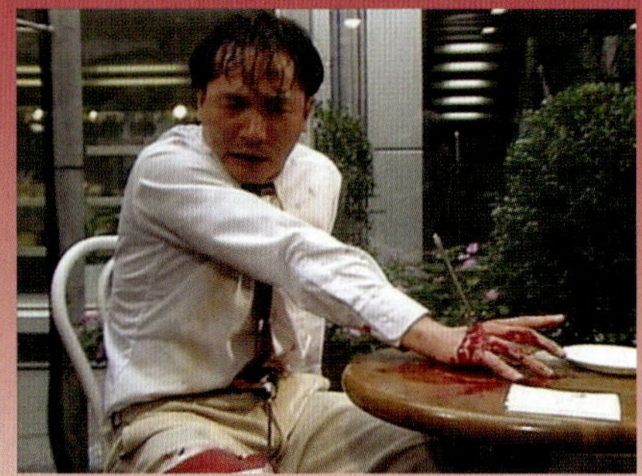

GUINEA PIG 4: DEVIL WOMAN DOCTOR

Japan, 1986
Director: Hajime Tabe. Producer: Satoru Ogura.
Screenplay: Hajime Tabe. Cinematography: Junichi Baba.
Cast: Mitsuru Fukikoshi, Kobuhei Hayashiya, Masami Hisamoto, Nezumi Imamura, Eve [Ivu], Tamio Kageyama.

The Japanese Guinea Pig series of films represents another example of a literary source being adapted to the big screen, in this case the graphic torture and violence-filled manga work of artist Hideshi Hino. The original series consists of six films and sources differ as to their release date order. Titles include **Devil's Experiment**, followed by **Flower of Flesh and Blood** (both 1985), **He Never Dies** (1986), and **Mermaid in a Manhole** (1988), with **Devil Woman Doctor** being either fourth or sixth (1986 or 1990). Whatever its chronological place, the film's story involves a transvestite doctor experimenting on patients, providing a series of gory vignettes. These include exploding heads, and the animated product of someone's bowels that might have influenced the creation of a certain character in Trey Parker and Matt Stone's animated series *South Park*. The 53 minute running time is played for the broadest type of Japanese comedy. You have been warned. Again, depending on sources, **Devil Woman Doctor** was followed in 1989 by **Guinea Pig 5: Android of Notre Dame**. It featured a dwarf scientist experimenting on subjects provided by a mysterious stranger, in an attempt to cure his sister's terminal illness. When the experiments fail the scientist hacks his subject to pieces.

The series is infamous for its scenes of extreme violence with minimal plots that serve as an excuse to show as much mutilation as possible. Actor Charlie Sheen saw **Flower of Flesh and Blood**, became convinced it was a snuff film and reported it to the US authorities, both adding to the series' reputation and prompting the filming of a 'making of' documentary in 1986, detailing how the special effects were done to reassure anyone concerned by such suspicions.

THE FLY

USA, 1986
Director: David Cronenberg. Producer: Stuart Cornfeld.
Screenplay: Walon Green, Charles Edward Pogue, David Cronenberg.
Music: Howard Shore. Cinematography: Mark Irwin.
Cast: Jeff Goldblum, Geena Davis, John Getz, Joy Boushel, Leslie Carlson, Gordon Chuvalo.

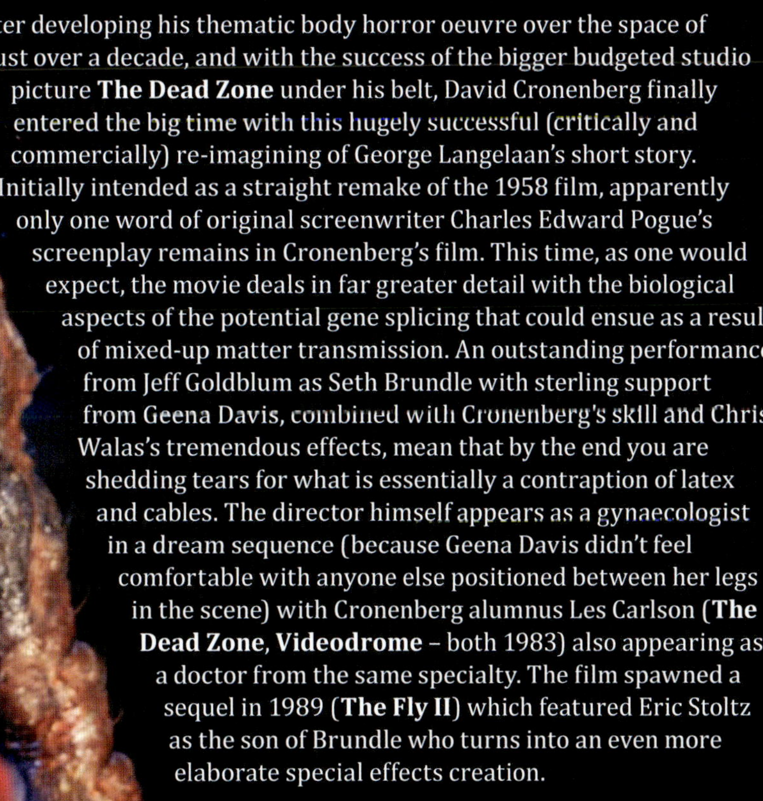

After developing his thematic body horror oeuvre over the space of just over a decade, and with the success of the bigger budgeted studio picture **The Dead Zone** under his belt, David Cronenberg finally entered the big time with this hugely successful (critically and commercially) re-imagining of George Langelaan's short story. Initially intended as a straight remake of the 1958 film, apparently only one word of original screenwriter Charles Edward Pogue's screenplay remains in Cronenberg's film. This time, as one would expect, the movie deals in far greater detail with the biological aspects of the potential gene splicing that could ensue as a result of mixed-up matter transmission. An outstanding performance from Jeff Goldblum as Seth Brundle with sterling support from Geena Davis, combined with Cronenberg's skill and Chris Walas's tremendous effects, mean that by the end you are shedding tears for what is essentially a contraption of latex and cables. The director himself appears as a gynaecologist in a dream sequence (because Geena Davis didn't feel comfortable with anyone else positioned between her legs in the scene) with Cronenberg alumnus Les Carlson (**The Dead Zone**, **Videodrome** – both 1983) also appearing as a doctor from the same specialty. The film spawned a sequel in 1989 (**The Fly II**) which featured Eric Stoltz as the son of Brundle who turns into an even more elaborate special effects creation.

THE KINDRED

USA, 1987
Directors: Jeffrey Obrow, Stephen Carpenter.
Producer: Jeffrey Obrow. Screenplay: Jeffrey Obrow, Stephen Carpenter, John Penney, Earl Ghaffari, Joseph Stefano.
Music: David Newman. Cinematography: Stephen Carpenter.
Cast: Rod Steiger, Kim Hunter, David Allen Brooks, Amanda Pays, Talia Balsam, Timothy Gibbs.

A favourite from the VHS era, Stephen Carpenter and Jeffrey Obrow's film boasts a screenplay credited to five people, including the directors and *Outer Limits* producer Joseph Stefano. There are at least two mad doctors (played by veterans Kim Hunter and Rod Steiger) in this somewhat Lovecraftian tale of a rambling old mansion housing the decidedly tentacular results of Hunter's genetic experimentation. She has named him Anthony 'after her favourite Saint' (well, everyone should have at least one). Steiger's been busy too, though, and has a basement full of genetic rejects handy for disposing of potential blackmailers. The script is peppered with 'science words' like hybridisation, electrophoresis, and haemocyanin (which is the invertebrate equivalent of haemoglobin with copper instead of iron). None of them are used particularly accurately. Not that it matters when our attention is on the nifty prosthetic effects used to realise the monster, that can only be calmed by a nursery rhyme on tape for when he's feeling 'rambunctious'. Steiger's Dr. Lloyd suffers an indignity similar to Bela Lugosi's Professor Vornoff at the end of Ed Wood's 1955 **Bride of the Monster**. Amanda Pays gets attacked by a fishy thing in a jar before turning decidedly fishlike herself. All this and one of the best poster tag lines of the era that also neatly sums up the central theme of genetic splicing: 'John's got a half brother. Half brother, half something else.'

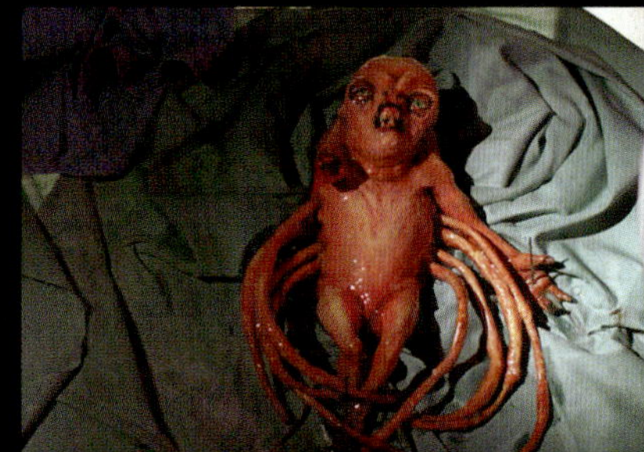

DEAD RINGERS

Canada/USA, 1988
Director: David Cronenberg.
Producers: Marc Boyman, David Cronenberg. Screenplay: David Cronenberg, Norman Snider.
Music: Howard Shore. Cinematography: Peter Suschitzky.
Cast: Jeremy Irons, Geneviève Bujold, Barbara Gordon, Shirley Douglas, Stephen Lack.

David Cronenberg followed up on the immense financial and artistic success of **The Fly** with this decidedly non-date movie (with the 'Faith Healer' episode of the *Friday the 13th* TV series sandwiched in between). It features twin gynaecologists, instruments for operating on 'mutant women', and a female patient with what the film describes as a 'trifurcate uterus', a congenital abnormality that would require someone to have had three Mullerian ducts during their embryological development. Women usually have two which fuse. If they don't they lead to a condition called uterus didelphys, and it's very hard to imagine a scenario where there would be three. Of course we've always been able to rely on Mr. Cronenberg to go one better, which naturally he also does here with Jeremy Irons, eliciting two great performances from the actor as twins Elliot and Beverly Mantle, smitten by patient Clare Niveau (Geneviève Bujold) leading to drug addiction and mental collapse. Stephen Lack, who had more or less retired from acting after starring in Cronenberg's **Scanners** seven years earlier, appears in this as Anders Wolleck, the creator of the Mantles' surgical instruments. **Dead Ringers** was adapted from a book by Bari Wood and Jack Geasland called *Twins*. The film was meant to be called that as well, but in the end the title went to a comedy starring Danny DeVito and Arnold Schwarzenegger from previous Cronenberg producer Ivan Reitman.

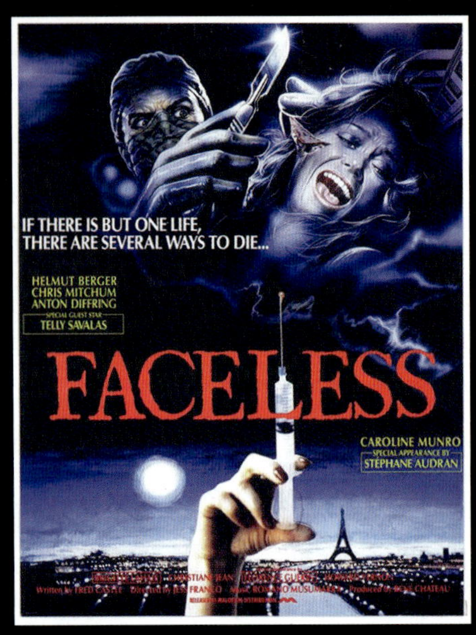

FACELESS

France, 1988
Director: Jess Franco.
Producer: René Chateau.
Screenplay: Pierre Ripert, Fred Castle [René Chateau], Jean Mazarin, Michel Lebrun.
Music: Romano Musumarra.
Cinematography: Maurice Fellous.
Cast: Helmut Berger, Brigitte Lahaie, Telly Savalas, Christopher Mitchum, Stéphane Audran, Caroline Munro.

French producer René Chateau provided director Jess Franco with sufficient funds to mount this slick, well-made surgical horror. It features a stellar cast of faces familiar to fans of European cinema, including Helmut Berger, Stéphane Audran, Anton Diffring, Brigitte Lahaie, and Telly Savalas, with Howard Vernon as an all-too briefly seen Professor Orloff and Franco's wife Lina Romay aptly playing Orloff's wife. With shades of 1960's **Circus of Horrors** (also starring Diffring) an unhappy patient throws acid at the face of Dr. Flamand (Berger), but misses their target and hits his sister instead, causing severe scarring. Thus the hunt is on for a replacement face for the doctor's sister. Only ex-Nazi surgeon Dr. Moser (Diffring, delivering a far more restrained, icily effective performance here than in Hammer's **The Man Who Could Cheat Death**) is capable of performing the surgery. Along with Flamand's partner Nathalie (Lahaie) they represent the type of cold, clinical, wealthy and privileged individuals that those familiar with Franco's oeuvre will have met many times before. The decent budget allows Franco to avoid the cutting of corners he often resorted to – which contributed to his unjustified reputation as an incompetent filmmaker – while the barbed script allows him to snipe effectively at the vapidity and superficiality of aspects of 1980s high society. There are some decent in-camera prosthetic gore effects, too. Be warned, though, that the theme song may linger in your head forever after watching.

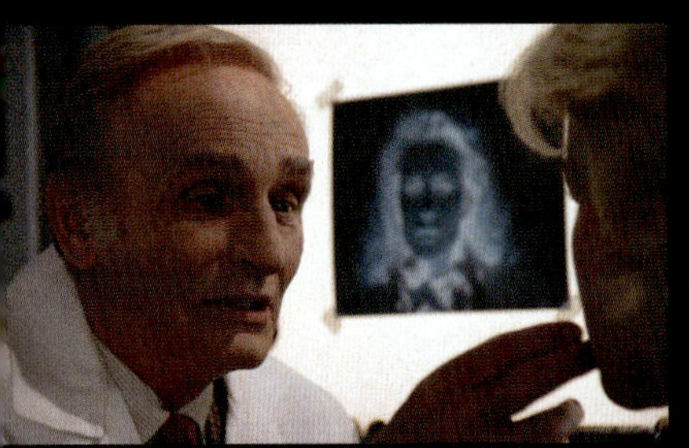

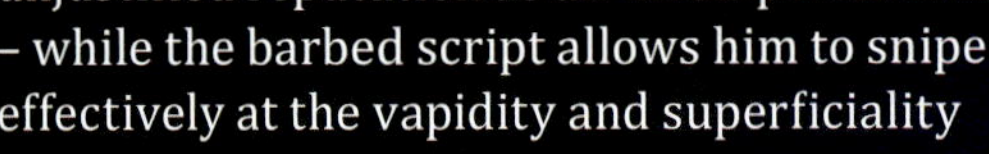

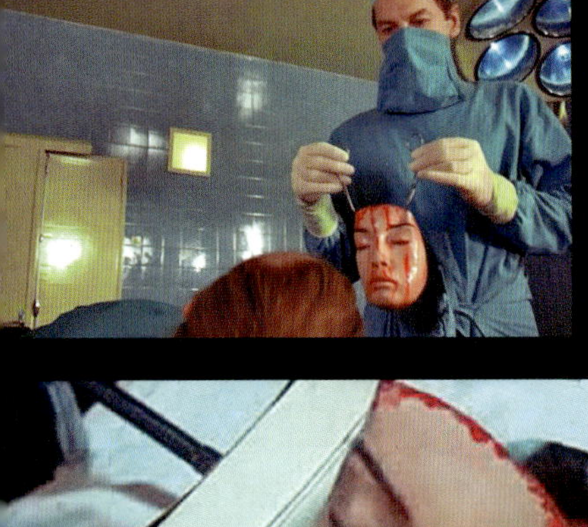

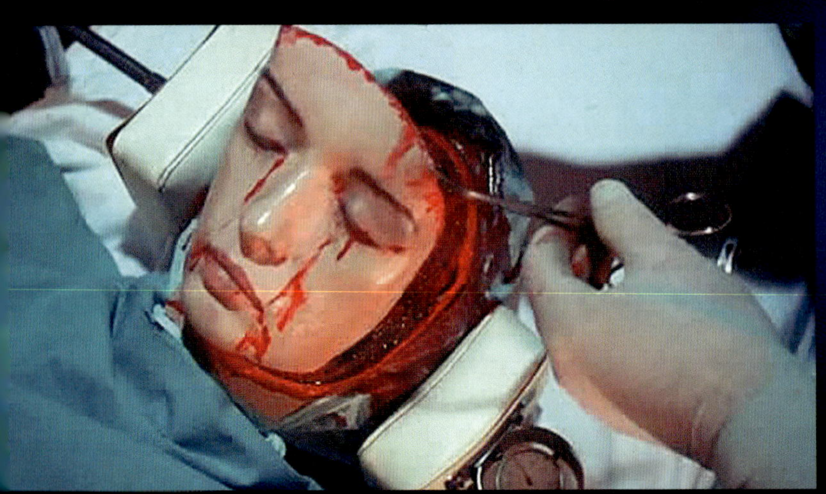

HELLBOUND: HELLRAISER II

UK, 1988
Director: Tony Randel. Producer: Christopher Figg.
Screenplay: Peter Atkins. Music: Christopher Young.
Cinematography: Robin Vidgeon.
Cast: Ashley Laurence, Clare Higgins, Kenneth Cranham, Imogen Boorman, Sean Chapman, Doug Bradley.

Horror author Clive Barker's UK-shot directorial debut **Hellraiser** (1987) was a low-budget hit for its American producer New World Pictures, and introduced the world to the Cenobites and their leader Pinhead (Doug Bradley) in a story very much modelled on Greek tragedy. The sequel tries for a more 'Midlantic' feel and introduces a new villain in the form of Dr. Channard (Kenneth Cranham) who runs the local lunatic asylum. Obsessed with solving the Lament Configuration (the puzzle box from the first film) he employs some of the patients to help him, resurrecting Queen of Hell Julia (Clare Higgins) in the process. Tony Randel, one of the uncredited executive producers on the first film, takes on directing duties this time, expanding the concept to include a panorama of Hell itself. Composer Christopher Young returns with the kind of over-the-top score one might expect to be playing there, employing not just the dissonant tritone (or devil's interval) played by the horns, but also having bass chanting spell out the word G-O-D in Morse code. Thus far the **Hellraiser** franchise has run to a startling nine sequels, the most recent being Gary Tunnicliffe's **Hellraiser: Judgment** (2018). A remake was on the cards for some years, with Pascal Laugier who made a splash with **Martyrs** in 2008, and Julien Maury and Alexandre Bustillo who were best known for 2011's **Livide**, among those attached to the project. The director's chair was finally filled by David Bruckner (**The Ritual**, 2017), and the **Hellraiser** reboot released in 2022.

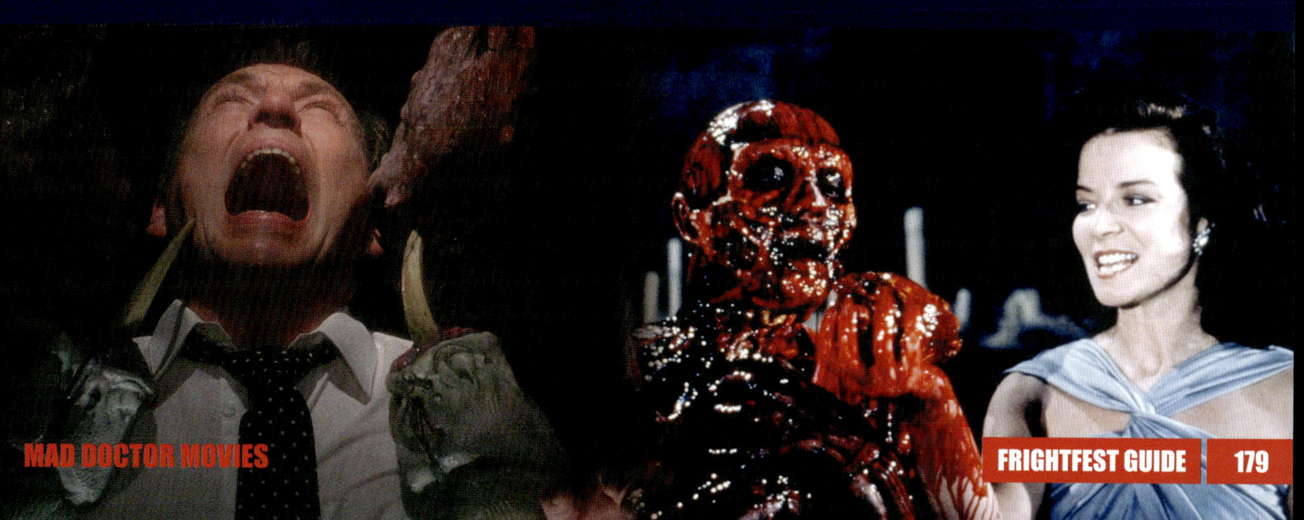

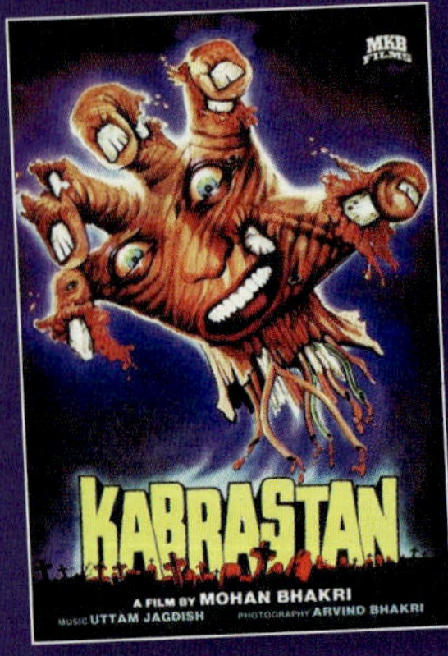

KABRASTAN

India, 1988
Director: Mohan Bhakri. Producer: Mohan Bhakri. Screenplay: Mohan Bhakri. Music: Uttam-Jagdish [Uttam Singh & Jagdish Khanna]. Cinematography: Arvind Bhakri. Cast: Hemant Birje, Kamna, Javed Khan, Kunika Sadanand, Raza Murad, Diljeet Kaur.

In the Hindu religion, when you die you are cremated. This creates a major stumbling block for any would-be Frankensteins planning to rob Indian graveyards for body parts. Legendary writer-producer-director Mohan Bhakri's solution for **Kabrastan** was to set the film within India's Christian community, apparently confusing and disappointing some of the nation's more provincial audiences who preferred their horror in more traditional settings. Aside from that, all of the standard ingredients of Bollywood movies are here – song and dance sequences, girls cavorting in states of undress that flirt outrageously with censorship restrictions and – ahem – 'homages' to contemporary popular western cinema, the most blatant here being a scene where the dead are resurrected in a graveyard to the music of Michael Jackson's 'Thriller'. Yes, there's a dance sequence here too. One might anticipate a film with characters named Rocky D'Souza and Hitler D'Costa to be a comedy, but Bhakri plays the whole thing straight, with a subjective camera standing in for the monster, even during a rape scene. Otherwise, the film is a heady melange of familiar horror tropes, including heart transplants, vengeful lovers, and acid thrown in the face. Unfazed by **Kabrastan**'s lack of success, Bhakri made **Khooni Murdaa (Deadly Corpse)**, which was 'heavily influenced' by Wes Craven's **A Nightmare on Elm Street**.

PIN

Canada, 1988
Director: Sandor Stern. Producer: René Malo. Screenplay: Sandor Stern. Music: Peter Manning Robinson. Cinematography: Guy Dufaux. Cast: David Hewlett, Cyndy Preston, John Ferguson, Bronwen Mantel, Terry O'Quinn, Helene Udy.

Director Sandor Stern's adaptation of Andrew Neiderman's 1981 pulp horror novel about two weird siblings – Leon and Ursula Linden – who live with their cleaning-obsessed mother and potty doctor father in a great big house. Dad (Terry O'Quinn) has a life-sized anatomical dummy in his doctor's office that he uses 'to explain things to patients with'. The dummy has been named Pin by the children, has no skin, a moveable head and, in one scene involving a nurse that wouldn't be out of place in a Joe D'Amato or John Waters picture, we discover that he is anatomically correct, er, downstairs as well. Who knows what you would use such a dummy for in a doctor's office, and Dr. Linden's actual specialty is somewhat glossed over, although at one point in the film he does perform an abortion on his own daughter, so perhaps his area of expertise is lack of ethics. And where would we trash film aficionados be without that particular discipline? When Leon and Ursula are approaching puberty, Dr. Linden uses Pin to explain the facts of life to them via a ventriloquist act so completely barmy this one scene alone makes this worth watching. Despite its flat and uninspired 1980s TV movie-like direction, **Pin** is so enjoyably crackers that anyone who likes outrageous nonsense will be more than willing to forgive the absence of style.

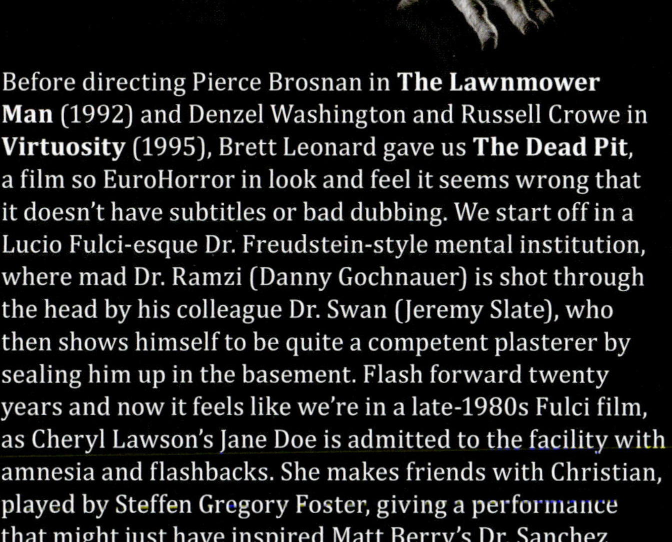

THE DEAD PIT

USA, 1989
Director: Brett Leonard.
Producer: Gimel Everett.
Screenplay: Brett Leonard, Gimel Everett.
Music: Dan Wyman. Cinematography: Marty Collins.
Cast: Jeremy Slate, Cheryl Lawson,
Steffen Gregory Foster, Danny Gochnauer,
Joan Bechtel, Geha Getz.

Before directing Pierce Brosnan in **The Lawnmower Man** (1992) and Denzel Washington and Russell Crowe in **Virtuosity** (1995), Brett Leonard gave us **The Dead Pit**, a film so EuroHorror in look and feel it seems wrong that it doesn't have subtitles or bad dubbing. We start off in a Lucio Fulci-esque Dr. Freudstein-style mental institution, where mad Dr. Ramzi (Danny Gochnauer) is shot through the head by his colleague Dr. Swan (Jeremy Slate), who then shows himself to be quite a competent plasterer by sealing him up in the basement. Flash forward twenty years and now it feels like we're in a late-1980s Fulci film, as Cheryl Lawson's Jane Doe is admitted to the facility with amnesia and flashbacks. She makes friends with Christian, played by Steffen Gregory Foster, giving a performance that might just have inspired Matt Berry's Dr. Sanchez in *Garth Marenghi's Darkplace*. Come to think of it, this entire film could have been an inspiration. The storyline becomes sufficiently random and the colour palette sufficiently Day-Glo that one is reminded of Norman J. Warren's **Terror** (1978) if not Argento's **Suspiria** (1977). That is until the end when the dead rise from the pit, ascend a spiral staircase reminiscent of **The Beyond** (1981), and attack the staff with all the verve of Jorge Grau's **The Living Dead at the Manchester Morgue** (1974). **The Dead Pit** tries hard to be stylish with obviously limited resources (including the acting talent available) and has a decent bucketload of good gore effects in its uncut version. Composer Dan Wyman did the synthesiser programming for John Carpenter's original **Halloween** (1978) and **The Fog** (1980). **The Dead Pit** was a big hit on its original VHS release, partly one suspects because the box came with a button you could press to make the zombie surgeon's eyes light up.

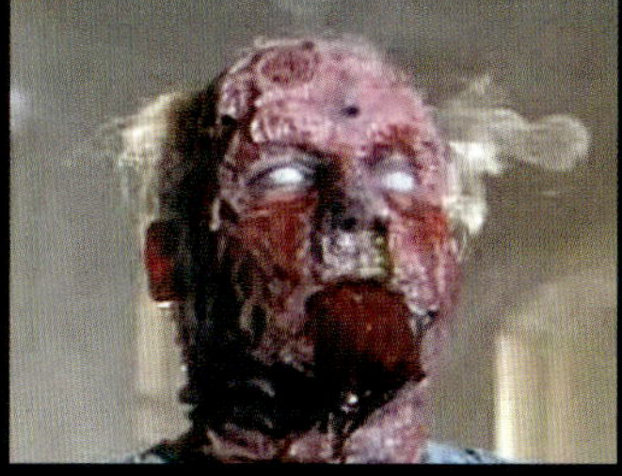

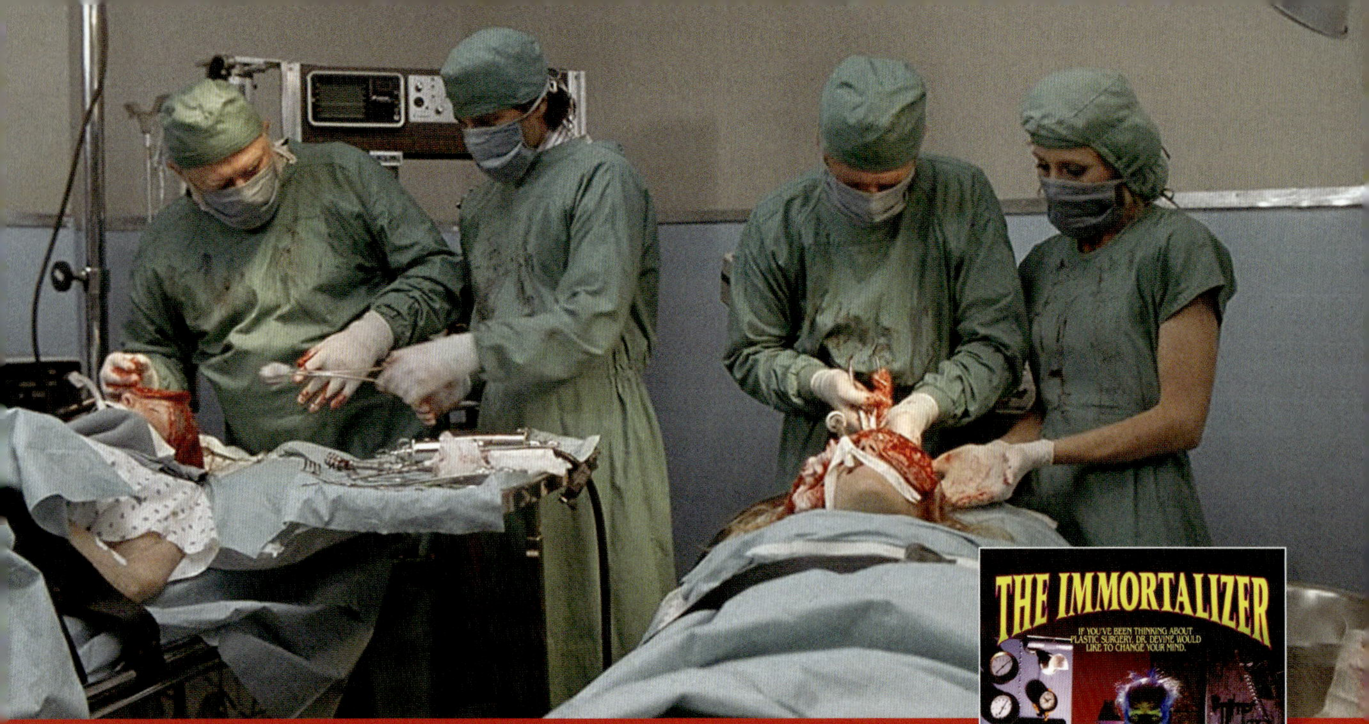

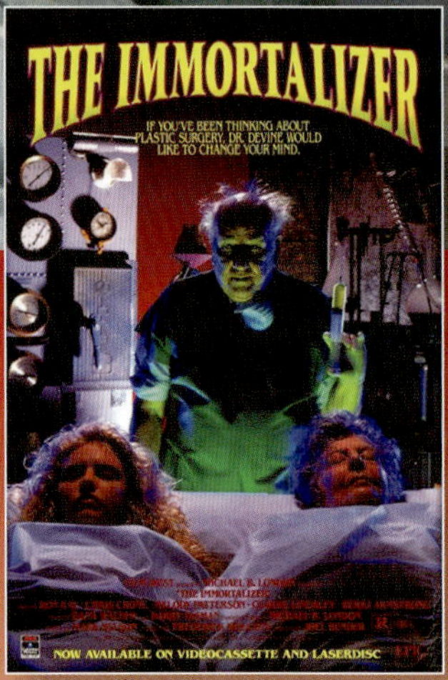

THE IMMORTALIZER

USA, 1989
Director: Joel Bender. Producers: Michael B. London, Fredrick Wolcott.
Screenplay: Mark M. Nelson. Music: Barry Fasman, Dana Walden.
Cinematography: Alan Caso.
Cast: Ron Ray, Chris Crone, Melody Patterson, Clarke Lindsley, Bekki Armstrong, Steve Jamieson.

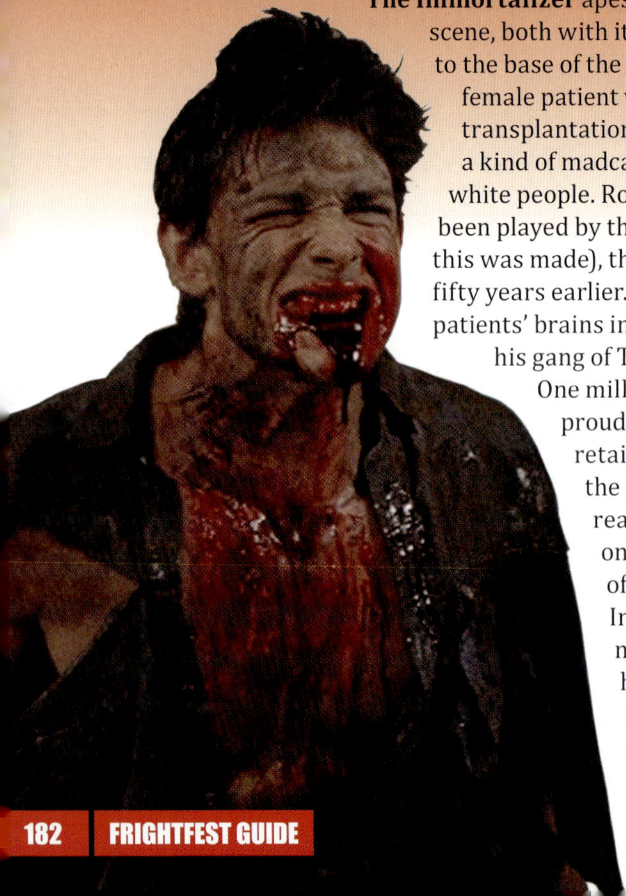

The Immortalizer apes Stuart Gordon's **Re-Animator** (1985) in its opening scene, both with its administration of an injection of glowing green liquid to the base of the neck and the camera angles used on the unfortunate female patient who is the recipient. Director Joel Bender's tale of brain transplantation as the secret of eternal youth soon settles down into a kind of madcap late-1980s version of Jordan Peele's 2017 **Get Out** for white people. Ron Ray is the corpulent Dr. Divine (if only he could have been played by the real Divine, who sadly was no longer with us by the time this was made), the kind of mad surgeon Lionel Atwill would have played fifty years earlier. He's perfected a technique of transplanting elderly patients' brains into the healthy young bodies of teenagers, kidnapped by his gang of Troma-esque zombies. His price for this treatment? One million dollars. Dr. Evil would be proud. For some reason, his patients retain their original voices, causing the already absurd climax to reach heights of ludicrousness only otherwise seen in episodes of *Garth Marenghi's Darkplace*. Indifferent acting and direction mean that while this one tried hard to give the world the next Herbert West, the result is nowhere near as stylish.

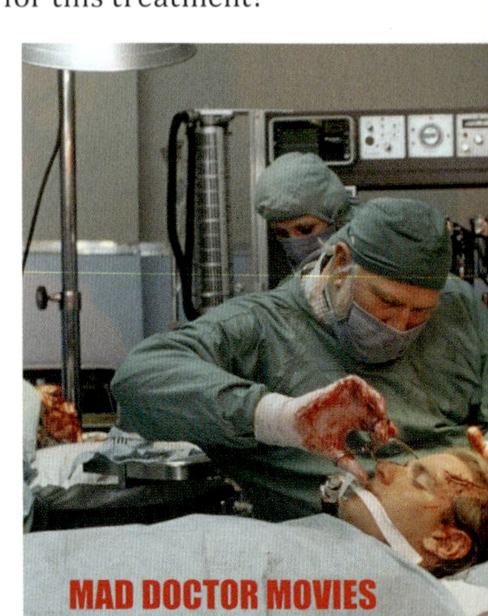

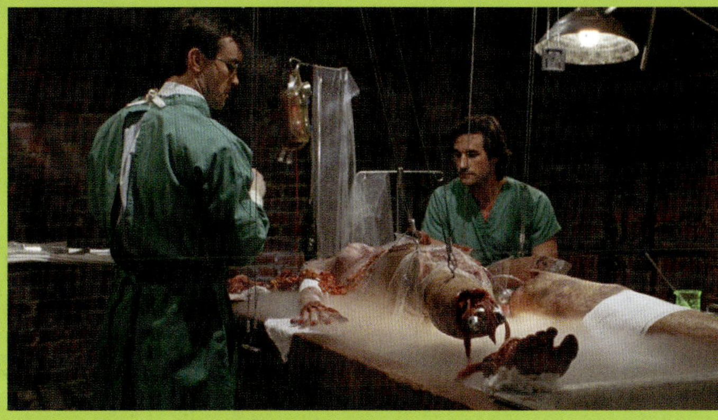

BRIDE OF RE-ANIMATOR

USA, 1990
Director: Brian Yuzna. Producer: Brian Yuzna.
Screenplay: Woody Keith [Zeph E. Daniel], Rick Fry.
Music: Richard Band. Cinematography: Rick Fichter.
Cast: Jeffrey Combs, Bruce Abbott, Claude Earl Jones, Fabiana Udenio, David Gale, Kathleen Kinmont.

Stuart Gordon's 1985 **Re-Animator** is one of the greatest horror films of all time, a frenetic and perfectly paced mix of outrageous splatter and well-timed humour, with some good old-fashioned horror tropes given a delightfully enthusiastic spin. The first film was something of a case of catching lightning in a bottle. However, this sequel is more someone who has seen the lightning caught, trying to do the same thing, but who doesn't really understand some of the major elements that caused that lightning to get trapped in the first place. The one really important factor **Bride of Re-Animator** lacks is the sense of vitality that infused every frame of its predecessor. Dialogue is flat, acting is flatter. Jeffrey Combs is still great as Herbert West, but his fiddling about with body parts 'for a laugh' doesn't feel consistent with the driven-and-mad young scientist we know from the first film. If anything, Herbert West seems as bored with this sequel as we are. The pacing is off, everything drags, and the hole-ridden script (which is nowhere near as exuberantly daft as the first film) gets shown up for being all a bit silly, really. It's a shame, but one really needed someone of James Whale's talents (never mind even Stuart Gordon's) to give this Bride some life. The film does score points, however, for featuring the University of Manchester's *Atlas of Human Anatomy* – the highlight for every medical student who watched this back in the 1990s.

FLATLINERS

USA, 1990
Director: Joel Schumacher. Producers: Rick Bieber, Michael Douglas. Screenplay: Peter Filardi. Music: James Newton Howard. Cinematography: Jan de Bont.
Cast: Kiefer Sutherland, Julia Roberts, Kevin Bacon, William Baldwin, Oliver Platt.

Joel Schumacher goes full Gothic in his brat pack, back from the dead pic, that's likely about as accurate about near death experiences as it is about medical school dissecting rooms. No modern-day medical student has ever taken apart bodies in moodily lit high-ceilinged oak-panelled rooms – apart from anything else, the cadavers are preserved with the kind of stuff that would make the paint peel from the Renaissance paintings decorating the walls. The corpses are also rather fresh-looking, as, in a cutaway from Julia Roberts' concentrated expression, we get a glimpse at someone's glistening innards in a stock insert worthy of 1972's **Superbeast**. Should we feel sorry for mad Kiefer Sutherland and his friends, up to no good daftness that causes them to revisit the past that haunts them? Perhaps not when it's as tepid as this. Come on, Joel – even back then Stephen King had shown how to make a career out of this sort of thing. Instead, we get Kevin Bacon not knowing that the best way to leave your student room is by the stairs and William Baldwin terrified of his guilty video collection (oh the possibilities there that went unexplored), with Oliver Platt to make up the numbers. At least Mr. Platt went on to make people defecate their guilt in 2016's **The Cleanse**.

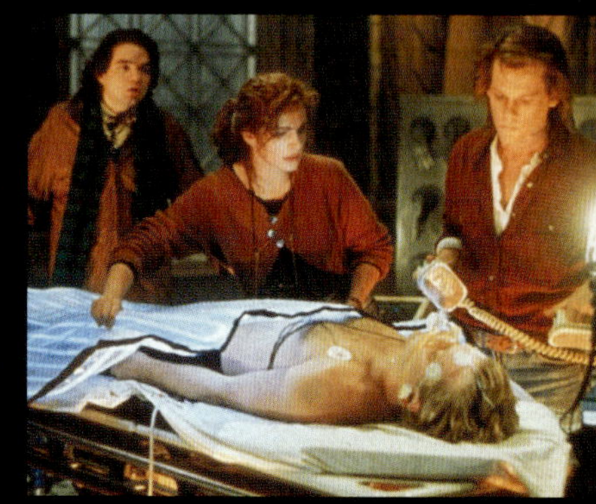

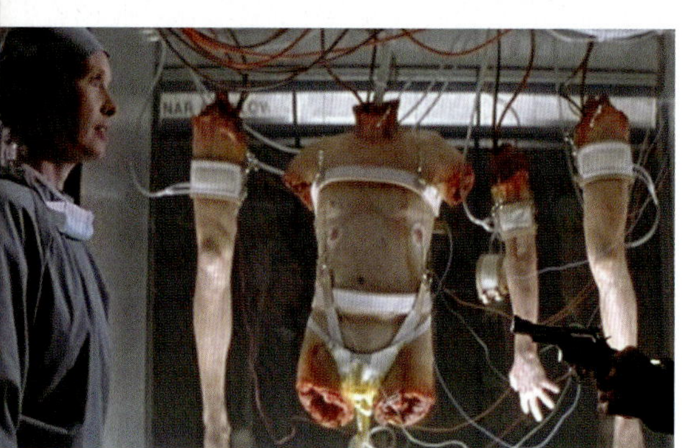

BODY PARTS

USA, 1991
Director: Eric Red.
Producer: Frank Mancuso Jr.
Screenplay: Eric Red, Norman Snider.
Music: Loek Dikker.
Cinematography: Theo van de Sande.
Cast: Jeff Fahey, Lindsay Duncan, John Walsh, Kim Delaney, Brad Dourif, Zakes Mokae.

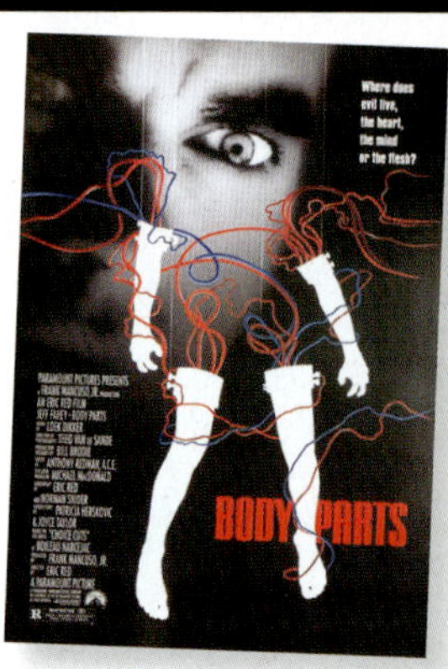

There's a strong **Hands of Orlac** feel to Eric Red's transplantation horror film. Jeff Fahey (from the likes of **The Lawnmower Man** in 1992 and **Planet Terror** in 2007) is the criminal psychologist who ends up with the arm of a convicted murderer, after losing his own in a spectacularly staged car crash. Lindsay Duncan (everything from 1975's **Further Up Pompeii!** to Jessica Hausner's 2019 arthouse Body Snatchers piece **Little Joe**) is the surgeon who does the operation. Pretty soon Jeff, or rather Jeff's arm, is slapping his kids and trying to strangle his wife. But is it the arm or is it Jeff? What could have been an interesting psychological study on the effects of transplantation (especially as Brad Dourif gets the other arm and starts creating weird art) is effectively scuppered by a climax that reveals it's all in the name of loony surgical experimentation. For those wondering, the kind of rotary saw Duncan employs is not commonly used in surgical procedures, not even to take someone's head off (not something that's commonly performed either). However, the film does score medical accuracy points for the armless legless headless torso in a tank that nevertheless has a catheter bag draining urine. Director Red (who made 1988's **Cohen and Tate**) is at his best handling action sequences – as well as the accident there's a terrifically tense car chase in **Body Parts** that alone makes it worth seeing.

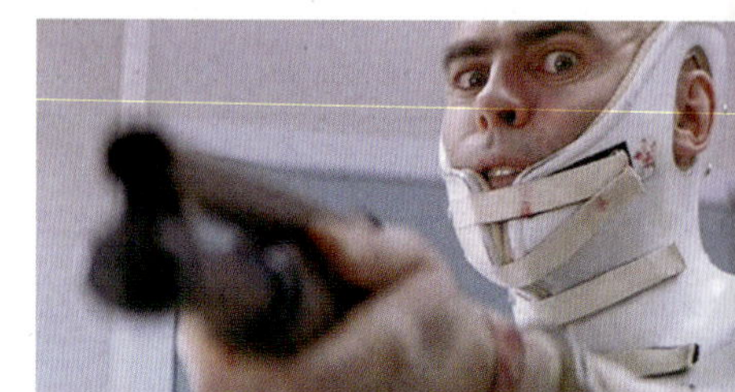

NAKED LUNCH

UK/Canada/Japan, 1991
Director: David Cronenberg.
Producer: Jeremy Thomas.
Screenplay: David Cronenberg.
Music: Ornette Coleman, Howard Shore.
Cinematography: Peter Suschitzky.
Cast: Peter Weller, Judy Davis, Ian Holm, Julian Sands, Roy Scheider, Monique Mercure.

Having succeeded (his early detractors would have claimed somewhat too well) in his aim to 'show the unshowable' with a string of original and highly creative science fiction horror movies through the 1970s and 1980s, Canadian director David Cronenberg announced the next step in his career development would be to 'film the unfilmable'. In other words, adapting literature considered by many too challenging to read, much less bring to the silver screen. His subsequent film projects have included adaptations of J.G. Ballard's **Crash** (1996), Patrick McGrath's **Spider** (2002), and Don DeLillo's **Cosmopolis** (2012). But first off was **Naked Lunch**, a film almost as insane as William S. Burroughs' 1959 novel, which he wrote as a series of vignettes to be read in any order. Peter Weller is William Lee, a bug exterminator and recreational drug user who starts seeing bizarre insectoid creatures. Their information eventually leads him to Dr. Benway (Roy Scheider) who may be running a narcotics operation specialising in a drug made from the intestines of giant Brazilian centipedes. Cronenberg's film benefits from its stellar cast and some impressive special effects, but the subject matter and very loosely linear plot mean this one's more for the arthouse circuit than the multiplex audience who it was aimed at on its initial release.

THE SILENCE OF THE LAMBS

USA, 1991
Director: Jonathan Demme. Producers: Ron Bozman, Edward Saxon, Kenneth Utt.
Screenplay: Ted Tally. Music: Howard Shore.
Cinematography: Tak Fujimoto.
Cast: Jodie Foster, Anthony Hopkins, Scott Glenn, Ted Levine, Anthony Heald, Brooke Smith.

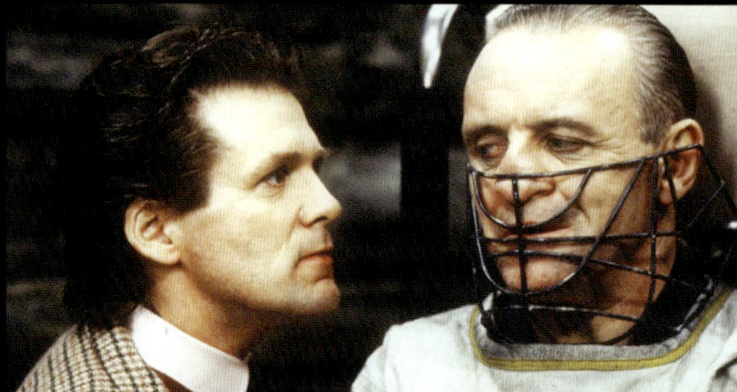

Thomas Harris' psychopathic cannibal psychiatrist Dr. Hannibal Lecter was introduced to cinema audiences in the form of actor Brian Cox in Michael Mann's **Manhunter** (1986). The character became world famous through Anthony Hopkins' iconic portrayal of him in this, Jonathan Demme's multi-Academy Award-winning film version of Harris's second Lecter novel. Demme essayed a deliberately different stylistic approach to Mann's film – the production design of the institution in which Lecter is being held is heavily Gothic compared to the building's ice-white clinical sterility in **Manhunter**. Demme also made sure to pepper his cast with nods to his exploitation roots (Tracey Walter, Charles Napier, cameos from Roger Corman and George A. Romero). The follow-up, **Hannibal** (2001) was inevitable, this time directed by Ridley Scott and with Julianne Moore replacing Jodie Foster as FBI agent Clarice Starling, as was a new version of the Mann film, this time under the source novel title of **Red Dragon** (2002) and directed by Brett Ratner. The Lecter legacy was far from over however. So far he has been the subject of three seasons of TV series *Hannibal*, starring Mads Mikkelsen as the doctor and Hugh Dancy as his nemesis Will Graham. The show, telling its story chronologically, ended (for now) with the climax of *Red Dragon*.

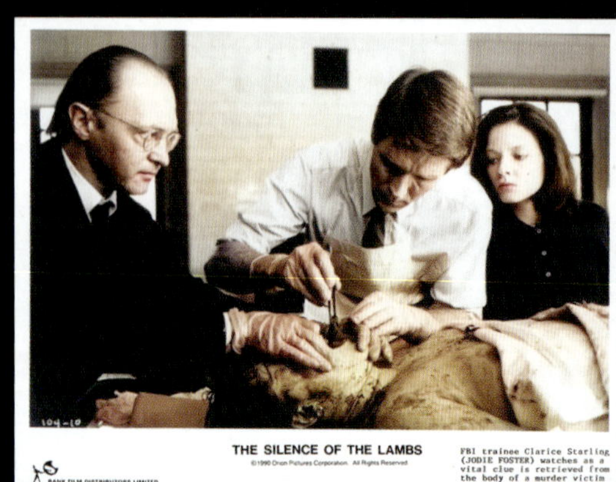

DR. GIGGLES

USA, 1992
Director: Manny Coto.
Producer: Stuart M. Besser.
Screenplay: Manny Coto, Graeme Whifler.
Music: Brian May. Cinematography: Robert Draper.
Cast: Larry Drake, Holly Marie Combs, Cliff De Young, Glenn Quinn, Keith Diamond, Richard Bradford.

An attempt to create a new wisecracking horror villain in the vein of Freddy Krueger, whose own franchise was in the process of limping to its end at the time (**Wes Craven's New Nightmare** would be the final entry in 1994, before a 2010 reboot). It's fashioned from a script that feels as if it was created by writing down as many commonly-used medical expressions as possible and then getting the titular character to utter them either before, during, or after a particular outrageous medical death. Dr. Giggles is a film that leaves its viewer with many questions, such as would a mental health institution really call a patient by that name because 'nobody knows his real one'? If Dr. Giggles has just escaped, where does he get a giant band aid, an enormous thermometer with a spike on the end, and all his other modus operandi from? Why has the police chief ordered Chinese food when he's clearly incapable of picking any of it up with chopsticks? With a cast composed of familiar faces including Holly Marie Combs (TV's *Charmed*), Michelle Johnson (Anthony Hickox's 1988 **Waxwork**), and in the title role, Larry Drake (H.G. Lewis' 1971 **This Stuff'll Kill Ya!**, Frank De Felitta's 1981 **Dark Night of the Scarecrow**, Sam Raimi's 1990 **Darkman**), this slasher movie is a ridiculous but highly entertaining timewaster, and at least Dr. Giggles puts his chest X-rays up the right way around.

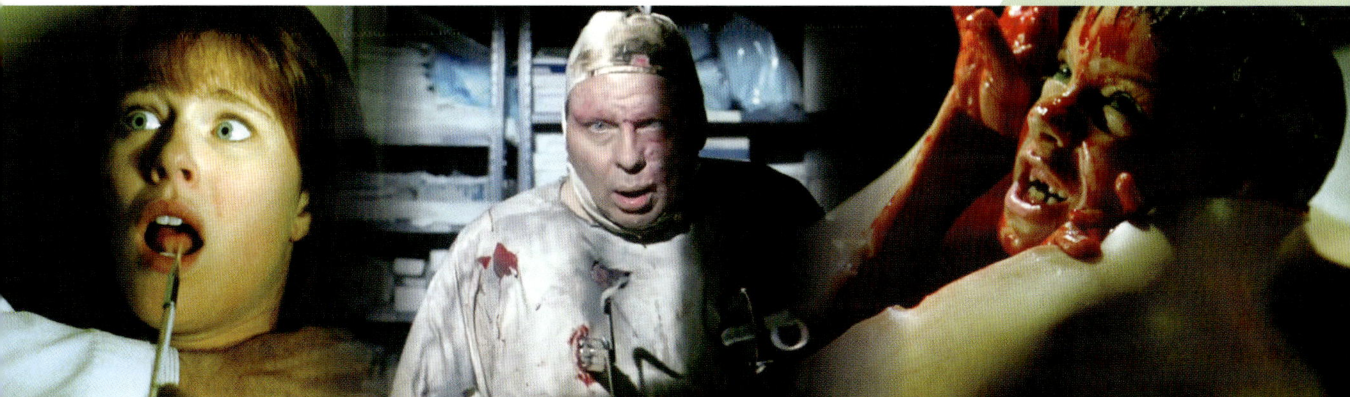

DR. LAMB

Hong Kong, 1992
Directors: Danny Lee, Billy Tang. Producer: Danny Lee.
Screenplay: Law Kam-fai. Music: Jonathon Wong.
Cinematography: Tony Miu, Kwan Chi-kan.
Cast: Danny Lee, Simon Yam, Kent Cheng, Lau Siu-ming, Parkman Wong, Emily Kwan.

It's amateur surgical dissection time in this Hong Kong Category III horror. **Dr. Lamb** is allegedly based on the true case of taxi driver serial killer Lam Kor-wan, arrested in 1982 for murdering female passengers, taking them home and dismembering them. Danny Lee and Billy Tang's film renames him Lam Gor-yue and begins like a Hong Kong version of an Italian *poliziotteschi*, with the police being tipped off about obscene photographs left for collection at a local developers. Lam (Simon Yam) is arrested, beaten up and eventually confesses to the killings, which we then see in gory detail. After his first murder – an annoying prostitute who sends him into a rage – Lam takes the body home and plays with it, eventually getting bored and hacking at the girl's left arm with a meat cleaver. Her eyes spring open in a scene reminiscent of the necrophilia-tinged films of Joe D'Amato at their more perverse. The D'Amato vibe persists during the subsequent buzzsaw dissections (Lam's work 'aided' by appropriate anatomy text books he purchases), and the accumulation of breasts preserved in jars, culminating in Lam's final victim, a teenaged graduate whose naked corpse he decides to marry, but not before he's given her an appropriate makeover. The 'wedding night' ends as one might expect and Lam videotapes it for good measure. Imprisoned for life, all he wants are his tapes and pictures back.

RAISING CAIN

USA, 1992
Director: Brian De Palma. Producer: Gale Anne Hurd. Screenplay: Brian De Palma.
Music: Pino Donaggio. Cinematography: Stephen H. Burum.
Cast: John Lithgow, Lolita Davidovich, Steven Bauer, Frances Sternhagen, Gregg Henry.

Brian De Palma's 'Greatest Hits' package of him, Hitchcock, and others, gives us the story of Carter Nix (John Lithgow), happily married to Jenny (Lolita Davidovich) and with a baby daughter, Amy. He also happens to be chloroforming and killing young mothers and abducting their children to deliver to his Norwegian mad scientist father (Lithgow again) who wants to use them in personality-splitting experiments. Dr. Nix has already been at it for years, though, and Carter himself is a mixture of the violent Cain, young Josh, and psychopathic Margo (all Lithgow, who is kept extremely busy in this film). We learn all this through a monologue from dying psychologist Dr. Waldheim during one of De Palma's trademark clever camera sequences – it's very good – you'll want to watch this bit at least twice. (Waldheim's played by the marvellous Frances Sternhagen – from 1978's **Fedora**, and the Stephen King adaptations **Misery**, 1990, and 2007's **The Mist** – here she makes the most of her awful wig.) Meanwhile Jenny is having an affair, the genesis of which is detailed in an awkward and clunky flashback that culminates in a 'shock shot' that made one wonder if De Palma wanted to homage sub-par Ulli Lommel, alongside all the other directors who are referenced in this. John Lithgow is excellent in all his roles. The same cannot be same of Lolita Davidovich in her one role, who just cannot evoke the levels of sympathy we felt for Angie Dickinson who played a similar character in **Dressed to Kill** (1980). **Raising Cain** isn't a bad film, but it is all rather daft, and while De Palma devotees doubtless welcomed it back in the day, it's not difficult to see why general audiences didn't go for it.

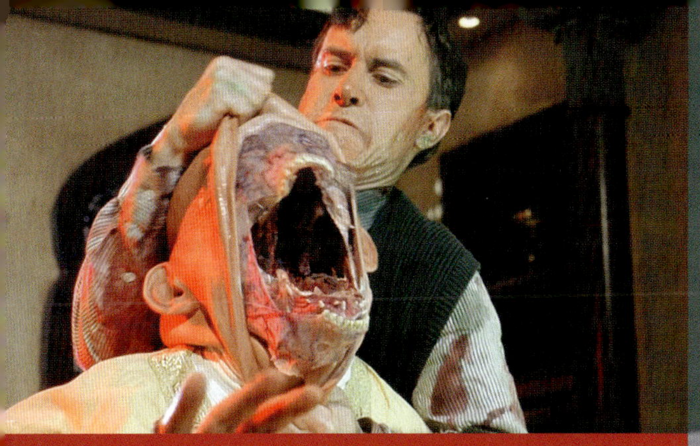

NECRONOMICON

USA, 1993
Directors: Christophe Gans, Shûsuke Kaneko, Brian Yuzna. Producers: Samuel Hadida, Brian Yuzna. Screenplay: Brent V. Friedman, Christophe Gans, Kazunori Itô.
Music: Joseph LoDuca, Daniel Licht.
Cinematography: Russ Brandt, Gerry Lively.
Cast: Bruce Payne, Richard Lynch, Belinda Bauer, David Warner, Bess Meyer, Millie Perkins.

H.P. Lovecraft's story 'Cool Air', about a mysterious doctor living in an abnormally cold apartment, has been filmed several times, including Bryan Moore's 1999 atmospheric 16mm black and white short, the rather tattier **Chill** (2007), an attempt by **The Sword and the Sorcerer** director Albert Pyun in 2006, and as a 1971 episode of Rod Serling's *Night Gallery* TV series, directed by Jeannot Szwarc. This Lovecraft-themed anthology movie adapts the story for its middle segment, and it's one of the better interpretations. It's directed by Shûsuke Kaneko (2006's **Death Note** and three 1990s **Gamera** movies) and stars David Warner as the scientist who has invented a machine to keep him alive after death. Bess Meyer is the girl who gets to know him better, and Dennis Christopher (from 1980's **Fade to Black**) is the reporter who gets more than he bargained for when he interviews her. The story is sandwiched nicely between Christophe Gans' Corman Poe-esque 'The Drowned' with Bruce Payne, Richard Lynch, and a Deep One, and Brian Yuzna's final tale about bone marrow-sucking flapping things from another dimension that might well have been inspired by both Frank Belknap Long's 'Hounds of Tindalos' and Clark Ashton Smith's 'The Vaults of Yoh-Vombis'. Jeffrey Combs plays HPL himself in a linking sequence between the stories.

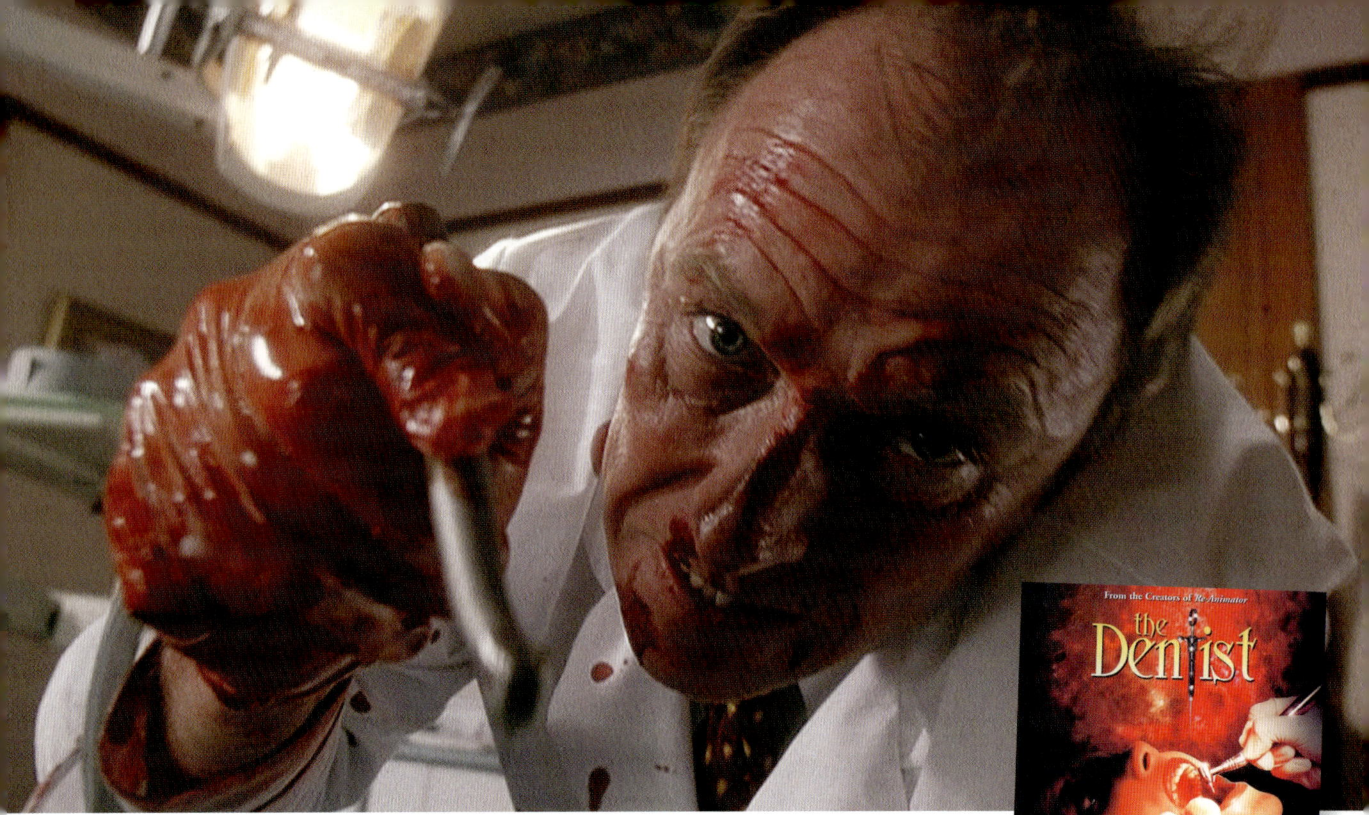

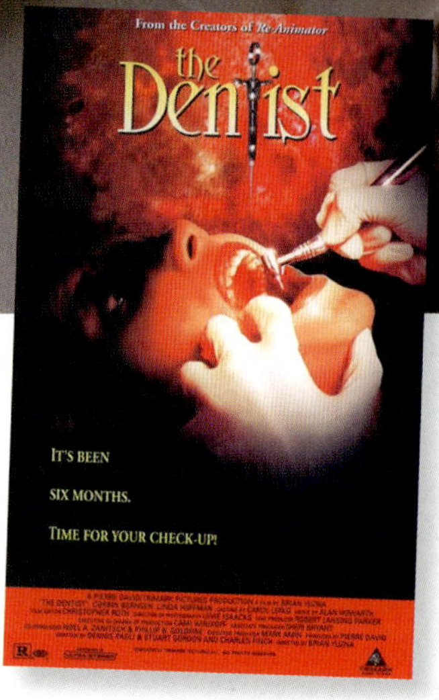

THE DENTIST

USA, 1996
Director: Brian Yuzna. Producer: Pierre David.
Screenplay: Dennis Paoli, Stuart Gordon, Charles Finch.
Music: Alan Howarth. Cinematography: Levie Isaacks.
Cast: Corbin Bernsen, Linda Hoffman, Michael Stadvec, Ken Foree, Tony Noakes.

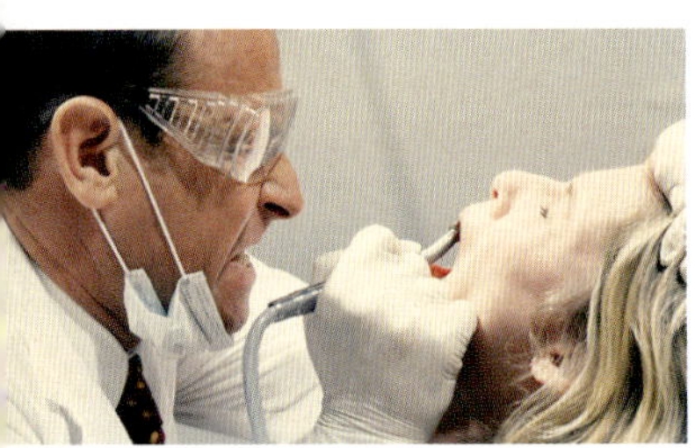

Laurence Olivier, with the aid of director John Schlesinger (and Dustin Hoffman as his unwilling victim), gave the world what is still considered the best single scene of dental horror in 1976's **Marathon Man.** Ten years later Steve Martin defined the insane screen dentist for many with his portrayal of the unhinged (and singing!) Orin Scrivello in Frank Oz's live action version of **Little Shop of Horrors**. It was not until 1996, however, that a dentist got to be the titular villain of his very own horror movie. Corbin Bernsen has a fine time as the rich and successful Dr. Feinstone who, due to mounting pressure from the IRS and concerns about his attractive wife's relationship with Matt the Pool Guy, goes off the rails, with mutilation and death as a result. Directed by Brian Yuzna, and co-written (with Charles Finch) by Dennis Paoli and Stuart Gordon, all three of whom collaborated on 1985's **Re-Animator**, the often witty dialogue and imaginative use of limited sets (the different consulting rooms in Feinstone's surgery were intended to show his different states of mind) mean **The Dentist** is a surprisingly well thought out and entertaining contribution to the genre. Audiences obviously agreed as the film was successful enough for **The Dentist 2** (also directed by Yuzna) to be released in 1998. Both star Bernsen and producer Pierre David were keen to collaborate with Yuzna on **The Dentist 3** but so far this has not come to pass.

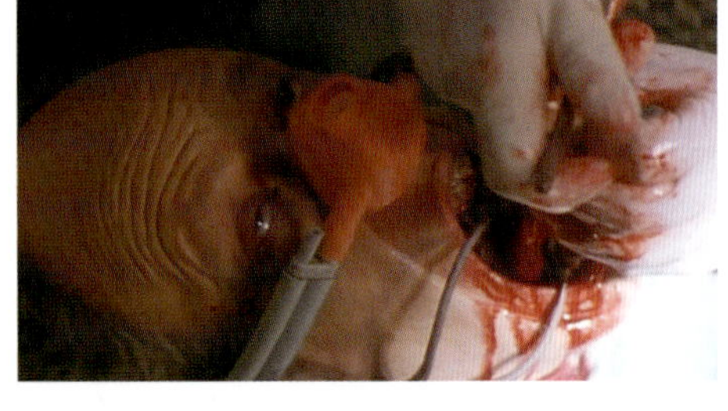

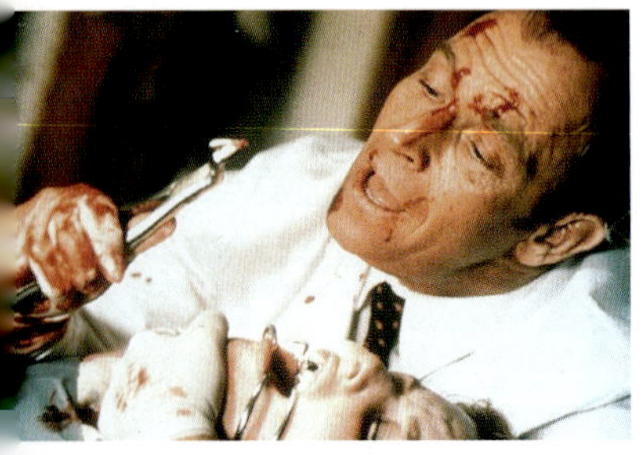

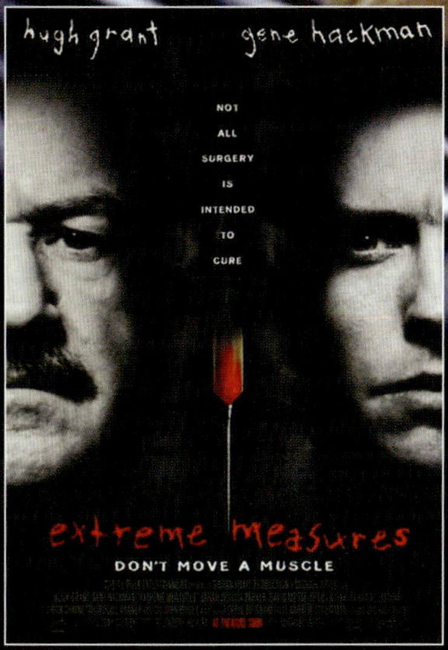

EXTREME MEASURES

UK/USA, 1996
Director: Michael Apted. Producer: Elizabeth Hurley. Screenplay: Tony Gilroy. Music: Danny Elfman. Cinematography: John Bailey.
Cast: Hugh Grant, Gene Hackman, Sarah Jessica Parker, David Morse, Bill Nunn, Debra Monk.

This takes a leaf out of Robin Cook's novel and Michael Crichton's film of **Coma** (1978), where a junior doctor working in a big city hospital discovers that a senior highly respected specialist at their institution is up to no good and finds their life under threat. **Extreme Measures** adds in a generous dollop of mad science with Gene Hackman as the surgeon trying to find a cure for spinal cord injuries and Hugh Grant (who co-produced the film with Liz Hurley) the doctor who finds out Hackman has been severing and then repairing the spinal cords of street people he has kidnapped to aid his research. The network of collaborators Grant's character uncovers is a fascinating idea and the film could have used it as an opportunity to explore more fully the lengths people are willing to go to in order to help a loved one. Unfortunately, Michael Apted's approach to such emotionally sensitive material is perhaps just a bit too restrained. A slightly more melodramatic touch might have worked wonders and made the film more memorable. As such, **Extreme Measures** still leaves us with some interesting ideas and good performances from Grant and Hackman (and Sarah Jessica Parker) in a film that deserves to be better known.

THE ISLAND OF DR. MOREAU

USA, 1996
Directors: John Frankenheimer, Richard Stanley [uncredited].
Producer: Edward R. Pressman.
Screenplay: Richard Stanley, Ron Hutchinson, Walon Green [uncredited], Michael Herr [uncredited].
Music: Gary Chang.
Cinematography: William A. Fraker.
Cast: Marlon Brando, Val Kilmer, David Thewlis, Fairuza Balk, Ron Perlman, Marco Hofschneider.

Oh goodness where to start with this one? Probably not with the film at all but instead with producer-director David Gregory's excellent documentary **Lost Soul: The Doomed Journey of Richard Stanley's Island of Dr. Moreau** (2014), which tells you all you need to know about how this ultimately disastrous project came to be. Marlon Brando plays Dr. Moreau in kabuki make-up, Val Kilmer is Montgomery his assistant, David Thewlis is Douglas the stranded castaway, Fairuza Balk is the panther woman. The whole resultant clash of egos, squandered millions, inappropriate location choices, and months of drug-fuelled parties was eventually credited to director John Frankenheimer, who somehow managed to get some sort of coherent end product out of New Line's ill-advised big-budget production. Original director Richard Stanley (who is left with a co-screenplay credit on the finished print) was fired from the production, but returned to the set during the shoot disguised as one of the beast men. H.G. Wells' *The Island of Dr. Moreau* didn't deserve this treatment, but it's a testament to the sometimes lunatic world of film production that the story told in Gregory's 'making of' documentary is almost as fascinating as the plot of the source novel. Which has yet to see a movie adaptation that truly does it justice – Erle C. Kenton's 1932 **Island of Lost Souls** remains the best so far.

NAKED BLOOD

Japan, 1996
Director: Hisayasu Satô. Producer: Hirohiko Satô.
Screenplay: Taketoshi Watari. Music: Kimitake Hiraoka.
Cinematography: Akiko Ashizawa.
Cast: Misa Aika, Yumika Hayashi, Mika Kirihara,
Sadao Abe, Masumi Nakao, Tadashi Shiraishi.

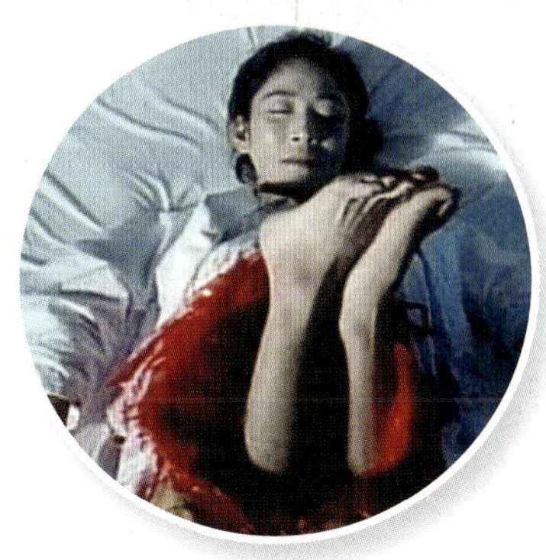

A slightly more restrained affair from Hisayasu Sâto, director of **Uniform Virgin: The Prey** (1986) and **Bondage Ecstasy** (1989) amongst many others, **Naked Blood** offers us a family tale of mad doctoring. Teenaged scientist Eiji has developed a substance he calls 'MySon' which increases the brain's endorphin levels, turning pain into pleasure. He mixes it with the experimental contraceptive which his researcher mother injects into three female test subjects. The one who loves to eat ends up turning her hand into tempura before eating her eye and generally becoming a gore prosthesis on the kitchen table. The one who loves to exercise goes piercing crazy, and the third, who suffers from insomnia brought on by her menarche, becomes homicidal. The film concludes almost literally on a bizarre climax, as Eiji and insomnia girl have sex in the presence of the massive cactus she has hooked up to a special machine. Then Eiji's long-lost father returns and dives into the open abdominal wound in his mother caused by homicidal insomnia girl. Except for the gore sequences, this is more of a quietly meditative, weird film, with the subtext that Eiji's research allows him to penetrate and influence women without having to go anywhere near them, filming them from rooftops to maintain his distance from base physical desires.

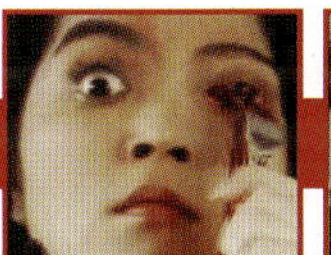
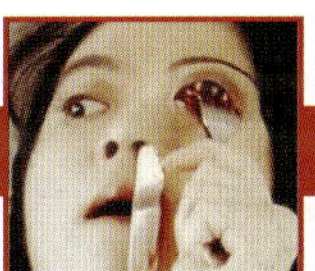
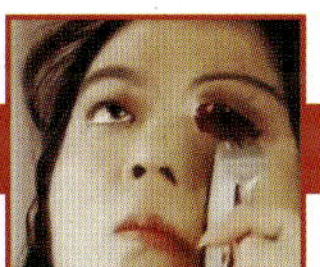

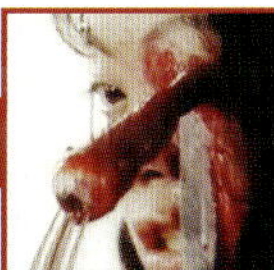
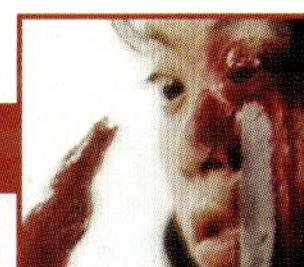

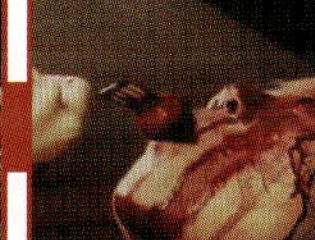

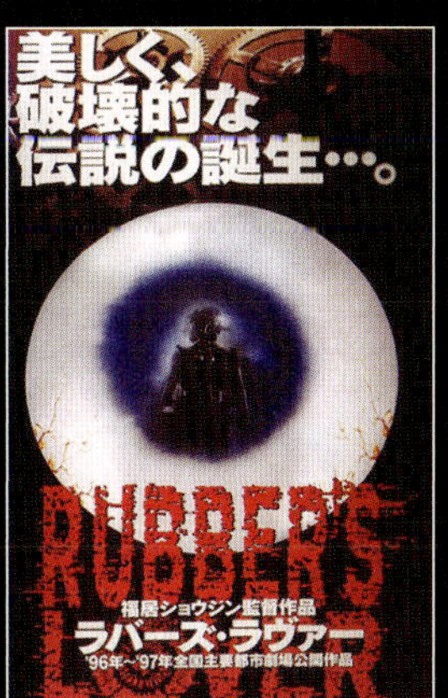

RUBBER'S LOVER

Japan, 1996
Director: Shozin Fukui. Producer: Takashi Nishimura.
Screenplay: Shozin Fukui. Music: Tetora Tanizaki.
Cinematography: Yoshio Tazawa.
Cast: Nao, Norimizu Ameya, Yôta Kawase,
Mika Kunihiro, Sosuke Saito, Ziko Uchiyama.

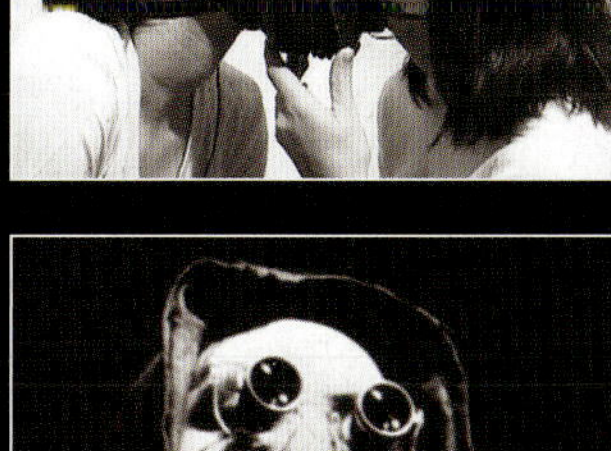

Japanese cyberpunk, its lunacy is unlikely to appeal to a wide audience. Two scientists have been attempting to give human subjects psychic powers by dressing them in rubber suits, giving them a massive injection of ether from one of the biggest syringes you will ever see, and then exposing them to intense sound frequencies and something called Digital Drive Technology. The subjects usually explode. The scientists' funding is cut, so they use their lab assistant for one final experiment which works, if works means lots and lots of screaming, as he uses his newly acquired psychic powers to get involved in a whole world of weird. Director Shozin Fukui also made 1991's **Screams of Blasphemy** (aka **964 Pinocchio**), a film about an escaped lobotomised cyborg sex slave, which some regard as a prequel to **Rubber's Lover**. Fukui's filmmaking style is less about plot and more about going for a visual and aural assault on the senses. The black and white photography is evocative of David Lynch, and some of the camera setups are inspired. But the frequent violence, torture, rape, general incomprehensibility, grinding soundtrack, and desire to be mad at any cost, mean those unfamiliar with movies like **Tetsuo: The Iron Man** (1989) would be advised to be eased into the genre by that instead.

GEMINI

Japan, 1999
Director: Shinya Tsukamoto. Producers: Toshiaki Nakazawa, Taishi Nishimura.
Screenplay: Shinya Tsukamoto. Music: Chu Ishikawa. Cinematography: Shinya Tsukamoto.
Cast: Masahiro Motoki, Ryô, Yasutaka Tsutsui, Shiho Fujimura, Akaji Maro.

Director Shinya Tsukamoto is probably best known for his cyberpunk trilogy of futuristic **Tetsuo** films, all three of which tell the story of characters driven to bizarre mechanical transformations as a result of their rage. **Gemini** also deals with rage and transformation, though we begin our story in 1910 with Yukio, an ex-military doctor who has settled down in a small town to a successful practice and a happy marriage. Meanwhile his twin brother Sutekichi, discarded by his parents at birth on the basis of a disfiguring birthmark, has grown up as travelling player. A chance occurrence causes the twin to learn of his abandonment. Sutekichi's revenge involves him imprisoning his brother in a well (no sign of Sadako), assuming his persona and killing off their parents. It's a more straightforward, less challenging watch than the **Tetsuo** films, and represents an attempt to tell a tale of extreme sibling rivalry seen in the mythology of many countries, through the medium of Japanese Gothic. (It could be argued the Hindi film industry has created an entire musical sub-genre devoted to this plot.) Based on an Edogawa Rampo story, **Gemini** isn't entirely successful but Tsukamoto still manages to come up with some arresting imagery, especially our first sight of Sutekichi in his travelling player make-up, cartwheeling his way through his own home invasion.

HOUSE ON HAUNTED HILL

USA, 1999
Director: William Malone.
Producers: Gilbert Adler, Michael K. Ross, Joel Silver, Robert Zemeckis.
Screenplay: Dick Beebe. Music: Don Davis. Cinematography: Rick Bota.
Cast: Geoffrey Rush, Famke Janssen, Taye Diggs, Peter Gallagher, Chris Kattan, Ali Larter, Jeffrey Combs.

William Malone's highly entertaining remake of William Castle's 1959 original provides a fabulous reason for the house (or rather hospital) in question to be haunted. Back in 1931 mad Dr. Vannacutt (Jeffrey Combs – hooray!) treats the criminally insane patients at his institution with a combination of torture, sadism, and extreme violence, all while getting his staff to film it. The patients rebel and the place goes up in flames. Cut to the present, and amusement park ride designer Geoffrey Rush – playing the genetically-spliced love child of John Waters and Vincent Price – invites five guests to his hated wife's (Famke Janssen) birthday party at the renovated Vannacutt Institute, only to discover that the doctor and his patients still lurk the corridors. A jumpy, shrieky haunted house picture in the William Castle tradition, this builds well, aided immensely by an atmospheric Don Davis score, but sadly the whole thing gets rather diffused by an excess of CGI effects towards the end. Chunks were cut before the film's release, and anyone hoping for answers from the 2007 sequel, **Return to House on Haunted Hill**, were to be disappointed. Gimmick fans, however, had that film's 'choose your own adventure' aspect to keep them entertained.

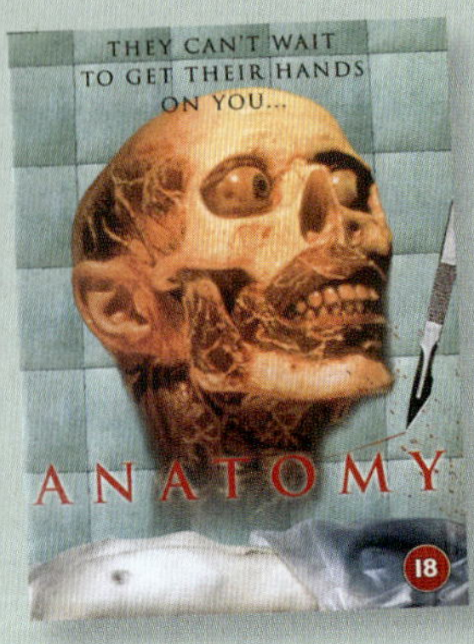

ANATOMIE

Germany, 2000
Director: Stefan Ruzowitzky. Producers: Jakob Claussen, Andrea Willson, Thomas Wöbke. Screenplay: Stefan Ruzowitzky. Music: Marius Ruhland. Cinematography: Peter von Haller.
Cast: Franka Potente, Benno Fürmann, Anna Loos, Sebastian Blomberg, Holger Speckhahn, Traugott Buhre.

Of course it had to happen. Anyone who has got this far through this book will have realised by now that there are a lot of mad doctors out there in movie land, so it was only a matter of time before some of them got together to form a secret society. In Stefan Ruzowitzky's film it's called the Anti Hippocratic Lodge, has been around for centuries, and its purpose is to conduct surgical experiments on patients without the need for considering ethics or any moral code. If nothing else their efforts have resulted in some very fine anatomy prosections (as partially dissected parts of human bodies are known). We get to see a lot of them in the film and very nicely – and on the whole accurately – designed they are too. There's also a good deal of accurate anatomical knowledge on display in Mr. Ruzowitzky and Peter Engelmann's script. The plot riffs a little on Robin Cook's *Coma*, with Franka Potente's junior doctor happening upon the practices of the AHL, and finding her life in peril as a consequence. There's a fictional drug that allows our mad doctors to induce rapid plastination and a necessarily simple way of reversing the process so not everyone ends up in display cases. (In reality plastination is an involved procedure to preserve human anatomical specimens for display, employed most famously by Gunther von Hagens.) **Anatomie** is a taut well-researched thriller, thoroughly deserving of being the biggest moneymaker in Germany on its year of release.

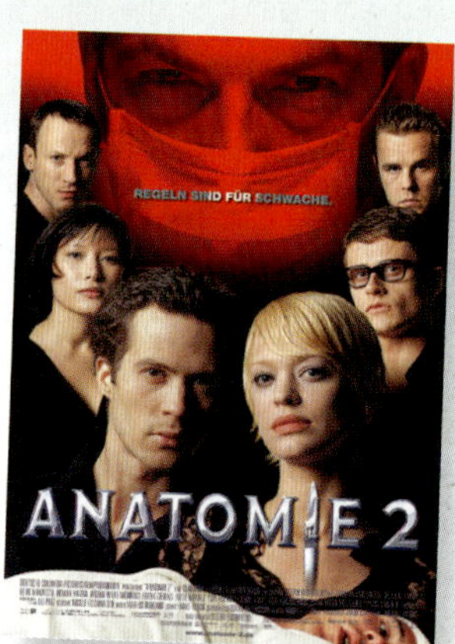

ANATOMIE 2

Germany, 2003
Director: Stefan Ruzowitzky.
Producers: Jakob Claussen, Andrea Willson, Thomas Wöbke. Screenplay: Stefan Ruzowitzky. Music: Marius Ruhland. Cinematography: Andreas Berger.
Cast: August Diehl, Ariane Schnug, Herbert Knaup, Birgit von Rönn, Klaus Schindler, Barnaby Metschurat, Franka Potente.

Stefan Ruzowitzky's sequel eschews the measured approach of his 2000 original in favour of going as far over the top as possible, kicking off with an impressive opening scene of bloodshed that points the direction for what is to come. The Berlin branch of the Anti Hippocratic League is at work on cybernetic implants, with the ruthlessly ambitious junior doctors on the research team allowing themselves to be used as the guinea pigs. Taking a far more comic book approach with its plot of the creation of atomic supermen who could take over the world, **Anatomie 2** sits comfortably in the style of B-movie science fiction programmers of the 1950s as much as it anticipates modern-day low-budget classics like Leigh Whannell's **Upgrade** (2018). Franka Potente's character from the first film pops up briefly. She's now a police investigator hunting down members of the AHL, which is no less believable than everything else that happens in the film. Such as being able to control all the experimental subjects by a laptop. Or the idea that a newly-qualified junior doctor could perform unofficial emergency brain surgery on a small child in a massive hospital without anyone knowing about it other than the family members, who also happen to be nurses who help him.

HOUSE OF A THOUSAND CORPSES

USA, 2003
Director: Rob Zombie. Producer: Andy Gould.
Screenplay: Rob Zombie. Music: Scott Humphrey, Rob Zombie.
Cinematography: Alex Poppas, Tom Richmond.
Cast: Chad Bannon, William Bassett, Karen Black, Erin Daniels, Joe Dobbs III, Judith Drake.

The drive-in / grindhouse influences are strong in this, rock musician Rob Zombie's feature debut as writer and director. The seedy, sleazy, menacing feel the director has striven for through much of his work – particularly the sequels featuring the characters introduced here – is in evidence from the opening credits. The rest of the film provides such a wild and crazy assault on the senses that a single viewing may not be enough to catch all the gags, like the fact the members of the insane sadistic Firefly family are all named after characters in Marx Brothers films. We learn of this film's mad doctor (Dr. Satan aka S. Quentin Quale – yet another Marx Brothers reference) early on, from roadside attraction host Captain Spaulding (a splendid, terrifying edge-of-sanity performance from Sid Haig). But it's not until the end that we get to see him in all his grotesque glory, carrying on his human experiments underground with the help of his mutated assistant. The Fireflys returned in **The Devil's Rejects** (2005) and **3 from Hell** (2019) but Dr. Satan didn't. Meanwhile Rob Zombie gave us another sort of mad doctor in the form of Malcolm McDowell's Sam Loomis in his remake of **Halloween** (2007) and its superior sequel **Halloween II** (2009).

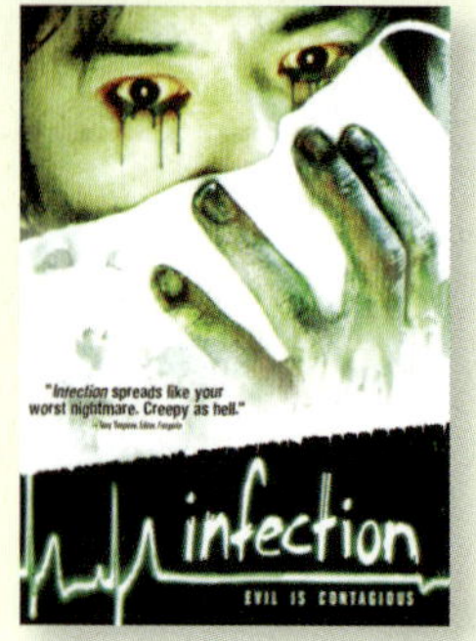

INFECTION

Japan, 2004
Director: Masayuki Ochiai. Producer: Takashige Ichise. Screenplay: Masayuki Ochiai. Music: Kuniaki Haishima. Cinematography: Hatsuaki Masui.
Cast: Michiko Hada, Mari Hoshino, Tae Kimura, Yôko Maki, Kaho Minami, Moro Morooka.

Before director Masayuki Ochiai shot the 2008 Japanese remake of **Shutter** (from the 2004 Thai original) and two sequels in the **Ju-On** series of movies – **The Beginning of the End** (2014) and **The Final Curse** (2015) – he made **Infection**, an original hospital-based horror film. A patient with seventy per cent burns is given the wrong drug when he has a cardiac arrest. He should get calcium chloride, which is a membrane stabiliser commonly found in arrest kits. Instead, he is given calcium chlorate, which is a herbicide, so it's anyone's guess what it's doing in a Japanese hospital's pharmacy. Though the hospital is pretty grotty and there's a distinct air of John Carpenter's 1976 **Assault on Precinct 13** to the rundown short-staffed building. An infected patient is brought there where they swiftly turn into green goo, and the staff agree to cover up the burn patient's death. The concept of a virus that spreads via consciousness and dreams, altering an individual's perceptions and making them prone to their weaknesses is fascinating. But it isn't terribly well presented in a film that tries to cram in too many disparate elements, doesn't deal with any of them especially satisfactorily, and remains disappointingly one-note in tone for most of its length.

TEARS OF KALI

Germany, 2004
Director: Andreas Marschall.
Producer: Olivera Becker. Screenplay: Andreas Marschall. Music: John Panama, India Bharti.
Cinematography: Heiko Merten, Michael Schuff.
Cast: Peter Martell, Anja Gebel, Adrian Topol, Michael Balaun, Mathieu Carrière, Cora Chilcott.

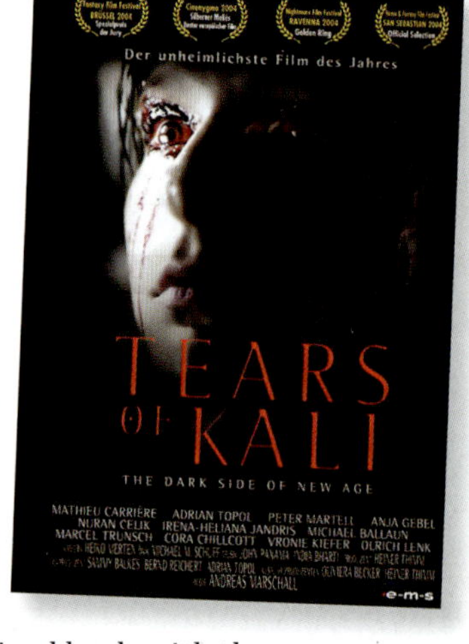

Andreas Marschall's exquisitely intense three-part anthology movie concerns itself with the activities of the India-based cult the Taylor-Eriksson group. Some members have made it back to Germany, bringing the horrors they acquired back with them. The middle segment, 'Devi' features a psychiatrist with some very radical ideas for treating his latest patient, a violent offender sent to him after putting a Polish victim into a coma. During the two-handed episode, tables are quickly turned as the perpetrator of the crime has his violent tendencies turned against him, leading to a satisfying blood-splattered finale. The other two stories deal with a girl imprisoned in a psychiatric institution for tearing her lover to pieces when it's actually a demon that's responsible, and the tale of a bogus faith healer who finds himself at risk of becoming the new host to the ancient demon one of his patients is harbouring. One of the commonest complaints levelled against anthology pictures is their uneven feel, but by having a very strong linking theme and consistently graphic disturbing and upsetting storylines **Tears of Kali** avoids this pitfall. If nothing else, it suggests if your psychiatrist starts chanting about Kali it's probably the signal to run.

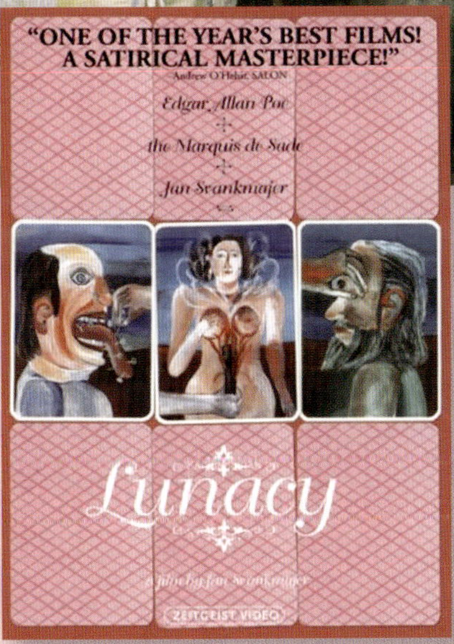

LUNACY

Czech Republic/Slovakia, 2005
Director: Jan Svankmajer. Producer: Jaromír Kallista.
Screenplay: Jan Svankmajer. Cinematography: Juraj Galvánek.
Cast: Jan Tríska, Pavel Liska, Anna Geislerová, Martin Huba, Jaroslav Dusek, Pavel Nový.

Czech surrealist filmmaker Jan Svankmajer turned his attention to adapting the works of both de Sade and Poe (specifically 'The Premature Burial' and 'The System of Dr. Tarr and Professor Fether') for this arthouse horror. Berlot, the lead, meets a man claiming to be the Marquis de Sade who, after some appropriate Sadean philosophising and a spell in a coffin, causes Berlot to end up in a chicken-filled asylum. A nurse claims the head doctor is an inmate and the real director is locked in the dungeon, but when Berlot frees him, the man's methods turn out to be far more horrible than his 'insane' replacement. Because this is Svankmajer the live action proceedings are regularly punctuated by bizarre stop motion animated sequences, many of them featuring meat, which slices itself and goes off for a walk, while eyeballs and brains toddle their way into cow skulls, all to the accompaniment of an organ grinder's repetitive tune. Svankmajer, a filmmaker who has influenced the Brothers Quay and Terry Gilliam amongst others, is responsible for a substantial body of short animated work – usually employing claymation or food as his media – commonly described as nightmarish, aggressive, or disturbing. His feature-length adaptations of literary works include 1988's **Alice** (from the Lewis Carroll novel) and 2018's **Insect** (from the Capek brothers play).

TURISTAS

USA, 2006
Director: John Stockwell. Producers: Marc Butan, Scott Steindorff, John Stockwell, Bo Zenga. Screenplay: Michael Arlen Ross. Music: Paul Haslinger. Cinematography: Enrique Chediak. Cast: Josh Duhamel, Melissa George, Olivia Wilde, Desmond Askew, Beau Garrett, Max Brown.

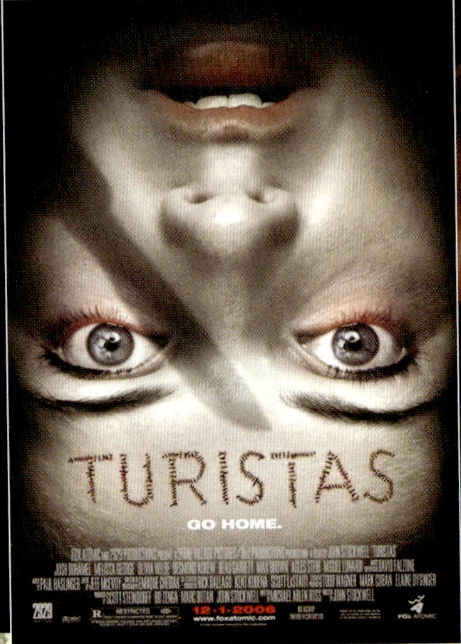

Released as **Paradise Lost** in the UK, director John Stockwell's picture is a 'holiday goes horribly wrong' tale of bright young attractive things who backpack to Brazil. There they get drunk on a beach and end up being drugged, and having their organs taken out by a psychopathic South American surgeon for transplantation into his local patients, as 'payback' for what the US has done to his country. Opportunities for political allegory and pithy dialogue are shunned in favour of bargain basement gross outs. Fans of medical inaccuracies in sleazy films can add this one to their list, as our villain disembowels a naked girl without anaesthetic and uses entirely the wrong kind of incision to take a kidney out. Produced in the wake of the success of Eli Roth's **Hostel** (2005) this entry in the 'going anywhere outside the United States will get you killed' subgenre provides some lovely locations, but otherwise this is strictly regressive grindhouse stuff, wasting the talents of actress Melissa George, and giving us a damp squib of an ending. Stockwell is best known for his acting roles in movies like John Carpenter's **Christine** (1983), and **Top Gun** (1986). At least he'll be remembered for something.

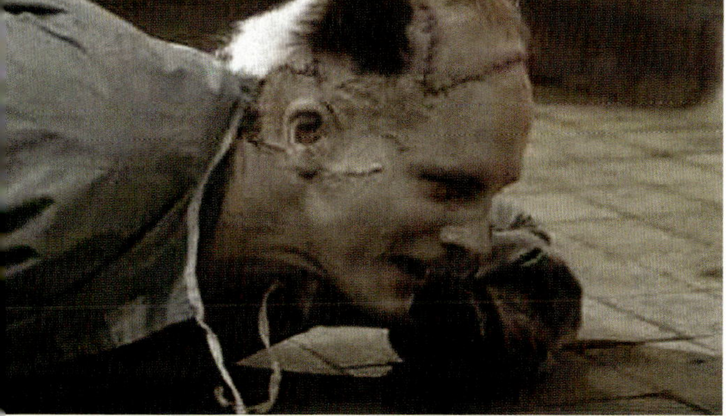

CHILL

USA, 2007
Director: Serge Rodnunsky.
Producer: Serge Rodnunsky. Screenplay: Serge Rodnunsky. Music: Nigel Holton, Kurt Oldman, Jeffrey Walton. Cinematography: Serge Rodnunsky.
Cast: Thomas Calabro, Ashley Laurence, Victor Grant, Shaun Kurtz, James Russo, Clark Moore.

H.P. Lovecraft meets Jess Franco in this ultra-low-budget homemade effort that uses the classic short story 'Cool Air' for its inspiration but throws in some topless prostitutes with their faces peeled off for good measure. Sam (Thomas Calabro) is an ex-doctor and writer who gets a job working in a supermarket owned by Dr. Munoz (Shaun Kurtz). Munoz spends most of his time living in a freezer in the back, when he's not driving around in his filthy white van urging his lumbering peeling-faced assistant Tor to abduct prostitutes so Munoz can use their skin to replace his own frequently shedding epidermis. He kidnaps Maria (**Hellraiser**'s Ashley Laurence) and wants Sam to become his assistant. Before he or anyone else can say 'Not on your *Necronomicon*' (the doctor has a copy, you see) the prostitutes' pimp turns up with his gang for a bit of a shoot-out and a twist ending that can at best be described as sub-par and at worst as incomprehensible. Reminiscent of 1970s EuroTrash, Tor should really be called Morpho in tribute to Jess Franco, while Dr. Munoz even wears a cloak and wanders around as if he's searching for the Spanish vampire picture in which he truly belongs.

THE GIRL REBEL FORCE OF COMPETITIVE SWIMMERS

Japan, 2007
Director: Kôji Kawano. Producers: Yôji Hirako, Masami Teranishi. Screenplay: Satoshi Ôwada. Music: Hideto Takematsu. Cinematography: Mitsuaki Fujimoto.
Cast: Sasa Handa, Yuria Hidaka, Ayumu Tokitô, Mizuka Arai, Hiromitsu Kiba, Hidetomo Nishida.

Who would have thought a zombie apocalypse would involve so much softcore schoolgirl lesbian groping? At least it does in director Kôji Kawano's film, which also goes by the titles **Undead Pool**, **Inglorious Zombie Hunters**, and **Attack Girls' Swim Team vs the Undead**. Doctors turn up at an all-girls school and proceed to inject its pupils and staff with a green glutinous substance on the pretext it's the vaccine for a virus. Cue homicidal zombies except for the girls' swim team who are mysteriously immune. New girl Aki (Sasa Handa) reveals that before enrolling in the school she was trained to be an assassin (mainly, according to the flashback, by wearing a ball gag and leather underwear) by a perverted mad doctor with a flute that, when played by him, causes all her clothes to fall off. The climax involves the doctor's return and yes he's got his flute with him. The final act forgets all about the zombies as everything goes crazy in that particular way unique to perverted Japanese cinema. Anyone researching Japanese schoolgirl fetishes will find the film a useful watch, as the director seems to have a penchant for quite a lot of them, including upskirt shots during dialogue scenes, lots of tight swimming costumes, and the aforementioned sapphic stuff.

SICK NURSES

Thailand, 2007
Directors: Piraphan Laoyont, Thodsapol Siriwiwat. Producers: Akarapol Techaratanaprasert, Prachya Pinkaew, Sukanya Vongsthapat. Screenplay: Piraphan Laoyont, Thodsapol Siriwiwat. Music: Lullaby Production. Cinematography: Chitti Urnorakankij.
Cast: Chol Wachananon, Wichan Jarujinda, Chidjan Rujiphun, Kanya Rattanapetch, Dollaros Dachapratumwan, Ase Wang.

Coming across a little like Norman J. Warren's 1978 **Terror** (which was itself inspired by Dario Argento's 1977 **Suspiria**) this Thai production offers us a group of pretty nurses who, led by a scheming doctor, are all involved in the black market trafficking of dead bodies. When one nurse threatens to expose the group, the others kill her, only for her ghost to return and subject each of them to a bizarre, creative, and neon-lit death in the hospital in which they seem to both live and work. The opening act does its best to depict the story's potential victims in as many 'playfully sexy' situations as possible, including weightlifting upside down, showering with their clothes on, and brushing their teeth while wearing only skimpy underwear. Once the murders get underway however, things take a distinctly nastier turn, not least the revelations as to how the doctor is ultimately the cause of it all. While neither as clever as 2004's **Shutter** nor as gory as 2009's **Meat Grinder**, the twisting plotline combines with some creative set pieces – involving tanks of blood, huge volumes of black hair, and one scene with hundreds of faceless clones – to make **Sick Nurses** a perfectly acceptable way to spend eighty minutes.

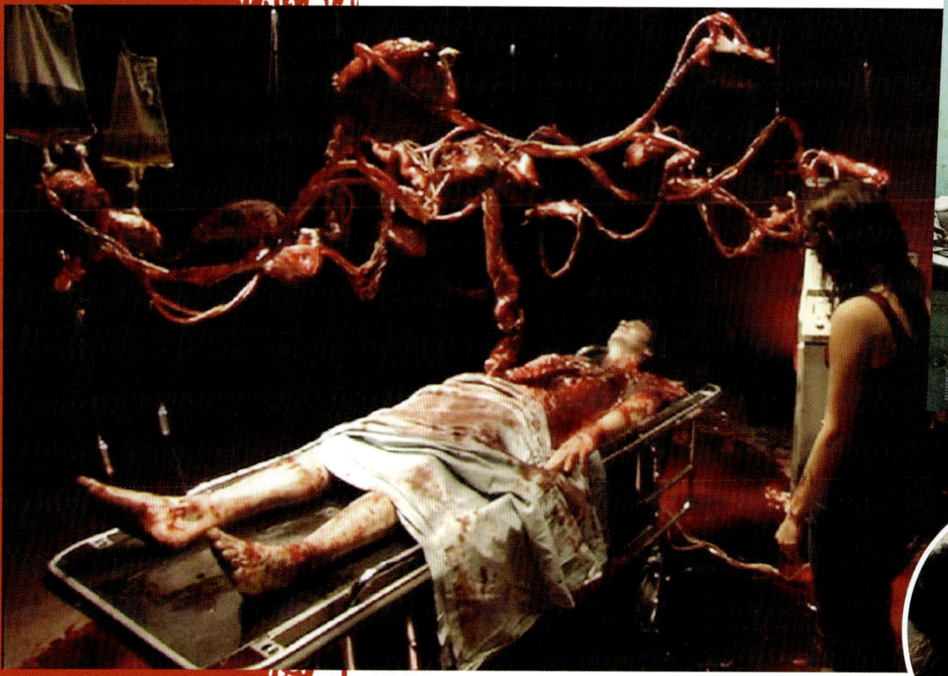

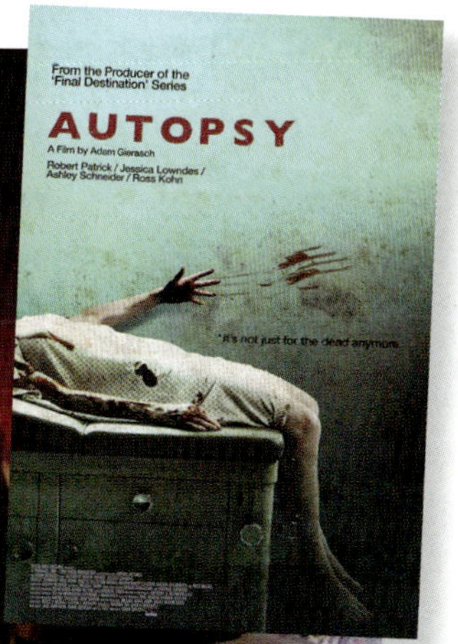

AUTOPSY

USA, 2008
Director: Adam Gierasch. Producers: Steve Markoff, Bruce McNall, Jessica Horowitz, Warren Zide.
Screenplay: Jace Anderson, Adam Gierasch, E.L. Katz.
Music: Joseph Bishara. Cinematography: Anthony B. Richmond.
Cast: Jessica Lowndes, Ross Kohn, Ross McCall, Ashley Schneider, Arcadiy Golubovich, Gregg Brazzel, Robert Patrick.

Five friends crash their car and end up being taken to a nearly deserted hospital run by Robert Patrick's mad Dr. Benway in Adam Gierasch's fairground fun-ride-style horror. There are some excellent special effects in an otherwise not terribly special picture, which has a plot structure that, bizarrely, mirrors Alvin Rakoff's **Death Ship** (1980) in which survivors of a disaster also wander around a lot on their own before succumbing to torture and death in varying scenarios, often for no good reason. In **Autopsy** a girl is subjected to the most inaccurate lumbar puncture ever depicted on screen, in which the quantity of spinal fluid drawn off would easily kill a giraffe, but here our heroine is sitting up fit and well straight after. Another victim has what one presumes to be their stomach removed, although the tense bloated organ Dr. Benway removes looks like no gastrectomy specimen any upper gastrointestinal surgeon would recognise. Towards the end things take a decidedly Italian turn. Director Gierasch name-checks Dario Argento in the end credits but the climax with Benway's near-dead wife is decidedly more from the Joe D'Amato school, with the killer revealed by a flash of lightning in true **Anthropophagous** (1980) fashion. Despite the title and all the gore on display, nobody actually undergoes an autopsy.

REPO! THE GENETIC OPERA

USA, 2008
Director: Darren Lynn Bousman. Producers: Mark Burg, Oren Koules, Carl Mazzocone. Screenplay: Darren Smith, Terrance Zdunich. Music: Darren Smith, Terrance Zdunich. Cinematography: Joseph White. Cast: Alexa Vega, Paul Sorvino, Anthony Head, Sarah Brightman, Paris Hilton, Bill Moseley.

There are very few horror musicals and even fewer that are entirely sung through. Kudos, then, to **Saw** franchise director Darren Lynn Bousman (Parts II, III, IV and 2021's **Spiral: From the Book of Saw**) who brought to the screen this tale of a future world where organ transplants are vital and are managed by the evil GeneCo. Anthony Stewart Head (Giles of *Buffy the Vampire Slayer* fame) is the 'Repo Man' of the title, repossessing organs from those who have failed to keep up their payments. His daughter Shilo (Alexa Vega) knows nothing of his 'night surgeon' alter ego or that he works for GeneCo boss Rotti Largo (Paul Sorvino). A bunch of quirky character actors (Bill Moseley, Paris Hilton, 'Ogre' from Skinny Puppy) are cast as the Largo family, who sing and go wild, while there's a role for Sarah Brightman (as 'Blind Mag') in this as well. The budget is kept low by the use of graphic novel-type splash panels for scene setting and backstory, the songs are often catchy, and the entire stylish endeavour is quite the unique and, if you can buy into the concept, entertaining item. Like **The Rocky Horror Picture Show** (1975), **Repo** initially received negative reviews but has gradually gained a cult following.

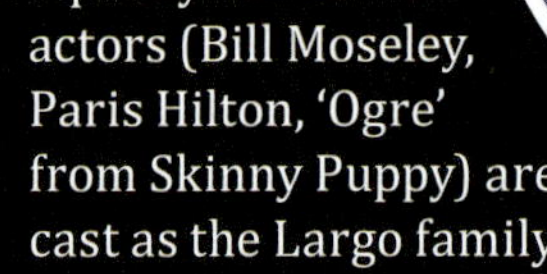

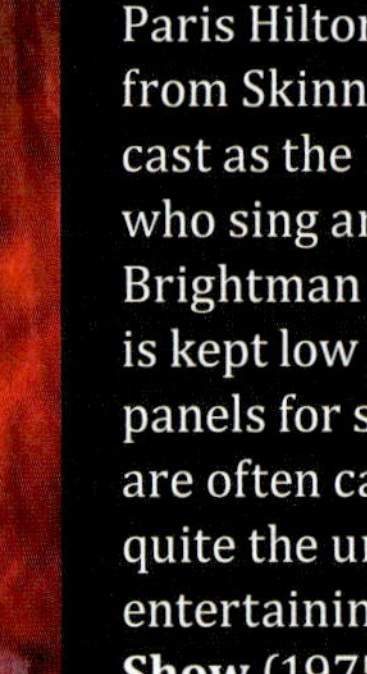

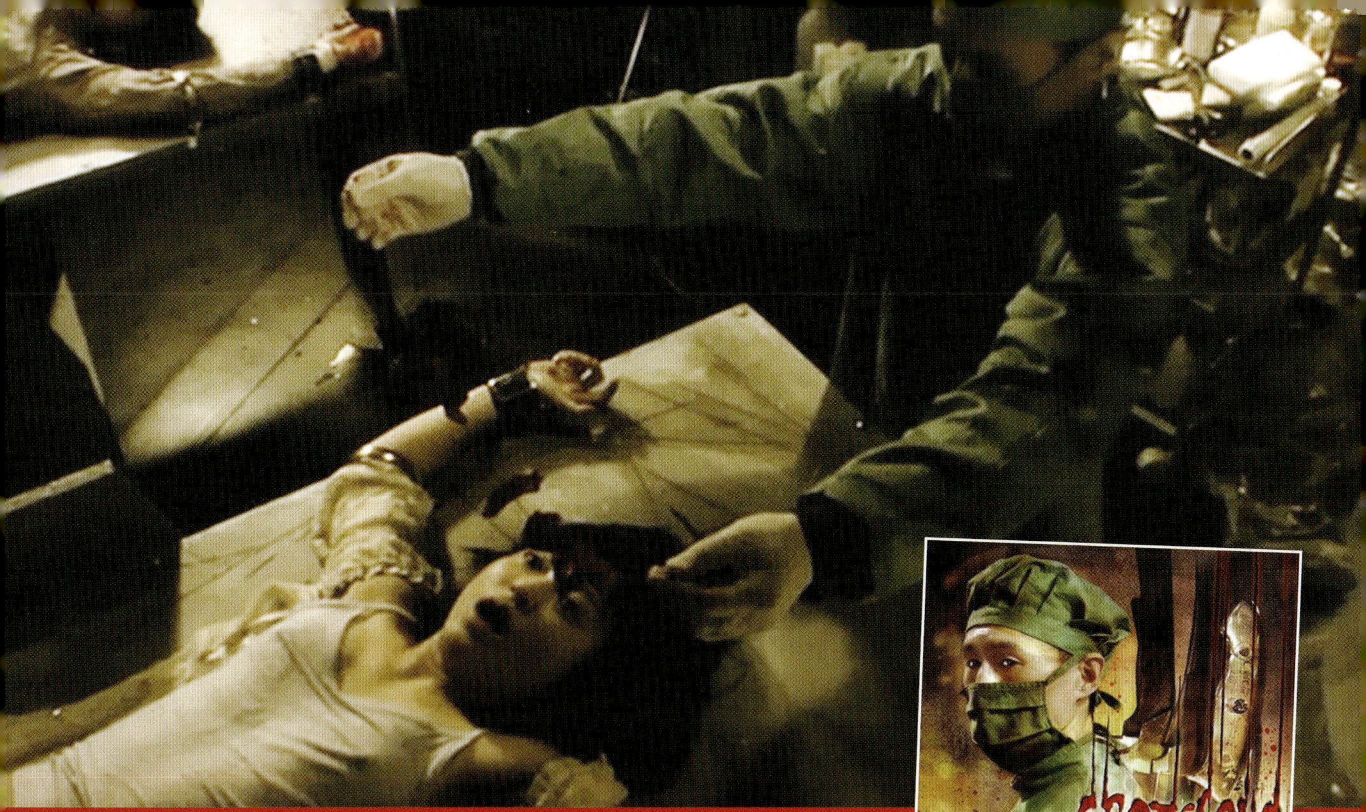

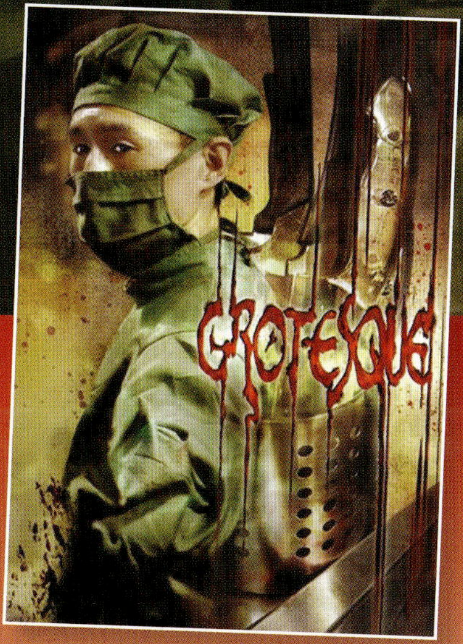

GROTESQUE

Japan, 2009
Director: Kôji Shiraishi.
Producers: Kazue Udagawa, Kyôsuke Ueno. Screenplay: Kôji Shiraishi.
Music: Kazuo Satô. Cinematography: Yôhei Fukuda.
Cast: Hiroaki Kawatsure, Shigeo Ôsako, Tsugumi Nagasawa.

In this grim piece of Japanese torture porn, a doctor (or at least he thinks he is) kidnaps a couple as they leave a restaurant and takes them to his torture dungeon. Here we spend most of the rest of the running time as he subjects them to various sexual violations and physical mutilations. Banned by the BBFC on submission even though the limb amputations and nipple slicings are all a bit Herschell Gordon Lewis (albeit done with rather more of a straight face). This is as good a place as any to take a moment to talk about how human intestines are rarely, if ever, accurately depicted onscreen. **Grotesque** makes the mistake found in many gore films. In reality, the small and large intestines are attached to the gut wall by a robust structure known as a mesentery, which helps to keep everything in order. It is therefore impossible to pop your hand into someone's abdomen (as our torturer does here) and pull out something akin to fifty feet of what looks like skipping rope, because the anatomy just doesn't work like that. Oh, and real bowel is a lot more delicate, so it won't support the weight of a human body, in case anyone was wondering. To add hilarity to inaccuracy, in **Grotesque** the torturer puts on 'Land of Hope and Glory' while conducting his inaccurate eviscerations, adding a surreal edge and raising a smile in anyone familiar with Spike Milligan's TV series *Q*...

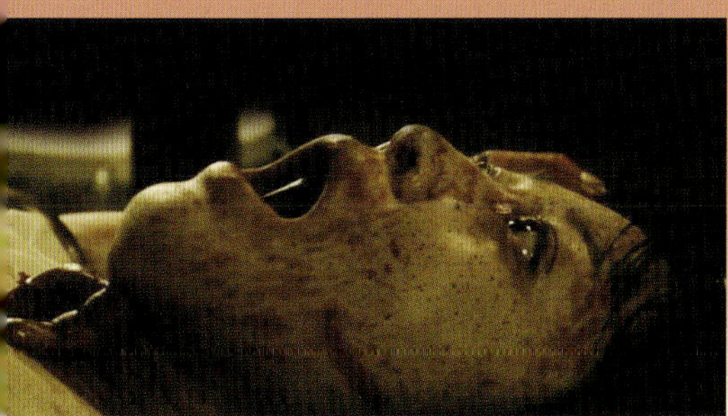

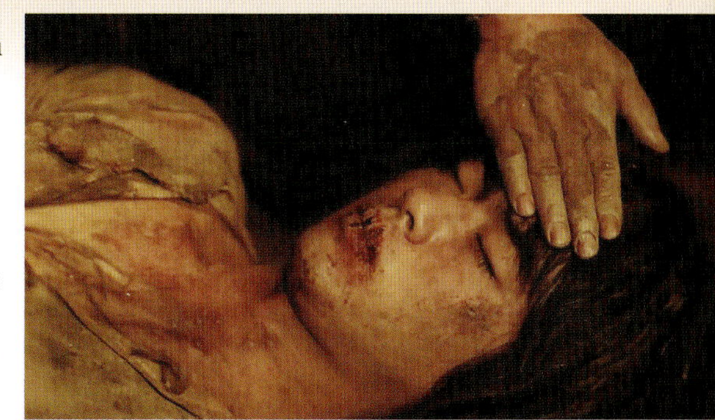

THE HUMAN CENTIPEDE (FIRST SEQUENCE)

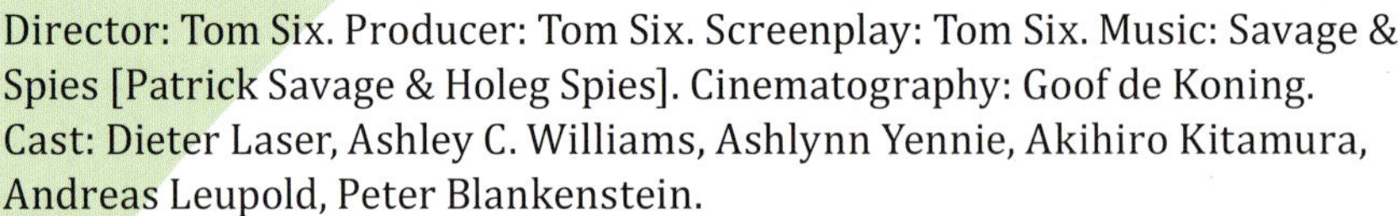

Netherlands, 2009
Director: Tom Six. Producer: Tom Six. Screenplay: Tom Six. Music: Savage & Spies [Patrick Savage & Holeg Spies]. Cinematography: Goof de Koning.
Cast: Dieter Laser, Ashley C. Williams, Ashlynn Yennie, Akihiro Kitamura, Andreas Leupold, Peter Blankenstein.

After his experiment with three Rottweiler dogs fails, mad genius Dr. Heiter (Dieter Laser in the role he was born to play after a forty-year career in film acting) decides to bury them in the garden and move onto something bigger. Perhaps he should have tried fusing smaller dogs than the Rottweilers first and made a Centipoodle. His plan: to join three human bodies together to form 'one long glorious gastrointestinal tract'. Tom Six's film is nasty, lurid, sensational, and exploitative in all the best senses of the word, and very much the 21st Century equivalent of a penny dreadful or 1930s horror comic. It's also very well made, with the photography so cold and crisp that the whole film feels like an outdoor operating theatre on a spring morning. Never dull, never boring, and with a couple of chase sequences that are properly suspenseful and ultimately cruel, this is a film for everyone who has been waiting for the movie equivalent of the nastiest pulp paperback stories of yesteryear. Widely publicised as being '100% medically accurate', it certainly is, although the suture techniques (and especially the skin clips) employed by Dr. Heiter wouldn't have provided a particularly strong anastomosis. For it all to hold together some good old fashioned silk deep tension sutures would have been advisable. The inspirations for the movie include exploitation standbys like Nazi war criminals, as well as the films of David Cronenberg, some of the more extreme examples of Japanese cinema, and Six's own fear of hospitals.

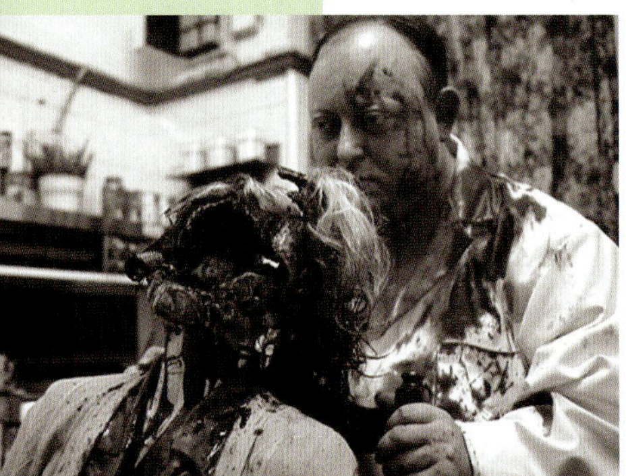

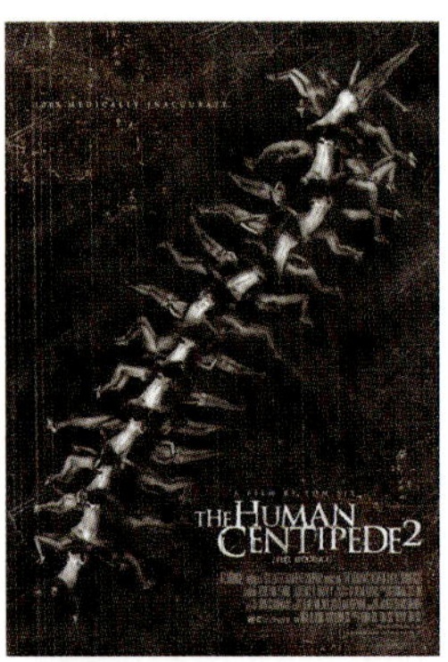

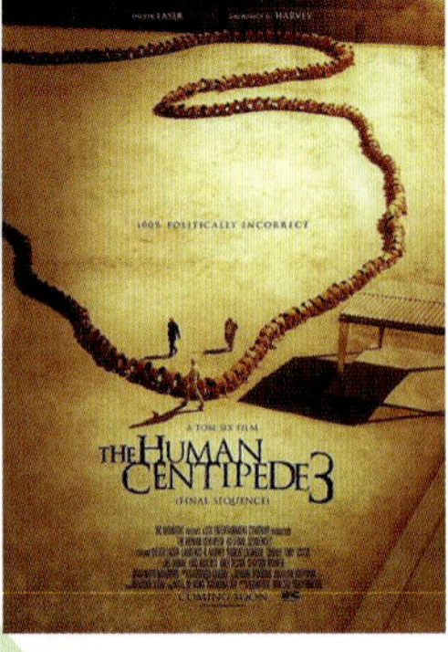

Six followed this with the distinctly different (in both tone and style) black and white, Lynchian **The Human Centipede 2 (Full Sequence)** in 2011. In the sequel Laurence R. Harvey plays Martin, an East London car park attendant obsessed with the previous film who, impressed by the character of Dr. Heiter, creates a 12-person centipede. Six proclaimed that this time his film was '100% medically inaccurate'. It would certainly be something of a challenge to achieve the surgical monstrosity Harvey's character stitches together, while the film as a whole was considered sufficiently controversial to be the subject of heavy censorship in many countries, including the UK. The trilogy concluded with 2015's somewhat metatextual **The Human Centipede 3 (Final Sequence)**, in that it managed to include the stars of both the first and second parts (in different roles, admittedly) as well as featuring Tom Six as himself. The action moves to the United States this time. Dieter Laser plays a prison warden who watches the second film and is inspired to create a 500 person-long centipede constructed from prison inmates. Academy Award nominee Eric Roberts and adult film star Bree Olson also featured prominently in the cast. An alternate ending to this final film suggested it was all a dream by part one's Dr. Heiter, allowing the cycle to start over again.

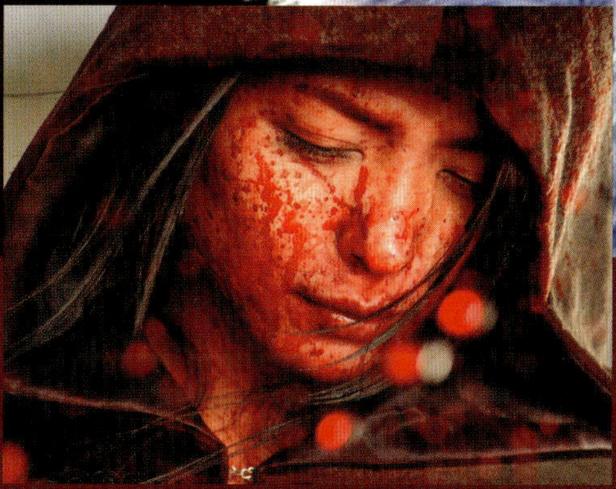

VAMPIRE GIRL VS FRANKENSTEIN GIRL

Japan, 2009
Directors: Yoshihiro Nishimura, Naoyuki Tomomatsu.
Producers: Masatsugu Asahi, Jun Nakajima.
Screenplay: Daichi Nagisa, Naoyuki Tomomatsu. Music: Kou Nakagawa. Cinematography: Shu G. Momose.
Cast: Yukie Kawamura, Takumi Saitoh, Eri Otoguro, Sayaka Kametani, Kanji Tsuda, Eihi Shiina.

It's back to the world of crazy Japanese exploitation cinema with the director of 2008's **Tokyo Gore Police**, Yoshihiro Nishimura, joining Naoyuki Tomomatsu (whose latest film appears to be 2018's **Scissorpenis**) to co-direct yet another tale of high school loves, jealousies, and intrigues – expressed using the media of over-the-top prosthetic effects and lunatic behaviour. This one's not for the easily offended as the school in question has a team that takes part in a 'Wrist Cutter Rally' and a clique of Japanese girls who try to dress as cliched Africans, including outrageous blackface. Members of both groups become fodder for Frankenstein Girl, created by her father the school Vice Principal, who in his spare time likes nothing more than to don a ludicrous long-haired white wig, daub his face in red and white paint and attempt to reanimate the dead with the aid of the oversexed school nurse. Mixing extreme gore with Saturday morning children's TV show-style histrionics, nods to Brian Yuzna's 1990 **Bride of Re-Animator** (a creature made from eyeballs and fingers), and the **Ju-On** films (a scene where a teacher gives a lesson about them) may raise a smile if you can tolerate things like casual racism and deliberate self-harm being played for (very bloodstained) laughs. There's a nod to Tony Scott's **The Hunger** (1983) at the end as well, before the film can't help but go out on a note of even greater daftness.

BEYOND THE BLACK RAINBOW

Canada, 2010
Director: Panos Cosmatos.
Producers: Oliver Linsley, Christya Nordstokke. Screenplay: Panos Cosmatos.
Music: Jeremy Schmidt [Sinoia Caves].
Cinematography: Norm Li.
Cast: Michael J. Rogers, Eva Bourne, Scott Hylands, Rondel Reynoldson, Marilyn Norry, Gerry South.

This one's set in 1983, the year the young Panos Cosmatos started visiting the video store where he was denied the films he most wanted to see, and so instead imagined what they might be like. When he finally got to make his own feature film, he also found the idea of setting a movie one year before 1984 amusing. Something terrible has happened at the New Age research facility created in the 1960s by the terrifically-named Dr. Mercurio Arboria (Scott Hylands). Now it's being run by the psychopathic Dr. Nyle (Michael J. Rogers) who wears a wig and contact lenses. He's also keeping a girl called Elena (Eva Bourne) prisoner in the basement so he can interrogate her to better understand the psychic abilities she possesses. A languid, slow, measured piece that will either entrance or infuriate, comparisons have been made to Stanley Kubrick's **2001: A Space Odyssey** (1968) and Andrei Tarkovsky's **Solaris** (1972). The film also name-checks William Burroughs' book *Naked Lunch* (Nyle gets his own medication from Benway's pharmacy). Cosmatos would go on to make the Nicolas Cage-starrer **Mandy** (2018) which is another film in the same style, both being a world away from the work of the director's father (George Pan Cosmatos of **Rambo: First Blood Part II** fame).

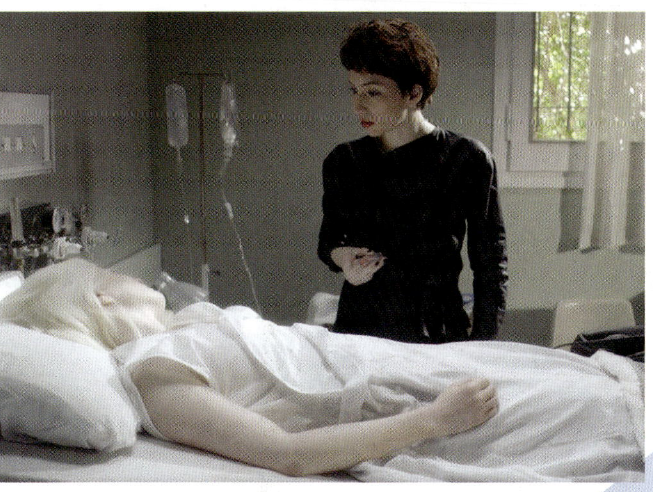

EXQUISITE CORPSE

USA, 2010
Director: Scott David Russell.
Producers: Michael Anderson, Scott David Russell, Christopher Sepulveda.
Screenplay: Scott David Russell.
Music: Jon Licht.
Cinematography: Nikolas Smith.
Cast: Steve Sandvoss, Nicole Vicius, Guillermo Diaz, Tessa Thompson, Larry Cedar, David H. Lawrence XVII.

This has nothing to do with the 1996 Poppy Z. Brite novel of the same name, about a necrophile serial killer, which was dropped by several publishers for being too violent. Or indeed the surrealist parlour game of garbled images or words. The tag line for this **Exquisite Corpse** would have you believe it's '**Re-Animator** Meets **Frankenstein**'. Actually it's more like Monogram's 1942 **The Corpse Vanishes** meets **Frankenhooker** (1990) but nowhere near as entertaining or creative as either. When Sophia (Nicole Vicius) drowns, her medical student boyfriend Nicholas (Steve Sandvoss) discovers he can bring her back with injections of large amounts of the hormone oxytocin produced during female orgasm. Unfortunately the donors die and Sophia needs regular infusions. Anyone expecting Frank Henenlotter levels of sleazy creative lunacy will be surprised to learn this ludicrous premise is treated way too seriously, performed – on the whole – by actors with little charisma, and directed with all the style and panache of a 1970s TV movie. Fans of celebrities-to-be in peril may enjoy the sight of future Marvel Cinematic Universe and **Men in Black: International** (2019) star Tessa Thompson tied to a table, but it's quite a drag to get there. Writer-director Scott David Russell has yet to perform similar duties on anything else.

KYOFU: THE SYLVIAN EXPERIMENTS

Japan, 2010
Director: Hiroshi Takahashi. Producer: Takashige Ichise.
Screenplay: Hiroshi Takahashi. Music: Hiroyuki Nakashima.
Cinematography: Akiko Ashizawa.
Cast: Mina Fujii, Yuri Nakamura, Sô Kusakabe, Yôichirô Saitô, Kimika Yoshino, Yôko Chôsokabe, Nagisa Katahira.

Prolific screenwriter Hiroshi Takahashi (The original **Ringu** movie trilogy and 2020's *Ju-On: Origins* TV series) wrote and directed this intriguing arthouse horror which doesn't entirely make sense but probably isn't meant to. After watching grainy black and white 16mm footage of brain stimulation experiments that yield a strange white light, neurosurgeon Etsuko Ota (Nagisa Katahira) continues the research by stimulating the lateral sulcus, or Sylvian fissure, of the brain (that's the bit that separates the temporal lobes from the parts that surround them). Her aim is to discover what 'true reality' looks like, her ultimate intention to cause humankind to undergo a 'spiritual evolution'. We touch upon cosmic horror, whether or not there even is an afterlife, and what happens specifically to suicides after death in this melting pot of astral projection, ectoplasmic manifestations, brain surgery, and a very strange bit where one of the subjects becomes pregnant with the afterlife itself. There are no simple explanations in this one but plenty to think about. Takahashi also directed 2018's **Occult Bolshevism** which is far more successful at combining science with the supernatural, with seven people who have had a brush with the supernatural taking part in a Nigel Kneale-style psychic experiment.

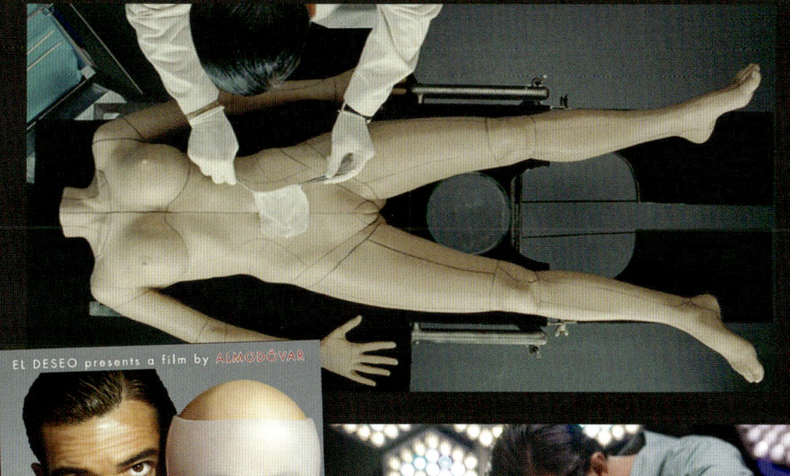

THE SKIN I LIVE IN

Spain/USA, 2011
Director: Pedro Almodóvar. Producers: Agustín Almodóvar, Esther García. Screenplay: Pedro Almodóvar, Agustín Almodóvar. Music: Alberto Iglesias. Cinematography: José Luis Alcaine. Cast: Antonio Banderas, Elena Anaya, Marisa Paredes, Jan Cornet, Roberto Álamo, Eduard Fernández.

Cult Spanish director Pedro Almodóvar explores the **Les yeux sans visage** subgenre of EuroHorror with gusto in this tale about plastic surgeon Robert Ledgard (Antonio Banderas). Ledgard keeps a girl locked up in his isolated clinic for reasons that are not at all clear until Almodóvar wants them to be. As well as a nod to Franju – Ledgard has participated in 'three out of the nine face transplants performed' – we also have Marisa Paredes in a key role (she was in fellow countryman Jess Franco's similarly-styled 1962 **The Awful Dr. Orlof**). A significant plot element is taken straight from the contes cruels of writers like Maurice Level (who pretty much invented the genre) and Sir Charles Birkin, with a surgeon's daughter being raped and subsequently committing suicide, whereupon her father employs his surgical skills to exact creative revenge. It's unsurprising, then, that with these literary antecedents **The Skin I Live In** is based on a more recent novel with that theme (*Mygale* by French author Thierry Jonquet, published as *Tarantula* in the UK and US). Almodóvar's movie is as fine a rendering of these themes as one could hope for, right down to this being one of the very few films where surgeons actually don their gowns and gloves properly, to say nothing of Banderas' impeccable explanation of the correct use of vaginal dilators.

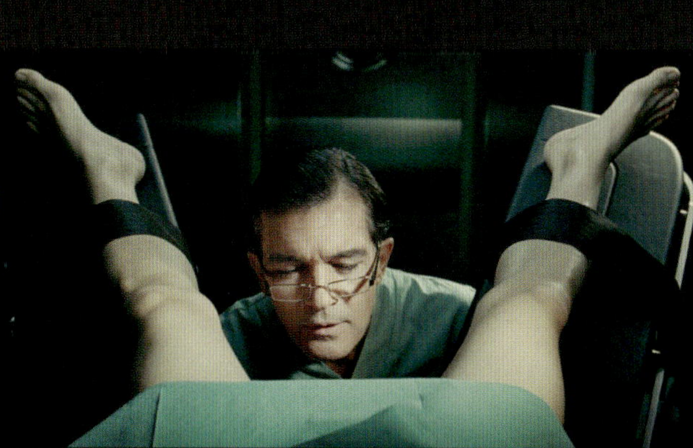

AMERICAN MARY

Canada, 2012
Directors: Jen Soska, Sylvia Soska.
Producers: John A. Curtis, Evan Tylor. Screenplay: Jen Soska, Sylvia Soska. Music: Peter Allen. Cinematography: Brian Pearson.
Cast: Katharine Isabelle, Antonio Cupo, Tristan Risk, David Lovgren, Paula Lindberg, Clay St. Thomas.

In need of money, medical student Mary (Katharine Isabelle) applies for work at a strip club, only to find her surgical skills to be in greater demand than her dance ones. After one case of treating straightforward injuries, Mary finds herself in full time employment as an illegal body modification surgeon, then taking revenge on the surgical lecturer who invited her to a sex party and raped her. Written and directed by twin sisters Jen and Sylvia Soska, who also appear in the film, **American Mary** uses broad strokes to create an extremely slick and witty revenge horror picture with a feminist agenda. It marked a considerable and assured step up in quality from their 2009 debut **Dead Hooker in a Trunk**. Since then, the Soskas have gained popularity both for their directorial work and hosting the *Hellevator* TV series, as well as maintaining a considerable presence on the festival circuit, displaying tremendous enthusiasm for the genre. Their subsequent features have been **See No Evil 2** (2014) and **Rabid** (2019), a sequel and remake respectively. After the creative peak of **American Mary** both these projects have felt like something of a retroactive step, and it is hoped the Soskas will once again come up with something as original and stylish as this picture.

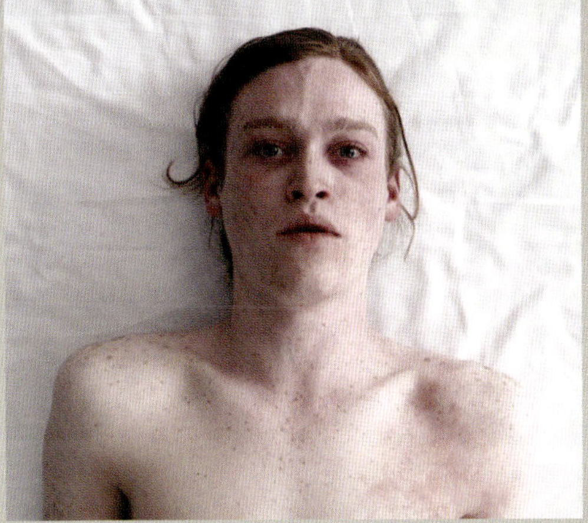

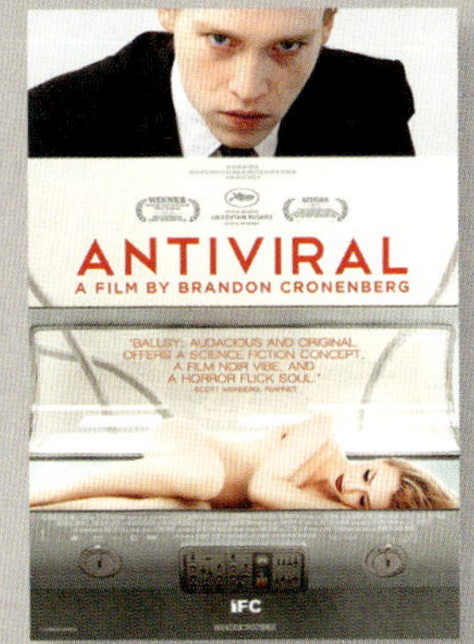

ANTIVIRAL

Canada/France, 2012
Director: Brandon Cronenberg.
Producer: Niv Fichman.
Screenplay: Brandon Cronenberg.
Music: E.C. Woodley.
Cinematography: Karim Hussain.
Cast: Caleb Landry Jones, Sarah Gadon, Lisa Berry, Douglas Smith, Nenna Abuwa, Donna Goodhand.

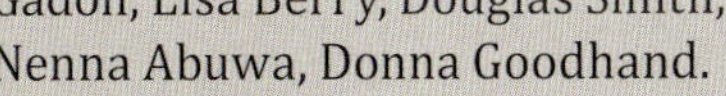

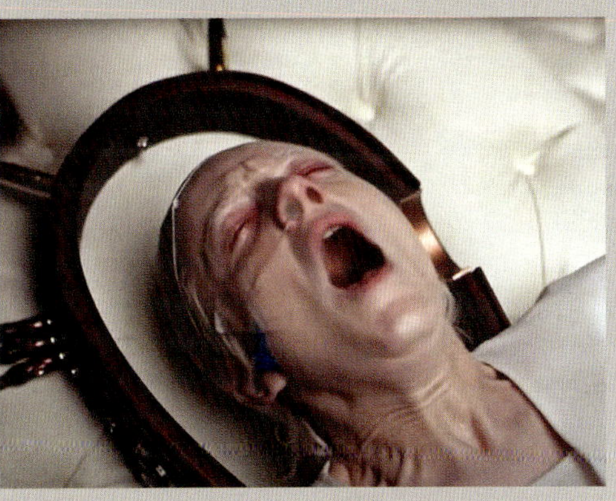

David Cronenberg's son Brandon proves to be a chip off the old block (or lobectomy off the old brain) with his debut feature, a body horror picture which explores the extrapolation of the commercialisation of celebrity to its most biological ends. Syd (Caleb Landry Jones) works at The Lucas Clinic, where clients can purchase the latest infections their favourite celebrities have suffered. Just like merchandising, these viruses are owned by various companies. The celebrity Hannah Geist is the Lucas Clinic's most profitable investment, and Syd deliberately infects himself with a virus she's caught in the hope of selling it on the black market. Then she reportedly dies of the disease, and Syd finds himself involved in a covert world of cutthroat corporate conspiracies, and to save his own skin, proposes new ways in which 'biological rights' can be exploited. Cronenberg Jr.'s visual style is certainly reminiscent of his father's early works – interiors are cold and sterile, and colour is mostly absent, with everything onscreen either black, white or shades of grey, right down to the celebrity meat grown from muscle cells that fans can buy to eat. Where modern day drug traffickers can resort to mules to carry illicit substances within their bodies, here a person's own circulatory system is used to smuggle the viruses. It's a grim view of the future, with little of the 'savage joy' exhibited in Cronenberg senior's body horror films. Except perhaps by the CEOs who run the clinics, but appropriately we never get to see that.

ERRORS OF THE HUMAN BODY

Germany/USA, 2012
Director: Eron Sheean. Producers: Mike Dehghan, Cole Payne, Darryn Welch.
Screenplay: Shane Danielsen, Eron Sheean.
Music: Anthony Pateras. Cinematography: Anna Howard.
Cast: Michael Eklund, Karoline Herfurth, Tómas Lemarquis, Rik Mayall, Caroline Gerdolle, Yusuke Yamasaki.

Geneticist Dr. Geoffrey Burton (Michael Eklund) comes to Dresden to work at Rik Mayall's research institute after describing 'Burton's Syndrome', in which the body develops tumours of every organ, and from which his young son died. The syndrome is fictitious but the science describing the mechanism (in this case mutation of what is known as a tumour suppressor gene – this one on chromosome 20) is sound. His old research associate Rebekka (Karoline Herfurth) has been speeding up limb regeneration in axolotls, while the much madder Jarek (Tómas Lemarquis) has ideas about using animals as gene vectors. In fact, the whole script is packed with interesting ideas expressed in some great lines of dialogue. Workers in the research institute are compared to cells in a single organism and there are random musings on the dreams of fruit flies. Where it falls down is in Eron Sheean's direction, which weighs far too heavily in favour of the political infighting that certainly can go on in such places, with too little emphasis on the body horror ramifications of the ideas being put forward. That the scientists all smoke, most likely creating tumours far faster than they can ever hope to cure them is a nice, nihilistic touch. But while the film desperately wants to be the stuff of Cronenberg's early films the execution is just a little too limp to bear comparison.

EXCISION

USA, 2012
Director: Richard Bates Jr.
Producers: Paul J. Alessi, Dylan Hale Lewis.
Screenplay: Richard Bates Jr. Music: Steve Damstra II, Mads Heldtberg.
Cinematography: Itay Gross.
Cast: AnnaLynne McCord, Roger Bart, Ariel Winter, Traci Lords, Malcolm McDowell, Ray Wise, Marlee Matlin, John Waters.

In writer-director Richard Bates Jr.'s feature debut – based on the short he made four years previously – AnnaLynne McCord is Pauline, a high school girl close to graduation but in danger of being expelled for her increasingly bizarre behaviour. She harbours dreams of becoming a surgeon, but parents Phyllis (genre icon Traci Lords) and Bob (Roger Bart from 2007's **Hostel: Part II**) insist she is delusional. Pauline's sister Grace (Ariel Winter) suffers from cystic fibrosis and needs a lung transplant, and with the girl across the road in Pauline's bad books, the scene is set for amateur surgery night in the family garage. **Excision** belongs to the same tiny subgenre of movies as Lucky McKee's 2002 **May**, starring Angela Bettis. Both depict delusional, troubled young women who find release through increasingly strange behaviour that runs the gamut from kooky to dangerously psychotic. Of the two, Bates' film is the more outré, peppering its narrative with deliciously gory and bizarre dream sequences and packing its cast with familiar faces including Malcolm McDowell, Ray Wise, Marlee Matlin, and the man **Excision** most feels like a tribute to, cult film director John Waters as a priest (oh the irony). It certainly doesn't take the greatest leap of imagination to see either Divine or Mink Stole as Pauline's mother, although Bates differs significantly from Waters in that some of his bloodstained imagery seems playfully (and undoubtedly deliberately) erotic, a charge that could never be levelled at the oeuvre of the man who gave us **Pink Flamingos** in 1972.

CAN'T COME OUT TO PLAY

USA, 2013
Director: John McNaughton. Producers: Steven A. Jones, Kim Jose, David Robinson, Meadow William. Screenplay: Stephen Lancellotti. Music: George S. Clinton. Cinematography: Rachel Morrison.
Cast: Samantha Morton, Michael Shannon, Natasha Calis, Charlie Tahan, Peter Fonda, Leslie Lyles.

When her mother and father die, twelve-year-old Maryann (Natasha Calis) goes to live with her grandparents in New England. Out wandering one day, she comes across a house that, if this were a Lucio Fulci film, would be located next to a cemetery. Through a downstairs window she spies Andy, a boy her age who is confined to a wheelchair by a mysterious disease that means he has to be kept at home. However, Andy's father Richard (Michael Shannon from 2010's **The Runaways** and 2017's **The Shape of Water**) doesn't mind Maryann visiting. Andy's mother Katherine (Samantha Morton from 2002's **Minority Report** and 2012's **Cosmopolis**) on the other hand, is dead against it. She works as a surgeon at the local hospital and has been caring for Andy at home ever since he was born. Maryann ignores Katherine's warnings and continues to see Andy on the sly. One day she ends up trapped in the house, ventures downstairs, and discovers something quite unexpected in the basement. Originally shown under the title **The Harvest**, director John McNaughton's well made, well acted film feels like the kind of thing that Britain's Children's Film Foundation might have come up with – had that company ever made a graphic horror film that would likely have ended up unsuitable for its target audience. The plot isn't remotely believable, but the skills of all involved keep you watching and there's a satisfying payoff at the end.

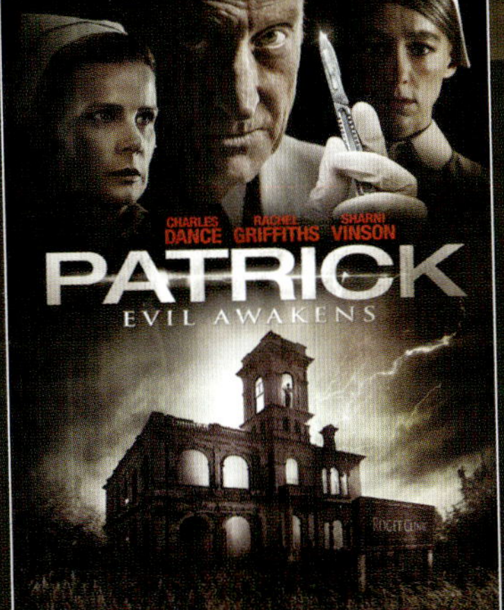

PATRICK

Australia, 2013
Director: Mark Hartley. Producer: Antony I. Ginnane. Screenplay: Justin King.
Music: Pino Donaggio. Cinematography: Garry Richards.
Cast: Sharni Vinson, Rachel Griffiths, Charles Dance, Peta Sergeant, Damon Gameau, Jackson Gallagher.

Mark Hartley's gloriously over-the-top operatic remake of Richard Franklin's 1978 original about a paralysed teenage boy who can control people with his mind was subtitled 'Evil Awakens' for its UK disc release. It stars Charles Dance in the mad doctor role originally played by Robert Helpmann, and whereas the hospital in the original version was a dull example of downtown city architecture, Dance's isolated mansion is full Gothic and so gloomy you wonder if he's late paying his electricity bill. Although he certainly has enough power available to repeatedly zap this film's Patrick (Jackson Gallagher). Sharni Vinson (from Adam Wingard's 2011 **You're Next**) is the nurse who works out what's going on when people start suffering bizarre accidents. The role was played by Susan Penhaligon in the original and one of the characters retains her surname as homage. Those who stay until the end of the credit roll will spot another intriguing little homage, not to the original film but to its sleazy nudity-filled unofficial 1980 Italian sequel **Patrick vive ancora** (**Patrick Still Lives**) directed by Mario Landi. Brian May composed the score to the original, which was used everywhere except in Italy where the Italian progressive rock group Goblin recorded a new music score. For the remake Hartley hired Italian composer Pino Donaggio.

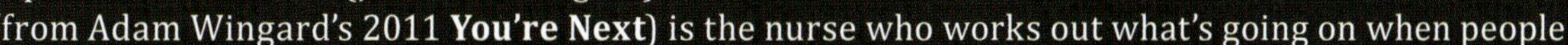

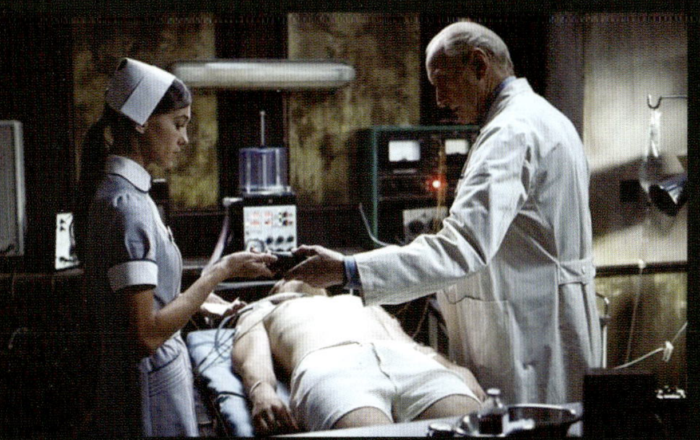

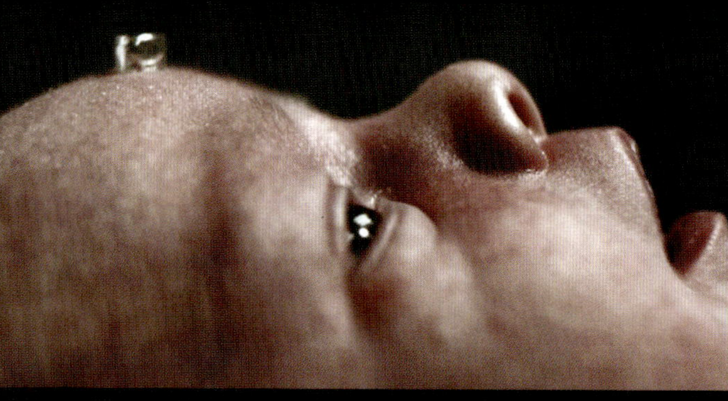

CLOSER TO GOD

USA, 2014
Director: Billy Senese. Producers: Jeremy Childs, Jonathan Rogers, Jennifer Spriggs. Screenplay: Billy Senese. Music: Thomas Nola. Cinematography: Evan Spencer Brace.
Cast: Jeremy Childs, Shelean Newman, Shannon Hoppe, David Alford, Isaac Disney, Olivia Lyle.

It's hard not to imagine how much better the legendary independent filmmaker Larry Cohen would have handled this subject matter. (In fact he did to some extent with **It's Alive** in 1974.) **Closer to God** is an uneasy mix of sober reflection on the morality of genetic engineering, saddled with inaccurate science, topped with a monster child subplot shoved in for good measure. Dr. Victor Reed (Jeremy Childs) announces he has achieved the first human clone using his own genetic material. It's a girl, which means it's not a clone at all. He then adds that he altered the DNA, so it would not be exactly like him, which makes it even more of a non-clone than it was before. This would be acceptable if there was an allusion later than he did this to prevent creating a psychopathic killer baby boy like his son Ethan, who he has locked up back at his house. As the religious protestors gathering outside the doctor's mansion get increasingly violent, Ethan escapes and starts bumping off members of the household, **The Brood**-style. At this point, the film should hurtle toward a climax involving both threats, but these two distinct elements of the film remain stubbornly separate, which is a shame because with better plotting this would be a far more memorable picture.

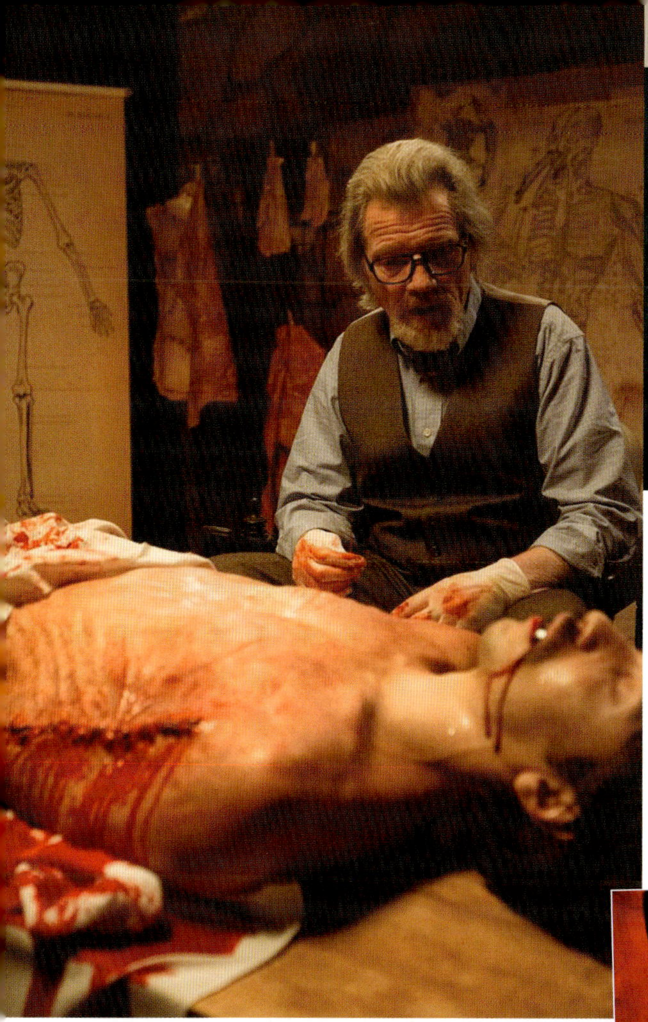

TUSK

Canada/USA, 2014
Director: Kevin Smith.
Producers: Sam Englebardt, David S. Greathouse, William D. Johnson, Shannon McIntosh.
Screenplay: Kevin Smith. Music: Christopher Drake.
Cinematography: James Laxton.
Cast: Michael Parks, Justin Long, Johnny Depp, Haley Joel Osment, Genesis Rodriguez, Harley Morenstein.

Michael Parks is Howard Howe, a retired seaman living in an isolated mansion in Canada. He tells interviewer Wallace Bryton (Justin Long) that he owes his life to a walrus – 'Mr. Tusk' – who rescued him when he was shipwrecked. Before he can say 'that tea tastes a bit funny' Bryton finds himself drugged and part of Howe's plan to use amateur surgical techniques to turn the journalist into Mr. Tusk. Another movie that, like Tom Six's **The Human Centipede** owes its thematic origins to the shudder pulps of the 1930s. The difference is that the film's attempts at humour sit uneasily alongside the outright cruelty of the depiction of Bryton's fate. Johnny Depp (under the pseudonym 'Guy LaPointe') and Michael Parks have a riot of a time facing off and doing silly voices, but the underlying nastiness means director Kevin Smith's attempt to mix the comedy and horror merely results in them overbalancing each other. **Tusk** was planned by its director as the first in a trilogy. The second, **Yoga Hosers** (2016) saw the return of Guy LaPointe on the trail of Nazis creating an army of sausage monsters. It did not do well. Neither did **Tusk**. The third, **Moose Jaws** (intended to be like Spielberg's 1975 **Jaws** but with a moose) has yet to go before the cameras.

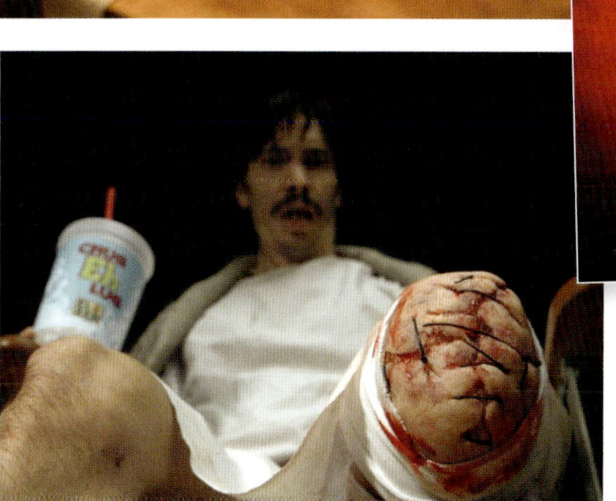

FRANKENSTEIN

USA/Germany, 2015
Director: Bernard Rose. Producers: Christian Angermayer, Gabriela Bacher, Klemens Hallmann, Heidi Jo Markel, Jennifer Holliday Morrison. Screenplay: Bernard Rose. Music: Halli Cauthery. Cinematography: Candace Higgins. Cast: Xavier Samuel, Carrie-Anne Moss, Danny Huston, Matthew Jacobs, Dave Pressler, Peter Adrian Sudarso, Tony Todd.

Danny Huston is Frankenstein and Carrie-Anne Moss is Elizabeth in Bernard Rose's version of Mary Shelley's tale. But this isn't their story, dispensing as it does with the buildup to the creation of the monster and beginning instead with the awakening of the digitally printed result (Xavier Samuel) who then proceeds to narrate his fate. Rose relocates the story to modern-day Los Angeles, gives the creature a short-lived friend in a stray dog, recreates the scene with the little girl by the lake (who doesn't die in this version) and has him escape police custody (where Elizabeth denies she knows him) to befriend a blind man in the form of Tony Todd's busking blues guitarist. The monster's tissues progressively degenerate in a manner reminiscent of Cronenberg, and while overall this version feels very modern and clinical, Rose allows his unflinching, touching, contemporary interpretation to end on the only truly Gothic note to be found in the picture. At the UK premiere at London's FrightFest, Rose – director of **Paperhouse** (1988), **Candyman** (1992, and also starring Tony Todd), and **The Kreutzer Sonata** (2008) – admitted he preferred adapting existing literary works rather than original ideas as it "gave him something to hide behind".

PATCHWORK

Canada/USA, 2015
Director: Tyler MacIntyre. Producers: Jason Klein, John Negropontes, Aaron Webman, Ethan Webman. Screenplay: Chris Lee Hill, Tyler MacIntyre. Music: Russ Howard III. Cinematography: Pawel Pogorzelski.
Cast: Tory Stolper, Tracey Fairaway, Maria Blasucci, James Phelps, Corey Sorenson, Eric Edelstein.

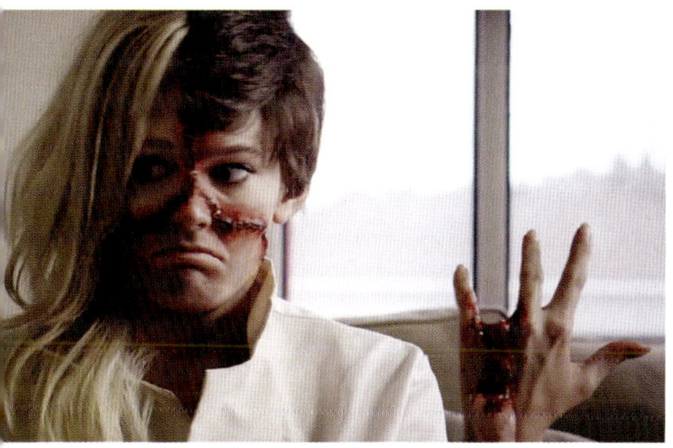

The spirit of NYC exploitation movie maestro Frank Henenlotter is strong in this one, which also channels Stuart Gordon's **Re-Animator** (1985) with its composite lead character brought back to life by a glowing green liquid, and James Whale's **The Invisible Man** (1933) with how she disguises herself once she's up and about and seeking revenge. Jennifer (Tory Stolper), Ellie (Tracey Fairaway), and Madeleine (Maria Blasucci) wake up on an operating table after a night on the town, to find parts of them have been used to create one single body which their minds all now collectively inhabit. The surgeon (Corey Sorenson) who performed the procedure looks like a graduate of the Henenlotter medical school of mad doctors, with his filthy lab coat and fingernails, cigarette placed strategically in the corner of his mouth as he wields his circular saw. The movie's narrative is itself a patchwork as we learn how the girls came to be in their current situation, and there are a few twists along the way, allowing director Tyler MacIntyre (who also made 2017's **Tragedy Girls**) to give us an entertaining feminist horror picture that never gets overly preachy amidst all the laughs and gore. One especially lunatic bit involving an animal close to the end is the icing on this particularly bloodstained cake.

VICTOR FRANKENSTEIN

UK/Canada/USA, 2015
Director: Paul McGuigan.
Producer: John Davis. Screenplay: Max Landis.
Music: Craig Armstrong. Cinematography: Fabian Wagner.
Cast: Daniel Radcliffe, Jessica Brown Findlay, Bronson Webb, James McAvoy, Andrew Scott, Charles Dance, Mark Gatiss.

A retelling of the Frankenstein story in the spirit of Jimmy Sangster's 1970 **The Horror of Frankenstein** but doing a much better job of it, Paul McGuigan's boisterous comedy version of Mary Shelley's novel is told from the point of view of Igor (Daniel Radcliffe). It details his journey from hunchbacked circus 'medical advisor' to assistant to a whooping, manic Victor Frankenstein (James McAvoy). Some flamboyant production design and a robust music score from Craig Armstrong all serve to embellish the by-now somewhat over-familiar story, but it's still an enjoyable ride, with Andrew Scott (BBC TV's latest incarnation of Professor Moriarty in *Sherlock*) as Frankenstein's nemesis Inspector Turpin, Charles Dance as a suitably stern Frankenstein senior, and a blink and you'll miss him turn from Mark Gatiss. The creation of a human creature is left until the very end of this, as the story concentrates on the events and relationships leading up to it, including a grotesquely funny set piece at the Royal College of Surgeons where Victor unveils his first attempt at breathing life into dead tissue. The cast enter into the enterprise with vigour, and the characters and situations are entertaining and endearing enough that it's a shame this didn't run to at least one sequel.

BAD BLOOD: THE MOVIE

USA, 2016
Director: Tim Reis. Producers: Michael Bremer, Tim Reis, James Sizemore.
Screenplay: Tim Reis.
Music: Christopher Ian Brooker.
Cinematography: John Manfredi.
Cast: Mary Malloy, Vikas Adam, Troy Halverson, Brian Troxell, Tomi Lavinder, Grayson Thorne Kilpatrick.

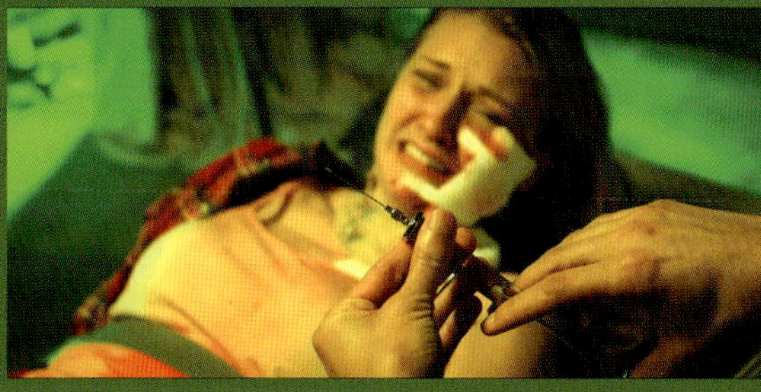

At FrightFest's UK premiere of **Bad Blood** writer / director / editor and general one-man band Tim Reis told the audience his desire was to make a film in the style of Frank Henenlotter. The spirit of the director of exploitation classics like **Frankenhooker** (1990) and **Bad Biology** (2008) is certainly evident in this potty film about an expelled medical student masquerading as a gas station attendant while working on frog-based experiments in the basement. In 1957 Whit Bissell caused Michael Landon to sprout hairs in **I Was a Teenage Werewolf**. Here Victoria (Mary Malloy) is attacked by the student's transformed mad doctor colleague (who has just broken out of prison) and ends up a teenaged werefrog, changing only during the full moon. How and why all this froggy research is intended to benefit mankind is only explained in the most superficial that's-not-the-point-of-this-one way. Frogs don't get used in horror as much as one would expect – George McCowan's 1972 eco-horror **Frogs** and the lunatic delights of Don Sharp's 1973 **Psychomania** (both actually shot in 1971 – the year of the horror frog?) come to mind. Perhaps to make up for this lack of amphibian exploitation, Reis includes quite a few of the creatures in **Bad Blood**, including a massive special effects one that lives in a glass tank and explodes at the end.

THE CLEANSE

Canada/USA, 2016
Director: Bobby Miller. Producers: Aaron L. Gilbert, Jordan Horowitz.
Screenplay: Bobby Miller. Music: Eskmo [Brendan Angelides],
Russ Howard III, Rob Simonsen. Cinematography: Michael Fimognari.
Cast: Johnny Galecki, Anna Friel, Kyle Gallner, Anjelica Huston,
Diana Bang, Kevin J. O'Connor, Oliver Platt.

Otherwise known as **The Master Cleanse**, this one sees *The Big Bang Theory*'s Johnny Galecki attending Oliver Platt and Anjelica Huston's detoxification clinic. Former UK soap star Anna Friel (perhaps better known now for Juraj Jakubisko's overlong 2008 **Bathory: Countess of Blood**) is a patient there as well. The therapy involves voiding one's negative emotions rectally. In an unexpected twist the products are cute little monsters of the sort one might find on a children's programme about faeces. There aren't that many films out there about peculiar rectal habits and their products, but they seem to be on the increase, making **The Cleanse** an example of a unique subgenre of films. It includes Lawrence Kasdan's **Dreamcatcher** (2003), adapted from the 2001 Stephen King novel. From quite the other end of the scales of both budget and taste comes Mark Pirro's **Rectuma** (2003), a film featuring a Mexican butt-humping bullfrog which causes a man's bottom to grow to Toho monster size (there's even a pair of tiny girls who sing in a urinal to make sure you get Pirro's point). In Jacob Vaughan's **Bad Milo!** (2013) a man's rectum is possessed by a demon. While in Tyler Cornack's 2020 **Butt Boy** the rectum is a gateway to an entire universe. A rectal-based villain / hero has yet to surface in the Marvel Cinematic Universe. Perhaps it's more suited to DC.

A CURE FOR WELLNESS

Germany/Luxembourg/USA, 2016
Director: Gore Verbinski. Producers: David Crockett, Arnon Milchan, Gore Verbinski. Screenplay: Justin Haythe. Music: Benjamin Wallfisch. Cinematography: Bojan Bazelli.
Cast: Dane DeHaan, Jason Isaacs, Mia Goth, Ivo Nandi, Adrian Schiller, Celia Imrie.

Gore Verbinski directed one of the better US remakes of a non-English language film (2002's **The Ring**) and managed a highly entertaining spin on the swashbuckling high seas adventure with the first three **Pirates of the Caribbean** films (2003-7). In this big-budget European horror, he grabs hold of a number of Gothic tropes and with eccentric aplomb shakes them until all the eels fall out. What is actually going on at the exclusive health spa in the Swiss Alps run by Dr. Heinreich Volmer (Jason Isaacs)? What has the ethereally sexy Hannah (Mia Goth) got to do with it? And will Lockhart (Dane DeHaan), sent to secure the signature of one of the patients, ever escape? A glorious mix of inspirations including Argento (**Suspiria**, 1977), Franju (sterile clinics and skin transplants), and Jess Franco (being more specific would be giving away the climactic reveal). As with **Suspiria**, Verbinski got his composer (Benjamin Wallfisch) to write the entire score before a single shot had been filmed, asking him for 'something for the dark spots on the X-ray of our conscience'. Just when **A Cure for Wellness** reaches what should be its natural climax (and with a great potential final line) we get a rollicking last hurrah of a final twenty minutes that represents Verbinski's hymn to Hammer Horror, with nods to the Frankenstein films, **The Reptile** (1966), and culminating in the best ever tribute to Don Sharp's **The Kiss of the Vampire** (1963). Don't worry that it doesn't all make sense – a lot of the best classic European horror films never did, so why should this? Instead revel in the kind of flamboyant, bizarre, crazy, sexy film that it was thought nobody made any more.

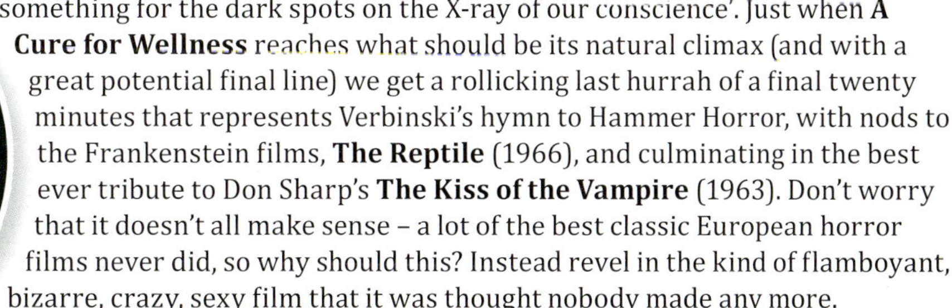

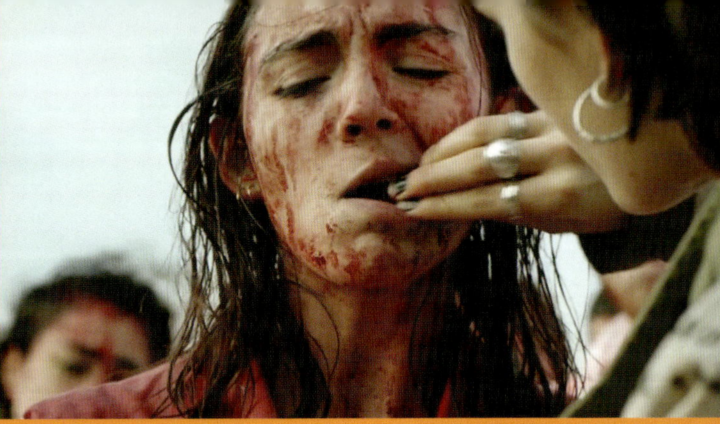

RAW

France/Belgium/USA, 2016
Director: Julia Ducournau. Producer: Jean des Forêts.
Screenplay: Julia Ducournau. Music: Jim Williams.
Cinematography: Ruben Impens.
Cast: Garance Marillier, Ella Rumpf, Rabah Nait Oufella, Laurent Lucas, Joana Preiss, Bouli Lanners.

There aren't that many films featuring mad vets and their associated occupations. The most overt is probably Billy O'Brien's 2005 **Isolation** (see the *FrightFest Guide to Monster Movies*) about mutant cow experiments on a grim Irish farm. There's also Lucky McKee's **May** (2002) starring Angela Bettis as a veterinary assistant who goes insane after developing a crush and decides to build her own boyfriend. Julia Ducournau's **Raw** is the story of Justine (Garance Marillier), who has been raised a vegetarian. When she goes to veterinary school, one of the bizarre and cruel initiation rites involves the consumption of flesh, triggering in her an increasing craving for human meat. Either times have changed, or life at French veterinary school is especially unpleasant, but the extent of UK medical school initiation gags usually never went further than being convinced to report to the Dean's office with a pot of your own urine for testing. Ducournau plays the subject matter of cannibalism straight, right up to the climax, when one begins to wonder if the intention all along was for **Raw** to be a comedy. It was the director's feature debut and marked her as a talent to watch. Her next project, **Titane** (2021) once again combined the reunion of family with horrible murders.

FLATLINERS

USA/Canada, 2017
Director: Niels Arden Oplev. Producers: Michael Douglas, Peter Safran. Screenplay: Ben Ripley. Music: Nathan Barr. Cinematography: Eric Kress. Cast: Ellen Page [Elliot Page], Diego Luna, Nina Dobrev, James Norton, Kiersey Clemons, Kiefer Sutherland.

It's time for some impossibly airbrushed students living in impossibly expensive-looking apartments – perhaps to distract us from the fact that, once again, women get defibrillated while still wearing their bras, causing fire hazards and electrical burns aplenty. Actually, we don't get any of that in this remake of Joel Schumachers' 1990 Brat Pack horror picture. This time Ellen Page is foolish / mad enough to want to locate the centres of the brain that deal with near death experience. She decides the best way to go about it is to induce a cardiac arrest for herself, have a brain scan, and then have her friends bring her back to life. Director Niels Arden Oplev's **Flatliners** ignores all kinds of opportunities for post-resuscitation brain damage horrors, or astral projection causing Lovecraftian things to spot you and follow you back to the real world, in the style of **From Beyond** (1986). Instead the plot follows the original, with our students having committed past misdemeanours of such soap opera quality you actually feel sorry that they haven't got more worthwhile **Grudge** or **Final Destination**-style forces after them. This is very much horror-lite (and horror-bland and pointless), slickly put together with studio efficiency and with **Hostel** (2005) composer Nathan Barr going all Philip Glass to help make it more endurable. Kiefer Sutherland fans get to see him play a grumpy senior doctor who waves his stick around, and full marks to whoever came up with a mnemonic for remembering the cranial nerves that isn't completely filthy.

GET OUT

USA/Japan, 2017
Director: Jordan Peele.
Producers: Jason Blum, Edward H. Hamm Jr., Sean McKittrick, Jordan Peele. Screenplay: Jordan Peele.
Music: Michael Abels. Cinematography: Toby Oliver.
Cast: Daniel Kaluuya, Allison Williams, Catherine Keener, Bradley Whitford, Caleb Landry Jones, Marcus Henderson.

Older readers may be reminded of John Blackburn's 1968 novel *Nothing But the Night* (filmed in 1973 by Christopher Lee's Charlemagne Productions) or even an episode of Brian Clemens' mid-1970s anthology TV series *Thriller* as they watch Jordan Peele's breakout award-winning horror. Those unfamiliar with the above will not have the surprises Peele has in store spoiled for them here. Suffice to say, with his debut feature the writer-director takes a basic mad scientist idea and, aided by some excellent performances (especially lead Daniel Kaluuya, probably best known to UK audiences prior to **Get Out**'s release from genre TV shows *Black Mirror* and *Psychoville*) delivers a movie that's both a cutting cultural and social commentary as well as being a rollicking good horror film. A hit with both audiences and critics, **Get Out** won the Best Screenplay Award at the 2018 Oscars, with nominations for Best Picture, Best Director, and Best Actor for Kaluuya. Its success helped pave the way for Peele to try his hand at becoming the new Rod Serling with a revamped *Twilight Zone* TV series, as well co-writing and producing Nia DaCosta's remake of **Candyman** (2021), producing TV show *Lovecraft Country* and writing and directing his follow up horror features **Us** (2019) and **Nope** (2022).

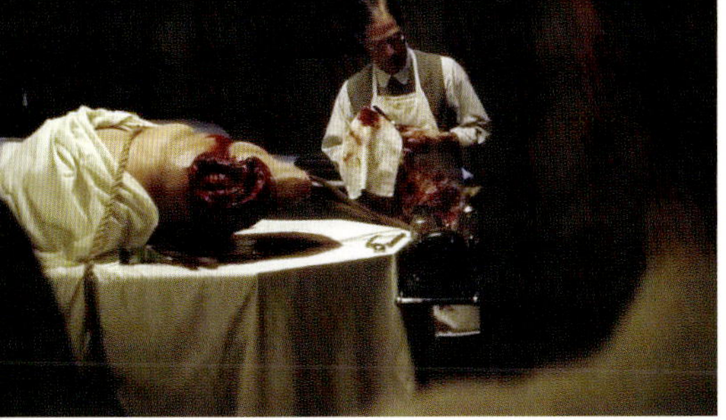

THE INSTITUTE

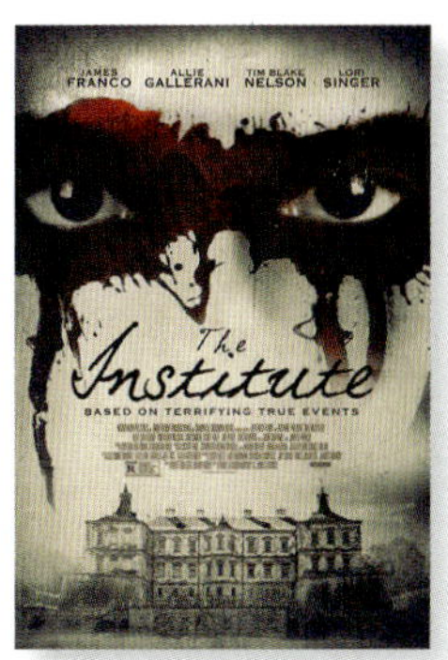

USA, 2017
Directors: James Franco, Pamela Romanowsky. Producers: Christa Campbell, Jay Davis, James Franco, Lati Grobman, Vince Jolivette, Scott Reed, Brian Esquivel [uncredited]. Screenplay: Matt Rager, Adam Rager. Music: Adam Crystal. Cinematography: Pedro Gómez Millán. Cast: Allie Gallerani, James Franco, Joe Pease, Scott Haze, Lori Singer, Amber Coney.

Co-director (with Pamela Romanowsky) James Franco stars as Dr. Cairn, head of a Baltimore psychiatric institute. In 1893, the gentle posh and pretty Isabel Porter (Allie Gallerani) checks herself in, after becoming traumatised by the untimely death of her parents. It's not long before she's being subjected to therapies that would be right at home in classic women in prison movies like Jack Hill's **The Big Doll House** (1971). **The Institute** is purportedly 'based on real events', which of course it isn't. Instead, it exploits a situation that really took place (a hospital for the treatment of women suffering from 'psychiatric conditions' actually being a front for human trafficking) and uses it as an excuse for a bit of good old-fashioned murder and mayhem spiced up with nudity. Not that you would expect it from the first thirty minutes or so. Perhaps Mr. Franco (James) grew up in a household where his mum watched the opening half an hour of a film to 'make sure it was suitable' before she went to bed. It certainly seems as if he has made a film for that particular situation, because after the tame opening scenes, we get topless ladies strung up, bare bottoms flogged, and all manner of perverse behaviour, culminating in a climax of utter daftness 'inspired' by Edgar Allan Poe. Franco (Jess) would be proud, especially at how little sense any of this makes. Those demanding historical accuracy should also be warned that they might find the shots of anachronistic full-frontal nudity another reason to find this film distressing.

THE SLEEP CURSE

Hong Kong, 2017
Director: Herman Yau. Producers: Albert Lee, Jason Siu, Yao Qinyi. Screenplay: Eric Lee, Erica Li. Music: Brother Hung. Cinematography: Joe Chan. Cast: Anthony Wong, Michelle Wai, Jojo Goh, Gordon Lam, Bryant Mak, Funaki Ikki.

We begin with camcorder footage of a man slowly losing the ability to sleep, followed by some audience-pleasing gory results. Then we're introduced to Dr. Lam Sik-Ka (Anthony Wong), an insomnia researcher and mad scientist (he's depriving white mice of sleep after all and that's never a good sign in a movie like this). When his research funding falls through he's approached by the daughter of the man from the opening scene. She has a huge cheque and the concern she may go the way of her father. In a lengthy flashback sequence, we learn of the events that triggered **The Sleep Curse**. A film that manages to combine some taboo-busting gore with a 'sins of the fathers'-style plotline about Chinese collaboration during Japan's occupation of Hong Kong during the Second World War, **The Sleep Curse** goes deliciously crazy at its climax, and if you fancy some uncomfortable splatter then it's probably worth the wait. The film's star Wong is probably best known to genre fans for his role in John Woo's **Hard Boiled** (1992), while director Herman Yau has over 70 movies to his credit, including the **Troublesome Night** series of comedy horror anthology films as well as over the top gore movies **The Eight Immortals Restaurant: The Untold Story** (1993) and **Ebola Syndrome** (1996), both of which also starred Anthony Wong.

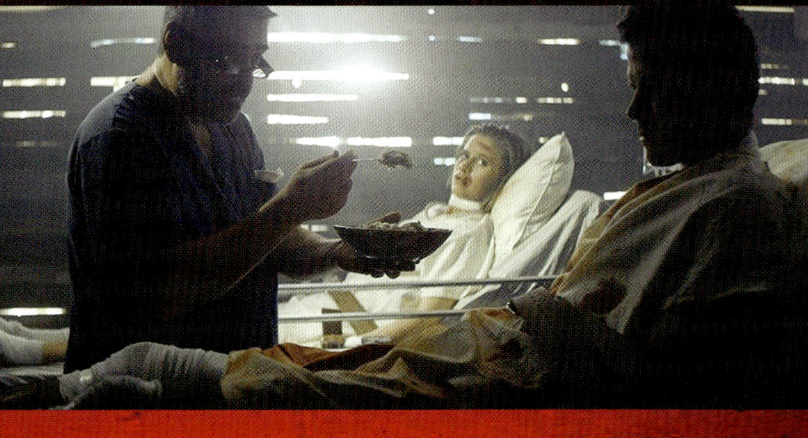

ALIVE

Canada, 2018
Director: Rob Grant. Producers: Lars Lehmann, Chuck McCue, Michael Peterson, Jules Vincent. Screenplay: Chuck McCue, Jules Vincent. Music: Michelle Osis. Cinematography: Charles Hamilton. Cast: Thomas Cocquerel, Camille Stopps, Angus Macfadyen, Chantal Perron, Gerrick Winston, Zoe Marlett.

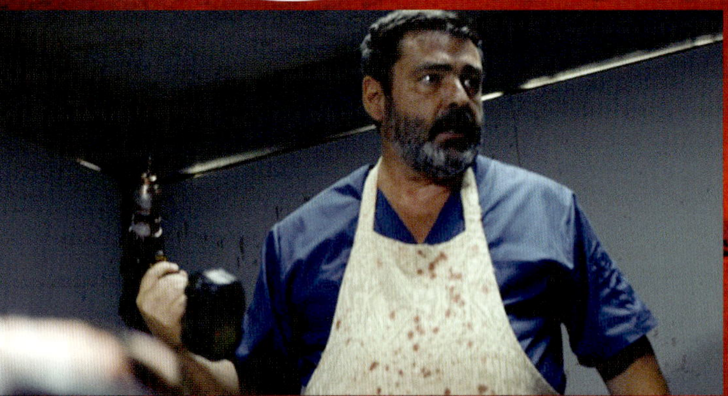

A man and a woman awaken nursing serious injuries in a rundown hospital where seemingly the only other person around is mad doctor (or is he?) Angus Macfadyen. Neither of them can remember who they are or how they got there. As they begin to recover, they quickly realise that the man who claims to be their saviour may in fact be their captor. Director Rob Grant is probably best known for his blackly humorous approach to horror. **Mon Ami** (2012) is the story of a couple of incompetent kidnappers who cause multiple deaths as a result of their mistakes, while the much slicker **Harpoon** (2019) is a virtual three-hander set on a yacht adrift in the middle of the ocean. **Fake Blood** (2017), in which Grant plays himself encountering the real world of violent crime is a cheeky 'semi-documentary', echoing Adam Green's meta-monster horror **Digging Up the Marrow** (2014). **Alive** is more serious, with an opening act that threatens to develop along the lines of Kôji Shiraishi's medical torture picture **Grotesque** (2009). Thankfully there's more to it than that, as the two leads escape their bonds and – looking a little like the two escapees at the start of Antony Balch's **Horror Hospital** (1973) – set about deciphering their past. The denouement is pleasingly nightmarish and Grant cannot resist ending the movie on a fittingly macabre joke.

ELIZABETH HARVEST

USA, 2018
Director: Sebastian Gutierrez. Producers: Dylan Baker, Leon Clarance, Sebastian Gutierrez, Brian Kavanaugh-Jones. Screenplay: Sebastian Gutierrez. Music: Faris Badwan, Rachel Zeffira. Cinematography: Cale Finot.
Cast: Abbey Lee, Ciarán Hinds, Carla Gugino, Matthew Beard, Dylan Baker.

A Netflix original film that shouldn't have its plot spoiled for those yet to discover it. Suffice to say **Elizabeth Harvest** deals with loss in that frankly physical but also barking mad way that's reminiscent of early-1970s European pictures, especially the work of Jess Franco. There's obsessive science, blood, sex, more obsessive science, and everything snowballs in that splendid 'nothing good can come of any of it' kind of way. A brilliant doctor marries a beautiful woman and brings her to his isolated mansion, where she is told she has the freedom of the place except for one room she must never enter. Inevitably, she disobeys this rule, but what she finds there and what ensues thereafter is best left to the viewer to discover. Ciarán Hinds plays the mad doctor in the kind of role Paul Muller would have played in the old days, with Abbey Lee taking the Soledad Miranda role, and Carla Gugino in the part Franco would have had Lina Romay play. There's weird fascinating architecture and odd dream sequences, while Venezuelan director Sebastian Gutierrez keeps everything stylishly ticking along, helping the viewer to maintain suspension of disbelief in the face of the ludicrousness on display.

OVERLORD

USA/Canada, 2018
Director: Julius Avery.
Producers: J.J. Abrams, Lindsey Weber.
Screenplay: Billy Ray,
Mark L. Smith. Music: Jed Kurzel.
Cinematography: Laurie Rose, Fabian Wagner.
Cast: Jovan Adepo, Wyatt Russell, Mathilde Ollivier,
Pilou Asbæk, John Magaro, Iain De Caestecker.

Right up at the big-budget, airbrushed, mainstream-audience end of the Nazisploitation sub-genre, Julius Avery's film kicks off with an excellent unnerving aeroplane crash. It strands our motley bunch of heroes some distance from the target of their mission – a French village which harbours a Nazi radio transmitter they've been tasked with destroying. Unfortunately, the church where the transmitter has been housed turns out to be less a house of God and more a place filled with naughty Nazi experimentation, where the dastardly villains are trying to create superhuman soldiers. They have got as far as a serum which, when injected, allows you to almost pull your own head off, as well as providing super strength, and a generally poor disposition towards others. Will our heroes save the day or will evil triumph? The mad doctor Nazi zombie / monster movie subgenre increased its numbers with all the rapidity of the laboratory creations themselves during the 2000s. Of all these movies – Richard Raaphorst's excellent **Frankenstein's Army** (2013) and the rather less excellent British **Outpost** trilogy of films (2008-2013) come to mind – **Overlord** is by far the most lavish. It's what in olden times would have been referred to as a Boys Own Adventure, a rip-roaring comic-book tale of good guys versus some very broadly drawn baddies indeed. The result is a slick, well put together World War II action horror film.

UPGRADE

USA/Australia, 2018
Director: Leigh Whannell.
Producers: Jason Blum, Kylie Du Fresne, Brian Kavanaugh-Jones.
Screenplay: Leigh Whannell.
Music: Jed Palmer.
Cinematography: Stefan Duscio.
Cast: Logan Marshall-Green, Betty Gabriel, Harrison Gilbertson, Melanie Vallejo, Benedict Hardie, Linda Cropper.

Writer-director Leigh Whannell's tribute to some of his favourite science fiction movies of the 1980s. After he is rendered quadriplegic in a car accident that kills his wife, Grey Trace (Logan Marshall-Green) receives a spinal implant with AI called STEM, from reclusive millionaire mad scientist Eron Keen (Harrison Gilbertson). STEM allows Grey to walk, but soon it's talking to him and helping him to find the men who caused the accident. Shot for very little money but looking like a lot more, **Upgrade** is the kind of Blumhouse production that makes you glad the company exists and further cements its reputation as the AIP or Empire Pictures of today. (Leigh Whannell calls them the latter-day New World Pictures.) Whannell wears his influences on his sleeve – **Robocop** (1987), **The Terminator** (1984), even **Death Wish** (1974) – without ever looking imitative, and he's aided immensely by excellent production design, a fine cast, and superb fight coordination. "As genre fans we run at all these pictures, wanting to love them", explained Leigh Whannell at the UK premiere of **Upgrade** at London's FrightFest. **Upgrade** is easy to love, and so is Whannell's 2020 follow-up, the first successful serious treatment of **The Invisible Man** in over seventy years.

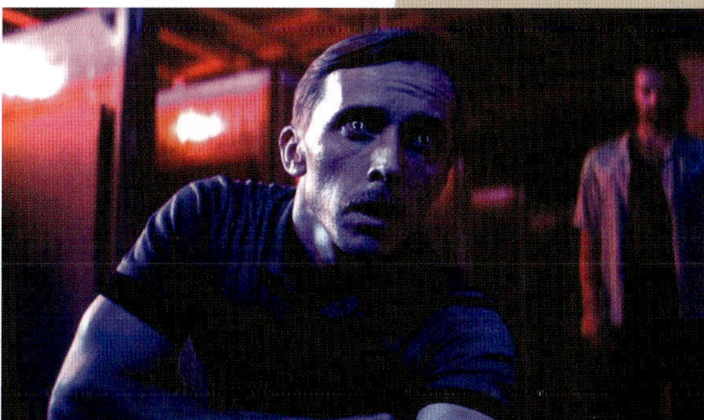

DEPRAVED

USA, 2019
Director: Larry Fessenden.
Producers: Larry Fessenden, Chadd Harbold, Jenn Wexler. Screenplay: Larry Fessenden.
Music: Will Bates. Cinematography: James Siewert, Chris Skotchdopole.
Cast: David Call, Joshua Leonard, Alex Breaux, Ana Kayne, Maria Dizzia, Chloë Levine.

Larry Fessenden's reimagining of the Frankenstein story takes a different approach to Bernard Rose, whose contemporary version was much closer to the novel (and previous movie versions) than this. Traumatised by his war experiences, surgeon Henry (David Call) is researching a method for transplanting limbs onto battle casualties with the financial aid of his medical school friend Polidori (Joshua Leonard from 1999's **The Blair Witch Project**). Henry perfects his technique, which leads to the creation of a man, Adam (Alex Breaux). Adam's kept alive in Henry's loft by a cocktail of (accurately researched) immunosuppressive drugs, plus Polidori's new research medication. Polidori takes Adam on a tour of New York's Metropolitan Museum of Art (filmed seemingly guerilla-style) and bends his ear with a diatribe on man's inherent tendency to both destroy and glory in that destruction (reflecting, perhaps Fessenden's own views). Inevitably Adam eventually rebels against his creators and escapes. **Depraved** echoes the original Universal **Frankenstein** as the film nears its end – and even has Polidori obliquely refer to Whale's film – with a resurrection scene and a thunder and lightning climax at Polidori's house. None of this detracts, however, from the very human tale Fessenden is telling here, and the movie ends on an appropriately touching note in this, his best picture to date.

GREYWOOD'S PLOT

USA, 2019
Director: Josh Stifter. Producers: Jason Scott Goldberg, Josh Stifter, Brandon Waites.
Screenplay: Daniel Degnan, Josh Stifter.
Music: Curtis Allen Hager. Cinematography: Daniel Lynn.
Cast: Daniel Degnan, Kim Fagan, Samantha Kirchoff, Aaron McKenna, Keith Radichel, Josh Stifter.

Definitely a film of two halves. For the first 45 minutes **Greywood's Plot** is the not-especially enthralling tale of likeable, bumbling losers Dom (director and co-writer Josh Stifter) and Miles (Keith Radichel) who set off on a hunt to film the chupacabra for their YouTube channel. Things take a decided right turn into *Island of Dr. Moreau* territory when they stumble onto land belonging to Doug Greywood (co-writer Daniel Degnan). Doug has been conducting some very strange experiments, and he intends Dom and Miles to become his latest subjects, as the film turns into a modern-day version of early-1930s mad scientist movies. Shot in black and white for virtually no money by the team responsible for 2018's **The Good Exorcist**, **Greywood's Plot** only really gets going in its second half, becoming decidedly disturbing by the end. Interviewed at FrightFest, director Stifter also cited Gerardo de Leon and Eddie Romero's 1959 **Terror Is a Man** as an influence.

BREEDER

Denmark, 2020
Director: Jens Dahl. Producers: Maria Møller Christoffersen, Amalie Lyngbo Quist. Screenplay: Sissel Dalsgaard Thomsen. Music: Peter Kyed, Peter Peter [Peter Schneidermann]. Cinematography: Nicolai Lok. Cast: Sara Hjort Ditlevsen, Anders Heinrichsen, Signe Egholm Olsen, Eeva Putro, Morten Holst, Jens Andersen.

Mad vet Doctor Isabel Ruben (Signe Eghom Olsen) is researching ways to prolong life, and wealthy men are prepared to pay for her services. Unfortunately, those services involve her kidnapping women, inseminating them with her clients' DNA, and then harvesting cells from the resultant baby to produce her youth serum. Mia (Sara Hjort Ditlevsen) discovers that her husband is helping fund the research and goes to investigate, ending up as one of the test subjects herself. Filled with brandings, beatings and women in cages forced to bear children, Jens Dahl's **Breeder** starts off a little like Brandon Cronenberg's **Antiviral** (2012) – clinical TV advertising, elite clientele – before veering off into Pete Walker **House of Whipcord** (1974) territory with its ineffectual male lead, ruthless villainess, and general sense of hopelessness. There's a stark contrast between the sterility of people's homes and place of business, compared with the grim and grimy 'factory' where the nuts and bolts of the biological processes are carried out. Despite talk of telomeres – at one point Dr. Ruben mentions Rapamycin, an immunosuppressive drug first isolated from organisms found on Rapa Nui (Easter Island) – no real attempt is made to explain the science of what is going on. The point here is social commentary in a similar vein to Alain Jessua's **Traitement de choc** (1973), though **Breeder** is focused on the exploitation of vulnerable female immigrants.

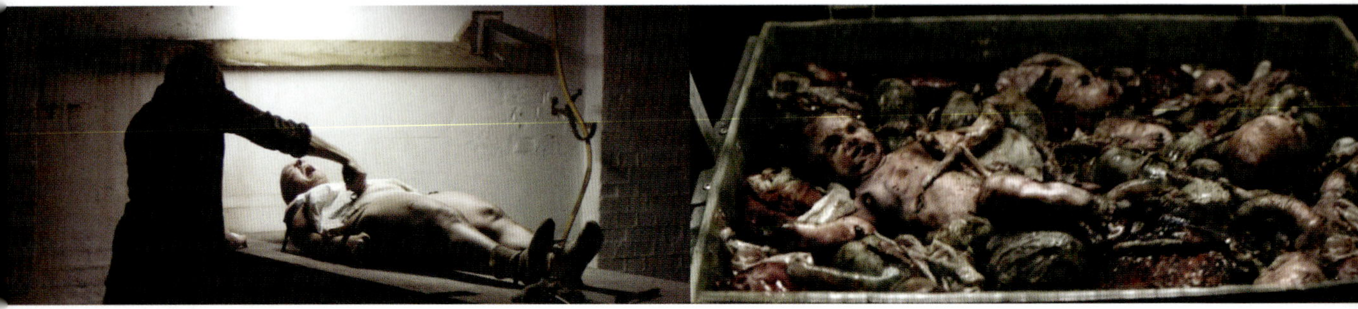

CEREBRUM

Switzerland/UK, 2022
Director: Sébastien Blanc.
Producers: Alessio Di Naro, Davide Marangoni.
Screenplay: Sébastien Blanc. Music: Daniel Nolan.
Cinematography: Jamie Touche.
Cast: Steve Oram, Tobi King Bakare, Ramona Von Pusch, Davide Marangoni, Chandrika Chevli, Lucia France.

Will (Tobi King Bakare) wakes up in an intensive care unit unable to speak. His neurosurgeon father Richard (Steve Oram) takes Will to their remote home where Will's mother is "upstairs asleep". Or is she? Who is that mysterious figure with glowing eyes, why does Richard keep bringing women of approximately Will's mother's age back to the house, and why do they disappear shortly after arriving? When Will confronts his father about his bizarre brain experiments, Richard responds "Think of what it will do for science!" Proving, if nothing else, that mad doctors seem to have learned little in the hundred years of cinema that have been documenting their exploits. Eighty years ago, Richard would have been played by Bela Lugosi, the modern, sterile country house in which he lives would have been a crumbling mansion, and the film would have had the look and feel of a typical Monogram production. Today, the confined setting and few characters, the mystery where we are drip fed clues to the solution, and the plentiful dialogue heavy with foreboding, are reminiscent of a feature length brain surgery-themed episode of the BBC TV series *Inside No.9*. The denouement is appropriately slick.

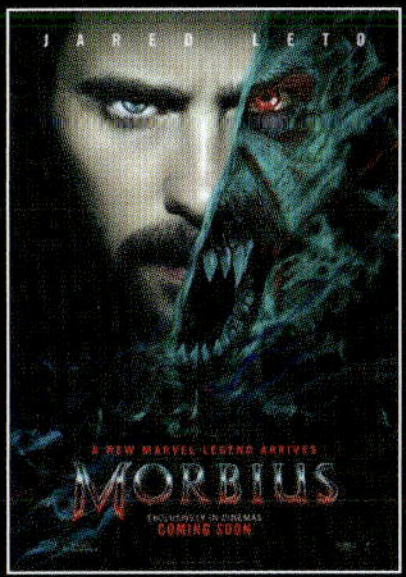

MORBIUS

USA, 2022
Director: Daniel Espinosa. Producers: Avi Arad, Lucas Foster, Matt Tolmach.
Screenplay: Matt Sazama, Burk Sharpless.
Music: Jon Ekstrand. Cinematography: Oliver Wood.
Cast: Jared Leto, Matt Smith, Adria Arjona, Jared Harris, Tyrese Gibson, Al Madrigal, Michael Keaton.

The Marvel Cinematic Universe (Sony Division) entered both mad doctor and vampire territory with director Daniel Espinosa's take on the comic-book character. Jared Leto is Dr. Michael Morbius, a brilliant haematologist who is himself suffering from a rare blood disease. Morbius injects himself with a serum he has isolated from a vampire bat, and is cured, but at a terrible price. Fortunately, he has also created a synthetic blood substitute that he can chug down overly dramatically (and somewhat repetitively) in moments of craving. If that all sounds convoluted that's because it is, but **Morbius** is also more fun than most reviews of the time made it out to be, with Matt Smith doing a fine turn as Morbius's childhood friend-turned-nemesis and an entertaining chase through an underground that's supposed to be in New York but looks a lot like London, because it is. The line most commonly associated with the film – "It's Morbin Time" – doesn't actually occur during the movie at all but was part of an ongoing joke by fans who also spread false rumours that the film had made a fortune (it didn't) and that after watching it Martin Scorsese had revised his previously loudly voiced negative opinion regarding superhero films (he hadn't).

INDEX OF FILM TITLES